THE LIBRARY
ST. MARY'S COLLEGE OF MARYLAND
ST. MARY'S CITY, MARYLAND 20686

INSULAR ROMANCE

INSULAR ROMANCE

*Politics, Faith, and Culture
in Anglo-Norman and
Middle English Literature*

SUSAN CRANE

UNIVERSITY OF CALIFORNIA PRESS
BERKELEY   LOS ANGELES   LONDON

University of California Press
Berkeley and Los Angeles, California

University of California Press, Ltd.
London, England

© 1986 by The Regents of the University of California

Library of Congress Cataloging in Publication Data
Crane, Susan.
    Insular romance.
    Bibliography: p.
    Includes index.
    1. Romances, Anglo-Norman—History and criticism.
2. Romances, English—History and criticism.   3. English
literature—Middle English, 1100–1500—French influences.
4. England in literature.   5. England—Intellectual life—
Medieval period, 1066–1485.   I. Title.
PC2948.C73   1986   843'.1'09942
85-13948
ISBN 0-520-05497-0 (alk. paper)

Printed in the United States of America
1 2 3 4 5 6 7 8 9

To My Beloved Parents

Contents

Acknowledgments	ix
Introduction	1
1. Romances of Land and Lineage	13
English Heroes and English History	14
Horn's Heritage	24
Havelok's Heritage	40
2. Land, Lineage, and Nation	53
Des Aventures e Pruesses Nos Auncestres	54
Justice	67
Style and Treatment	74
Insularity and the Romances of English Heroes	83
3. Religion in Pious Romances	92
Veyn Carpyng	94
Þe Kniȝt of Cristene Lawe	104
Faithful Friends	117
Insularity and the Pious Romances	128
4. Measuring Conventions of Courtliness	134
Courtly Literature and the Insular World	135
Tristan: Love and Suffering	146
Ipomedon: Love and Pleasure	158

5. Adapting Conventions of Courtliness	175
Tristan Revised	181
Ipomedon Revised	198
In Few Wordes Ys Curtesye	211
Conclusion	216
Abbreviations	225
Bibliography	229
Index	253

Acknowledgments

My longest-standing debts are to the teachers whose dedication to students and inspiring scholarship encouraged me to undertake medieval studies: David Herlihy, Chauncey Wood, and Georges Duby in undergraduate classes, and Charles Muscatine, R. Howard Bloch, and Phillip Damon in graduate seminars. Their example and advice have sustained my work in countless ways.

Many friends and colleagues have made suggestions that improved this study. I am especially grateful to Robert Gottfried for historical references, to A. J. Holden and William MacBain for advice on translations, and to Morton Bloomfield, Whitney Bolton, Jed Dannenbaum, Dee Garrison, Judith Gerson, Charles Muscatine, and Carol Nackenoff for specific suggestions about my argument that helped me toward its final articulation. The task of reviewing the entire manuscript in its later stages was cheerfully undertaken by Mark Barenberg, Susan Gal, John Ganim, Samuel Hamburg, Brian Merrilees, Paul Strohm, and Andrew Welsh. These readers' incisive comments and good humor made the final months of revision particularly enlightening and happy ones.

A Mellon Faculty Fellowship at Harvard University in 1980–81 allowed me to gather much of the material for this study, and grants from the Rutgers Research Council have supported its completion. I am grateful as well to Doris Kretschmer, Barbara Ras, and Rose Vekony of the University of California Press for their editorial efficiency. The faults that remain are all my own.

Introduction

In the decades following the Norman Conquest, a new dialect of Old French expressed England's gradual detachment from continental influence. Usually called Anglo-Norman after the political and geographic divisions that gave rise to it, this dialect originated in the many continental vernaculars spoken by the conquerors and their followers, but it soon became "a language apart," defining aurally the separation of its speakers from France.[1] The romances written in Anglo-Norman dialect, while not much noticed on the continent, had a profound influence on emerging Middle English romance. In this study I argue that Anglo-Norman romances and their Middle English versions form a distinctively "insular" body of works, closely related to one another and to their situation in England. Divided from continental romance in emphases as in language, the insular works share poetic concerns and techniques that respond forcefully to issues of their time and place.

To acknowledge a poem's engagement in the world is not to refuse its validity as poetic object. While many postformalist theories continue to deny the text any substantive historical affiliations, much can be discovered about insular romances by investigating the temporal conditions of romance writing and the historical dimensions of the texts themselves. Even if the ways in which literature and history overlap and interact are elusive, even if the past is

1. Rothwell, "Anglo-Norman Perspectives," p. 42; see also [Crane] Dannenbaum, "Anglo-Norman Romances."

only imperfectly accessible to us, the effort to reconnect literature to history is vital for those who believe that literary texts are social communications that played a part in the lives of their first audiences. The insular romances deal with the historical world just as surely as they reflect on and liberate themselves from the world. In studying these relations, I examine fundamental historical conditions of order, justice, power, and the like to which the romances particularly attend. I then consider how those conditions were conceptualized in the romances, and why they might have been conceptualized as they were.

The Norman Conquest reduced English to a subjugated language and literature for a time. However, to imagine that the Normans simply superposed continental French power on English life and literature is inaccurate. In many ways the settlers could soon be distinguished from their continental contemporaries; in many ways they grew less distinguishable from the English with whom they lived. The patterns of their assimilation deny the simpler view that for two centuries English and the English were suppressed, French and the French dominant. Rather, the interaction between cultural groups in England contributed to the formation of a new insular culture, one distinct from cultural formations in France.

A second change in rule, nearly as momentous for literary purposes as the Norman Conquest, further divided Anglo-Norman language and literature from the continent. With the coronation of Henry II in 1154, Norman control of the English crown was lost to the Angevin dynasty. Whereas the Normans had treated England and Normandy as a political and cultural unit, the Angevins did not attempt to integrate England so fully in their much more extensive provincial holdings.[2] By the later twelfth century the growing political isolation of England was manifested in feudal institutions and laws that differed in some respects from those of French provinces. England's differences inspired insular settlers with new visions of ideal achievement and right social order; and as literature written in Anglo-Norman dialect assessed and responded to those visions, it diverged from the norms of continental literature.

While Anglo-Norman literature was becoming more thoroughly insular, the Angevin courts were encouraging other literary developments. The courts of Henry II, Eleanor of Aquitaine, and their

2. The differences between Anglo-Norman (AN) and Angevin rule, including the increased isolation of England from holdings in France, are stressed by Le Patourel, *The Norman Empire*, pp. 102–17; and by Hollister, "Anglo-Norman *Regnum*."

sons were great centers of cultural activity. But the taste and the vernacular of this new dynasty were not primarily Anglo-Norman. Rather, Champenois, Norman, and even Provençal literature flourished in the peripatetic Angevin courts. The *Roman de Thèbes*, *Enéas*, and works of Benoît de Sainte-Maure, Robert Wace, Chrétien de Troyes, Marie de France, Bernart de Ventadorn, Bertran de Born, and Arnaut Daniel can be associated with the Angevins. Their courts clearly favored imaginative literature of the continent, and indeed the Angevin ruling family probably found England the least cultured of its many dominions.[3]

During the later twelfth century, then, French literature in England can be divided into continental (including Norman) works that flourished in the royal courts, and works in Anglo-Norman dialect that were more deeply rooted in insular history and society. Precise boundaries for Anglo-Norman literature cannot be established: some literary historians would prefer to include all French works composed or copied in England, while others would exclude all but the most strongly dialectal. I take the presence of any dialectal peculiarities in the composition of a work as the essential criterion of Anglo-Norman identity, since this dialect is a concrete sign of distance from the continent and participation in England's daily life.[4] As England grew socially and politically more separate from the continent in the thirteenth and fourteenth centuries, Middle English literature predictably drew its first strength from the dual insular sources of English tradition and Anglo-Norman literature.

Historical investigation offers a fresh approach to a literature that has discouraged critical analysis. Anglo-Norman romances do not meet the standards of Old French literature, as modern critics and medieval French audiences seem to agree.[5] Scholars accuse

3. See Chapter 4, nn. 17–34. Dronke reviews patronage studies in "Peter of Blois.".

4. This criterion excludes from my study such works as *Fergus*, set in Scotland but probably composed in northeast France (see Owen, "*Fergus*"), *Guillaume d'Angleterre*, and the *lais* of Marie de France (on her continental dialect see Ewert, ed., *Lais*, pp. xx–xxi). These works are to some degree in touch with insular life and thus share some interests with AN romance. Of works I include, the *Lai d'Haveloc* has the fewest AN dialectal traits despite its obvious insular origin and appeal.

5. E.g., "Les productions anglo normandes ont très tôt acquis sur le continent une réputation fâcheuse"; they appear "barbares" in dialect, composition, and style (Le Gentil, "*Amadas et Ydoine*," p. 372). Next to Old French (OF) romances, C. B. West concludes, AN works "show comparatively little interest in the analysis of emotional states"; they are "more pedestrian" than the troubadours, more "practical" and "prosaic" than Chrétien de Troyes (*Courtoisie*, p. 168). From her continental perspective, West is unable to suggest why AN poets might have modified continental patterns and what values they substituted for continental French *courtoisie*.

Middle English romances of many aesthetic weaknesses and are perplexed that these works could have been favored to the extent that the manuscript evidence indicates.[6] In looking elsewhere for these texts' sources of power, we might well stop asking if they are aesthetically simple or subtle, or realistic or escapist, and explore instead what they did for their insular audience, how they measured the issues of their day, and what strength could be taken from them for sustaining or resisting the ideas of their time. These questions are not narrowly historical. Rather, they insist that the romances' aesthetic dimensions carry important meanings in the world as well as in the text. My investigation attends less to the literary sources and influences of insular romances than to their own voicing of social relations, their challenges to contemporary belief, and their reformulations of the life they observe.

The distinction I make between works composed in Anglo-Norman dialect and works in continental dialects that were composed or copied in England is based on the division in social experience that Anglo-Norman dialect signals. During the first century following the Conquest, the settlers intermarried with the English, who adapted quickly to Norman rule, and probably raised their children to speak English as their mother tongue and French merely as an acquired accomplishment.[7] Just over a century after the Conquest, a royal official remarked that

> iam cohabitantibus Anglicis et Normannis et alterutrum uxores ducentibus uel nubentibus, sic permixte sunt nationes ut uix decerni possit hodie, de liberis loquor, quis Anglicus quis Normannus sit genere.
>
> nowadays, when English and Normans live close together and marry and give in marriage to each other, the nations are so mixed that it can scarcely be decided (I mean in the case of the freemen) who is of English birth and who of Norman.[8]

Anglo-Norman dialect, bilingualism, and artificial preservation of French express the cohesion of the English and Normans and their

---

6. E.g., "From the point of view of literary and critical understanding, it is difficult to understand why poems that are so bad according to almost every criterion of literary value should have held such a central position in the literary culture of their period" (Pearsall, "Understanding Middle English Romance," p. 105).

7. Short, "Bilingualism," summarizes recent research; see also Shelly, *English and French*, pp. 85–88, 94; and Galbraith, "Nationality and Language," pp. 120–21.

8. Richard, Son of Nigel [Richard FitzNeale], *Dialogus de Scaccario*, ed. and trans. Johnson, p. 53; Short, "Bilingualism," p. 478.

isolation from the continent. In the eleventh and twelfth centuries, the dialect's development shows "the combination of conservatism and neologism that ordinarily characterizes a speech that is severed from its parent stock," conserving some elements that on the continent had become archaic while creating new forms through the influence of English and irregular contacts with a variety of continental French dialects.[9] The lower strata of society, by far the majority of the population, clearly did not acquire Anglo-Norman as a second language; rather, the dialect characterized those in power. That it was not a national vernacular no doubt encouraged bilingualism among its speakers. Intermarriage between the continental settlers and the higher strata of English society during the first century after the Conquest also encouraged bilingualism among the powerful.[10]

Because Anglo-Norman connoted status and refinement, its users sought consciously to retard its full displacement by English. From quite an early date—perhaps as early as the 1160s—Anglo-Norman had to be deliberately preserved as a "language of culture," taught to the children of prominent families as the proper medium for social, legal, and literary communication.[11] Artificial preservation was inevitably imperfect preservation. Even in the second half of the twelfth century, when the use of Anglo-Norman and the writing of Anglo-Norman romances were at their height, one writer apologizes for her "false French of England"; Walter Map ridicules the impure "Marlborough French" of King Henry's illegitimate son Geoffrey; and Marie de France and Guernes de Pont-Sainte-Maxence, writing in England, call attention to their continental birth. From this period on, Anglo-Norman dialect was derided in French courts, chronicles, and fabliaux.[12] Although in England's shires this dialect

9. Pope, *From Latin to Modern French*, p. 425 et passim; Vising, *Dialecte anglo-normand*; Tanquerey, *Evolution du verbe*; and Petit, "Anglo-Norman—English Linguistics."
10. Rothwell, "Français en Angleterre"; Clark, "Women's Names"; Short, "Bilingualism," pp. 474–79.
11. The designation "language of culture" and the early artificial preservation it implies are discussed by Rothwell, "French in Thirteenth-Century England"; and by Short, "Bilingualism." See also Lefèvre, "Usage du français."
12. The Nun of Barking declares, "un faus franceis sai d'Angleterre," *Edouard le Confesseur*, ed. Södergård, line 7; Walter Map, *De Nugis Curialium*, ed. James, pp. 246–47; Guernes de Pont-Sainte-Maxence writes "Mis languages est bons, car en France fui nez," presumably contrasting his language to the AN around him (quoted and discussed by Short, "Bilingualism," p. 473). For other evidence of criticism of AN dialect in the twelfth and thirteenth centuries, see Langlois, "Les Anglais du moyen âge"; Rickard, *Britain in Medieval French Literature*, pp. 163–205.

was a mark of power and refinement, from continental perspectives it was a sign of exile and inferiority.

The users of Anglo-Norman, then, were those settlers who had lived for some time in England and their descendants raised in England who were taught the insular dialect of Old French. Just as Anglo-Norman dialect betrays isolation from the continent, romances written in this dialect depart from continental norms and establish insular ones that are continued in Middle English romances. Their difference brought the Anglo-Norman romances little popularity on the continent. Although Old French versions of *Boeve de Haumtone* and *Amis e Amilun* exist, they diverge widely from the Anglo-Norman and allied Middle English versions. Only the few Anglo-Norman romances primarily concerned with love—*Tristan*, *Amadas et Ydoine*, and perhaps *Ipomedon*—gained an audience in France.[13]

In contrast to their limited appeal abroad, virtually every Anglo-Norman romance had a Middle English descendant,[14] constituting a group of some twenty insular romances that have not yet been studied together despite repeated calls for research.[15] I investigate these works' relations to one another in the light of England's particular social, political, and religious structures. To be sure, the life and literature of England generally resemble those of France during this period, yet England's institutional differences resonate significantly with the differences that characterize the insular romances.

Central to my investigation is the history of the barony, those who held land in fief from the king and more often from lesser lords. Two characteristics of the English barony in this period are especially pertinent to the concerns of insular romance. First, the barons' status as members of the second estate, the *bellatores*, was less relevant to their power than was their control of land; thus they are more appropriately defined as a class, however nascent, than as the estate of "men who fight." Many indeed did not fight, while many knights did not manage to become titled landholders. Chiv-

---

13. Legge, "Archaism and the Conquest"; Livingston, "*Roman d'Ipomedon*"; Paris, "Sur *Amadas et Ydoine*."

14. *Protheselaus* and *Amadas et Ydoine* are exceptions. The ME descendants of *Fouke le Fitz Waryn* and *Waldef* are lost; evidence for them is given in *Fulk Fitz Warine*, ed. Wright, pp. x–xiii; *Johannes Bramis' Historia Regis Waldei*, ed. Imelmann, pp. xxviii–xxxix; Wilson, *Lost Literature*, pp. 112–13, 116.

15. Kane emphasizes the need for studies of AN influences: "Middle English Scholarship"; see also Dean, "Fair Field."

alric ideals were important to the cultural identity of this class, but England's barons also had important economic interests as feudal landholders, and they shared social and political concerns related to their control over agrarian production. Second, the barony's economic and social position deteriorated between 1066 and 1400 in ways that altered their cultural engagement with literature.

The conquerors adapted quickly to an integrated English and Norman life in England, and developed uniquely regular, stabilizing feudal structures there. In contrast to the fragmentation of power and the complicated, often conflicting oaths of fealty that made administration difficult on the continent, William I's power was clear and complete: he claimed all land in England for the crown, then granted land in tenure only.[16] The strength of the early Norman kings, together with a tenure system that was more clearly stratified than those on the continent, favored the peaceful development of a securely landed aristocracy.

Extensive Angevin reforms further distinguished England's baronial life from that of other feudal monarchies. From the time of Henry II, private war was prohibited; all landholders were sworn in fealty to the king no matter whom their immediate oath of fealty bound them to; and an effective system of royal and baronial courts controlled issues of *novel disseisin* and *mort d'ancestor*.[17] In these conditions, tensions within the barony and between baronial and royal interests were usually played out in the courts rather than on the battlefield. Conditions were more turbulent in many provinces of France, where in the absence of a functional, effective judicial system, private war remained a right and often the only available means of redress. There the period of transition from feudal organization to the centralized state was one of resistance and loss for the aristocracy.[18] In England barons had fewer privileges to lose to royal power from the first. More significantly, their own impulses

16. Good introductory surveys of AN feudalism are R. H. C. Davis, *Normans and Their Myth*, pp. 103–32; and Douglas, *Norman Achievement*.

17. Warren, *Henry II*, pp. 278, 317–61; Painter, "Family." Particular emphasis is placed on the separate and unique aspects of AN culture by Southern, "England in the Twelfth-Century Renaissance"; Legge, "Précocité"; Barlow, "Effects of the Norman Conquest."

18. The long resistance of continental barons to royal attempts to suppress private war and judicial duels, and the inadequacy of continental judicial systems, are outlined in relation to literary history by R. H. Bloch, *Literature and Law*, pp. 63–70, 108–21; see also Cazelles, "Réglementation royale"; Duby, *Région mâconnaise*, pp. 201–3, 569–77.

were predominantly in consonance with the movement toward the national state. Their wealth was considerable, and their power was dependent not on military strength but on the administration of land; accepting their role as managers and submitting to judicial procedures were for them the means to prosperity rather than painful sacrifices.

The relatively peaceful, even domestic nature of the Anglo-Norman barony derived not only from its particular legal and feudal character but also from its relatively inclusive, flexible organization. Unlike the continental hereditary *noblesse*, this barony "was not yet so rigid that it attempted to exclude the *nouveau riche*, the soldier or the administrator by laying down strict qualifications of blood and birth as conditions of entry."[19] Moreover, moving out of baronial status was as easy as moving up to it: England's law of primogeniture "made the development of a *noblesse* impossible in England because it drove younger sons into the ranks of the inferior gentry, into the professions, and even into trade."[20] In these conditions the English barony could not rely on ancestry or title for self-esteem. Power lay in effective administration and service, not in birth alone.

The barony continued to be preoccupied with the control of land and rights under law in the later thirteenth and fourteenth centuries. The economic and political power of the class, however, was considerably eroded during this period by royal encroachments on the jurisdiction of baronial courts, by the growth of trade and towns relative to the agricultural sector, and later by famine, plague, and widespread labor unrest.[21] Mobility characterized the class more and more; careers in law and government became typical routes to gentry standing.[22] These factors challenged the barony's dominance in the later Middle Ages and encouraged the class to draw on sources of status external to its landholding and its more

19. Holt, *Magna Carta*, p. 26. Perroy contrasts the thirteenth-century English and French nobility in his "Social Mobility." Duby finds very little class mobility in France's eleventh and twelfth centuries: see "Enquête"; also M. Bloch, *Société féodale*, II, 73–77.

20. McFarlane, *Nobility*, p. 276. McFarlane modifies this generally accepted formulation (see nn. 22, 23 below) as the barony discovered ways of protecting its interests; still, McFarlane characterizes this barony as an "unformed, almost liquid" class (p. 272). See also Thrupp, *Merchant Class*; Starkey, "Age of the Household."

21. Painter, *English Feudal Barony*, pp. 193–97; McKisack, *Fourteenth Century*, pp. 182–209; Postan, *Mediaeval Economy*, pp. 61–72; Waugh, "Profits of Violence."

22. McFarlane, *Nobility*, pp. 8–15; Jefferies, "Social Mobility"; Bennett, *Community*.

distant warmaking functions. Chivalric ideals, religious and secular orders of knighthood, and "courtly" social behaviors became important sources of justification for the barony's remaining rights. Literature became a guide to these sources and a model for their execution in life.

The fundamental concept of gentle status survived and continued to incorporate both the high baronage and the newest landholders of some substance. Only in the later fourteenth and fifteenth centuries was this fluid society gradually fixed in defined and stratified ranks, so that the peerage, serving in parliament, became clearly superior to the much larger and now subordinate category of gentry.[23] But during most of the fourteenth century, the English barons' identity and concerns evolved directly from those of their Anglo-Norman predecessors. This relationship suggests that the barony constituted the audience for the Middle English adaptations of Anglo-Norman romances.

No one disputes that the Anglo-Norman romances of the twelfth and early thirteenth centuries addressed gentle audiences. But Middle English romances have often been assigned bourgeois and peasant audiences, usually because of their language—English instead of Anglo-Norman—and because of their limited poetic resources. Some English romances may have had ignoble publics, but those considered in this study probably retained the high audience of their Anglo-Norman antecedents and at the same time extended their appeal to include the newly powerful. This degree of continuity in audience is strongly suggested by the thematic sympathies uniting the insular romances. Moreover, the verbal simplicity and naturalism of the English works need not denote a less sophisticated audience.[24] Nor is the use of English a sign of ignoble appeal. There are many indications that even before 1250, knowledge of French was on the decline. Rather than being taught in all gentle families with social aspirations, French gradually became an accomplishment typical only of the highest nobility.[25] Before the close

---

23. Prestwich, *Three Edwards*, pp. 137–64; McFarlane, *Nobility*, pp. 268–78; Coss, "Social Terminology"; Saul, *Knights and Esquires*.

24. We know that even the fabliaux had aristocratic audiences (Muscatine, "Social Background"). Against associating naturalism with a middle-class audience, see Gombrich, rev. of *The Social History of Art*.

25. Records of Richard II's books, Thomas, duke of Gloucester's library, and other great lords' wills and purchases testify to the continued use of French in England (R. F. Green, "Richard II's Books"; Scattergood, "Literary Culture"; Strohm, "Chaucer's Audience"). But at the broader level of the barony as a whole, there is

of the thirteenth century, *Arthour and Merlin* noted the increasing marginality of French for the barony:

> Freynsche vse þis gentilman,
> Ac euerich Inglische Inglische can;   Englishman / knows
> Mani noble ich haue yseiȝe,   seen
> Þat no Freynsche couþe seye:
> Biginne ichil for her loue   I shall / their
> Bi Iesus leue, þat sitt aboue,
> On Inglische tel mi tale.²⁶

The modification that the second couplet makes to the first is telling: although French should be or once was a class marker, the fact is that "mani noble" do not have facility in French. For them—the direct antecedent is the nobles, although "euerich Inglische" may also be included—the poet will proceed in English.

Like Anglo-Norman romance, Middle English romance seems to have developed outside the royal courts of England, as the broad range of lesser baronial courts and households were turning from Anglo-Norman bilingualism to English. The literature most naturally suited to the later barony's station and concerns was to be found in Middle English adaptations of the literature of their predecessors, the Anglo-Norman barony.

Because I am most interested in describing the historical situation of Anglo-Norman and Middle English works, I avoid basing my discussion on a single generic definition of romance. Genre was not an important concept for medieval theorists, nor did poets restrict the term *roman/romaunce* to one set of characteristics.²⁷ Even the works usually called romances today differ widely; thus insofar as observations about the generic nature of medieval romance can be made, they must be fluid and contingent, seeking to clarify the nature of single works rather than to classify them. Broadly speaking, medieval romances are secular fictions of nobility, "storial

---

much to indicate a shift from bilingualism to an acceptance of English as the only comfortable means of communication: see Blaess, "Abbaye de Bordesley"; and Wilson, "English and French."

26. *Arthour and Merlin*, lines 23–29. Albert Croll Baugh's work is the most thorough rebuttal of minstrel and oral composition theories; see, e.g., "Middle English Romance." Ramsey argues that the Middle English (ME) romances had noble audiences in *Chivalric Romances*; and Thrupp's evidence on the libraries of merchants indicates that they were not given to imaginative literature (*Merchant Class*, pp. 161–63, 248–49).

27. See Strohm, "Middle English *Romaunce*"; Gradon believes "it is doubtful whether the romance can be indeed regarded as a genre at all" (*Form and Style*, p. 269; see also pp. 212–72).

Introduction   11

thyng that toucheth gentillesse."[28] Romances do not claim to be coextensive with the contemporary world, as do chronicles, but to reshape and meditate on the world. Like epics, they tell the stories of whole careers; but unlike epics, they do not envision their heroes primarily in service to society's collective need. Instead, romances contemplate the place of private identity in society at large. Their thematizations of stress and harmony between hero and world make this genre an eminently social one which nonetheless proposes that private identity exists somehow above and apart from collective life.

Insular romances flesh out these generic tendencies with concerns specific to England's social conditions. As Hans Robert Jauss and others have persuasively argued, generic variations deserve close attention as signs of differing institutional and ideological structures.[29] I will examine both kinds of structure here. England's feudal institutions provided a way of life distinct from that in other feudal territories. The church was making increasingly bold institutional efforts to influence daily behavior. Finally, the cultural power of Angevin royal and French courts affected the development of romance in England. These broad political, religious, and cultural formations generated belief systems that I term ideologies insofar as they sought to justify or alter their generating conditions.[30] The English barony developed in its own defense an ideology of right rule, social order, and noble virtue. The insular romances show a consistent awareness of all these interconnecting and conflicting claims to value and power. Romances do not engage in the overt polemicism of ideological arguments; in this sense they are disinterested texts. But they do enact and comment on various confrontations among dominant ideologies in relation to England's barony.

28. *Works of Geoffrey Chaucer*, ed. Robinson, *Miller's Prologue*, 3179. Three stimulating discussions of the genre's edges from three perspectives (thematic, structural, stylistic) are: Southern, *Making of the Middle Ages*, pp. 219–57; Bloomfield, "Episodic Motivation and Marvels in Epic and Romance," in *Essays and Explorations*, pp. 97–128; and Zumthor, *Langue, texte, énigme*, pp. 237–48.
29. "Theorie der Gattungen"; other examples are Köhler, *Ideal und Wirklichkeit*; Duby, "'Jeunes'"; and R. H. Bloch, *Literature and Law*. Jameson, *Political Unconscious*, similarly historicizes his analyses of postmedieval romances.
30. I do not use "ideology" pejoratively but rather only to describe a set of interrelated beliefs that informs a particular way of life and works to validate that way of life in its attempts to win and maintain a place for itself in the world. Surely no modern reader adheres fully to any medieval ideology, and this is only one of the ways in which medieval literature is difficult of access (see White, *Metahistory*, pp. 5–7, 22–29; Baechler, *Idéologie*).

In subsequent chapters I delineate three aspects of the insular romances' identity. The romances of English heroes (Chapters 1 and 2) examine the centralizing political belief that national interests must be sustained above all. These works draw on chronicle and epic for conviction, validity, and heroic scale, yet construct a world in which self-advancement is in consonance with defense of the community. In securing his lineal rights the English hero secures the nation; his strength is not simply military but rests in the strength of law, custom, and justice. Rather than functioning as "ancestral" demonstrations of a single family's merit, the romances of English heroes generate an ideal of achievement that responds broadly to the feudal situation of the insular barony.

Church reform and the rise of hagiography provide a second context for the development of romance in England (Chapter 3). Some heroes' careers imitate hagiographic patterns of dedication, sacrifice, and submission. Yet the romances' expanding moral sensitivity clashes with their growing resistance to the abnegation and transcendence modeled in saints' legends. Although the pious insular romances accept faith as a new poetic dimension that can affect heroic behavior, they subvert the deeper implications of Christian teaching. Ultimately, the pious elements in insular romance validate the subordination of faith to worldly values and preoccupations.

Finally, the cultural detachment of Anglo-Norman and Middle English writers from the continental wellsprings of *courtoisie* affects insular approaches to ideals of love and chivalry (Chapters 4 and 5). Courtly convention undergoes a coherent revisionary process in England that resonates with the barony's shrinking resources and loss of status. Anglo-Norman writers tend to be skeptical of courtly poetics, testing *fine amor* against alien conceptions of passion and rejecting the optimistic convention that love interacts fruitfully with prowess. Later insular poets accept a profoundly modified version of courtliness that revises the tradition's claims to exclusivity and high refinement. The didactic openness of the late romances offers their audience a figurative claim to status.

Across their literary interactions, the insular romances are attuned to the realities of English life. As these works draw on and distance themselves from epic, hagiography, and courtly romance, they shape their voices to England's questions. The insular romances' aesthetics are intimately connected to their ideals, and their social and literary history clarifies those interrelations.

Chapter One

Romances of Land and Lineage

English heroes are the subject of half the romances in Anglo-Norman dialect we know of today: the *Romance of Horn, Lai d'Haveloc, Boeve de Haumtone, Gui de Warewic, Fouke le Fitz Waryn,* and *Waldef*. Omitted from Jean Bodel's list of "trois materes . . . / De France et de Bretaigne et de Romme la grant," the "matter of England" continues strongly in Middle English: every Anglo-Norman romance of this group had an English descendant, although the Middle English *Fulk* and *Waldef* are lost. Conversely, of all the Middle English romances of English heroes, only the comparatively late *Athelston* and *Gamelyn* are not demonstrably related to Anglo-Norman sources.[1] This large and cohesive group of romances comments on the English barony's feudal strength and vulnerability by weighing the class convictions that sustained baronial claims.

The romances of English heroes differ thematically from the medieval fictions most familiar to twentieth-century readers. The Old French romances of love and adventure emphasize love's power to transform heroic identity, and trace love's role in precipitating crises between private identity and public expectations.[2] The romances of English heroes instead present external, political crises

---

1. Bodel, *Saxenlied* [*Les Saisnes*], ed. Menzel and Stengel, lines 1–2. On lost ME and AN romances of English heroes see Intro., n. 14.
2. Critics of diverse persuasions agree that the central thematic tension of OF romance is between the individual and society (love and adventure): e.g., Köhler, *Ideal und Wirklichkeit*; Hanning, "Social Significance," pp. 3–4; Zumthor, *Poétique médiévale*, pp. 355–57.

that are met by a fully worthy and capable hero who senses no problematic conflict between his own desires and those of his society. In this respect they may seem close to epic, but none of their heroes is entirely a representative of his community, bent on winning its survival even at the expense of his own life. The English hero is self-interested; his goals are personal, typically involving his protection of feudal rights and the honor of his family. This pattern, in turn, resembles that of the Old French *gestes des révoltés*, whose rebel barons defy their lords in defense of private rights. But in the insular works, adherence to legality and tradition always brings success and stasis, while the *gestes des révoltés* move inexorably toward chaos, misfortune, and disillusion—"a torn, ambiguous world, where the norms of feudal society are no longer conducive to existence."[3] In contrast to the *gestes des révoltés*, the romances of English heroes have faith in traditional systems and confidence that justice will prevail.

These romances are not concerned with the revelatory experience of love, nor with an ideal of service to the nation, nor with rebel barons' dark affairs. Rather, they explore an imaginative response to the insular barony's peculiar situation. Unusually wealthy and peaceful, England's titled landholders were in cause and consequence unusually restricted by the crown. Virtually without military recourse, barons relied on the courts and on the right of inheritance to perpetuate their control of land. The romances of English heroes picture baronial claims that rise above the merely legal to the unquestionably just, and join blood lines inextricably to property rights. Political interests become universal goods as the hero's impulse toward personal achievement supports a broader, impersonal impulse toward social stability. Beyond this wide-ranging harmony are the pagans, usurpers, monsters, and wrong-headed kings who challenge properly established order. This poetic conception of noble life is grounded in the barony's history.

English Heroes and English History

The Anglo-Norman romances of English heroes developed in fruitful interaction with chronicles during the twelfth century. The chronicles inspired by Norman rule have so literary a cast that des-

---

3. Calin, *Epic of Revolt*, p. 115; see also pp. 127–32 on the historical context for these works in France; and R. H. Bloch, *Literature and Law*, pp. 100–103.

ignations such as "historiographie littéraire" and "poetic histories" are coined for them.[4] Both the chronicles and the Anglo-Norman romances of English heroes glorify England's past, with the direct or secondary effect of justifying Norman presence in England. The aims which these chronicles and romances share, however, should not obscure their essential differences.

William the Conqueror took the throne of England on the ground that Edward the Confessor had designated him next in the line of succession. His somewhat specious claim, eagerly endorsed by the barons, higher churchmen, and merchants who came to settle in England, gave political impetus to works relating pre-Conquest history to Norman rule. Wace dramatized Edward's designation of his successor in the *Roman de Rou;* William of Malmesbury and Henry of Huntingdon included political justifications for the Conquest in their accounts of England's glorious past; Geoffrey Gaimar's *Estoire des Engleis* presented insular history in a continuum from the heroic past through the death of William II.[5] The royal asseveration that the Conquest was legal, and that continuity characterized insular life despite the Conquest, encouraged chroniclers to discover English heroes and to present them as *antecessores* (forebears, understood as ancestors) for the Normans. By this alchemy even historical figures such as Waldef and Hereward who opposed the very Conquest itself receive praise and generate pride in the chronicles.[6] Although such transformations and inventions necessarily partake of the fictional, chronicles present their material both as if it were fully historical and as if it demonstrated the worth of the current heritors of a glorious past.

The Anglo-Norman romances of English heroes accomplish a different task, and in a less direct manner. Whereas the chronicles justify the power of rulers in England openly,[7] the romances argue for the rights of vassals covertly, under the cloak of imagination and

---

4. Foreville, "Typologie du roi," p. 276; Hanning, "Beowulf," p. 78; see also Meneghetti, "'Estoire des Engleis'"; and Partner, *Serious Entertainments,* esp. pp. 194–211.
5. *Maistre Wace's roman de Rou,* ed. Andresen, lines 5565ff.; William of Malmesbury, *Gesta Regum Anglorum,* ed. Stubbs; Henry of Huntingdon, *Historia Anglorum,* ed. Arnold; Geoffrey Gaimar, *L'Estoire des Engleis,* ed. Bell.
6. R. H. C. Davis, *Normans and Their Myth,* pp. 130–31; "Waltheof"; Hart, "Hereward 'the Wake.'"
7. R. H. C. Davis, *Normans and Their Myth,* pp. 122–31; Köhler, *Ideal und Wirklichkeit,* pp. 54–61; Gransden, *Historical Writing,* pp. 92–104, 173–74, 186–218. An interesting discussion of the differences between chronicle and romance is Gouttebroze, "Henri II," pp. 106–9.

invention. The chronicles address specific patrons and advertise openly the associations they invent or discover between Norman rulers and heroes of history; but the romances of English heroes explore more broadly the issues of insular baronial life, and offer a poetic image of that life's value.[8]

To explain the preoccupation of these romances with legality and feudal tenure, some literary historians favor the theory of "ancestral romance" or "roman généalogique." The ancestral theory proposes that four of the six Anglo-Norman romances of English heroes—*Boeve, Gui, Waldef,* and *Fouke*—owe their genesis to a particular family's commission, which itself had been sparked by a specific crisis in the rights of the family to its lands or titles.[9] This theory is unpersuasive. None of these romances praises a patron, mentions the contemporary family holding the title of the celebrated hero, or even takes careful note of the alleged patrons' history and possessions. If *Boeve* was written for the Albinis, why is Southampton, which they never possessed, made Boeve's home; and why is the hero buried at St. Laurent rather than at Wymundham, the traditional burial abbey of the Albini family?[10] Only the title to Arundel associates the family's circumstances with the romance. If *Gui de Warewic* was designed to celebrate the union of the lands of Margery d'Oilly (Wallingford) and Henry de Newburgh (Warwick), why does Guy alienate Wallingford from his holdings by giving it to his old tutor's family? If Osney, anxious to ensure its continuing role as a family abbey, is responsible for the composition of *Gui*, why is Gui's holy death set not there but in a hermitage and his burial not there but at a new abbey in Lorraine? *Fouke le Fitz*

---

8. Since patronage was so tenuous, we would expect a patronized work to address the patron; thus, the absence of dedication in the romances of English heroes is significant. Because poets held professional jobs (like Chaucer's) they were not dependent on patronage for regular income; see Bolton, "Literary Composition," pp. ix–xxxvi.

9. Mason, "Beauchamps' Ancestors"; Legge, *Anglo-Norman Literature*, pp. 139–75; Ewert, ed., *Gui de Warewic*, I, iv–viii; Levy, "Ancestral Romance" and "Waltheof."

10. Levy, "Ancestral Romance," pp. 448–51; Tierney, *Arundel*, I, 191. Similarly, in the absence of any direct information, it is possible to conjecture that *Waldef* was written for the Bigod family, which endured from 1177 to 1199 a great legal crisis in its holdings (Legge, *Anglo-Norman Literature*, pp. 145–46; Painter, "Family," p. 12); but equally possible to conjecture that its patrons were the Mortimers of Attleborough, whose holdings corresponded in many respects to those of Waldef (Levy, "Waltheof," p. 196; Robert Anderson, "Waldef," in *Grundriss*, ed. Frappier et al., p. 290.

Waryn, in spite of its far more specific and contemporary historical setting, includes as well so many inexplicable mistakes in family history that it is unlikely the Fitz Warin family could have been associated with its composition.[11] Indeed, the random errors in genealogy, the absence of reference to any patron, and the general vagueness of setting all suggest that these romances were designed and written for a wider audience than a single family.

The attempt to support the conjectured relationship between a specific family and an ancestral romance with evidence of a motivating crisis in family rights or titles is likewise unconvincing, simply because of the abundance of possible crises. Literary historians have variously related the genesis of *Gui de Warewic* to a union of the rival Newburgh and Oilly families (ca. 1200); the death of the last Oilly male and praise of the heiress's husband, Henry de Newburgh (1232); the claim of Thomas, the heiress's son, to his mother's lands; and the engagement of Richard, brother of Henry III and tenant of Wallingford (1242).[12] The earldom of Warwick suffered many other depredations in the thirteenth century that could also be viewed as motivating crises: several appropriations of land by the king to reward services; various financial burdens; and perhaps most dramatic, the king's attempt to force marriage with John du Plessis on the widowed Countess Margery (1242).[13] For *Boeve de Haumtone*, William of Albini II's acquisition of the title to Arundel (1154), his son's attempts to recover Arundel from Henry II (1189–90), and William of Albini IV's insecure position with Henry III after the baronial uprising under John (ca. 1215–21) have each been suggested as the critical moment responsible for the romance's composition.[14] To these possibilities could be added the censure of Nigel of Albini's son for siding with King Henry the Younger

11. For details of major historical inaccuracies in *Fouke*, see Painter, "Sources of *Fouke*"; E. M. Martin, "Shropshire Lad," p. 93. Painter suggests that *Fouke* was written in response to public demand for a compilation of local legends. Meisel agrees that the romance was not written for the family (*Barons*, pp. 132–38).

12. Mason, "Beauchamps' Ancestors"; Ewert, edition, I, v–vi; Legge, *Anglo-Norman Literature*, p. 162; Levy, "Ancestral Romance," pp. 224, 228–39. Wathelet-Willem, *Chanson de Guillaume*, pp. 42–45 believes, as does Mason, the hand of a *Pseudo-Turpin* MS of ca. 1214 to be identical to that of *Gui* MS E, but *Gui's* composite plot and some elements of dialect and versification (Ewert, I, xxiv–xxv) argue a later date for its composition.

13. Mason, "Earldom of Warwick."

14. Legge, *Anglo-Norman Literature*, p. 159; see also her "Influence of Patronage," pp. 140–41; and Levy, "Ancestral Romance," pp. 444–45.

against Henry II (1173) and royal seizures of the family lands for periods of time after the deaths of William of Albini IV (1221) and William of Albini V (1224).[15]

This multiplicity of crises in baronial holdings not only reduces the likelihood that any single crisis motivated the creation of a romance but, more important, indicates that these works respond to pervasive qualities of English feudalism. The relation of these romances to their world is better understood by acknowledging their pertinence to the situation of the Anglo-Norman aristocracy as a whole than by seeking, on so little evidence, to limit their expressive import to a particular crisis in a particular family. Furthermore, once we set aside the ancestral theory, we can group the *Romance of Horn* and the *Lai d'Haveloc* with the other four romances of English heroes. *Horn* and *Haveloc* seem not to conform to the ancestral model because their heroes are kings rather than barons. The distinction is specious, however. Horn and Haveloc, like the other English heroes, control only small areas of England; more important, all six romances are marked by strong similarities in narrative design, in theme, and in social values. The narrative pattern of departure and return that characterizes these works is typically incorporated in a pattern of dispossession and reinstatement, the hero regaining through his admixture of courage and legal knowledge a rightful inheritance wrongfully seized from him. By translating a basic revenge pattern into terms of feudal reinstatement and translating love motifs into terms of family stability and continuity, this literature accommodates fundamental Anglo-Norman baronial concerns.

The dynamic of Anglo-Norman feudalism, that of an unusually strong royal power in tension with a smoothly running landed baronial hierarchy, was well established in England by the second half of the twelfth century. Feudal and legal systems in England differed in some ways from those on the continent. The autonomy of barons in England was comparatively slight: they had lesser rights of jurisdiction over their fiefs, no right to private war or to ownership of castles; and they were universally sworn in allegiance to the king, rather than enjoying private or partially private rights.[16]

---

15. Painter, "Family," p. 6; Levy, "Ancestral Romance," pp. 440–43.
16. All these measures are important in determining the character of a tenure system, according to Brown, "Tyranny"; and Bisson, "Feudal Monarchy." See also Warren, *Henry II*, pp. 277–78.

Perhaps in part because of these constraints and in part because of their considerable landed wealth, the Anglo-Norman barony experienced a relatively peaceful and productive development.[17] Under Henry II, however, the ordered strength of this barony was challenged by the Angevin policy of increasingly careful and intrusive supervision of baronial lands, titles, marriages, and inheritance rights. Feudal custom already gave the king power to forbid marriages of his vassals, to choose husbands for orphaned and widowed women, and to levy succession duties on lands and titles. All the Angevin kings extended these powers more or less extralegally to include forced marriages of the king's choice, outright seizure of lands, and refusal of inheritances.[18] Paradoxically, these characteristic abuses of royal power were accompanied by a series of reforms and developments aimed at regulating baronial disputes and establishing a uniform national taxation system. In the Angevin exchequer and royal courts can be found the roots of modern state bureaucracy.[19]

The Angevin kings' subversion of law and custom aroused great resistance among the Anglo-Norman landholders. But with the exception of the revolt of 1173, the landed interests of the barony cast the struggle into legal rather than violent terms. As Angevin attention turned to the continent, and particularly during King Richard's prolonged absences from England, baronial strength and responsibility increased. Landholders practiced subinfeudation within their own families, thereby placing portions of their holdings a step further from the king's control, and patiently followed legal procedures for obtaining and regaining land.[20] This readiness to work within bureaucratic structures is what is so interesting, and so important to understanding Anglo-Norman romance, about the barony's response to England's feudal and legal systems. King and

17. Poole, *Domesday Book*, writes that during the few years of civil strife known as the Anarchy under the last Norman king, Stephen, "it may be doubted whether the state of England was very different from that which prevailed almost continuously in the twelfth century in many parts of Europe where the feud and the private castle were not prohibited. . . . The English people had been 'spoilt', as we might say, by more than half a century of peace and strong rule for a state of things which on the Continent was almost a commonplace" (p. 150).

18. Painter, "Family," pp. 1–16; Warren, *King John*, p. 175; Jolliffe, *Angevin Kingship*, p. 13.

19. Warren, *Henry II*, pp. 317–61; on growing professionalization in law see Turner, "Judges."

20. Appleby, *England Without Richard*, p. 234; Painter, "Family," p. 16; M. Bloch, *Société féodale*, II, 227–31; Petit-Dutaillis, *Monarchie féodale*, pp. 150–52.

barons alike accepted the new bureaucracy as advantageous. Taxation and royal justice kept landholders under the king's eye, but at the same time the royal courts' new legal procedures controlling inheritance and disseisin expedited and clarified the administration of baronial rights as never before. What the barony opposed was royal *abuse* of law and royal refusal to submit to the law's newly refined procedures.

England's barons also acquiesced to Henry II's revision of their military role. John Schlight concludes that the "driving force behind Henry II's use of mercenaries was not disloyalty nor disunity but the disinterest of his nobles in military affairs."[21] This was the most striking of many developments that countered the purpose and character of a military aristocracy. But since England's ruling class had never been a true nobility of blood nor a solely military class, the developments of the twelfth century were evolutionary rather than deleterious. The personal power of barons had long been and continued to be primarily dependent on the control and administration of their lands: on agricultural labor, roads and bridges, dowries, marriages, and above all inheritances.[22]

The high value of inheritances in the Anglo-Norman system presented unusual difficulties. Theoretically, in any feudal system a vassal holds land from his lord only by personal oath; he cannot pass it on to heirs. In practice, especially as the personal and military quality of the feudal relationship faded, lords normally permitted the transfer of fiefs from one generation to the next upon performance of homage and payment of a relief fee. In England these transfers were at the forefront of legal dispute and reform during the later twelfth and thirteenth centuries.

William Marshal's biographer, who admired continental chivalric life, censures the displacement of England's power struggles from the military to the judicial sphere:

> Mais or nous ront mise en prison
> Chevalerie li halt home:
> Par perece qui les asome,
> E par conseil de coveitise
> Nous ront largesse en prison mise,

21. *Monarchs and Mercenaries*, p. 74.
22. Warren, *Henry II*, pp. 232–34, 367–80; in *King John*, Warren describes Magna Carta as "largely concerned with succession dues and wardship, with widows and fish-weirs, with forest laws and forced marriages" (p. 180).

E l'esrer e le torneier
Si sunt torné al plaideier.²³

But now, those in power have imprisoned chivalry for us: through laziness that weighs them down and through the advice of covetousness, they have imprisoned largesse for us, and errantry and tourneying have turned to court pleading.

The Anglo-Norman barony was uniquely peaceful, and its domesticity was well served by the Angevin moves toward legal systematization. Magna Carta (1215) was the greatest single expression of this peculiarity of Anglo-Norman life. Magna Carta sought not to reestablish freer relations between king and barons, but to incorporate the king into his own legal system, to restrain him, too, within the fine new net of law he had cast around his barons. Far from being a radical challenge to royal rights, Magna Carta affirms the trend toward systematic, centralized government operations.²⁴

Such was the milieu, tenaciously legalistic yet adaptable and practical, in which the romances of English heroes were written. The composition of the last Anglo-Norman romances in the group, *Gui de Warewic* (ca. 1230) and *Fouke le Fitz Waryn* (ca. 1280, extant prose version ca. 1330) overlaps with that of the earliest Middle English versions, *King Horn* (ca. 1225) and *Havelok the Dane* (ca. 1280). Even the latest of the English hero romances descended from Anglo-Norman, those in the Auchinleck book (ca. 1330), give the group a fairly restricted chronological range.

The social and political situation of the later Anglo-Norman and the Middle English works remained largely the same through the early fourteenth century. Magna Carta did not reshape the central issues of concern between king and barons, nor did it permanently alter the kinds of conflict generated by those issues. Rather, Magna Carta exemplifies the nature of aristocratic conflict throughout the period: it seeks to apportion royal and baronial economic, legal, and customary rights in the context of general principles benefiting both parties. Subsequent developments extend these concerns and

---

23. *Guillaume le Maréchal*, ed. Meyer, lines 2686–92; on inheritance and feudal custom see Warren, *Henry II*, p. 342.

24. Holt, *Magna Carta*, p. 30 et passim; Warren, *Henry II*, pp. 380–96. For further emphasis on the barony's legalistic nature, see Treharne, *Baronial Plan*, pp. 30–37: during the dispute with King John, the barony "never ceased to bear a constitutional character, being generally reasoned and moderate, aiming at the redress of definite grievances, and taking its stand upon the law and custom of past days" (p. 35).

counter "the curious view that king and barons were natural enemies."[25] The baronial reform movement of 1258–67 based its work in Magna Carta and attempted to improve administration of the charter's principles in the context of ever-increasing royal systematization. Like the revolt against King John, the revolt of 1258 "was not primarily a revolt against over-centralisation. It was essentially directed against the king's incapacity to direct this centralised system of government along the right lines."[26] The reform's important legal documents, the Provisions of Westminster (1259; reconfirmed 1263, 1267) and the Statute of Marlborough (1267), provided new structures for carrying out the central ideal of Magna Carta, that uniform and consistent government based on the law of the land is the concern of king and barons alike.[27] Thus, although tension between the royal and baronial factions over how to apportion power was constant, their shared interest in rationalized government generated a deeper complicity between them in the transition from localized feudal organization to a centralized national state.

The later reforms incorporated a wider social spectrum. Although the right of all classes to participate in government was not yet considered, the later thirteenth-century parliaments called for local knights and burgesses to represent shires and towns, signaling a new awareness that national administration could not rest in the exclusive control of king and barons. Moreover, the English barony's vision of equitable, legally responsive government tended to coincide with the interests of other groups, so that the barons' reform movement won widespread support.[28] Further, the sense of common cause that the movement created was sustained by the openness of England's class structure. Except at the highest level of the nobility, where during the thirteenth and fourteenth centuries the expiration of great lineages tended to concentrate estates in fewer hands, mobility was relatively widespread.[29] Several factors

---

25. Powicke, *Thirteenth Century*, pp. 1–8 (quote at p. 6). The "curious view" is more credible for relations between barons and king in France; see Köhler, *Ideal und Wirklichkeit*, pp. 21–22, 35–36.
26. Treharne, *Baronial Plan*, pp. 46–47; cf. pp. 37–40.
27. Powicke, *Thirteenth Century*, pp. 132–47, 215–18; Treharne, *Baronial Plan*, pp. 343–48.
28. Treharne, *Thirteenth Century*, pp. 355–56 (see also pp. 348–58); Coss, "Sir Geoffrey de Langley," pp. 3–34; Powicke, *Thirteenth Century*, pp. 142, 197.
29. McFarlane, *Nobility*, pp. 6–9, 122–26, 172–76. See also Jefferies, "Social Mobility": Edmund Chelrey began a commoner, through a career in law rose to hold in wardship the lands of the Fitzwarin family of romance, won knighthood, and estab-

militated against a sense of isolation and class interest among the barony: primogeniture could displace the highborn from gentility; social flexibility could reward with gentle status the hard work and ambition of commoners; and the barony's landed power united it with other groups (except the largest and most exploited) in the desire for orderly and predictable government.

Throughout the period of the romances of English heroes, then, baronial society was based on landholding. Barons defended their fiefs by bequest and litigation, but the crown's power, the centralizing process of state formation, and class fluidity constrained baronial action in various ways. Their concerns first receive literary expression in the Anglo-Norman romances of English heroes. Tales of departure and return are hardly unique to insular literature, but that formula's treatment connects these romances to their time and place, and to their Middle English versions. A persistent confidence in custom, law, and social order infuses their accounts of dispossession and reinstatement, translating the barony's historical situation into terms of absolute justice and providential certainty. In these works the political and economic interests of the realm turn out to derive from those of the hero, validating his preoccupation with private concerns. The English hero is an adopted ancestor whose exploits and nobility establish and enhance the status of the insular aristocracy. His story typically traces the loss and recovery of his inherited lands and titles, not through historically mimetic fines, inheritance duties, and petitions to the king, but through a glorious exile, a righteous and sometimes bloody return, and a marriage blessed with sons who extend their father's holdings in a cyclical repetition of his story.

The linguistic shift from French to English enlarges the potential audience beyond those members of the nobility and clergy who artificially maintained Anglo-Norman as a "language of culture." Reduced attention to differences of rank in the Middle English romances suggests that their audiences were indeed broader socially than those of their Anglo-Norman sources, although we have seen that the English barony itself was revising its already modest sense of separateness in the thirteenth and fourteenth centuries. Also suggesting an expanded audience for Middle English romance

---

lished his heirs in gentle status. M. Bloch discusses the later evolution of the barony (*Société féodale*, II, 73–77).

are the thematic simplifications and appeals to emotion that supplement or replace appeals to law and reason,[30] and treat the original themes of the Anglo-Norman romances in a more subjective, less politically committed mode. Yet the Middle English works have close structural, thematic, and stylistic sympathies with their sources' depictions of dynastic aspiration, social order, and baronial rights. This chapter and the next will trace those sympathies across two centuries.

Horn's Heritage

The *Romance of Horn* by Thomas (ca. 1170) and *King Horn* (ca. 1225) are the earliest extant versions of Horn's story and probably the two earliest Anglo-Norman and Middle English romances of English heroes.[31] In theme they integrate the heroic defense of family rights with a sense of common purpose. They affirm, in poetic fictions, that the feudal community is essentially a just order that will prosper. In method they differ considerably. The *Romance of Horn* is ornamental and archaizing in style, yet acutely contemporary in its concerns and aristocratic in its sympathies; *King Horn* achieves a timeless, elemental quality through extreme narrative concision and sharply reduced social detail and class sympathy.

The doubled expulsion-and-return pattern of the *Romance of Horn* is identical in outline to that of *King Horn*. The child Horn and his followers, set adrift by the pagan conquerors of Horn's father Aälof, arrive in the country of Hunlaf (Ailmar *KH*), where they grow to manhood. Horn accedes to the pleas of the king's daughter Rigmel (Rimenhild *KH*) and they exchange vows. He wins knighthood and fights pagan invaders, but his traitorous follower Wikele (Fikenhild *KH*) brings about his second exile by misrepresenting the lovers' relationship and Horn's ambitions to the king. Alone this time, Horn travels to a new land disguised as a humble knight, but here he does so well against pagan invaders that he is offered the succession and the hand of the king's daughter. Receiving the news that Rigmel is about to marry another, Horn returns to Hunlaf's

---

30. Duby, "Cultural Patterns."
31. The author "Thomas" is a different poet for each of the three Anglo-Norman romances so designated; see Wind, "Incertitudes," pp. 1130–31. I use Pope and Reid's edition of *The Romance of Horn* (hereafter cited as *RH*) and Hall's edition of *King Horn* (*KH*; my quotations are from MS C unless otherwise noted). The incomplete *Horn Childe* (ed. J. Caro) derives from *KH* and will not be considered here.

kingdom, rescues and marries her, and pardons Wikele. He then recaptures his father's throne from the pagans, and warned by a dream he returns in disguise a second time to rescue Rigmel from Wikele's stronghold. Horn kills Wikele, rewards his followers, and returns with Rigmel to rule his homeland.[32]

The *Romance of Horn* is a beautifully balanced achievement that at once acknowledges and ideally resolves vital conflicts of insular baronial life. Each narrative element in the work's doubled pattern of expulsion and return echoes and expands a previous element in an even progression toward the achievement of land, power, and stability. Each stage in the story's progress marks, both in itself and in its echoing of a previous stage, the steady movement from deprivation to reacquisition and from moral wrong to right. This movement is itself double, represented both by the usurpation and rewinning of Horn's birthright and by the separation and reunion in marriage of Horn and Rigmel. These two narrative lines, two aspects of the movement toward family stability, support and echo each other throughout the romance. Horn's first service in exile, during which the king and his daughter are involved in the hero's struggle "'De purchacier mun regne'" (1809), is repeated in full during Horn's second exile as the second king approves his strength and the second princess reenacts the aggressive courtship of Rigmel. Horn's first single combat and full battle with pagan invaders in Brittany, which play the double role of a first proof of love and "sa premere venjance" (1321), are paralleled in his second exile by vengeance on Aälof's murderer himself, in single combat with the help of Rigmel's ring, and by a second battle victory. The treacherous accusation that Horn threatens Hunlaf's power and his daughter's honor is repudiated in King Gudreche's offer of both his kingdom and his daughter in reward for Horn's services. Horn twice returns disguised to rescue Rigmel from competing suitors. Finally, he balances his initial expulsion with a last battle against the pagans on his home soil, so that the usurper himself "set ben ke par Horn la mort ert revengee / De sun pere Ááluf, ki de meint ert ploree" [knew well that Horn had revenged the death of his

---

32. Diverse conjectures about the source of the Horn story are "little more than guesses": Leach, *Angevin Britain*, p. 331; also Legge, *Anglo-Norman Literature*, p. 98. Recent studies plausibly conclude that *KH* is a direct descendant of *RH*, and that *RH* is not drawn from a lost source but is a new creation drawn from contemporary material: Christmann, "Verhältnis"; Hofer, "Horn et Rimel."

father Aälof, who was lamented by many] (4704–5). Horn's moving reunion with his mother may even parallel his association with Rigmel, since both relationships express his restoration of family stability and continuity. Thus, the fundamental design of regaining lost social position is doubled in motive—revenge and love—as well as in events.[33]

The poet's great affinity for doubles extends inward to small textual details and outward beyond the boundaries of the romance itself. Repetitions of significant developments, often as laisse links, emphasize the plot's doubling; and short passages occasionally recall earlier scenes.[34] On the largest scale, the whole romance forms a sequel to that of Horn's father, Aälof (1–5).

What is the attraction of doubling for Thomas, an attraction so strong that it patterns his work from the broadest structural to the smallest stylistic levels? That Horn's own double is his father suggests an answer. Horn's career takes much of its value from reaffirming, by repeating, the career of his father Aälof. As a foundling in Hunlaf's court, Horn recalls his father's life as a foundling in Suddene, Aälof's marriage to the king's daughter there, and his inheritance of that kingdom (250–81). When considering Horn's request to be knighted in order to fight invading pagans, Hunlaf remembers that Aälof saved his benefactor from pagan invaders (1386–89, 1425–26). Horn's favorite follower, Haderof, is the son of Aälof's best knight (362–68). Of Horn's betrayer Wikele, whose grandfather falsely accused Aälof, the poet says pointedly: "Fel traïtrë iert cist, pur taunt iert alignez" [he was an evil traitor, thus he was true to lineage] (1835). This emphasis on the continuity from Aälof's life to Horn's suggests that a son both duplicates his father's career and extends it into a new one. From this perspective the doubles in the text, like its cyclical patterns, endorse structurally the theme of a family's renewal and extension, generation by generation, of its vitality and its rights. In almost all the romances of

---

33. Although the romance is set in three countries (Suddene, Brittany, Westir), the first is only a frame for the doubled development—that is, the first setting is necessary in order for there to be two exiles, two returns, two periods of servitude, and so on.

34. Rigmel's maid dreams that Horn presents Rigmel with a falcon that she holds to her breast; the disguised Horn reveals himself through veiled references to a goshawk he fears may have been harmed during his absence (729–36, 4257–68). Horn insults his father's murderer by referring to the myth that Mohammed was devoured by pigs; on the eve of Horn's final victory the usurper Rodmund dreams that he is attacked by murderous swine (3019–24, 4644–53).

English heroes, duplication expresses an envisioned consonance between lineal descent and perpetual rights to land. Although the question of the land's heritability is elevated to a clear moral level by making Horn's enemies pagans rather than a rightful king, Thomas emphasizes repeatedly that Horn's goal is dynastic—to avenge his father and to regain his land.[35]

The poet Thomas concludes Horn's achievement by announcing that the hero's son, Hadermod, will in turn extend his father's work by conquering Africa and avenging "tuz ses parenz" on the pagans there (5227-28). Simultaneously Thomas announces that his own son, Gilimot, will tell the story of Hadermod: "Controvures ert bon: e de mei ce retendra" [he is a good composer, and he inherits that from me] (5233). The fictional veil is pierced; the son doubles his father not only in romance but in romance writing. Surely this implies a promise of something more than vicarious fictional fulfillment for the audience as well. In a gesture remarkable for its artistic boldness and its social optimism, the poet suggests that the just and fruitful extension of one generation's achievements into those of the next generation is not simply a literary ideal but an attainable social reality.

King Horn is so radically condensed an account of Horn's life that it might be expected to lack much of the sense of the Anglo-Norman account. But the two works are closely allied despite great divergences in presentation. *King Horn*'s rapid, action-centered narration still interprets the story's underlying themes of revenge and love in terms of the characteristically insular concern for regaining a rightful heritage and achieving family stability.[36]

That *King Horn* takes the stances of the *Romance of Horn* is remarkable in view of the two works' vastly different verbal resources. Thomas writes the *Romance of Horn* in laisses, without *laisses similaires* but with occasional one-line concatenation between laisses. His conservative form is in keeping with the mysterious or archaic place-names, the distant historical setting, and the frequent reference to old customs and ceremonies that pervade the work. At the same time, Thomas modernizes the laisse by using a twelve-

---

35. E.g., *RH* 323-25, 336-37, 1083-88, 1136-39, 1313-18, 1465-71, 2900-10, 2918, 2934.
36. On the use of the motifs of revenge and love in *KH* see Hartenstein, *Studien zur Hornsage*, pp. 49-50; Mehl, *Middle English Romances*, p. 50; McKnight, "Germanic Elements," pp. 222-23; Hall, *KH*, p. lvi.

syllable line, enjambment, a lyric caesura, and rhyme rather than assonance. These modifications suggest that Thomas's lyrical laisse was a deliberate archaism, designed to confer a sense of authenticity and tradition on his story, as in some English alliterative poetry of the fourteenth century.[37] This modified laisse strikes a handsome accord between formality and narrative flexibility, between dignity and expressiveness. The slowly-paced, elegant alexandrines develop both court and battle scenes with leisurely assurance, taking equal pleasure in the objects of noble life and in the skill with which Horn handles them. Horn's performance of the *lai* of Batolf (2824–44), for example, is by far the most complete technical description we have of *lai* performance, yet its details are suffused with a compelling sense of the moment's dramatic importance: Horn reveals his personal excellence for the first time in Westir, not arrogantly but in veiled devotion to Rigmel through the *lai* by her brother Baltof. Characteristically, great richness of detail charged with a deep sense of purpose gives Thomas's verse its intensity.

Small flashes of humor and irony occasionally lighten, but do not subvert, the serious tone of the work. With macabre finesse Thomas associates his inability to describe a scene of carnage with the victims' own silence: "Taunt i veïssez morz gesir gole baéé, / Nes savreit acunter nule buche letréé" [there you'd have seen so many dead lying openmouthed that no educated mouth could reckon them] (1622–23). This gentle ironizing, particularly subtle in its simultaneous awareness of the scene's horror and of its fictionality, suggests the range of expression Thomas achieves within a generally sober and slowly cadenced narrative.

King Horn could hardly have a more different stylistic texture. This earliest Middle English romance, rising from a seriously weakened if not interrupted English verse tradition, is in the process of

---

37. Pope, *RH*, II, 6, concludes on the contrary that Thomas's form illustrates "a stage in the passage from epic to romance," while Legge, "Influence of Patronage," conjectures that the form may be a literary regression representing the changed atmosphere of the court after the defeat of King Henry the Younger. The first conclusion assumes that AN literature is best measured in terms of continental genres and further that Thomas had no conscious control over his form; the second depends on the unlikely theory that *RH* was written in the court of Henry II—unlikely both in view of the poem's baronial sympathies and in view of Horn's military campaign against the Angevins (lines 1737–50). For recent work on English alliterative poetry, see Lawton, ed., *Alliterative Poetry*; and Levy and Szarmach, eds., *Alliterative Tradition*.

finding the very rhythms and locutions fundamental to narrative verse, through reference to Layamon, to French verse, and no doubt to unpreserved popular verse.[38] The most striking contrast in verbal resources between the *Romance of Horn* and *King Horn* is in social and physical detail. A profusion of Anglo-Norman customs, stratagems, and word-plays; a host of uncles, cousins, and retainers; a wealth of spiced wines, white greyhounds, brocades, and jewels are swept entirely from the Middle English scene, stranding each character and each encounter in apparently desolate space.

As if to emphasize this rigorous limitation of detail, *King Horn* often resorts to one formula in narrating repeated similar circumstances. Couplets expressing Horn's planned reconquest of Suddene may be meant to recall previous pagan threats:

> Payns him wolde slen   slay
> Oþer al quic flen.   Or skin alive
>
> 'Alle we hem schulle sle
> & al quic hem fle.'
>   (85–86, 1369–70)
>
> 'Þis lond we wulleʒ wynne   seek to conquer
> & sle þat þer is inne.'   those therein
>
> 'Wulle ʒe þis lond winne
> & sle þat þeris inne?'
>   (603–4, 1357–58)

Repetition is unquestionably the defining quality of *King Horn*'s style: it marks the narration of similar episodes throughout the story and also heightens crucial moments, emphasizes particularly important scenes such as Horn's knighting (445–504) and his mother's withdrawal from society (73–78), and conveys emotional states as diverse as Rimenhild's silent frustration (253–60) and her imperious desire (535–40).

In part, this style is a function of the romance's early date; *King Horn* is not yet at the point of toning and varying formulaic locutions to fit different situations. It is not clear whether the recurrence of formulas represents deliberate verbal echoing or simply the application of a limited number of locutions to a relatively larger number of situations. Whatever medieval ears heard in these

---

38. H. S. West, *Versification of King Horn*; McIntosh, "Alliterative Verse." The role of oral performance is reexamined by Quinn and Hall, *Jongleur*.

repetitions, M. Hynes-Berry argues that for us they "actively function in the romance to create a cohesion and emotional coherence."[39] This analysis counters the old assumption that because repetition is a necessary function of limited poetic means, it must have no aesthetic value, or even a negative one.[40]

But we can go farther, to link *King Horn*'s repetitive style to its thematic emphases. The very insistence, the pervasiveness, of repetition in *King Horn* and in Middle English romance as a whole indicates that its presence is neither fortuitous nor without aesthetic purpose. In a structural study of repetition in Middle English romance, Susan Wittig concludes that "within the repeated patterns of formulaic language there is a kind of psychological comfort, an assurance that the social institutions in which the audience has invested itself are stable and secure, that the traditions have been preserved, that the future is safe."[41] This understanding of the meaning generated by repetitive style corroborates the thematic emphases of the romances of English heroes. Their conservative faith in established social patterns is appropriately embodied in a verbal style that connotes the same conservative faith. *King Horn*'s repetitive style achieves, through more restricted poetic means, an effect of assurance and tradition analogous to that conveyed by Thomas's calm, deliberate, archaizing alexandrines.

Deprived of the thickening press of detail that in Anglo-Norman gives themes their solidity and conviction, *King Horn* must use other measures to validate its themes. One such measure is powerful emotion. The Anglo-Norman Rigmel's quiet pensiveness at her forced wedding and her ready acquiescence to a life of poverty with Horn (4122–28, 4284–308) are replaced by Rimenhild's vehement and tearful protests at her wedding and her dramatic suicide attempt when she believes Horn to be dead (1032–50, 1191–208). Both versions reunite the lovers after testing the lady's loyalty, but the first casts the scene in an emotionally controlled mood and gives the test a socioeconomic function, while the second is freely asocial and passionate. In many other instances in *King Horn* violent emotions, particularly sorrow and frustration—bitter tears, bloody tears, wringing hands, waxing wild, hot blood, burning hearts[42]—suffuse themes with energy and conviction.

39. "Cohesion," p. 662.
40. An interesting summary of and response to this venerable assumption is Calin and Calin, "Medieval Fiction"; see also Allen, ed., *Horn*, pp. 82–83.
41. *Narrative Structures*, p. 44; cf. Ganim, *Style and Consciousness*, pp. 28, 46.
42. E.g., KH 112, 252, 296, 608, 948, 980, 1406, 1481–82; O 1005, 1275; L 1240.

A second way that *King Horn* shapes value is through natural instead of social imagery. The *Romance of Horn* measures Horn's merit in terms of specific noble graces, physical beauties, and personal virtues, and emphasizes his perfection through constant comparison with his followers or the court in general:

> D'eskermir en tuz sens n'est a li cummunal
> Nul ki vest' el païs u burel u cendal;
> Nul ne siet envers lui bien mener un cheval,
> Nul si porter escu od bucle de cristal.
> Fort e bel le fist Deus, li sire esperital,
> Ne mais tiel n'iert truvé nul home charnal.
> Od tut çoe si est mut e humbles e leal,
> Qu'il ne freit de sun cors huniement vergundal
> Pur tut l'or ki onc fust trové en un jornal.
> (378–86)

In every kind of swordplay no man in the country, dressed in coarse wool or fine silk, could equal him; none knew how to handle a horse compared with him; none could so carry a crystal-bossed shield. God, the heavenly father, made him strong and handsome; never had earthly men seen one like him. But in addition he was so very humble and loyal that he would never do himself shameful dishonor, not for all the gold that was ever found in a day.

Horn's social virtues and accomplishments can demonstrate his superlative merit in the Anglo-Norman work, because the work itself generates and values a complex social world. In *King Horn* a series of hyperboles without context place Horn alone on a timeless pinnacle of merit:

> Fairer ne miste non beo born.   might none be
> Ne no rein vpon birine,   rain upon
> Ne sunne vpon bischine: shine
> Fairer nis non þane he was,   is none than
> He was briȝt so þe glas,
> He was whit so þe flur,
> Rose red was his colur.
> In none kinge riche   kingdom
> Nas non his iliche.   equal
> (10–18)

The primarily natural images demonstrate Horn's excellence by measures that lie beyond the social, even beyond the human. The rain, sun, and flowers display Horn's uniqueness as if the world were new, in perfect freshness.

The strongest natural force in *King Horn* is the sea. The sea's power, to which the pagans originally confer the execution of Horn and his followers, dominates all but Horn himself: it terrifies the children, drowns Rimenhild's messenger and casts him up at her feet, makes Fikenhild's castle impregnable—but Horn can row his followers to safety, travel over the sea just as he likes, and arrive by boat at Fikenhild's castle at precisely the crucial moment. Of the many social graces and systems in which the Anglo-Norman Horn excels, in *King Horn* only passing references to harping and hunting, to high birth, and to very simple distinctions in power among the characters survive. Horn's control over the elemental power of the sea demonstrates his superiority in the absence of an impressive set of social accomplishments for him to master.

That *King Horn*'s social context is greatly reduced does not mean that social issues are ignored. Rather, *King Horn* cuts to the base of aristocratic consciousness, moving back through the pacifications of the twelfth and thirteenth centuries to uncover the aggressive sources of baronial power. Georges Duby ("La Féodalité? Une mentalité médiévale") extracts the distinguishing features of feudal consciousness from the later manifestations that consciousness could take. Feudal mentality, he proposes, begins with a conviction of difference and superiority among the military elite of a society. This awareness leads to a belief that the practice of certain virtues is incumbent upon the elite. Finally, social bonds are imagined as extensions of military bonds of association. *King Horn* respects these distinguishing features, even in the absence of contextual detail. Knighthood is presented as essentially military, worthier than nonmilitary life, and basic to social relationships.[43]

Despite its military expression, Horn's desire seems peaceable enough. Avenging his father is largely a means of getting his land back and securing his mother and his wife so as to continue the family. Horn is not an adventurer, an expansionist, or even an aggressor. His prowess merely signals his freedom and his right to determine the course of his life. In this respect *King Horn*, like other romances of English heroes, poetizes an ideology that sustained the insular barony's status. What Horn wants (land and autonomy) is presented as a birthright (heritable, deserved, and justly his).

---

43. The ceremony in which Horn and his followers are knighted is military and hierarchical (*KH* 499–522; see Hall's note). Horn's relationship to his followers is there established as one of superiority and mandates his later rewards to them for their loyalty and "meoknesse" (*KH* 549–50, 829–30, 996–98, 1496; O 1131).

Only evil opposes these rights, while the dependence of Horn's followers on their leader's fate further validates his efforts to regain what is lost.

The pagans themselves acknowledge and fear the rightness of Horn's cause, setting him and his twelve companions adrift to avoid atonement for Allof's death:

> 'Þe se ȝou schal adrenche,   drown
> Ne schal hit us noȝt ofþinche;   we will not regret
> For if þu were aliue,
> Wiþ swerd oþer wiþ kniue,
> We scholden alle deie
> & þi fader deþ abeie.'   pay for
> (105–10)

The crisis Horn faces is inextricably personal and public. Horn's interests are identical with those of his society; only when he regains his patrimony and wins his wife will his followers in exile and his captive countrymen at home have peace and stability. Horn voices this congruence of purposes by juxtaposing messages to his family and to the usurper in his emotionally charged words to the boat:

> 'ȝef þu cume to Suddene,
> Gret þu wel of myne kenne,   Greet / kin
> Gret þu wel my moder,
> Godhild quen þe gode;
> & seie þe paene kyng,
> Jesucristes wiþering,   enemy
> Þat ihc am hol & fer   whole and sound
> On þis lond ariued her;
> And seie þat hei schal fonde   feel
> Þe dent of myne honde.'   blow
> (143–52)

Subsequent encounters with the pagans are only irregularly associated with Horn's plan of vengeance,[44] but these two initial passages, in their moral weight and their appeal to the power of the sea and of time, give the theme of family continuity great natural force.

Horn's dynastic purpose also informs his courtship. Here, indeed, it has been argued that *King Horn* achieves a fuller integration of the hero's purposes than did the Anglo-Norman poem, by attributing actions over long spans of time to Horn's love, in order

---

44. But cf. "His fader deþ wel dere hi boȝte" (884); "his fader deþ & ys lond / awrek godmod wiþ his hond" (L 899–900); "he sloȝ in felde / Þat his fader quelde" (987–88).

to emphasize the relation of love to military success.⁴⁵ Similarly, Rimenhild gives a protective ring to Horn and another to his closest comrade, Aþulf (561–78); later, Horn is concerned to rescue not just Rimenhild but Aþulf as well (1081–90). When Horn replies to the false charge that he has plotted to kill his benefactor and marry Rimenhild (693–94), he emphasizes that his political and personal goals are inseparable:

'Þu wendest þat iwroȝte	thought I did
Þat y neure ne þoȝte,	What I never
Bi Rymenhild for to ligge,	lie
& þat i wiþ segge.	deny
Ne schal ihc hit biginne,	
Til i suddene winne.	
Þu kep hure a stunde,	time
Þe while þat ifunde	proceed
In to min heritage	
& to mi baronage.	
Þat lond ischal ofreche	reach
& do mi fader wreche.	avenge
Ischal beo king of tune	
& bere kinges crune,	
Þanne schal Rymenhilde	
Ligge bi þe kinge.'⁴⁶	

The linking of the two narrative lines is completed when Horn at last brings Rimenhild to Suddene, "Among al his kenne," and makes her his queen (1517–19).

In the Anglo-Norman poem the relationship between Horn and Rigmel is similarly integrated into Horn's dynastic purpose. Despite the wakeful nights, tears, and sighs that embroider their affair, it is from the first a politically advantageous match, a second line of action in Horn's campaign to reestablish his patrimony in Suddene. In love Rigmel is the suppliant, as she will be in marriage the social dependent.⁴⁷

---

45. Arens, *Fassungen des Hornstoffes*, pp. 113–23; Hynes-Berry, "Cohesion," p. 657.

46. Lines 1273–88. There is no evidence for Mildred Pope's statement that Fikenhild's accusation of sexual intimacy was justified ("*Romance of Horn and King Horn*," p. 165), although the lovers do some snuggling (e.g., *KH* 705–6). Cf. *RH* 1927–36.

47. For example, in contrast to similar topoi from the literature of *fine amor*, Rigmel's maid dreams of a falcon given to Rigmel by Horn, representing not his heart but their son Hadermod (729–36); both Horn and his benefactor Herland realize that the relationship depends on the rewinning of Suddene (1083–88, 1109–18a, 1172–78).

Wikele's attempts to undermine Horn's winning of Rigmel make him an enemy not simply to love, but to the interests of his feudal lord:

> Ben se vengera Horn de sun mal traïtur,
> Ki volt partir de lui e de Rigmel l'amor:
> Issi deit avenir tuz jors a boiseor,
> Car unc ben ne finat ki trichat sun seignur.
> (5171a–74)

Horn will avenge himself well on his evil betrayer, who sought to undo the love between him and Rigmel: thus it should always befall a deceiver, for no one ends well who betrays his lord.

Horn's free access to his heritage is the poem's dominant measure of right. His love draws value from contemporary courtly ideals of beauty and passion, but without contradicting its vital function. As in *King Horn*, unity derives from the hero's determination to re-establish his patrimony, with military action and courtship as means to that end.

We have seen how the tensions of insular feudalism shape and enrich the two narrative movements—revenge and love—in the story of Horn. In addition, the character of Horn himself is made to illustrate these tensions in idealized equipoise. His traits are static, present and complete in his character even as a boy, so that the story proceeds not through the gradual development of his personality but through a series of enemy actions which he progressively reverses by his own actions. A sense of providential certainty sanctions the course of the hero's life, contributing further to the tone of optimistic assurance that pervades the romances of English heroes.

In the *Romance of Horn* God's providence guides the pattern of events at every turn.[48] Thomas's assurance that "ja avienge neent / A nul home del mund de sun purposement, / Si Deus n'en ad aunceis fait sun ordenement" [nothing that any man in the world plans ever happens unless God has already ordained it] (3586–88) characterizes the atmosphere of quiet inevitability in which Horn, born completely a hero, simply follows the foreordained course of events

---

48. The pagans do not harm Horn as a child "kar ne fud destinez" (22); God chooses Horn rather than another husband for Rigmel (412–14); God destines Horn's first defeat of the pagans, his victories in Ireland, and his final vengeance in Suddene (1570–71, 3604–12, 4622–23).

to reach his goal. Even as a child, he is "Plus hardi de parler e li mielz doctrinez" [bolder of speech and the most learned], a balanced combination of courage and intelligence.[49] The legal wisdom he demonstrates as a foundling, in demanding pledges of peace and of freedom from servitude before trusting King Hunlaf,[50] informs his actions throughout the romance, perhaps most strikingly in response to Wikele's false accusations in Brittany.

It is not the accusations themselves but the legal method by which Horn may deny them that leads to his exile. The king, at the suggestion of Wikele, demands that Horn acquit himself "par serrement" (1925), while Horn insists that the only suitable proof for a man of his birth and country is "par bataille" (1945a). As their argument develops during fifty lines of increasingly short-tempered dialogue, it becomes clear that the king in his anger demands that Horn swear his innocence in order to humiliate him, while Horn clings doggedly to the custom of his lost homeland and the principle of his lost rank:

> 'Horn,' çoe li dist Hunlaf, 'par la fei ki est meie
> Vus m'en frez serement, si volez ke vus creie;
> Si fere ne·l volez, si tenez vostre veie. . . .'
> Dunc respundi si Horn: 'Ci ad male maneie.
> Bien jurer le pousse, si faire le deveie,
> Mes m'est vis en mun quoer, ke faire ne le deie,
> Ainz me larraie traire e le quoer e le feie
> Ke serement face. . . .
> Le parage de mei, s'il vus plest, ne·l otreie.'
> (1960–62, 1973–77, 1979)

'Horn,' said Hunlaf, 'by my faith, you will take an oath on it if you want me to believe you; if you don't want to do that, go your own way. . . .' Then Horn answered, 'Here is cruel mercy. I certainly could swear to it, if I were bound to do so, but in my heart I believe I should not do it; I'd rather let my heart and liver be torn out than take an oath. . . . My lineage, if you please, does not permit it.'

That a major narrative crisis here takes the form of a dispute over law, a dispute containing more than twenty technical terms, is a testament to the depth of interest in legality that marks these ro-

---

49. *RH* 33; cf. "li pruz, li sené" (390); "le pruz sené" (674); "Li greindre e li plus fort, li meuz endoctrinez" (1013). Curtius traces the development of this topos in *European Literature*, pp. 170–76.

50. *RH* 164–66, 246–49; cf. the binding pledge taken from Wikele (4549–66, 5049–57); the acceptance of Modin as a vassal rather than an enemy (4530); promises to Gudreche (3823–35).

mances and the insular baronial class itself. But the subject of this dispute elevates it above the level of contemporary legal procedure. Judicial combat was fast becoming a thing of the past in twelfth-century England, in favor of jury decisions based on written or sworn testimony. In particular, judicial reforms of 1179 guaranteed jury trials in questions of disputed inheritance rights and permitted the defendant to refuse outright the unpopular judicial duel as a means of proof.[51] Like the English poet's return to military action as a sign of noble power, Horn's proud insistence on judicial combat translates Anglo-Norman respect for and reliance on the law to a higher, more archaic level of expression where fierce courage unhesitatingly enforces feudal rights.

Horn's demand for the legal proof appropriate to his rank even while in exile, like his pledge to recover his benefactor's seized lands (3760–61, 4538–42) and his battles defending the right of two kings to their land, support his principal claim to his own right of inheritance: Horn's ultimate interests always subsume the interests of the kings whom he serves "vassalement."[52] Particularly apt is his disguise in Ireland as a vassal of his dead father and his avenging of his father's death in that adopted role (3175–234). Similarly, he defends his father-in-law "vassalement" in the closing battle of the romance (5210–11). Thus the ideal of feudal service reinforces the more central ideal of protecting family rights. Horn's vasselage is so very bold, proud, and ultimately self-interested that some critics misunderstand it as a negative model;[53] rather, in this model of vasselage, feudal service simply facilitates dynastic ambitions. Horn's vasselage, like the poem's stylistic effects and its thematic em-

---

51. Bossuard, "Institutions," I, 61–63; Warren, *Henry II*, pp. 292–93, 336–42; Petit-Dutaillis, pp. 150–52; R. H. Bloch, *Literature and Law*, pp. 119–21. The AN and continental baronies contrast sharply in their attitude toward the judicial duel. In France, it remained the right of nobles until the late 1250s in spite of royal efforts to suppress it; and as late as 1306 Philip the Fair permitted some judicial duels under pressure from his barons. In England, the judicial duel was never popular. The contrast again illustrates the insular barony's less military, more legalistic cast. Pope discusses the two dozen legal terms in this scene of *RH* in "Vocabulary."

52. In each encounter with pagan invaders, Horn acts both "vassalement" and in vengeance of his father's death (in Brittany: 1470, 1723; in Westir: 2907a–10, 2918, 2934, 3195, 3208, 3216, 3222, 3234). As Hunlaf's deputy he acts at once "cum vassal noblement" (1742) and as a ruler himself, destroying the castles and towns of those who have done wrong and making peace "Tut al pleisir dan Horn a ki la merci pent" [entirely at the pleasure of lord Horn, on whom mercy depends] (1746).

53. Pope, *RH*, II, 15; Legge, *Anglo-Norman Literature*, p. 102. The misunderstanding is discussed and countered in Burnley, "'Roman de Horn'"; see also Pensom, "Lexical Field."

phases, presents a remarkably positive view of what baronial life can mean.

King Horn also sustains its dramatic development toward justice and stability with morally weighted portrayals of character. The Anglo-Norman Horn acts always in accordance with the direction and intention of God; the Middle English Horn acts charismatically as an embodiment of God's will. He stands curiously "alone, / Also [as if] he sprunge of stone" (1025–26), isolated in his ability to choose and change the future. He rows his followers to Westernesse and fights pagan invaders singlehandedly. With quiet self-containment he locks what he hears in his heart (243–44, 379–80), revealing his private plan for the course of events only at the appropriate moments, to the relief of his friends and the discomfiture of his enemies. Until his final victories, his followers confine their actions to sending one message and anxiously watching for his return (930–32, 1091–96, 1443–46). Parallels to Christ also set him apart from other men.[54] Fikenhild, unlike the simply spiteful and envious Wikele, is an inherently evil character, "þe wurste moder child" (648); and his forced marriage with Rimenhild is a sinister inversion of Horn's brightness (14, 385–86):

> ffikenhild or þe dai gan springe
> Al riȝt he ferde to þe kinge,   went directly
> After Rymenhild þe briȝte,
> To wedden hire biniȝte.   by night
> He ladde hure bi þe derke
> In to his nywe werke;
> Þe feste hi bigunne
> Er þat ros þe sunne.
>   (1427–34)

In the drastically reduced social context of the Middle English romance, these alignments with ultimate good and evil do much to reinforce Horn's claim to his land and to Rimenhild.

Finally, in both Anglo-Norman and Middle English Horn is more than a fully capable and virtuous hero. He is a repository of national custom, bearing the greatness of his people closed within himself like a seed. This function is revealed in his distinctive elo-

---

54. Horn has twelve followers rather than the Anglo-Norman fifteen; he is of Christ-like perfection, "fairer bi one ribbe / Þane eni Man þat libbe" (315–16; see [Crane] Dannenbaum, "Fairer"); and he identifies the usurper of his kingdom as "'Jesucristes wiþering [enemy]'" (148).

quence, his ability to narrate his own and his people's history. When the shipwrecked children are discovered on the beach, "Horn spak here speche, / He spak for hem alle" (170–71). In Ireland the Anglo-Norman Horn's account of his life wins the praise "'bien est enromauncez'" (2320): the term and the context suggest storytelling power as well as simple verbal facility. In the English Horn's most important statement of his plans, he recounts his own life as if it were a romance, and prophesies his success poetically before achieving it in deed:

> 'King,' he sede, 'þu luste   listen to
> A tale mid þe beste.
> Ine seie hit for no blame,
> Horn is mi name.
> Þume to kniȝte houe,   you lifted me
> & kniȝthod haue proued.'
> (1263–68)

The hero's self-justification is here conflated with the storyteller's conventional call for attention, plea for the audience's goodwill, and introduction of the hero's name and life story.[55] The Anglo-Norman Horn similarly performs his own life as art when he sings the *lai* concerning his love for Rigmel, a *lai* that has made their names and excellence known far beyond the boundaries of Brittany (2782–844). In both works Horn voices and lives by his own traditions, ones the people around him in exile often seem not to follow.[56]

That Horn carries his heritage and his story through exile adds a further dimension to the assurance and continuity he represents. Horn's followers can rely for their identity on such a hero until the homeland is regained; the nation is safely contained in his person. When Horn wins his heritage and his wife, the seed of nationhood he carries can once more flourish in the lives of his people and his descendants.

Despite their very different verbal resources, these two romances draw on baronial ideals in their exaltation of landed stability, their conservative faith in custom, and their presentation of these values as beneficial to the nation as a whole. Following the typical pattern

---

55. Wittig (*Narrative Structures*, pp. 54–61) analyzes the structural units typical of Middle English romance openings. The first six lines of *KH* follow the same structure as Horn's own account: address and exhortation to audience (two lines), introduction of a hero's name (two lines), synopsis of hero's life.

56. E.g., *RH* 308–16, 1939–44, 2609–10, 2735–38, 2752–55; *KH* 419–24, 543–60, 829–36.

for the romances of English heroes, Horn begins a dispossessed vassal and, after long struggles in exile, ends a lord in full control of his rights. The perfect balance of courage and wisdom in his character ensures his success, while the narrative, in its cyclical design and its constant interweaving of the double movements toward feudal reinstatement and marriage, elevates to a glorious struggle blessed by providence the fundamental economic conflicts of insular baronial life.

Havelok's Heritage

The *Lai d'Haveloc* and *Havelok the Dane*, like the *Romance of Horn* and *King Horn*, are distant from each other textually but share a close thematic harmony. Like the Horn romances, they invest legality and social order with great importance in the justification of inheritance rights. The hero again carries the destiny of his people and provides them with a sense of common purpose. *Havelok the Dane*, bearing these concerns further into the thirteenth century, illustrates their evolution from a relatively local and feudal understanding of rule toward a broader, less class-specific understanding.

Havelok's career so resembles Horn's that I will treat some of its features only briefly here. The *Lai d'Haveloc* (ca. 1200)[57] draws from Gaimar's Anglo-Norman chronicle *L'Estoire des Engleis* (39–318) the story of a Danish prince dispossessed in childhood and raised in England by his guardian Grim. There he is married to a king's daughter, Argentille (Goldeboru *HD*), who has also been unjustly disinherited. Havelok subsequently regains his heritage and that of his wife as well. *Havelok the Dane*'s dependence on the *Lai d'Haveloc* is likely but not fully demonstrable, since the Middle English poet has "fele nihtes waked" [stayed awake many a night] (2999) to enrich the story's telling.[58]

The Havelok poems, like the Horn romances, develop the expulsion-and-return pattern in terms of the wrongful usurpation of in-

---

57. *Le Lai d'Haveloc and Gaimar's Haveloc Episode*, ed. Bell (hereafter cited as *LH*). For other insular versions of the story, see Heyman, *Havelok-tale*, pp. 109–38; and *The Lay of Havelok the Dane*, ed. Skeat (hereafter cited as *HD*), pp. xv–xx.

58. On the relation of *HD* to *LH*, see *HD*, pp. xix–xx; Heyman, *Havelok-tale*, pp. 139–48. Meyer-Lindenberg, "Datierung des *Havelok*," proposes an early date for *HD* (1203–16) and suggests that it was a source for *LH* rather than vice versa. But see Jack, "Date of *Havelok*"; further argument for a date in the last decades of the thirteenth century is offered by Delany and Ishkanian, "Kingship"; and by Staines, "Havelok the Dane."

herited rights, with a supporting emphasis on legality in other situations.⁵⁹ In the *Lai d'Haveloc* Grim and his family leave Denmark solely to protect the "dreit eir" (92), whom they regard as "lur seignur" (109) even though he is only two years old. When Haveloc is a young man Grim sends him to the court of Lincoln to learn its ways, "Kar il quidot en sun corage / K'uncore avreit sun heritage" [because he believed in his heart that he (Haveloc) would have his heritage again] (165–66). And indeed, when he returns to Denmark, all swear fealty to him as soon as they hear that he is the true heir (915–27). Like Horn's, Haveloc's final gains are land tenure and its associated social power; in the end he rules three kingdoms: his inherited Denmark, Argentille's Norfolk, and her uncle's Lincoln and Lindsey.⁶⁰

A sense of providential favor suffuses the story's developments with an assurance that justice will prevail. The arranged marriage of Haveloc and Argentille is especially interesting in this respect. The *Lai*'s account details the barons' insistence that Argentille's guardian Edelsi fulfill his oath to marry her "al plus fort home" [to the most powerful man] (361) and traces Edelsi's maneuvers to override his barons (283–380). Edelsi's attempt to subvert justice through a falsely literal interpretation of his oath is thwarted by the convergence in Haveloc of physical and lineal strength; instead of obscuring Argentille's claim to her heritage, the marriage leads directly to the recovery of both spouses' rights. Haveloc's return to Denmark is similarly providential, a visitation coinciding with God's: "'Deus nus ad revisitez. / Veez ici nostre dreit eir'" ["God has returned to us: behold here our true heir"] (912–13). Besides being graced with divine sanction, Haveloc also meets concrete requirements that demonstrate his lineage: his appearance, his mark of flame, and his ability to blow a horn that none but the true heir

---

59. *Waldef* (ed. Holden), a work of about 1200 whose ME descendant is lost (see Intro., n. 14), corroborates the concerns and patterns of the romances of English heroes. Waldef, like Horn and Havelok, is driven from his heritage (the kingdom of Norfolk) in youth but returns to avenge his father and reclaim the patrimony when he matures. The pattern of exile and return is doubled, and Waldef's sons extend their father's conquests in England and Europe. Brian Levy remarks on the characteristic insularity of *Waldef*'s themes "d'une famille en péril et d'un patrimoine compromis," noting relationships to the stories of Horn, Havelok, and Bevis of Hampton ("Waltheof," p. 184; see also Holden, edition, pp. 23–32). Holden opposes the ancestral theory (pp. 33–36).

60. Haveloc receives oaths of fealty from the barons of each kingdom (*LH* 915–22, 1097–98, 1103–4). His right by inheritance or through marriage is mentioned for each kingdom (*LH* 971–72, 1091–92, 1101–6).

can sound. Here as in the romances of English heroes generally, a doubled pattern of deprivation and reacquisition is made to express the convictions that lineage should guarantee landed security and that claims to inheritance will prevail through the agency of earthly and heavenly justice.

Havelok the Dane offers a sophisticated reworking of these convictions. The heroine's story becomes a fuller and more evocative double for that of Havelok. A series of parallel passages on the rule and death of their fathers, the trickery and later the trials of their wicked guardians, and the hardships the two children suffer give this work the most handsomely articulated double structure of all the romances of English heroes.

Havelok confers added importance on the theme that children both duplicate and extend their parents' lives by representing the rituals through which the dying fathers seek to extend their rights to their children (184–209, 383–99). These quasi-religious, quasi-legal ceremonies dramatize the proposition that children partake of their parents in some inalienable way, so that to separate them from their inheritances would defy moral and natural law. The *Lai d'Haveloc* expresses the relation very simply through physical resemblance: when Denmark's seneschal sees the returning Haveloc,

> Entientivement l'esgarda,
> De sun seignur li remembra,
> Del rei Gunter k'il tant ama.
> Anguisusement suspira.
> Cil li resemblot de visage
> E de grandur e de corsage.
> (741–46)

He looked closely at him and recalled his lord, King Gunther, whom he had loved so much. He sighed sorrowfully. This man resembled the king in face, stature, and build.

Physical resemblance is a sign of less tangible affiliations, as illustrated by the failure of the guardians' scheme to restrict "strongest" and "highest" to their literal senses in marrying off the heroine. Even in his low station as kitchen boy, the English Havelok resembles a "king or cayser" (977). His imposing size and Goldeboru's beauty assure us that once the fated pattern of their fortune is traced out, their station will again reflect their inborn nature.

That characteristic features of the romances of English heroes receive emphasis and endorsement in *Havelok the Dane* is important to assessing just what social attitude is implicit in the work. Early criticism of *Havelok* took it for a minstrel composition designed to entertain the poor.[61] No extant manuscript of Middle English romance can be labeled a minstrel's book nor a copy from a minstrel's book,[62] supporting recent revision of the earlier judgment that *Havelok*'s verse is unsophisticated hack work. This remarkable romance has attracted high praise in recent years for its verbal richness, structural subtlety, and effective manipulation of formulaic style.[63] But despite the widely recognized quality and sophistication of its poetry, some readers still find the work a "peasant fantasy" designed to please and to express the attitudes of a "lower-class audience."[64] This reading is not plausible.

A narrative that traces a hero's journey through the social classes to kingship may seem calculated to please the peasantry. But our only evidence of the story's transmission prior to its appearance in *Havelok the Dane* finds it in the circles of power. Gaimar's *Estoire des Engleis*, which was written for Constance FitzGilbert, wife of a powerful baron, and the *Lai d'Haveloc*, which was accessible only to that cultured sector of the insular population who knew French, clearly did not seek to appeal to a lower-class audience. Equally, some features of the English text that seem to fit a simple audience—such as the catalogue of fish, the attention to menial occupations, the wrestling contests, the absence of love scenes, and the sensitivity to poverty and its economics—do have antecedents in Gaimar and in the *Lai d'Haveloc*.[65]

It is important to remember that in the later thirteenth and fourteenth centuries the English barony was not closed and was more domestic than military. Its openness sustained in its members a

---

61. E.g., Creek, "Author of *Havelok*"; but see Baugh, "Middle English Romance." Pearsall notes the literary imitation of AN laisse form at lines 87–105 (*Middle English Poetry*, p. 115).
62. Hirsh, "*Havelok* 2933"; Gallais, "Mentalité des romanciers," 1964, p. 488.
63. E.g., Mehl, *Middle English Romances*, pp. 162–68; Weiss, "Structure and Characterisation"; Hanning, "*Havelok the Dane*."
64. Halverson, "*Havelok the Dane*," pp. 149–50; Staines, "*Havelok the Dane*," pp. 610–23 (quote at p. 612 n.).
65. Staines and Halverson suggest that these features in HD demonstrate a lower-class audience, but cf. the AN (aristocratic) versions in Bell's edition of LH: Gaimar, lines 442–52 (catalogue of fish and course of Grim's economic success); LH 137–40, 244–50, 791–92 (Grim's work, Havelok's work); LH 168–76, 188 (Haveloc is to seek profit in Lincoln, Grim gives him new clothes for the trip); Gaimar 109–18, LH 266–78 (wrestling); Gaimar 453–78, LH 563–64, 619–20, 645–50 (Kelloc's merchant husband gives Haveloc clothes, money, and advice). In both Gaimar and *LH*, villains are characteristically inhospitable and good people charitable; in both, the psychology of love is of no interest at all.

preoccupation with achievement and a conservative attitude to law and property rights. The romances of English heroes speak to these concerns, and *Havelok the Dane* treats them with an increased economic specificity that would appeal to the deepening insecurities of an ever more porous upper class.[66]

Discussions of medieval audience usually consider noble and common interests to be mutually exclusive, but *Havelok* attends to some interests that the barony shared with the emerging professional and mercantile class. In this period the strongest lines of class difference were not drawn between commoners and barony, but between the peasantry (whether bonded or free) and the middle class, and between the highest nobility and the broad ranks of the barony.[67] As we have seen, considerable mobility, both upward and downward, linked the ranks of the barony to the middle class. Both groups enjoyed degrees of power and status; both were benefited by economic prosperity, sound justice, peace, and maintenance of the existing social order.

Havelok the Dane builds an imaginary world in which these values sustain a utopian vision of harmony and happiness. The good rule of Athelwold opens the romance; the first cause of his people's love is that "gode lawes / He dede maken, and ful wel holden" (28–29). Strict law enforcement permits trade, travel, and social harmony (45–66). Although Athelwold is also charitable to the weak, he seems to concentrate his energies on a powerful array of wrongdoers, whom he has (according to the crime) bound, hanged, brought to sorrow, made poor, castrated, cast in fetters; in sum, "He made hem lurken, and crepen in wros [corners]: / Þei hidden hem alle, and helden hem stille, / And diden al his herte wille" (67–70). The protection of property, trade, and the social order that fosters them remains a constant value in the romance,[68] most importantly in Havelok's model behavior as a worker. In his youth the hero gladly tramples other laborers to win his job, then works as tirelessly as a beast, without ever complaining (879–948). He sug-

---

66. See Intro., nn. 19–22, and n. 75 below; also Pearsall, "Alliterative Revival."
67. Hilton, *Bond Men*, pp. 25–62; Mollat and Wolff, *Popular Revolutions*, pp. 15–22; McFarlane, *Nobility*, pp. 122–25, 268–78. From the twelfth century, Duby claims, the ambition of wealthy merchants was not to establish an urban cultural elite but "to integrate themselves into the rural nobility, to be accepted into its circle, to share its way of life and its culture" ("Knightly Class," p. 250). These desires characterize England's bourgeoisie in the thirteenth and fourteenth centuries as well.
68. Money and investment also figure in nonthematic measures of worth: *HD*, 907–8, 1635, 1693, 2034–36, 2146–47, 2614–15; see also Mills, "Havelok's Return."

gests menial tasks he might add to his chores and even rejects a proffered board-and-hire arrangement to work for board alone (905–26).

The ethic of *Havelok the Dane*, then, hardly recommends itself to a lower-class audience. Havelok's tireless submissiveness to his employer is exceeded only by the joyful abasement of Grim's family when Havelok returns to them. Adopting again the bonded status they had borne in Denmark but surpassed in England, they surrender all their property and their persons to Havelok: "'Þou maght us boþe selle and yeue [give]. . . . / We hauen shep, we hauen swin, / Bi-leue her [remain here], louerd, and al be þin!'" (1218, 1227–28). As John Hirsh writes, "Such romances as *Havelok* tell us not so much what the lower classes thought of the upper, as what the upper classes liked to think the lower classes thought of them."[69] The history of the peasantry in England reveals not cheerful acquiescence to the basic social order, but rather a series of movements against that order, which sought by its very nature to distribute the social product to the disadvantage of the poor.[70] *Havelok the Dane*, in idealizing the virtues of a stratified and judicially repressive order, hardly offers a "peasant fantasy" of social change.

Yet within the restrictions of its class focus, this romance boldly constructs an ideal of transcendent and universal social harmony. A brief analysis of the more limited vision of the *Lai d'Haveloc* will illuminate by contrast the conception to be found in *Havelok the Dane*.

The *Lai d'Haveloc* has a primarily aristocratic context; it is introduced as "L'aventure d'un riche rei / E de plusurs altres baruns" [the adventure of a mighty king and of numerous other barons] (12–13). Grim is a wealthy lord whose many household retainers set out for exile with his family (57–60, 97–104). Only because of a pirate attack does Grim turn to fishing and selling salt in order to support Haveloc. Soon, anxious that Haveloc be educated in accordance with his noble birth, Grim sends him off to the court of Lincoln, hoping he may there "entendre / Afetement e sens aprendre"

---

69. "*Havelok* 2933," p. 343; further examples of willing acceptance of class difference are Grim's triple repetition that he will never take freedom from anyone but Havelok (615–31) and Grim's concern only for Havelok, to the exclusion of his own children, in time of famine (835–38).

70. Postan, *Mediaeval Economy and Society*, pp. 150–55; Landsberger, ed., *Rural Protest*, pp. 67–141; Maddicott, *English Peasantry*, pp. 23–24, 64–67.

[hear instructive things and learn wisdom] (163–64), as he cannot among the poor inhabitants of Grimsby. At Lincoln, Haveloc demonstrates his innate nobility of character: despite his great strength he is generous, "francs e debonere," and attentive to the needy (251–56). So restricted is the social vision of the *Lai* that these virtues, conventionally associated with the nobility, seem laughable in Haveloc the kitchen boy: "Pur la franchise k'en lui ot / Le teneient entr'els a sot, / De lui feseient lur deduit" [They held him for a fool because of his high generosity; they made fun of him] (257–59). The conviction that certain virtues have no place in lower stations serves to distinguish noble from common nature.

Class division also restricts Argentille's identity. Although she shows considerable initiative and acumen in comparison to Rigmel, her potential is nonetheless circumscribed by the narrow imperatives of her social and legal roles. Her cleverness has no independent value but is purely functional in advancing Haveloc's cause and finally "deserves" his affection (978). Her social standing is contingent on marriage (221–24, 1095–98, 1105–6) and childbearing: the barons who demand her inherited rights for her note that "ja esteit creue e granz / E ben poeit aveir enfanz" [now she was grown and matured and could well bear children] (289–90; cf. 575–76, 656–60, 681–86). Like her intelligence, her sexuality is directed only toward perpetuating the lineal rights claimed by her class.

Havelok the Dane manifests a different kind of class consciousness. Although rank is fundamental to the social structure in *Havelok*, no hierarchical imperative requires that the hero be defined as fundamentally different from the common man. The same holds true for women: Goldeboru knows that her marriage disinherits her, but apprehends her fate more vividly in terms of gender and earthly destiny: "Sho þouhte, it was Godes wille: / God, þat makes growen þe korn, / Formede hire wimman to be born" (1166–68). Here Havelok's behavior as a kitchen boy inspires not the scorn but the love of "Boþen heye men and lowe" (958).[71] Havelok's strength tempered by mildness (927–98, 1066) offers a perfected lower-class version of Athelwold's law-enforcing severity tempered by charity. Both men are strong first and mild second at the work

---

71. Similarly, the English of all ranks love Athelwold (*HD* 30–34); all ranks detest and fear Godrich (260–79).

they have been assigned in life, and both are loved by all for their excellence.

This ideal of common understanding pervades the romance. The dispossessed young Havelok formulates for himself the work ethic of laborers:

Swinken ich wolde for mi mete.	Work / food
It is no shame forto swinken;	
Þe man þat may wel eten and drinken	
Þar nouht ne haue but on swink long;	Ought not
To liggen at hom it is ful strong.	shameful
(798–802)	

That a royal heir can voice this ethic does not imply a radical disregard for social stratification. Havelok simply validates the form that idealized commitment to the common good takes among laborers. Similarly, when he returns to Denmark fitted out as a merchant, he wins the gratitude of burgesses for protecting his host's property from a band of sixty thieves. Havelok's journey through the classes, from a thrall's family to the throne, expresses an ideology of cohesion in which all people share an understanding of good and right, and each class's duties contribute to the common purpose of achieving and maintaining social order.

Nor does the ennobling of helpful commoners at the end of the romance (2346–53, 2856–927) diminish the validity of social stratification.[72] On the contrary, Havelok's gesture recognizes the power of the hierarchical structure by treating status as a valuable reward for a chosen few. At the same time, within the general restrictions of class difference, Havelok's exceptional rewards signal the communal nature of his enterprise.

Havelok the Dane reinvigorates the characteristic structures of the romances of English heroes, and extends their appeal to the bourgeoisie by associating traditional themes of baronial concern to middle-class concerns for profit making and social stability. *Havelok* creates a world remarkable for its social complexity and breadth, yet unites that world in harmony with the hero's purpose. After briefly relating these developments to ideas about kingship and the

---

72. Delany and Ishkanian, "Kingship," pp. 299–300, give historical parallels for the exceptional rewards in *HD* and argue that *HD* represents in this respect "the social reality and realistic ambitions of the upper bourgeoisie and knighthood" (p. 300).

realm, we must ask how *Havelok*'s poetry sustains developments so wide ranging, appeals so inclusive.

Havelok the Dane is truly a romance of the law. The familiar question of inheritance rights here expands to a comprehensive interest in legality as it affects all of society. Many passages emphasize that all ranks are bound, both theoretically and effectively, by good or evil rule.[73] This principle extends to the functional corollary that parliaments can review and moderate the exercise of power. Noble councils handle some legal matters, but the traitors Godard and Godrich are judged by parliaments that represent their victims throughout society.[74] In comparison to the earlier *Romance of Horn* and *King Horn*, less can now be entrusted to divine providence, but more to human justice.

This literary transformation assesses important historical changes. The baronial class acquired a broader political consciousness during the turbulent reform period that accompanied the barony's gradual losses in economic, social, and political dominance during the thirteenth century.[75] Developing conceptions of social interdependence were sustained by a new emphasis on law as essential to rule, expressed most fully in Henry of Bracton's *De Legibus et Consuetudinis Angliae*.[76] Ernst Kantorowicz describes the later thirteenth century as "the most critical period" in the development

---

73. Athelwold's good government and Godrich's severe government are presented entirely from the point of view of the governed (*HD* 27–105, 260–79). Even Ubbe, a good man, inspires fear rather than love in his people, presumably because he is not the rightful ruler of Denmark (2289); cf. the fear of Godrich among the English (277–79, 2568–69).

74. Parliaments of judgment are depicted in *HD* 2464–87, 2818–37; cf. other councils, 999–1006, 1326–28, 2180–85, 2252–73, 2302–11, 2794–807. Barons and knights alone choose Havelok's and Goldeboru's guardians, perhaps implying the weakness of less representative decisions (*HD* 176–83, 366–81).

75. On the breadth of social concern in the baronial reform movement, see Powicke, *Thirteenth Century*, pp. 142, 148–49; on the loss of baronial powers through the century, see Painter, *English Feudal Barony*, pp. 193–97; on the bourgeoisie's growing agitation for power in England in the second half of the thirteenth century, see Petit-Dutaillis, *Monarchie féodale*, pp. 390–91, 413–17; and Wood, *Age of Chivalry*, pp. 114–17.

76. Relationships between Bracton and *HD* are developed by Staines, "Havelok the Dane," pp. 615–16; Delany and Ishkanian, "Kingship," pp. 290–91. Both essays argue that *HD* makes specific references to Edward I and his rule. I believe it more accurate to find in *HD* a general and unspecific response to the social and political climate of the later thirteenth century. Edward did not hold the first representative parliaments or the first parliaments at Lincoln: see Powicke, *Thirteenth Century*, pp. 191–92, 341–42; Petit-Dutaillis, *Monarchie féodale*, p. 391; van der Gaaf, "Parliaments."

of English political thought: "It was then that the 'community of the realm' became conscious of the difference between the king as a personal liege lord and the king as the supra-individual administrator of a public sphere."[77] This development finds a poetic corollary in *Havelok the Dane*, where Havelok's mystical signs of flame and glowing cross preserve an older conception of theocratic lordship, while the emphasis on law and the community introduces a newer version of rule based on contractual agreements. Like the heavenly signs of flame and cross, the ability to govern fairly becomes a distinguishing mark of the true heir.

Turning back perhaps half a century to the *Lai d'Haveloc*, we find only nascent suggestions of these ideas. The Havelok plot is well suited to demonstrating that a community benefits through its leader's success, but the *Lai* does not exploit the design by emphasizing the hero's participation in many levels of social life. At scattered points, however, the good of the realm is associated with Haveloc's personal success. When Haveloc returns to Denmark and demonstrates his right to rule,

> De totes parz i acoreient
> E riche e povre, ki l'oeient,
> De lui firent lur avoé,
> A chevaler l'unt adobé.
> (925–28)

Both rich and poor who heard about it ran there from all sides; they made him their protector and dubbed him knight.

This emotional demonstration of support prefigures those in *Havelok the Dane*; but the *Lai d'Haveloc* more typically develops the right to lordship in technical and legal terms involving only the barony.[78]

The strongest demonstrations in the *Lai* of the hero's bond with his community are Haveloc's expressions of concern for his soldiers. In Denmark, he stakes his rights against Odluf in single com-

---

77. *King's Two Bodies*, p. 191; also pp. 143–92 on Bracton. French kingship throughout the Middle Ages was less defined and limited by law and more charismatic.

78. When Haveloc's forces defeat the English forces at the end of the *Lai*, the usurper Edelsi consults with his closest advisers and by their counsel arranges a truce guaranteed by hostages (1079–94), after which Haveloc "Des baruns recut les homages / Si lur rendi lur heritages" [received homage from the barons and reconfirmed their hereditary rights] (1097–98). In *LH* the control of land (rather than of subjects' devotion) is the source of political power (26, 38–39, 313–14, 581–82, 932–34, 1005–12).

bat out of pity for "la gent menue" who would otherwise die for his cause (941–45); and subsequently in England, the deaths among his troops are so upsetting to him that he would have departed "si la reïne li suffrist" [if the queen had allowed him], but she urges him on to victory (1055–59). Examples of good and bad rule also are limited in Anglo-Norman: when Argentille's father ruled in England, "Mult ot en lui noble barun" [many had a noble lord in him] (206), whereas the Danish usurper governs "Tant par destreit, tant par pour" [as much by oppression as by fear] (41); Haveloc, by contrast, "En la terre bone pes mist. / E des feluns justise fist" [made good peace in the land and brought felons to justice] (975–76).

Thus the *Lai d'Haveloc* makes clear in several ways that the common purpose of hero and people will be served by protecting his inheritance rights. But the *Lai* speaks to these concerns in the restricted vernacular and the limited aristocratic terminology of the barony alone—in an Anglo-Norman language of homage, heritage, fief, and feudal law. As we have seen, *Havelok the Dane*'s thematic treatment stretches to encompass the concerns of a wider community. In verbal treatment as well, this work enhances the appeal of familiar insular patterns.[79]

The effect of rhetorical ornament in *Havelok the Dane* is not, as in the *Romance of Horn*, that of elegant, digressive elaboration. In *Havelok* each device has a practical use in exposing the fundamental elements of the story, giving the romance an economical, powerful forward movement at all times: Grim's possessions are catalogued as he sells them in flight from Godard (699–705); his fish are detailed while he catches them for market, demonstrating his merit as a provider and guardian (753–59). "Hise swink ne havede he nowht forlorn" (770), comments the poet, approving in Grim the efficient handling of good things that characterizes the very style of the poem. *Havelok*'s many simple ornaments—catalogues, proverbs, similes, patterned repetitions, descriptions—achieve, in Dieter Mehl's phrase, "an unassuming and yet ceremonious tone."[80] This inclusive style seems at once to provide simplicity and sophistication, leisure and efficiency, unaffected directness and high serious-

---

79. By contrast, the *Lai*'s style is unobtrusively simple, remarkably regular in emphasis, and lacking in rhetorical decoration. Only threefold repetitions of important facts give any stylistic emphasis to points in the story: naming Grimsby (*LH* 132, 143–44, 795–96), marriage promise (325–28, 360–62, 373–74), Haveloc's strength (245, 265, 278), the pirate attack (111–18, 609–12, 783–86), Haveloc's attack on the wife-stealers (691–703, 715–21, 757–66).
80. *Middle English Romances*, p. 165.

ness. It is an art of aspiration tempered by practicality. It is the poetic equivalent of those broad central strata of English society where birth counted for something but performance for more, and where engagement in daily affairs was necessary to achieving the life of abundance that *Havelok* celebrates.

Havelok the Dane also expands the accessibility of Anglo-Norman themes with emotional and moral emphases. When the usurper seizes Denmark in the *Lai d'Haveloc*, the nobles in charge of young Haveloc discuss the political situation and decide to leave the country (79–88). In *Havelok the Dane*, this fundamentally political crisis is rendered as a direct confrontation between the usurper and the orphaned Havelok, who witnesses the murder of his two sisters. Havelok's desperate pleas give dramatic intensity to the abstract concepts of disinheritance and repossession:

Ful sori was þat seli knaue,	innocent
Mikel dred he mouhte haue;	Great
For at hise herte he saw a knif,	
For to reuen him hise lyf.	take from him
But þe knaue, þat litel was,	
He knelede before þat Iudas,	
And seyde, 'Louerd, merci nou!	
Manrede, louerd, biddi you!	Fealty / offer
Al Denemark i wile you yeue,	give
To þat forward þu late me liue.'	agreement / let
(477–86)	

The ceremony of feudal submission and the subsequent renunciation of heritage rights (487–95) take fire and universality from the horror of Godard's bloody murders, the religious measures of evil and good, and the pathos of childish suffering that pervade the scene.

The many-faceted appeal of this episode typifies the poem's narrative procedure.[81] A single idea or event receives both rational and pathetic support, both political and moral meaning. By multiplying

---

81. Other examples of pathos are: sorrow at the deaths of the good kings (*HD* 152, 164, 234–35); the children's regret for their births (461, 1129–30); the murder of children (415ff., especially pathetic in taking advantage of their credulity [467–69, cf. 1106–10]). Mehl, *Middle English Romances*, p. 163, notes the use of the deaths of Havelok's sisters as "a concrete image of his sufferings" (*HD* 1364–68, 1411–16). Examples of religious appeals complementing political developments are: attribution of good rule to piety (102–5, 214–16, 226); use of holy objects in political ceremonies (185–203, 388–97, 1077–82); God's protection of Havelok (600, 648, 1175–80, 2226); angel's announcement that Havelok is the true heir (1263–74); return to Denmark in context of prayer (1359–84); characterization of Godrich and Godard as Judas and Satan (319, 425, 482, 496, 506, 1100, 1134–35, 1409–11, 2512).

the kinds of significance given to any episode, the poet ideally harmonizes the claims of law with those of morality and the interests of all classes with those of the hero. In presenting an ostensibly universal social reconciliation that in fact embodies the barony's concern for landed stability and the middle class's affinity for social order, *Havelok the Dane* boldly transforms the interests of society's middle and upper ranks into a literary vision of fulfillment in which hard work and dignity are compatible, profit and virtue coincide.

The stories of Horn and Havelok, in all their versions, join seriousness of purpose to buoyant optimism. Horn and Havelok contrast as heroes, but their differences only emphasize their stories' shared themes. Havelok is a disarmingly affectionate man who needs much encouragement to win back his heritage.[82] Horn, in contrast, wields active power over his destiny with autonomous confidence. Yet both models of behavior, the loving and the leading, define the hero in terms of his relationship to his followers and identify his fate with that of his people.

The later romances of English heroes follow the direction of *Havelok the Dane* toward greater accessibility. Social meanings are increasingly sustained and even overshadowed by affective and religious appeals. Diminishing political and social energy coincides with a growing interest in the hero's personal success and in action and event as purely narrative phenomena. Yet the later romances' diversity, rather than countering their underlying attentiveness to baronial issues, seeks to reformulate those issues in less class-defined, more universal terms.

82. Havelok is generous and kind, tolerant of insults, innocent of guile and sin (*LH* 251–62, 385–94, 486–88, 800–2; *HD* 945–54, 991–98). In *LH* he never initiates aggression or mentions his feudal rights but is pushed along the road to kingship by his guardian Grim, Grim's daughter, his wife Argentille, and the powerful Dane Sigar Estal. The ME Havelok shows a little more initiative, but he too must on several occasions be led or encouraged to win back his heritage.

Chapter Two

Land, Lineage, and Nation

The conventional notion of what constitutes medieval English romance—much bloodshed, great length, marvels and wonders, action rather than reflection—comes close to perfect embodiment in the stories of Guy of Warwick and Bevis of Hampton. Lord Ernle's assessment typifies modern reaction to these romances: "The austere simplicity of the older forms is overlaid with a riot of romantic fancy; their compactness of structure is lost. The romances are swollen to a prodigious length, in which incident is threaded to incident, adventure strung to adventure, and encounter piled on encounter."[1] They are as long as novels, and their detractors often fault them for failing by modern fictional standards,[2] while their admirers class them with popular detective novels or thrillers.[3] But "novel" content, design, technique, and invention by no means characterize the aesthetic of these works, nor are they particularly strong on mystery or thrills. Rather, they develop earlier romances' interest in baronial issues of land and lineage; their design, the kinds of events and problems they treat, and their stylistic proce-

1. Ernle, *Light Reading*, p. 78.
2. Charles W. Dunn writes that *Guy of Warwick*'s "incidents are unduly repetitive and prolix; the Middle English adapters show no inventiveness or critical sense. . . . The extent of its appeal is presumably dependent more upon the fame of Warwick Castle than upon its literary merit" (Severs, ed., *Manual*, I, 31).
3. E.g., Richmond, "*Guy of Warwick*: A Medieval Thriller"; McKeehan, "*Guillaume de Palerne*: A Medieval 'Best Seller'"; Ramsey, *Chivalric Romances*, pp. 1–7.

dures convey images of noble life that give their "riot of romantic fancy" a meaning worthy of the success they enjoyed.

This chapter treats the thirteenth-century Anglo-Norman romances of English heroes, their English descendants, and some later fourteenth-century romances as well. *Sir Beues of Hamtoun*[4] and *Guy of Warwick* (both ca. 1300) are so closely related to Anglo-Norman versions that some critics have treated them as translations. But textual studies demonstrate that no English manuscript translates an extant Anglo-Norman manuscript, so that their differences cannot be considered evidence of direct poetic reworking. Instead, the various versions of each story, like the versions of Horn and Havelok, are related works whose differences may be more accurately understood in terms of insular generic and historical developments than in terms of textual revision.

The longer romances of English heroes usually connect exile and return to feudal dispossession and reinstatement, and double the hero's winning of land with his winning a bride to continue the lineage. As for Horn and Havelok, the law and the courts are important sources of justification for Bevis, Guy, and Fulk—though this confidence in law breaks down in the later *Athelston* and *Gamelyn*. In addition, the diffuse longer works incorporate new sources of validation for noble heroes. Motifs from epic, saints' legends, and courtly poetry demonstrate heroic worth by other standards than winning a heritage. Where these standards conflict, uneasy accommodations reestablish the heritage as the dominant value for adventuring heroes.

Des Aventures e Pruesses Nos Auncestres

Central to all these works is the English hero's status as fictional forebear and defender of his nation. The opening lines of *Fouke le Fitz Waryn* (ca. 1280) illustrate this emphasis by revising the topos that spring's renewal stimulates human activity. Rather than inspiring love as in much lyric poetry, or warfare as epitomized in Ber-

---

4. *Beues of Hamtoun*, ed. Kölbing. On its dependence on the AN *Boeve*, see Kölbing, edition, p. xxxv; and Baugh, "Improvisation," pp. 431–32. The eight MSS and early printed versions used in Kölbing's edition differ considerably, although three main versions may be classified from them. See Kölbing, pp. vii–viii; Baugh, "Convention and Individuality," pp. 126–29. I cite the Auchinleck (A) MS, except where variants are significant to the discussion.

tran de Born's "Be'm platz lo gais temps," here springtime prompts reflection on the deeds of English ancestors:

> En le temps de averyl e may, quant les prees e les herbes reverdissent e chescune chose vivaunte recovre vertue, beauté e force, les mountz e les valeyes retentissent des douce chauntz des oseylouns, e les cuers de chescune gent pur la beauté du temps e la sesone mountent en haut e s'enjolyvent, donqe deit home remembrer des aventures e pruesses nos auncestres, qe se penerent pur honour en leauté quere.[5]

> In the season of April and May, when meadows and plants become green again and every living creature regains its nature, beauty, and force, the hills and valleys echo with the sweet songs of birds, and people's hearts soar and gladden at the beauty of the weather and the season, then we should remember the adventures and deeds of prowess of our ancestors, who labored to seek honor in loyalty.

Fulk is loyal to his lineage and to feudal law: the "aventures e pruesses nos auncestres" typically continue to arise from disputed land tenure and a family's cyclical self-renewal. This is evident in the first of the later romances of English heroes, the Anglo-Norman *Boeve de Haumtone*, composed somewhat later than the *Lai d'Haveloc* but probably not long after 1200. More than in the Old French *Bueve de Hantone*, in *Boeve* a clearly discernible line of interest in land and family runs through a varied range of motifs and adventures.[6]

Boeve, which closely resembles the story of Horn in plot,[7] unites the hero's first exile loosely around his first disinheritance. Like Horn, Boeve becomes a model vassal who defends the feudal hierarchy at home and in exile, refuses to marry until his patrimony is

---

5. *Fouke le Fitz Waryn*, ed. Hathaway et al., p. 3, lines 1–8. The editors summarize research on the relationship between the extant prose version (ca. 1330) and its lost verse source (ca. 1280), pp. xxxiii–xlvii.

6. *Boeve de Haumtone*, ed. Stimming. Legge, *Anglo-Norman Literature*, p. 157, suggests a late twelfth-century date, but cf. Stimming, edition, pp. lvii–lviii. Stimming, pp. clxxx–cxciii, and Matzke, "Beves Legend," summarize debate over the origin of the story and the relationship of the AN version to the three continental versions (*Bueve de Hantone*, ed. Stimming). Recent opinion supports continental dependence on the AN version (Rickard, *Britain in Medieval French Literature*, pp. 140–41).

7. During Bevis's first period of exile from his patrimony in England he is wooed by Josian, the daughter of the foreign king he serves, and in consequence suffers a long imprisonment in Damascus. A second exile from England (after his horse Arundel kicks King Edgar's son to death) follows Bevis's marriage to Josian and a temporary reacquisition of his lands and titles. This exile repeats the pattern of foreign success and wooing by a foreign princess found in Bevis's first exile, with many added adventures of separation and reunion. Finally, Bevis's twin sons participate in the acquisition of three kingdoms, those of Josian's father, Josian's pagan husband Yvor, and England.

56   *Insular Romance*

secured, and makes plans to avenge his father's death and rewin his own rights.⁸ His subsequent confrontations with King Edgar inspire the most politically cogent section of the work. Unique to the insular versions of the story are Boeve's refusal to pay the inheritance fee because of Edgar's failure to protect his rights, his request for permission to build Arundel Castle, and his warning to Edgar not to interfere with his land while he is again in exile.⁹

Boeve's second exile develops insular concerns in the more emotive sphere of family feeling. The hero's line of descent and that of his old tutor Sabaoth become intermixed in one extended family that shares Boeve's exile, conquests, and return to power in England.¹⁰ Boeve and his companion Tierri, Sabaoth's son, value their wives primarily as mothers and take great delight in their children.¹¹ Boeve's two sons obediently play up to their father's pride in their emerging likeness to himself:

> Dist l'un a l'autre: 'le champ traversez,
> si pensom de joster! Contre moi venez;
> ke ne savom, kant serrom esprovez.
> Kant nus vera mun pere li alosez
> nos armes porter, si serra mult lez.'
> Ore purrez vere cops de chevalers.
> 'Par mon chef!' dist Boves, 'cil erent bachelers;
> s'il vivent longes, il atenderunt lur per. . . .
> Sainte Marie, dame!' dist Boves li alosez,
> 'dame, merci! les enfans me gardez.'
>   (3346–53, 3357–58)

One said to the other: 'Cross the field, and let's think on jousting! Come at me, for we don't know when we will be tried. When our renowned father sees us bearing our arms, he will be very happy.' Then you could see the blows of knights! 'By my head!' said Bevis, 'these are fine aspirants to knighthood; if they live long, they'll catch up to their father. . . . Holy Mary, Lady!' said worthy Bevis, 'Lady, your grace! Guard these children for me.'

---

8. *Boeve*, 635–46, 683–87, 977–79, 1412–16, 1945–46, 2375–77, 2380–82. Martin [Weiss], "Middle English Romances," pp. 95–107, believes that different poets composed the first 165 laisses and the remainder of the poem. Errors and illogicalities do trouble the later stages of narration, e.g., the designation "François" for Boeve's supporters (3156–59, 3604–28). Cf. Stimming, edition, pp.xxii–lvii.

9. *Boeve*, 2428–50, 2508–22, 2545–50, 2615–21.

10. Boeve gives Sabaoth his land (2598–600); Boeve's second (chaste) wife subsequently marries Tierri (3001–6); Boeve is godfather to their son Boeve (3200), who is to be married to Boeve's daughter Beatrice (3520).

11. The account of Boeve's marriage stresses the conception of his sons (2389–96); see also 3064, 3195–200, 3205–6, 3265–71, 3512–13.

Land, Lineage, and Nation

The family continuity that Boeve sees represented in his children culminates when his two sons share in achieving his heritage and when he realizes at his death two weeks later that his children can successfully hold his property:

> 'Sire, ke tendra vos riches cassemens?'
> 'Dame, jeo n'en ai cure, a deu lur command;
> la merci deu, uncore ay trois enfans,
> ke purrunt tenir nos riches cassemens.'
> (3814–17)

'My lord, who will hold your great fiefs?' 'Lady, I have no concern for them, I commend them to God; thanks to God I still have three children who can hold our great fiefs.'

Here the familial devotion running through the work finally comes to support the political concept of land tenure.[12] Through much of the romance, however, the influence of baronial concerns operates on the level of emotionally felt impulse rather than of consciously articulated political principle.

In *Fouke le Fitz Waryn* the "aventures e pruesses nos auncestres" all center more closely around the disputed patrimony. This romance, exceptionally, tells not of legendary pre-Conquest figures but of a historical family's fortunes from the time of the Conquest through the reign of King John. Nearly half the romance recounts (with many historical distortions) the exploits of Fulk's ancestors as they establish the lineal claims he must defend from King John's depredations. Fulk's defense is double, with two escapes abroad from John's unjust anger, two promises of restoration, and numerous minor adventures that support the legal rights of family members and other barons to land.

The central crisis occurs when, upon the death of Fulk's father, King John denies Fulk's inherited right to Whittington in favor of another's claim. Fulk turns outlaw with a resounding denunciation of John's failure to provide just administration:

'Sire roy, vous estes mon lige seignour, e a vous su je lïé par fealté tant come je su en vostre service, e tan come je tienke terres de vous; e vous me dussez meyntenir en resoun, e vous me faylez de resoun e commune ley, e

---

12. In addition, a few events in the second half of the work reinforce or echo Boeve's political claim in England: he defends the claim of the Dame de Civile (2824–47) and of Sabaoth's son (3702–5); he returns to England, as he warned Edgar he would, when Edgar dispossesses Robant, who holds Boeve's lands for him (2611–21).

unqe ne fust bon rey qe deneya a ces franke tenauntz ley en sa court; pur quoi je vous renk vos homages.' (24.26–32)

'Sir king, you are my liege lord, and I am bound to you in fealty as long as I am in your service and as long as I hold lands from you; and you ought to sustain me in justice, and you fail me in justice and common law; and there was never a good king who refused his free tenants law in his court; wherefore I renounce my allegiance to you.'

Fulk's language of fealty and his appeal to law recall the *Romance of Horn*, yet here the situation is directly historical. The era of Magna Carta is the only post-Conquest period for which it is easy to imagine baronial victories comparable to those in the romances of English heroes. The historical John, like the fictional Edgar in the story of Bevis or Edelsi/Godard in the story of Havelok, appeared a wrongheaded and in the end intimidated king who had to concede the rights he unjustly sought to deny. Similarly, the Welsh border is perhaps the only post-Conquest setting that provided something like the military autonomy with which the English heroes demonstrate the worthiness of their claims. The Marcher lords enjoyed rights to private armies, to waging war and winning land, and to considerable judicial freedoms, in contrast to the rest of England's barony.[13] In *Fouke* a remarkable historical moment, an exceptional setting, and a heavily romanticized account of the Fitz Warin family's affairs allow the ideal fictional pattern of baronial victory to play itself out in a situation from the insular barony's own history.

To regain his holdings, in these later romances as in earlier ones, the hero must establish or sustain his family dynasty. Women's roles (except in the story of Guy) support the hero's efforts and contrast to roles from the literature of *fine amor*. Fulk secretly marries Matilda, whom he has never even seen before the wedding, partly to discomfit her suitor, King John, and partly because he "savoit bien qe ele fust bele, bone e de bon los, e qe ele avoit en Yrlaunde fortz chastels, cités, terres e rentes e grantz homages" [knew well that she was fair, good, and of good reputation, and that she had in Ireland strong castles, towns, lands and income, and great fiefs] (30.20–22). The insular Bevis versions lack even the superficially decorous customs of deference that ornamented political alliances in the *Romance of Horn*. Rather, Josian courts Bevis with pleas and

---

13. Davies, *Lordship and Society*, pp. 67–85, 149–75, 217–28; Meisel, *Barons*, pp. 34–54, 87–100, 132–38.

insults, while he shows energetic pique at her advances, walks out on her show of indignation, and, when she follows him to his room, snores in a futile attempt to get rid of her (AN 670–772, ME A 1093–199). After their betrothal, this freedom from the conventions of *fine amor* allows Josian to become an active helper to the hero, very like his wonderful horse Arundel, with whom she is in fact sometimes equated. Bevis's wife and horse both assist him in his dynastic victory and, despite their servile status, achieve a measure of dignity and repute as the appanage of Bevis's great merit.[14]

Sir Beues of Hamtoun undertakes an important development, whose beginnings are barely discernible in *Boeve*, from the perception of the baronial family as a political unit owing personal allegiance to rulers on the basis of reciprocal support, to a wider perception of national identity and the importance of national interests. The adventures of Horn and Havelok as they lose and gradually regain power correspond directly with the loss and the need of their people. This is a simple and effective means of heroic justification: what is good for Horn and Havelok turns out to be good for everyone. *Fouke le Fitz Waryn* shares this confident assessment. In the romances of Bevis and Guy, the needs and desires of the whole nation do not constantly coincide with those of the noble hero. But in compensation, patriotic sentiment reinforces the value of the hero's actions. Whatever his private baronial goals, he nonetheless represents his nation by occupying England's fictional history as an ancestral figure of diverse and superlative accomplishments.

The process is just beginning in *Boeve de Haumtone*, where a marginal sense of the hero's Englishness may be suggested by echoes of the legend of St. George, whose feast day became a national holiday in 1222.[15] Boeve's crusading fervor against pagans and his imprisonment in Damascus, as they recall St. George's exploits, reflect the gradual development of England's national identity through the impact of the Crusades, the loss of Normandy in 1204 and of the Angevin territories by 1243, and the increasing centralization of rule: "By the thirteenth century the fully developed medieval state [of England] had reached a momentary equilibrium, and if it was

---

14. Arundel is her gift to Bevis; both she and the horse are one-man creatures who resist appropriation by others (e.g., Yvor's attempts, AN 981–1031, ME A 1457–534, 2031–35). In two AN warning dreams losing Arundel represents losing Josian (2731–42) and harm to Boeve indicates the loss of one or the other helper (3436–43).

15. Matzke, "Contributions," p. 125; Weiss, "*Sir Beues of Hamtoun*," p. 72.

still 'feudal,' it was also, in its way, a national state."[16] To sustain the national state, a sense of pride in and commitment to it developed, expressed during the thirteenth century in antiforeign sentiment and more positively in the country's mobilization against the crises of the 1290s. Maurice Powicke concludes from Edward I's handling of these crises that "it was in Edward's reign that nationalism was born."[17]

A powerful sense of national commitment renders obsolete and even subversive the older feudal belief that lord and vassal have mutual duties and that vassals can maintain some spheres of autonomous action. Fulk's resistance to John goes unquestioned, but the Middle English *Beues* recognizes and adjusts to the challenge of nationalism by adding references to England and Bevis's Englishness on the one hand while supporting and even strengthening Bevis's feudal claims on the other.[18] Introducing an interpolated combat with a dragon, the poet ranks Bevis's achievement with similar victories by the English Wade and Guy of Warwick (2599–608). Told in the manner of a saint's legend, the dragon-killing extends the correspondences suggested in Anglo-Norman between the hero and St. George, patron saint of the English army from the earliest Crusades.[19] By these associations the Middle English version implies that Bevis's merit is national, even while extending references to his personal claims.

The conclusion of *Beues* also recognizes that the more dominant national ideology becomes, the more questionable a baron's commitment to his family and resistance to royal authority will become. *Boeve de Haumtone* reaches its resolution when Boeve, in response to Edgar's disseisin of Sabaoth's son, returns to England to bring the king into line. Edgar sweats with fear at the news of Boeve's arrival and, deferentially greeting the hero as "'sire roi'" (3767), settles Boeve's claim by arranging with his parliament to offer his daughter

---

16. Galbraith, "Nationality and Language," pp. 113–14; Powicke, *Thirteenth Century*, pp. 29–31, 100–103, 218–19; Wood, *Age of Chivalry*, pp. 125–38; Rickard, *Britain in Medieval French Literature*, pp. 38–40.

17. *Thirteenth Century*, p. 528; see also Keeney, "Military Service."

18. The English adapters add these references to Bevis's claims: *Beues*, A 1126–28, 1263–88, 1339–44, 2916–20, 2938–40, 3039–46, 3070, and M 901. But they omit passages on the children's charms and their growing prowess; Terri has no son and Bevis no daughter.

19. A 2597–910; Weiss argues that "patriotic sentiment" inspires these and other developments in *Beues* ("Sir Beues of Hamtoun," p. 72); see also Matzke, "Contributions," pp. 125, 150–56.

in marriage to Boeve's son (3738–49). The tensions in the feudal hierarchy that provide the terms of *Boeve*'s conclusion are obfuscated in the conclusion of *Beues*. The vassal no longer intimidates the king; even though Edgar had wrongly denied Bevis's rights he simply returns the heritage "bleþeliche" (A 4301). But the inescapable tension between them erupts in a street battle instigated by the king's steward, who recalls Bevis's role in the death of Edgar's son during the son's attempted theft of Arundel:

'Hureþ þe kinges comaundement:	Hear
Sertes, hit is be-falle so,	Truly
In ȝour cite he haþ a fo,	
Beues, þat slouȝ þe kinges sone;	slew
Þat tresoun ȝe ouȝte to mone:	lament
I comaunde, for þe kinges sake,	
Swiþe anon þat he be take!'	Right away
Whan þe peple herde þat cri,	
Þai gonne hem arme hasteli.	
(A 4332–40)	

It may seem surprising that a hero would be memorialized in British literature for slaughtering so many citizens of London "þat al Temse was blod red" (A 4530).[20] The carnage does resolve the charge that Bevis had betrayed the king: "'Þus men schel teche file glotouns [vile rascals] / Þat wile misaie [speak evil of] gode barouns,'" the hero concludes self-righteously as he delivers the coup de grace to King Edgar's steward (A 4387–88). In terms of the poem's professed national feeling, the best we can do is to read this episode nonmimetically as a "good baron" triumphing over slander.[21]

But it is important that, however Bevis's Englishness or his relations with Edgar may be *described*, his *actions* still defend his heritage, defy the king, and maintain his autonomy. Deprived of direct confrontation with Edgar, he exercises indirect opposition with relish; during this battle his sons' devoted support is crucial (A 4415–

20. That the steward's chief ally is a Lombard, or in later versions crowds of Lombards (A 4497–516; MO 4102, 4233), gives the episode a more conventionally nationalist coloring, yet in all versions surely most of the thirty thousand or more citizens whom Bevis slays must be Englishmen. On antiforeign sentiment in the thirteenth century, see H. W. C. Davis, *England under the Normans*, pp. 415–16, 421–22, 433–34; Rickard, *Britain in Medieval French Literature*, p. 40.
21. Mehl recognizes the problem but assumes it would not be recognized by an audience of "less refined tastes" (*Middle English Romances*, p. 216); Weiss seeks national feeling in the street fight's analogies to certain oppositions between barons and London merchants during the reform period ("Sir Beues of Hamtoun," pp. 73–76).

18, 4457–74, 4523–26). The romance denies its own assertions with respect to nationhood whenever those assertions interfere with Bevis's access to rights and rank. The underlying impetus of *Beues of Hamtoun* remains baronial, and any conflicting elements of national ideology are resisted.

The latest of the paired romances of English heroes, *Gui de Warewic* (ca. 1230) and its closely related Middle English versions,[22] supplement the underlying baronial impetus with further criteria of merit. Guy's story is based on the doubled expulsion and return pattern, extended into a brief parallel section on his son Reinbrun. But this typical pattern is modified by ideals from courtly literature, hagiographic values, and (as in *Beues*) respect for nationalism.

Guy's first exile from England is voluntary, inspired by his love for Felice, the proud daughter of his lord. Having fulfilled her demand that he become among knights "'del mund tut le meillur'" (1076) ["'best doinde / In armes þat animan mai finde'" (A 1157–58)], Guy marries her. Soon, however, he repents of so many victories in the name of love and undertakes a second voluntary exile to seek similar victories for God. As a humble pilgrim he revisits the Near East, the continent, and England, the three scenes of his youthful victories, and takes on three single combats of national importance; he then retires to a hermitage on his own property and dies a pious death.

Although many elements new to the romances of English heroes appear in the story of Guy, they are subordinate to the older issues of baronial rights. Early episodes portray a squire beset by conventional lovesickness who looks to Amor, a personified force, as his source of strength. But although the Guy poems say far more about the nature of love and its effects than do the other insular romances of English heroes, Guy's love is no more than the initial stimulus for the thousands of lines of adventure that follow. Guy hardly gives Felice a thought during the adventures she sends him on, and she never suffers reciprocal pains for love of him. Guy even curses his passion at times:

22. *Gui de Warewic*, ed. Ewert, is based on twelve AN MSS; two fourteenth-century English MSS are edited by Zupitza, *Guy of Warwick: The First or 14th-century Version*. Quotations are designated A (Auchinleck) or C (Caius); MSS described in Zupitza, *Guy of Warwick: The Second or 15th-century Version*. Several fragmentary AN and ME MSS have been separately published. The relationships among MSS are discussed by Weyrauch, "Mittelenglischen Fassungen"; and by L. H. Loomis, "Auchinleck Manuscript," pp. 607–8, 612.

'Las! tant fu dure ma destinee,
Kant a Felice fud enveie!
Felice, pur la vostre amur
De chivalerie vi perir la flur. . . .
Ahi! sire coens Rualt!
Vostre conseil mult par valt. . . .
Ki ne vult oir sun piere,
E despit la priere sa miere,
Mal li avendra sanz delai,
Kar esprové ja bien le ai.'[23]

'Al to iuel it fel to me,	evil
Felice, þo y was sent to serue þe;	when
For þi loue, Felice, the feir may,	
Þe flour of kniȝtes is sleyn þis day. . . .	
Allas! Allas! Rohaut, mi lord,	
Þat y no hadde leued þi word! . . .	believed / advice
Who so nil nouȝt do bi his faders red,	follow / counsel
Oft-siþes it falleþ him qued.'	badly
(A 1557–60, 1583–84, 1589–90)	

Guy's lament recalls the plea of his parents and of his lord that he put duty to them before his quest to win Felice (AN 1099–166, ME A 1183–246). In valuing the claim of lord and family over that of love, his lament anticipates the practical arrangements surrounding the lovers' eventual marriage, which Felice's father proposes to Guy with emphasis on the lands and titles involved (AN 7453–526, ME A st. 5–15). As in the *Romance of Horn, fine amor* merely ornaments and serves dynastic ends.

Religious feeling is hardly more salient in the second half of the romance than love in the first. Ostensibly, Guy now avoids recognition as carefully as he previously sought it, but he does reveal his identity after each of his combats;[24] and he is in any case so firmly established as the greatest knight by the time of his pilgrimages that the skepticism with which the oppressed accept this anonymous pilgrim as their champion in place of Guy of Warwick, whom they have been seeking desperately, simply emphasizes his stature as a living legend. Piety often enhances heroic merit in the romances of this group: Fulk goes into holy retirement like Guy before his death, Bevis converts his wife and the giant Ascopart, and

---

23. *Gui* 1424–40, with variants from MS C. The C-variants of this passage are fully translated in *Guy*, A 1559–66, 1583–84, 1589–94. Compare to this rejection of love *Gui* 317–19, 460–61, 7603–18; *Guy* A 361–63, 493–94, 24.1–12; C 7413–18.

24. *Gui* 8935–38, 10671–72, 11330–31; *Guy* A 138.1–6, 225.11–12, 274.1–7.

these heroes undertake numerous battles for Christianity. Yet in every case, piety is a praiseworthy quality that sustains public renown rather than transcending it.

Renown is a worldly value, as are other values Guy follows in the combats he undertakes as a pilgrim. He defends the right of his companion Terri to his heritage and the right of the English over the Danes to hold England.[25] In both cases Guy's impetus is double: he hopes primarily to avenge Terri but does express faith in God's assistance (AN 9703–24, ME A 159.6–160.9); he accepts the duel with the Danish champion in defense of the land, but also for love of God (AN 10996–98, ME A 248.4–5). Guy's attitude is more pious than in his youth, but his causes have not really changed. His parting speech to Terri after winning back his lands typifies the work's infusion of faith into baronial substance:

> 'Vostre seignur lealment servez,
> Gardez que orguil n'en aiez,
> A bosoig ben le socurez,
> De home desheriter ja ne pensez,
> Car si a tort nul desheritez,
> Ben voil que vus le sacez,
> Del regne Deu desherité serrez.'
> (10744–50)

'. . . be nouȝt to prout, y þe rede:	advise you
To serue þi lord at al his nede	
Þou proue wiþ þi miȝt.	try
Desirite no man of his lond:	
ȝif þou dost þou gos to schond;	you are lost
Ful siker be þou, apliȝt.	sure / indeed
For ȝiue þou reue a man his fe	if / rob / fief
Godes face schaltow neuer se,	
No com in heuen liȝt.'	Nor / heaven's
(A 230.4–12)	

Here Guy justifies rights to land, the oldest of Anglo-Norman themes, by appealing to feudal custom and piety together. His ser-

---

25. *Gui* 9709–10, 9716, 9793, 10241–45, 11063–64, 11204–5; *Guy* A 159.10–12, 165.4, 197.5–12, 248.4–6; C 9328, 9787–99, 10567, 10693–94. His first combat as a pilgrim, more difficult to summarize, settles an argument arising from a quarrel over chess between two pagan kings. It is undertaken primarily "Pur amur Deu" (8195) ["for the love of god all-myght" (C 7897)] as well as for pity of Jonas, but his victory apparently never results in the amnesty for Christians promised by King Triamor before the duel (AN 8337–62, ME A 87.4–88.9).

mon on feudal duty presents disseisin simultaneously as a breach of legal responsibility and as a morally reproachable act.

Despite the prominence of erotic and religious ideals, *Gui de Warewic* and its Middle English descendants express baronial concerns more fully than any of their group except the *Romance of Horn*. In his youth Guy's three major achievements defend the right of lesser nobles to their land against the claim of great lords, and even as a pilgrim knight his causes defend property and land from unjust seizure. Like Bevis's sons, Guy's son Reinbrun imitates his father, undertaking adventures that parallel those of his father's chivalric youth and even thinking of his father for inspiration in combat (AN 12480-90, ME A 93.1-94.7). In his culminating adventure Reinbrun rescues Guy's old squire Amis by using a magical sword to defeat a fairy knight, while Guy simultaneously rescues Amis's heritage through his battle against disseisin in Germany.[26] Father and son perform parallel services to Amis, but Reinbrun's adventure in fairyland is as suited to his youthful fancy and exuberance as Guy's judicial duel is to his maturity and moral dedication. The parallels convey both the generation that separates them and the blood uniting them, thus preparing for Reinbrun's return to England to take his father's place as Earl of Warwick.

Religious and courtly elements, then, affect the structures of Guy's story but not its strong baronial sympathy. National feeling, however, does affect that sympathy. As the Middle English versions move toward expressions of nationalism, the baronial perspective fades: feudal terminology, names of titles and holdings, and Reinbrun's echoing of his father's life are less important in the Middle English versions than in the Anglo-Norman. Granted, *Gui de Warewic* brings us the first hero to defend all England against its enemies.[27] In Anglo-Norman, though, the terms of Gui's defense are still baronial rather than national. Athelstan's plea for a champion against the Danes enumerates the central concerns of England's barons in narrow class terms:

> 'Francs chevalers, ore vus purveez!
> Voz sunt les chastels e les citez,
> Les larges terres e les maneres
> E les forestz de bestes pleneres;

---

26. *Gui* 12537-68, *Reinbrun* [*Guy* A] st. 97-98.
27. In addition to driving off the Danes, Guy kills a dragon that endangers the whole land of King Athelstan (7243-408).

Sovenge vus de voz tenemenz granz,
De voz femmes, de voz enfanz;
Si par voz feblesces les perdez,
A tut dis mes honiz serrez.'
(10871–78)

'Noble knights, now prepare yourselves! Yours are the castles and the walled towns, the broad lands and the manors, and the forests full of beasts. Remember your great possessions, your wives, your children; if by your weakness you lose them, you will be shamed forever.'

Gui's combat with the Danes' champion is similarly formulated: Athelstan sends word that he has found a knight who "Le dreit sun seignur defendra" [will defend the right of his lord] (11018), and Gui prays that he may successfully "de servage defendre la tere" [defend the land from servitude] (11064). The king argues that each baron's manor, wife, and forest bear witness to the Danish threat: here as throughout the romances of English heroes, individual fiefs and families stand for the barony's class interest and even for wider national interest. Yet Gui's courageous vassalage and the avoided threat of servitude do not really refer to the status of peasants or even that of the clerical first estate.

The Middle English versions of this episode formulate Guy's action in more fully national terms, usually omitting Athelstan's exhortation to the barons entirely and expressing the purpose of Guy's combat differently: he will fight not as Athelstan's vassal but "for Inglond" (A 248.12); he prays that he may "'To-day saue Inglondes riȝt'" (A 252.11). The shift from baronial to national allegiance is accomplished more easily than in Bevis's story, where the king challenged his vassal's own heritage. Here the need of the baronial class coincides more fully with the desire of a national community to enjoy England in peace.

In the later romances of English heroes, the pressure of ideologies not fully compatible with baronial concerns gradually increases. Religious issues become important in Guy's story, and their role will be treated more fully in Chapter 3. Courtly convention, too, affects the structure of *Gui de Warewic* and its descendants.[28] Most of all, nationalism challenges the local and lineal preoccupations of baronial heroes. Answering the challenge, poets assign national significance to the careers of these heroes by giving them

---

28. Pp. 196–97; courtly motives also influence *Degrevant*, whose plot begins with a challenge to land but continues with a doubled courtship.

specific combats in defense of England, by presenting them as fictive ancestors in Englishness, and by associating their excellence in adventure to the merit of the English as a whole. Yet in action these heroes seem to withdraw from national identification, Fulk in his outlawry as Bevis in his street carnage and Guy in his solitary wanderings. The tendency is even greater in the later *Gamelyn* and *Sir Degrevant*,[29] whose English heroes are engaged in a purely self-interested defense of inheritance rights with no national overtones. Yet even when nationalism is an important force in romances of English heroes, a strong underlying allegiance to the political ideals of the barony remains.

Justice

One measure of this allegiance is that like the earlier romances of English heroes, the stories of Bevis, Guy, and Fulk express faith in the capacity of judicial procedures to establish both the hero's claim and all subsidiary claims he defends during his adventures. So deeply do insular heroes believe in law as the proper instrument of baronial justice that they often welcome its substitution for open armed conflict and urge its application to kings. Although capricious kings may attempt to act unjustly, the institutions of justice are themselves sound and can successfully resolve the problems submitted to them.

Misuse of power by the mighty presents difficulties to all the insular heroes. When Arundel kills King Edgar's son, the king swears that Bevis will hang without trial, but the assembled barons constrain the king's wrath by reminding him of traditional law concerning homicide:[30]

> Diunt al roi: 'Vus nos volez escharnier,
> nos li veyum devant vus server,
> o vostre coupe aler e revener;
> ceo n'est pas dreit ke tu le facis occier.
> C'il refuse le bon chival de pris,
> nus i veum qu'il deyt estre garis.'
> (2587–92)

---

29. *Gamelyn*, ed. Skeat; *Degrevant* (ca. 1400), ed. Casson.
30. Medieval law exhibits cases both of executing animals that had killed and of fining the animals' owners. Domestic animals were sometimes tried for homicide, on the principle that they were as responsible for their actions as humans; see R. H. Bloch, *Literature and Law*, pp. 32–33.

> Þe barnage it nolde nouȝt þole   allow
> & seide, hii miȝte do him no wors,
> Boute lete hongen is hors;   Than / his
> Hii miȝte don him namore,
> For he seruede þo þe king be-fore.
> (A 3570–74)

The barons' adherence to law and the English king's eventual submission to it contrasts with the pagan king Bradmund's perverse transformation of his parliament into a posse to chase the escaping Bevis (ME A 1713–20). Edgar's submission foreshadows his response to Bevis's second return to England, when king and council agree to restore Bevis's heritage (AN 3738–72, ME C 4249–65).

King John allows personal enmity to overrule just procedure more fully, in enfeoffing Fulk's rival with land to which Fulk has right by inheritance. Fulk protests that "'vous me faylez de resoun e commune ley, e unqe ne fust bon rey qe deneya a ces franke tenauntz ley en sa court'" ["you fail me in justice and common law; and there was never a good king who refused his free tenants law in his court"] (24.29–31), an objection confirmed by the earlier examples of Henry II and Richard I, who kept the peace and renewed the Fitz Warin family's rightful claims to land (20.35–21.17, 23.18–23). Fulk's protest is just, and in consequence his outlaw life, rather than repudiating law, opposes to the breakdown of justice under King John a principled forest society.[31] King John rightly trembles with fear when Fulk, having kidnapped him, threatens him with his own wrathful arbitrariness: "'Tel jugement froi je de vous come vous vodrez de moy, si vous me ussez pris'" ["I will judge you in the way you would judge me, if you had taken me"] (49.36–38). But Fulk's threat is only educative; having made his point about the king's vengefulness, he frees John on the strength of the king's promises to grant him peace and to restore his land—promises that John promptly breaks.

The threat to just procedure emanates primarily from kings in the earlier romances of English heroes as well, although the kings in those works are irregular in some way: usurpers, pagans, foreign rulers. In every case, then, the English heroes speak out against royal injustice, and the right that is on their side compensates for

---

31. Fulk's band steals only from King John and his men; Fulk hunts down an imposter who committed crimes against the people in his name (27.7–34, 30.32–32.3).

their inferior political power. This fictional pattern makes a telling comment on the particularly litigious relationships between barons and king in England. Considerable tension arose in the legal sphere between the barony, who were asked to follow court procedures to determine and defend their holdings, and the king, who held himself to be both lawgiver and above the law.[32] The idealized process of these romances intimates not only that law and custom are on the side of the baronial hero and will fulfill the barony's desires, but also that justice is above even kings and will prevail against royal attempts to subvert it.

Even *Athelston*, which has no Anglo-Norman antecedent, makes the latter point about royal power.[33] Like Edgar in the story of Bevis, King Athelston wishes to execute an assumed traitor without trial. So willful is Athelston in his wrath that when his wife pleads that a parliament be called to determine the guilt or innocence of the accused, the king physically attacks her for disobeying his "comaundement," killing her unborn child (253–93). The problem of royal capriciousness is deeper here than in the main group of romances of English heroes, in that no baronial hero speaks for law in opposition to the king's injustice—indeed, the romance has no hero in the familiar sense, since the story's dominant figure, Athelston, must be overcome if justice is to triumph.

The heroic defense of legal procedure is particularly characteristic of *Guy of Warwick* and *Fulk Fitz Warin*. Guy's three great victories as a pilgrim knight are in judicial combats whose binding terms and formal oaths are extensively presented.[34] In youth as well, Guy supports legal or diplomatic solutions over military ones.[35] Fulk similarly persuades Prince Llewelyn to reconcile himself to a baron the prince had planned to attack:

Fouke fust sages e bien avysee, e savoyt bien qe le tort fust al prince; si ly dist en bele manere: 'Sire, pur Dieu,' fet il, 'mercy! Si vous ce fetez qe vous avez devysee, vous serrez molt blamé en estrange regneez de totes gentz. E, sire, si vous plest, ne vous peyse qe je le vous dy: tote gent dient qe vous

---

32. Chap. 1, nn. 18, 20–24; Kantorowicz, *King's Two Bodies*, pp. 149–50, 162–71.
33. *Athelston*, ed. Trounce (untitled in the unique MS).
34. *Gui* 8343–62, 8425–32, 9135–42, 9921–76, 10029–60, 11071–88; *Guy* A 87.4–88.9, 94.7–95.3, 176.1–179.12, 184.1–185.5, 253.1–255.2; C 8802–9, 9612–34; *Reinbrun* [*Guy* A] 17.7–18.3.
35. In a war between the emperor of Germany and certain barons whose cause Guy supports, the hero resolves the conflict by arranging a private parley between the opposing sides and a public ceremony of submission to the emperor's judgment (AN 2541–798, ME C 2485–716).

avez pecchié de ly, e pur ce, sire, pur Dieu! eiez mercy de ly, e yl se redressera a vous, a vostre volenté, e vous servira de gree, e vous ne savez quant vous averez mester a vos barouns.' (34.15–22)

Fulk was wise and observant, and knew well that the prince was in the wrong; so he spoke eloquently to him: 'Sire, for God's sake,' he said, 'have mercy! If you do what you have planned, you will be much blamed in foreign countries by all people. And sire, if you please, do not be offended that I say this to you: everyone says that you have wronged him. And therefore, sire, for God's sake have mercy on him, and he will return to you at your pleasure, and will serve you willingly; and you do not know when you will have need of your barons.'

Through his knowledge of deferential language and baronial rights, Fulk turns the prince's plans for war into no more than a lengthy discussion. He "talks and preaches" Llewelyn into acting fairly (34.23), just as by argument he finally convinces King John of his rights: "molt de paroles furent, mes a dreyn le roy lur pardona tot son maltalent, e lur rendi tot lur heritage" [there were many words, but at last the king pardoned them all his anger, and restored all their heritage to them] (57.26–28). The faith these heroes place in fair and reasoned argument contrasts with the evasions of wicked barons as well as of kings. Otes de Pavie stages a false parliament, with false oaths and kisses of peace, to entrap Guy and his friends (AN 5696–789, ME A 5619–84); the Fitz Warin family makes peace with a rival family through the court procedure of the loveday, but the rival family breaks the agreement at the deceptive advice of a "faus chevaler" (16.11).[36]

In all these instances two interrelated concepts of right are at work. The institutional procedures that can secure justice or peace are many—law and custom, parliament, loveday, judicial combat, inquest—and all are championed by various English heroes. But the reliability of these institutions rests on the more fundamental and, in these romances, pervasive reliability of language itself. The procedures that the English heroes demand are based in the validity of language in arguments, promises, testimony, depositions, and oaths. And since the language of good people is trustworthy and even the language of deceivers is usually transparent and read-

---

36. *Fouke* 14.6–10, 16.2–11; on lovedays, law, and literature, see Heffernan, "Poem on Lovedays."

ily exposed, the heroes' faith in the capacity of legal pleading is neither misplaced nor disappointed.

The later fourteenth-century romances *Athelston* and *Gamelyn* lose this bold confidence in institutional justice. Yet *Athelston* (ca. 1370) is deeply concerned with law. No wars, combats, or marvelous adventures supplement the central action of injustice and redress. Rather, the movement from calumny to vindication unfolds in a series of verbal gestures. Four messengers "Þat wolden yn Yngelond lettrys bere, / As it wes here kynde [was natural to them]" (14–15) meet at a crossroads and swear an oath of brotherhood. Later, when one has become king and the others are barons and archbishop, one baron lies under oath of secrecy that the other is a traitor. The king sends a false message to lure the accused baron and his family into royal control; then the king refuses to call a parliament of inquiry to verify the baron's guilt or innocence. The archbishop pressures Athelston with excommunication and interdict into surrendering judgment to the church. In the archbishop's ordeal the accused and his family swear their innocence and are vindicated. Athelston, sidestepping his oath of secrecy, reveals the accuser's name to the archbishop in the privileged language of confession: "'Be schryffte off mouþe telle I it þe'" (688). Then the archbishop's false message brings the accuser to court, where he fails the ordeal, confesses, and is executed.

The parade of diverse statements constituting this plot—oaths, lies, accusations, true and false messages, confessions—intimates that *Athelston* is concerned with the nature of communication, as well as with justice. Meaning in language, like truth in law, is far more elusive in this romance than is typical of the romances of English heroes. All characters accept all statements made to them as literally true, yet often the good characters as well as the bad make false statements or oaths that will be broken.

That the four main characters begin as messengers concretizes a distinction between language itself and effective communication. Subsequently, when the original four messengers take on their different roles as accusers and defendants, they are linked by a new messenger's activities, which occupy fully a quarter of the text's length. The preoccupation this suggests with the problem of transmitting meaning through words is borne out by the central messenger's treatment of his messages as mere commodities. His amoral readiness to transmit false as well as true messages, his desire for rewards, and his very dominance in the text cumulatively convey that speech is a fallible vehicle that often obscures the speaker's intention from the listener.[37]

The importance of language to this story of justice is further signaled by the assignment of a single name to king and messenger; the latter "bar his owne name: / He was hoten [named] Athelstane; / He was foundelyng" (184–86). Is the subject of this romance really the elusiveness of justice, embodied in the capricious king, or the unreliability of language, enacted by the blustering messenger? Ultimately the two problems are identical, as are the two characters' names, because justice can only be realized when language has determinate and reliable meaning. In *Athelston* the reliability of language disintegrates to the point that justice seems unattainable.

The archbishop snatches justice from the jaws of false speaking, but only by substituting an ordeal for a parliamentary inquiry.[38] Unlike the inquest, which depends on men's understanding of verbal testimony by witnesses, the ordeal reaches beyond its institutional structures to the ear of God. Unlike the judicial duel, the ordeal is unilateral. In bilateral judicial duels, depicted in other romances of English heroes, two champions swear before God to the rightness of their causes, and the outcome of their duel is taken as God's judgment. Theirs is a physical and social contest in which divine sanction, while it determines the outcome, is not at the center of the drama. In the unilateral ordeal private power and control are more fully surrendered to the judicial process, and God's power acts through the process more directly and immediately. In the earlier romances of English heroes, testimony and military skill and reasoned argument could contribute to putting down liars and wrongdoers. There no unilateral ordeals are to be found; but in *Athelston* the deviousness of good and evil people alike has cor-

---

37. Like coins, words can be put to good or bad uses. False messages bribe barons into coming to court; Athelston claims that the accuser's false words killed the queen's child: "'For þy falsnesse and þy lesyng / I slow3 myn heyr'" (762–63, see also 294–96).
38. Initially the archbishop pleads, like the queen, for a secular inquiry (445–49). Instead, and wisely in view of how the characters misappropriate language, he establishes an ordeal. On inquest versus ordeal: R. H. Bloch, *Literature and Law*, pp. 121–44.

rupted even speech, and justice is recoverable only by purifying speech through a direct appeal to the primal word of God.

Gamelyn (ca. 1375) betrays a similar sense that justice is elusive. This romance, like *Havelok the Dane*, opens with a dying father passing on his lands to his sons, of whom Gamelyn is youngest. Gamelyn's right to his inheritance is opposed not, as in earlier romances, by enemies from without, but by the very social units that should support him: the neighbor knights who advise the dying father and draw up his will, the regional churchmen with whom Gamelyn pleads for assistance, and the older brother who repeatedly deceives the hero in youth and ruins the land that should be Gamelyn's.

Soon Gamelyn's cause is judicially embattled as well, when his brother becomes sheriff, declares Gamelyn an outlaw, and bribes a royal jury of inquiry to vote against the hero's cause.[39] Corruption runs so deep in the world of *Gamelyn* that to resolve his claim, Gamelyn must move beyond both his unsuccessful verbal pleas and the unsupportive local institutions to a direct physical attack on the suborned royal jury. Hearing that the jury is certain to vote against him,

Thanne seyde Gamelyn to the Iustise,
'Now is thy power y-don, thou most nedes arise;
Thow hast 3euen domes that ben yuel dight,　　given sentences / wrongly done
I wil sitten in thy sete and dressen hem aright.'　　repair
The Iustice sat stille and roos nought anoon;
And Gamelyn in haste cleuede his cheeke-boon;　　cleaved
Gamelyn took him in his arm and no more spak,
But threw him ouer the barre and his arm to-brak.
(845–52)

Gamelyn himself then replaces the justice on the bench, his outlaw band constitutes a new jury, and the entire court and the sheriff are condemned to be "honged hye, / To weyuen [swing] with the ropes and with the wynde drye" (879–80). This road to vindication is diametrically opposed to that of the earlier English heroes, despite suggestive similarities between Gamelyn's and their causes and ad-

---

39. Like Fulk Fitz Warin, Gamelyn resists social injustice for a time by living in the society of outlaws, whose king he becomes. This is an order of proud men who live by a code of fairness that seeks to rectify injustices (779–82). On law and violence in *Gamelyn*, see Kaeuper, "Historian's Reading."

ventures.[40] The earlier heroes' profound faith in the capacity of justice and its institutions to determine right, based in their faith in the power of language, here degenerates to the point that only force can accomplish what pleading and inquests once did.

Athelston and *Gamelyn*, in presenting the achievement of justice as elusive and problematic, show a favorite theme of insular romance in its later development. The sense of crisis in the late romances enacts the social and political unease of the later fourteenth century, as virtually every medieval institution faced powerful challenges from all sides.[41] In *Athelston* and *Gamelyn*, the structures of family and feudal hierarchy, the institutions of justice, and even language itself no longer seem to promise security and success. But through the time of the Auchinleck manuscript, the insular romances of English heroes sustain a simple and direct faith in the accessibility of right and in the capacity of law, custom, and their language to regulate social action.

Style and Treatment

The romances of Bevis, Fulk, and Guy sustain the concerns of earlier works: disinheritance and repossession, dynastic disruptions and continuities, and institutional justice. The salient difference in the longer works is their diversification of interests and multiplication of episodes. The long romances also discover tensions between baronial commitments and national or religious ones. Although baronial and national ideals are largely compatible, some difficulties arise in presenting a hero whose interests are predominantly personal and lineal, yet whose significance is partly national. We have seen how narrative reconciliations tend to subordinate all to baronial themes, and poetic treatment works to the same end. As the

---

40. The failures of law throughout *Gamelyn* are the more remarkable for the sound knowledge of contemporary law the romance demonstrates; the nuncupative will and primogeniture, indictment, outlawing, mainprise and bail, trial by jury, and jurors as witnesses are examined in terms of legal history by Shannon, Jr., "Mediaeval Law"; Kaeuper, "Historian's Reading," pp. 58–59.

41. Studies on the upheavals of the fourteenth century are surveyed in Wallerstein, *Modern World-System*, pp. 20–37; Postan, *Mediaeval Economy*, pp. 61–72; and Duby, *Rural Economy*, part 4: "Change and Upheaval in the XIV Century" (pp. 289–357). Although these changes began before 1330 (date of Auchinleck MS), conditions were relatively stable until then: see, e.g., Dyer, *Lords and Peasants*, pp. 51–83. Cultural and literary expressions of crisis in the later fourteenth century are treated by Muscatine, *Poetry and Crisis*; and Coleman, *Medieval Readers*, pp. 58–156.

heroes' national identity calls dynastic allegiance into question, stylistic energy and eventfulness deflect attention from the import of specific episodes to action itself as a sign of worth and competence. Emphasizing action diffuses thematic oppositions, contributing to the reconciliation of national and baronial impulses.

The pressure of narrative in these works leaves no room for subtle or consistent stylistic effects. Still, even versification can convey a general attitude toward material. Unusual features of *Gui*'s and *Boeve*'s verse seem to strive for the balance between modern and archaic style that also characterizes the *Romance of Horn*'s verse. *Boeve* modifies the epic laisse with rhyme in a gesture that Albert Stimming understands as modernizing; Jean-Charles Payen suggests that *Gui*'s irregular verse may betray the partial modernizing of an earlier decasyllabic version, or may signal "le souci éprouvé par le poète de se référer à l'épopée traditionnelle."[42] In either case *Gui*'s unusual couplets, like *Boeve*'s rhymed laisses, combine elements of older, traditionally epic verse and newer syllabic rhymed verse, reinforcing on a stylistic level the narrative claims to both modern significance and historical validity. The English hero champions causes of practical and current interest to England's barony, but he is at the same time an exalted forebear, distanced from and elevated above the contemporary scene.

Middle English tail-rhyme's derivation from Old English meter and its archaic vocabulary have historical and national connotations. The Auchinleck versions of *Beues* and *Guy* change verse form once or more, but like other English versions they use tail-rhyme stanzas intermittently.[43] According to Elizabeth Salter, "the distinction of this Middle English verse is its power to invest an old measure with contemporary splendor and relevance." Verbally archaic,

---

42. Stimming, edition, *Boeve*, pp. xlvii–xlviii; Payen, in *Grundriss*, ed. Frappier et al., p. 478. *Gui*'s lines range from six to thirteen syllables (see Ewert, edition, I, xxvi).

43. Baugh suggests that the Auchinleck *Beues* reflects *Boeve*'s first shift in laisse pattern, in its change at a corresponding point from six-line tail-rhyme stanzas to couplets ("Improvisation," p. 432). On classification of *Beues* versions by verse form, see Baugh, "Convention and Individuality," p. 129. The Auchinleck *Guy* reorganizes the AN romance into a four-stress couplet section on Guy's youth, twelve-line tail-rhyme stanzas on Guy's marriage and expiation, and finally another tail-rhyme section on the extracted matter of *Reinbrun, Gij sone of Warwike*. The resulting division between the two halves of Guy's story is less marked than that between Guy's story and Reinbrun's (Bliss, "Auchinleck Manuscript"). Other ME versions of *Gui* do not attempt the Auchinleck version's reorganization.

yet compatible with a "maturing sense of 'Englishness,'" alliterative verse supports the romances' thematic emphasis on England's *antecessores* in relation to the country's feudal present.[44]

But this thematic emphasis is obscured by vastly increased eventfulness. Dorothy Everett notes in her characterization of English medieval romances that their action most often moves forward "under the impulse of love, religious faith, or, in many, mere desire for adventure. . . . What is certain is that medieval readers and hearers thirsted for tales of all kinds, enjoyed the mere narration of a series of events."[45] Everett's observations describe the later Anglo-Norman romances of English heroes just as accurately as their Middle English descendants. Their emphasis on action extends heroism from its earlier expression in the defense of family and heritage to a range of secondary expressions involving the hero's personal energy and capability. Poetic style grows vivid and lively, compensating for the diffused thematic energy of the later romances. Examples from the stories of Bevis and Guy will illustrate these tendencies.

The *Romance of Horn* and *Boeve de Haumtone* are so similar in design that a common source has been suggested for them.[46] Yet even in the initial section of each poem, where they are most clearly parallel, a significant difference separates them. The purposeful seriousness of the *Romance of Horn*, the constant regard for baronial self-justification and political principle, are in the story of Bevis often submerged in a great variety of added events. Bevis's expulsion from England draws on the motifs of May–December marriage, young wife's infidelity, cruel mother's remarriage, compassionate executioner, disguise, staged execution, and sale of the hero into slavery. This multiplicity contrasts with the relatively spare design of enemy invasion and rudderless boat in the story of Horn, and moves the usurpation of Bevis's rights from the purely political sphere to one of sexual intrigue, deceptions and disguises, and oedipal jealousies. Only in this connection does Bevis present his plan of vengeance:

> A donkes mounte li emfes en le paleis en haut,
> a l'emperur devaunt touz il parla com baud.

---

44. "Alliterative Revival," pp. 235, 150.
45. *Middle English Literature*, pp. 3, 12.
46. Stefan Hofer, "Horn et Rimel," pp. 283–90; see also Matzke, "Beves Legend," p. 41; Mehl, *Middle English Romances*, p. 213.

Li emfes vint devaunt le emperur a vis fer,
hardiement comença a parler:
'Entendez vers moi, beau duz sire cher,
ky vus dona congé cele dame acoler?
Ele est ma mere, ne vus enquer celer,
e kaunt a moi ne volez congé demaunder,
jeo vus frai sa amur mou cher achater;
rendez moi ma tere, jeo vus voil loer.

Beau sire emperur,' dist Boefs li sené,
'vus acolez ma mere estre mon congé;
mun pere, ke taunt amai, vus avez tué.
Pur ceo, sire, vus pri ke moi ma tere rendez,
que vus fausement tenez tut saunz ma voluntez.'
Lui emperur respondi: 'Fol, kar vus teisez!'
(287–302)

Al aboute he gan be-holde,	
To þemperur he spak wordes bolde	
Wiþ meche grame:	anger
'Sire,' a sede, 'what dostow here?	he / are you doing
Whi colles þow aboute þe swire	embrace / neck
Þat ilche dame?	very
Me moder is þat þow hauest an honde:	
What dostow her vpon me londe	here
Wiþ outen leue?	permission
Tak me me moder and mi fe	Give me / fief
Boute þow þe raþer hennes te,	Unless / quickly / go
I shel þe greue!	
Nastow, sire, me fader slawe?	Have you not
Þow schelt ben hanged & to-drawe,	
Be godes wille!	By
Aris! Fle hennes, I þe rede!'	advise you
Þemperur to him sede:	
'Foul, be stille!'	Fool

(A 421–38)

The many motifs of Bevis's dispossession, and of his exile as well, are engaging in themselves, but they cloud the thematic significance of his departure and return.[47] Stylistically, these two versions of Bevis's confrontation with his stepfather demonstrate that the

47. Other later romances of English heroes show a similar diffusion of interest: Guy's pet lion, Fulk's trick of shoeing his horses backward to confuse pursuers, and numerous giants, magical gemstones, dragons, and the like provide the "merveilles e aventures" (*Fouke* 45.16) that characterize the later romances. The story of Guy is most strongly affected in that his two exiles are voluntary, inspired by love of Felice and love of God, despite the prominence of baronial themes in his story.

English poet imitates Anglo-Norman phrasing, repetition, laisse boundaries, and laisse linking, yet the final effect is quite different from the density and elevation of the Anglo-Norman verses. Removing Anglo-Norman descriptive epithets and multiplying questions and exclamations contribute to the English version's generally less formal tone. *Beues*'s few similes are universal or agricultural—bees about the hive, hail striking stones—while those of *Boeve* revolve largely around hawking.[48] *Beues*'s rather frequent and often humble physical details—workmen going to work, a handkerchief stopping a wound, a child pulled along by the ear—contrast with the rare and purely ornamental use of a gilded stirrup or a marble staircase in *Boeve*.[49] The Middle English narrator is far less aloof than the Anglo-Norman counterpart, regularly cursing, lamenting, praying for, and commenting on the characters and encouraging a like emotional commitment from the audience.[50] These stylistic changes, like the multiplication of narrative motifs, contribute to *Beues*'s energy and accessibility—but again by broadening the narrative's appeal rather than by sustaining themes of land and lineage directly.

Emotional emphases also supplement thematic ones in *Gui de Warewic*, the only Anglo-Norman romance of English heroes that anticipates the Middle English desire (first evident in *Havelok the Dane*) to discover opportunities for pathos in episodes of political and legal importance. When Seguin comes to the parliament that Gui has arranged to reconcile him to his lord, the poignant spectacle of his humble approach to the emperor prepares for his subsequent legal defense:

> Puis ad sun bliand osté,
> Maint home en ad de lui pité,
> Remis est en sa chemise;
> Ore oez en quele guise

---

48. *Beues* A 1407–8, 2771–72; see also 792, 2485–86, 2673–77; *Boeve* 593–94, 601–2, 1736, 1755, 3422. A few alliterative phrases elevate the tone of *Beues*'s first section: *Beues* A 18, 48, 312, 348 (all in tail lines); see Kölbing, "Alliteration."

49. *Beues* A 3228–30, 1934–36, 492; *Boeve* 2481, 2602, 3135 ("estru doré"), 2407, 2525 ("marbrin degré").

50. A similar transformation enlivens *Guy*'s style. The proportion of direct to indirect speech rises, and colloquial vigor increases: "'Þou lexst amidward þi teþ,'" "'Thou art not worthe a mouse torde!'" (A 4385, C 3704). Occasionally a more formal speech, such as Gui's "'Seignurs, ore tost nus armuns, / Les Sarazins irruns assaillir, / Chescun se peine de ben ferir'" (3004–6), gains energy in keeping with its content: "'To armes,' he seyd, 'euerichon! / Þe Sarrazins we willen agast. / For godes loue, smiteþ on fast!'" (A 2928–30).

> A l'empereur en volt aler:
> En sa main porte un raim d'oliver,
> Par les rues en va nuz piez,
> Duxcs e cuntes od lui asez,
> Que l'empereur requerrunt
> Tant tost cum il le verrunt.
> Quant el muster sunt entrez,
> A l'empereur chairent as piez.
> (2691–702)

Then he removed his tunic (many men pitied him for this); he kept on only his shirt. Now hear how he wishes to go to the emperor: in his hand he carries an olive branch; through the streets he goes barefoot accompanied by many dukes and counts who will plead with the emperor as soon as they see him. When they entered the church, they fell at the emperor's feet.

Seguin's enactment of his longing for conciliation with the emperor culminates in his legal testimony (2703–24) that he killed the emperor's nephew in self-defense, in the presence of a third party, and that he will defend himself in judicial combat from any charge of *felonie*. Six witnesses testify to Seguin's good character and innocence, and the emperor accords his pardon (2725–98). The matter of the scene is clearly judicial, the manner both descriptive and supportively emotional.

As the story of Guy develops, its pathetic content increases. The later Anglo-Norman manuscripts G and R, which date from the period of the early Middle English versions, add to the older version of Seguin's pardoning a hangman's noose (G) and a haircloth (R) worn in token of submission and repentance.[51] The Caius *Guy of Warwick* adopts both these variants, in addition to the emotive details of the older Anglo-Norman version, transforming the original emotionally supported legal proceeding into a colorful and dramatic pageant centered on a figure of greatly increased pathos (C 2598–625). Weighted with the many symbols of his penitence, the Caius Seguin is so abashed and miserable that he no longer speaks in his own defense. If his expressions of pure regret (C 2633–46) had not been supplemented by his witnesses' pledges of his innocence (C 2647–704), the scene would have lost the substance of a legal proceeding altogether.

Here treatment supplements content as the legal proceeding itself becomes less compelling than it was in Anglo-Norman. The

---

51. *Gui*, variants, II, 196; on dates of MSS G and R, see I, iv–vii.

heightened pathos, like vivid colloquial language and direct speech, involved and involving narrators, and sharpened detail, extends the capacity of the narrative to command attention.[52] Thus while older concerns (in these examples, disinheritance and judicial procedure) still lie at the heart of the narrative, increasingly diverse motifs and intensified stylistic appeals render those themes in more emotive, less overtly political, and more universal terms. Style animates the reoriented themes and helps to steady the episodic sprawl of the later works.

That wild sprawl has another domesticator, the hero himself. Whatever the achievements of style, the longer romances are undeniably episodic. Rather than simply executing a thematically determined development, events often stand on their own as so many independent embodiments of the hero's greatness. For the relation of hero to world is typically one of domination: he kills dragons, abashes pagans, escapes prisons, tames lions, beheads adversaries, and converts or marries princesses. The hero's frenetic activity, like the style, compensates for diminished thematic substance. This process tends to dissociate the hero's merit from his objectives (heritage and family; now extended to nation, lady, and salvation) and to stress instead the means to those objectives—prowess and initiative. Since the means are relatively constant, emphasis on them rather than on a collection of ill-sorted ends makes sense of heroic action in the long romances. Much of heroic merit now resides in the freedom and the capability to manage events.

For example, in *Boeve de Haumtone* the thematic relations of episodes and even their inner logic are often obscure, but always clear is Boeve's presence and centrality. His confession to the patriarch in Jerusalem illustrates the challenge to coherence posed by the imperious power of event:

> Enver Jerusalem ad son chemin torné,
> a la patriarc se ad il confessé,
> tretuz se pechez li ad contez
> e coment son pere fu tué
> e com il servi Hermine, le fort coronez,

---

52. *Beues*, like *Havelok*, supports political developments with the pathos of innocent suffering (e.g., A 1457–62); Guy pities a defeated lion (A 4118–19) and pities the English lords who face the Danish threat (A 247.12). These two changes from AN are significant but do not warrant the judgment that in ME all Guy's adventures illustrate "the knight's pity and desire to help the oppressed" (Mehl, *Middle English Romances*, p. 226).

> e com il pris Brandon, le roi mult provez,
> e com il fu a Damacle enveyez
> e com il fu en la preson gettez
> e com il fu de iluc eschapez
> e com il conquis le geant menbré.
> E le patriarc si en prent pité
> e li dona un mulete afeyté
> e trente e quatre besans de fin or esmeré
> e li bonement a deu comandé.
> (1346–59)

Toward Jerusalem he made his way, and confessed himself to the patriarch; he told him all his sins, and how his father was killed, and how he served Hermine the strong king, and how he captured Brandon the proven king, and how he was sent to Damascus, and how he was thrown into prison, and how he escaped from there, and how he conquered the famous giant. And the patriarch took pity on him and gave him a well-trained mule and thirty-four besants of refined gold, and commended him graciously to God.

The additive drive of this passage's syntax accurately condenses the poem's episodic character. The patriarch's useful gifts to the hero demonstrate that even he, like Boeve, is distracted from the Christian function of their encounter into a full sympathy with adventure. What matters to both characters is that Boeve has done much and will soon do more.

Often narrative style can relate and subordinate certain episodes to others,[53] yet this amounts to fairly superficial ordering of what remains an intractable fecundity of episodes. Hence it falls to the hero to direct and control the onslaught of events. This is hardly a new observation, but it is difficult to see just how the hero gives sense to these works when we attempt to read across their narrative parataxes. Is the story of Guy an *exemplum* of loyalty, or of pity?[54] Or perhaps it is an *Entwicklungsroman* tracing Guy's "growing

---

53. *Beues* supplies more motivation and coherence than *Boeve*: e.g., A 58–66, 286–91, 569–70, 837–40, 1511–12, 1263–84, 1976–84, 2080–98, 4036–38. The ME versions of Bevis's encounter with the patriarch summarize rather than list the hero's escapades (he speaks "Of is [his] wele and of is wo"), and the patriarch provides him not with perpetuating gifts but with advice: "Þat he neuer toke wif [take a wife] / Boute [unless] ʒhe were clene maide [virgin]" (A 1964, 1968–69; see also variants SNM). No more confessional than the AN version, the ME versions do introduce reflective and admonitory elements that highlight the transition between the adventures demonstrating Bevis's superiority to his pagan captors and those culminating in his marriage.
54. Legge, *Anglo-Norman Literature*, p. 169; Mehl, *Middle English Romances*, p. 226.

awareness of who he is and his enunciation of a distinctive scheme of values."[55] Certainly Guy's conversion to God's service demonstrates moral growth, but that interest is only one of several in the story. Episodes in which the young Bevis is reproached or in which he rejects his friends[56] may imply an immaturity corrected by his later defense of and concern for friends and family. But the story of Bevis does not attend consistently to inner growth: like Horn, Bevis is as bold and as deserving of his heritage at his first exile as at his last return.

The slender attention to heroic growth in the stories of Bevis and Guy demonstrates that to look for significance in the hero's personal development is to desire, inappropriately in these romances, the quality of *romans psychologiques* or even novels. We are not invited to worry about the maturation of these characters, only to admire them at every stage. Nor is any one trait, such as loyalty or pity, dominant in any hero. The alternating tensions and resolutions that power all the romances of English heroes have little to do with personality and personal development. The hero is not self-reflective but active; his life is a series of encounters through which he defines his effectiveness as conqueror, father, defender of land and nation, defender of faith, and so on.

Stylistic treatment gives force and new appeal to the many events that demonstrate the hero's capacities. Yet despite their heightened verbal energy the later romances, like the earlier ones, are heavily conventional and formulaic in phrasing.[57] Their underlying conventionality inhibits liveliness and returns us to the sense of familiarity, assurance, and stability inherent in the much earlier verse of *King Horn* and the *Romance of Horn*.

The massively eventful later romances, however their style may strain toward coherence and however their conventionality may tame their violence, give us a world of turbulent action where doing and achieving are the essential occupations of life. By mastering each event the hero reveals himself to be remarkably capable. The focus on capacity rather than cause helps to reconcile baronial ideals to new challenges, especially those of nationalism. Bevis

---

55. Richmond, *Popularity*, p. 152.
56. E.g., *Boeve* 321–24, 846–61, 1570–86, 1609–28; *Beues* A 469–74, 1305–32.
57. See Baugh, "Middle English Romance"; Wittig, *Narrative Structures*; and Gradon, *Form and Style*, who argues that conventional imagery "irradiates" the specific with a sense of the universal or "archetypal" (pp. 170–74, 212–72).

makes peace with Edgar but kills the king's steward and masses of citizens, all the while insisting that he is a "gode baroun." In Germany Guy fights in God's name, but the substance of his cause is Terri's feudal right to his land. Such episodes are not openly contradictory when action and military success are the point, rather than precisely what principle the hero is acting on.

This orientation respects the value that England's barony placed on defending some rights from national control, while encompassing as well the value that merchants and professionals placed on aggressive achievement. Class focus softens when the later romances blur issues of heritage and law, while heroic autonomy and violence—merely the atavistic servants of landed and peaceable concerns in Horn's and Havelok's romances—come to the fore as values in themselves. Still Bevis, Guy, and Fulk continue to fulfill baronial ideals, to look to the heritage as the ultimate source of security, and to protect the interests of others as they follow their own. In addition, heroic capability in the later romances imaginatively expands the special worth of "those who fight" from the military sphere to many other areas of endeavor and domination. Whether converting a pagan or tricking a jailkeeper, winning a wife or defending a nation, the hero wields the ability to bring all his adventures to an assured, stable, and peaceful close.

Insularity and the Romances of English Heroes

The Anglo-Norman and Middle English romances of English heroes show no interest in the dominant continental themes of divided self or divided society, but their divergence cannot be understood merely as a failure to imitate or to comprehend Old French romances. Rather, as outlined in these two chapters, the insular romances of English heroes work changes on romance that allow them to transform, idealize, and respond to some of England's social and institutional conditions. In so doing these works present a different model of human existence from that of most Old French romance. Conflict between a hero and his society is not central and problematic. Rather than locating the human drama in self-discovery, the insular romances propose that the human drama is collective, a communal search for stability that takes place through the hero's search.

This characteristic perspective is evident in early crises from the *Romance of Horn* and *Havelok the Dane*. In the *Romance of Horn* and its descendant *King Horn*, the young hero loses his patrimony as invading pagans set him and his twelve companions adrift. Horn's crisis is external and political, a challenge imposed on him by cruel enemies. That Horn's companions share his fate emphasizes the social nature of this crisis and of its subsequent resolution. Havelok faces a similar challenge as the wicked regent Godard prepares to kill him. Havelok saves his life only by throwing himself on his knees, in the feudal gesture of submission, swearing fealty to Godard and promising to renounce his parentage. Thus in saving his life he must place himself and his countrymen at the mercy of a virtually merciless tyrant. Havelok's subsequent actions continue the identification of his own fate with that of the Danish: he passes his youth anonymously in England, where a tyrannous ruler treats the people just as Godard must be treating the Danish; when Havelok returns to Denmark he regains his throne through a popular uprising and has Godard judged by a parliament drawn from all ranks of society.

The identification of heroic striving with social good is less direct in the later romances, but the connection between hero and society remains fundamental. When Bevis and Guy fight in the name of Christianity, when Fulk and Guy in exile champion barons against injustices, when Guy defends England from Danish servitude, they strive for causes that extend beyond personal advancement to affect the lives of numberless others. In correcting the injustices of kings, from whom justice should emanate, they correct the legal system itself. Fulk represents the barony as a whole when he menaces King John "pur le grant damage e la desheritesoun qu'il avoit fet a ly e a meint prodhome d'Engleterre" [for the great damage and disinheriting he had done to him and to many a good man in England] (49.39–50.1). Bevis, refusing to submit to Edgar's wrath and subsequently attaining such power that his son marries Edgar's daughter, wins for noble aspirations a more vicarious victory, through an imaginative association between the hero's achievement and a wider ideal of baronial potential.

Why is it that the romances of English heroes perceive the good of hero and people as interdependent? The perception has profound thematic effects, dictating that crises and their resolutions be enacted in political rather than psychological terms, and that they place whole social groups in jeopardy before moving toward a harmonious realization of the interests of rulers and ruled. In part the political orientation of these romances stems from their close affiliations with insular historiography. Havelok, Waldef, and Athelstan appear in chronicles before they become figures of romance; Guy and Havelok are found in chronicles throughout and even beyond the medieval period.[58] Their histories often overlap: Havelok may well be Horn's father Aälof; Athelstan's attributes in chronicles prepare for his appearances in both *Athelston* and the story of Guy; in the *Petit Brut d'Angleterre*, Guy challenges the kingdoms of Havelok's son.[59] Local relics of Guy at Warwick, Havelok at Grimsby, and Bevis at Southampton, although they postdate the romances themselves, reemphasize that the works' origins were considered to be historical.[60] In romances the *antecessores* of the chronicles, who provided the Normans with an Anglo-Saxon past, continue to defend their people's causes. But now the significance of these heroes is only in part genealogical; they come to champion new causes, those of the insular baronial structure.

The barony's landed wealth in the twelfth and early thirteenth centuries, its restricted military power and, in contrast, its access to a functioning legal system that controlled the questions of land rights on which its strength depended—together these conditions inform the ideal model of heroic resistance to royal injustice that the Anglo-Norman romances of English heroes offer. This reading of the works reinforces historians' assessment of England's barony as a pragmatic nobility that confronted its problems with directness and energy: "It was mainly by keeping close to the practical things which give real power over men and avoiding the paralysis that overtakes social classes which are too sharply defined and too dependent on birth that the English aristocracy acquired the dominant position it retained for centuries."[61] The themes of the Anglo-

58. Heyman, *Havelok-tale*, pp. 109–22; Brian J. Levy, "Waltheof"; Trounce, ed., *Athelston*, pp. 28–30; L. H. Loomis, *Mediaeval Romance*, pp. 128–31 (on Guy); R. S. Crane, "*Guy of Warwick*."
59. Legge, *Anglo-Norman Literature*, pp. 99, 101; Heyman, *Havelok-tale*, p. 112.
60. See Timmins, *History of Warwickshire*, pp. 17–19, on Guy's relics; John Ross, *Earls of Warwick*, ed. Hearne, pp. 225–27, which claims Guy as ancestor; *Havelok the Dane*, ed. Skeat, pp. xx–xxii, on local traditions concerning Havelok; and Dunn, in *Manual*, ed. Severs, I, 27, on statues of Bevis and Ascopart. Even *King Horn*, most bereft of social or historical context, is for Mehl "the biography of a famous ancestor, a vivid portrayal of the past" (*Middle English Romances*, p. 51).
61. M. Bloch, *Société féodale*, II, 77 (trans. *Feudal Society*, II, 331); see also McFarlane, *Nobility*; and Holt, *Magna Carta*.

Norman works correspond to issues so vital and so pervasive for the insular barony that the ancestral romance theory does not best explain their composition.[62] Each of these romances, far from responding to a particular crisis in a particular family's history, springs from the history of England's entire barony and transforms that barony's daily realities into literature. The complete continuity of the romances of English heroes from Anglo-Norman to Middle English versions demonstrates the continued vitality of baronial issues through the thirteenth century and into the fourteenth.

To some extent the rise of nationalism threatens the traditional values of these works. If the historiographic origins of these heroes gave them their political and collective stance, their use in romance orients that stance toward a specific class situation. Royal centralization asks barons to subordinate dynastic interests and landed autonomy to the good of the realm: the king is the head, barons only the hands, of the body politic.[63] The romances of English heroes resist this ideology in their models of baronial action. The hero's free search for private goals and even his outlawry and defiance of kings always end well and benefit the community. Such plots imply that baronial interests are universal principles that provide well for everyone. Gradually in the later romances, upholding the heritage does take on patriotic colors, and legal preoccupations expand to involve national questions. These accommodations to nationalism have historical correlatives in the barony's acceptance of increasing centralization, the lessening of baronial power, and the broadening role of the commons in government.[64] But the place of national spirit in the romances is uneasy, as Fulk's defiance of John and Bevis's slaughter of Londoners illustrate.

The romances of English heroes give their insular world literary expression through a range of structural and stylistic procedures that transform and assess a complex social experience. At the

62. See pp. 16–18. I insist on the arguments against this theory in part because it is widely accepted in studies of ME romance, with distorting effect: e.g., Mehl, *Middle English Romances*, pp. 211, 218, 224; Richmond, *Popularity*, pp. 5, 148–49; Lillian Herlands Hornstein, in Severs, ed., *Middle English Scholarship*, pp. 56, 71–72; Watson, ed., *Cambridge Bibliography*, pp. 447–50.

63. The metaphor is from John of Salisbury's *Policraticus* (ed. Webb, 5.2 and 6.29; trans. Dickinson, pp. 64–66, 276–77), which Duby calls "the first systematic formulation of a secular ideology of power and social order" (*Three Orders*, p. 264; see pp. 263–68, 271–92). A fourteenth-century example is discussed in Thomson, "Walter Burley's Commentary."

64. See pp. 21–23; and Painter, *English Feudal Barony*, pp. 193–97; Treharne, *Baronial Plan*, pp. 378–79.

broadest structural level, these romances share the narrative pattern of departure and return, which usually takes the specific form of dispossession and reinstatement.[65] The hero, through his courage and his legal knowledge, regains a rightful inheritance wrongfully seized from him. A concern for just procedure often transforms crises that could be occasions for warfare into lessons in legality. Horn exiles himself from Hunlaf's kingdom over their dispute about oath-taking and judicial combat; Bevis wins back his heritage from King Edgar not by invasion but by pressing his legal claim and winning the support of the king's counselors. Fulk loses his heritage in a dispute over the rights of king and barons, and he wins his lands back by arguing King John into pardoning him. Crises in which heroes and villains act as litigants abound, emphasizing the preoccupation with law and custom that characterizes the romances of English heroes.

In the related Anglo-Norman and Middle English works, legality safely delivers justice, and justice sustains heroic defense of the heritage and later of the nation. The dream of ferocious animals and trees bowing in cowed homage to Haveloc in the Anglo-Norman *Lai* (401–38) expresses a purely seignorial desire for landed power, whereas the English Havelok's dream of all Denmark clinging with love to his embracing arms (1285–1303) expresses both his own desire and a reciprocal spirit of national harmony. Even in the story of Guy, most diffuse in interests and appeals, the adventures the hero dedicates to God are dedicated as well to defending Jonas's and Terri's seignorial claims and England's claim to independence from Denmark. In every case, then, these works attend to issues of legality and landed identity, so that judicial questions direct the plots' critical turning points and feudal principles often inform even minor adventures in the heroes' exile.

A further refinement of the pattern of departure and return underlines the preoccupation in these works with rights to land. The romances of English heroes double their fundamental design, containing two departures, or disinheritances, two recoveries, and two pivotal victories over oppression or injustice. This doubling has various structural manifestations—Bevis is dispossessed and exiled

---

65. General comments on structure apply less to *Gamelyn* and *Athelston* than to the other romances of the group. *Gamelyn*, however, does move from dispossession to reinstatement, a pattern doubled by the brother's false promise to return Gamelyn's land (155–68).

in childhood by his cruel mother, in adulthood by the king; Horn is driven from two different countries, then wins rule over both; Havelok's dispossession in Denmark is echoed by that of his wife in England. The nature of the double suits perfectly the central concern of these works, whereas the more common tripartite structure of folktales, fairy tales, and many continental romances would counteract that concern. A triplet forms a closed sequence, a whole and finished figure. Its uses in traditional narrative and in religious and magical symbolism demonstrate the completeness and inner unity attributed to the number three.[66] But a double structure implies any number of additional victories. Doubling involves difference, but also echoing or equation. Its difference connotes extension or progression, while its sameness connotes assurance and stability. The two implications are often evident in the conclusions to these romances: almost all end with a dual summary, first of the hero's achievement of peaceful rule and then of the son's extension of that rule in a repetition of the father's victories. Such conclusions recognize overtly that doubling supports the proposition that landed stability can be threatened but will endure.

As these observations imply, the romances of English heroes are socially conservative. They respect and value the institutions of marriage and the family as well as the class system, strong rule, and strong justice. Their conception of personal potential is equally conservative. An English hero does not typically experience remarkable personal growth or enlightenment; rather, he is fully himself—fully noble and worthy of his heritage—from birth. The crises he faces are external ones: How is he to win back his heritage? Can he protect his family's honor, find a suitable wife, and ensure perpetuation of the family's line? Rimenhild's seduction of Horn, although at first appearing to be an antisocial, rebellious act, turns out to be not a physical seduction but a temptation to marriage. So strongly institutional are Rimenhild's motive and Horn's consent that, when Rimenhild's father accuses Horn of having seduced her, Horn rejects even the idea of marriage until he has achieved his heritage. Many insular romances share this view of marriage as a social institution that helps to define feudal status.

66. See Hopper, *Medieval Number Symbolism*, pp. 4–8, 11, passim (on three as completeness); pp. 3–4, 11, passim (on two as ambiguously both completeness of pairs and incompleteness). Studies on tripartite design in Chrétien de Troyes's romances are surveyed in Zaddy's *Chrétien Studies*; see also Kelly, *Sens and Conjointure*, pp. 166–203.

Children extend that status by carrying on their parents' achievements. The knowledge that his sons and daughter can hold his land reconciles Boeve to his own death; of Havelok's fifteen sons and daughters, all kings and queens, the poet concludes sententiously, "Him stondes wel þat god child strenes" [he is secure who begets good children] (2983). The idea that children double their parents' lives, by stressing continuity rather than disjunction between generations, validates the principle of land inheritance. Thus the stability won by the hero through his appeals to justice will outlive the hero himself.

In structures as in themes, then, the romances of English heroes provide images of continuity, stability, and confidence. Their variously archaizing verse and the conservative impulse of their conventional style sustain these images. The ambivalence of the later romances *Athelston* and *Gamelyn*, confronting the seignorial losses of the later fourteenth century, emphasizes by contrast the remarkable assurance of the main body of works. The future these earlier works project does not differ from the bold present of their heroes' lives: barons are and may be variously challenged, but their power to control and transcend threats to their security is absolutely certain.

The calm optimism of these works also contrasts with the profound sense of crisis that, critical studies argue, afflicted the continental aristocracy and affected Old French literature of the twelfth century. Erich Köhler's work explores social and political conditions that produced unresolvable and keenly felt contradictions for the nobility in France between personal and social interests and between noble rights and royal programs. The later epics recognize these destructive contradictions; the *romans d'aventure* reintegrate the interests of hired knights with those of the higher nobility, attempting a unification of aristocratic purpose that was no longer possible in this divisive period.[67] Georges Duby suggests for much continental literature a similarly beleaguered audience, those men of noble birth who because of continental inheritance patterns were only irregularly able to wield the power of nobility.[68] In a more ex-

---

67. "Quelques observations," pp. 26–27; and *Ideal und Wirklichkeit*, pp. 66–128. Eugene Vance believes Chrétien's works were "ideologically in the service of the high aristocracy and opposed to the interests of the lower aristocracy" ("Signs of the City," p. 558).

68. "'Jeunes'"; in contrast, Painter, "Family," shows the smoother handling of inheritance in England.

tended study, R. Howard Bloch argues that continental literature confronts the aristocracy with its losses of power and acts to reconcile the aristocracy to those losses: "The 'performed text' is seen less as a mechanism by which aristocracy affirmed its own solidarity and resisted change than as a forum for adaptation to the political realities of the postfeudal world."[69]

England provided an aristocratic experience less contentious and bitter than that of France: a flexible class structure made the difference between noble birth and noble rights clearer than in France; the powerful English kingship and its highly developed court system early displaced most power struggles from the military to the judicial sphere; indeed, the barons' landed prosperity encouraged them to support the transition to a centralized national state. This more peaceful and cohesive society felt less conflict between past and present, between feudal and national systems, and between baronial ambitions and social realities. The barony's position did change from the twelfth to the fourteenth century, particularly around the time of Magna Carta when the "old-style struggle for baronial independence was virtually over; but a new kind of struggle to impose restraints upon monarchy was just beginning."[70] But England's barons were throughout the period less isolated in their struggle, less disaffected from the interests of the commons on the one hand and of royalty on the other, than was the continental aristocracy.

The romances of English heroes convey a less anguished image of society than the troubled and profoundly reflective continental works of the twelfth century. The insular works understand the interests of barony and commons to be mutual, and baronial rights to be largely compatible with royal centralization. Both the historical record and the disharmonies of *Athelston* and *Gamelyn* testify that the interests of commons, barons, and king did not really pivot around baronial aspirations. But until the later fourteenth century England's relative wealth and harmony could sustain the romances' vision that commitment to the noble hero's success amounted to commitment to the common good. As if in imitation of England's "unformed, almost liquid" class structure,[71] this literature proposes that life's struggles are joyously collective. And if our desires are

69. *Literature and Law*, p. 258; see also Borst, "Rittertum."
70. Warren, *Henry II*, p. 382.
71. Treharne, *Baronial Plan*, p. 272.

truly identical, then chaos endangers us all, and it is the hero's restoration of social order that will unite us in peace. Only when tradition, hierarchy, and feudal custom prevail everywhere will they prevail anywhere, because the interests of all are mutual and interdependent.

Chapter Three

Religion in Pious Romances

Religious and moral commitment is strong in England's medieval fictions. Constance Birt West noted that a "strain of deep piety" affects Anglo-Norman romances, and the perception has become a commonplace, echoed most recently in the preface to the Anglo-Norman *Alexander*: "There is to be found throughout . . . a strong moral tone of the type familiar to students of Anglo-Norman literature."[1] The continued presence of moral and homiletic approaches in Middle English romance provides one of the most direct connections between Anglo-Norman and Middle English literature. Studies of Middle English romance even propose, with increasing frequency and conviction, that some of the morally committed romances are so distinctive as to constitute a separate genre of "exemplary romance" or "secular hagiography."[2] On the continent, by contrast, romances rarely incorporate motifs or standards of value from saints' lives.[3]

England's pious romances interact extensively with hagiography and, through that literature, respond strongly to changes in the status of church and Christians. To many readers Guy of Warwick's conversion to God's service, Amis and Amiloun's perfect faith in

---

1. *Courtoisie*, p. 23; Thomas of Kent, *Alexander*, ed. Foster, II, 64. Parts of the following discussion appeared in [Crane] Dannenbaum, "Guy of Warwick."
2. See below, n. 34.
3. Of the few OF works that do have close hagiographic connections, *Guillaume d'Angleterre* may have been composed in England and *Robert le Diable* has an English version, *Sir Gowther*.

brotherhood, and Athelston's repentant submission to his archbishop exemplify a harmonious and mutually supportive union of religious and secular material. The absorption of Christian fervor in romance is, however, less complete than may at first appear. The tenets of the church are not fully compatible with the secular values that inform romances. Where these conceptions are at odds, the romances uphold secular values of self-determination, family strength, and worldly success. Piety enriches and broadens the importance of heroic action, but in so doing it becomes in some ways merely an attribute of secular heroism.

The issue is inextricably historical and generic. Hagiography, the immediate context for pious elements in romance, flourished when the church turned some of its resources from consolidating its institutional strength and appropriating state power, most spectacularly in the calls to Crusades, to undertaking pervasive reforms directed toward the laity. From the early thirteenth century into the fourteenth, these reforms stimulated an outpouring of texts designed to educate the clergy and sustain the spiritual health and development of lay Christians. Saints' legends are part of this powerful movement, and it is easy to imagine the pious romances swept up in it too, carried beyond their generic origins into full sympathy with reform doctrine. But the history of church reform itself resists this conclusion.

To be sure, thirteenth-century reforms profoundly altered the relationship between lay Christians and the church. They brought to the laity on the one hand improved and more regular pastoral care, but on the other hand increased supervision and restraints on behavior. Enforced confession, for example, allowed parish priests unprecedented control over the daily behavior of parishioners, while sermons and manuals of instruction similarly sought to regulate many features of traditional village and developing town life. William of Pagula instructs priests to admonish their parishioners not to use charms to treat illness or injury, never to turn the care of their children over to wet nurses, and to shun usury in all its forms.[4] The best-known example of medieval instruction for penitents, Chaucer's *Parson's Tale*, condemns those who take pleasure in property, dress, and social station; those who joke and gossip, even without malice; and those who willingly exercise perquisites

---

4. Pantin, *English Church*, pp. 189–219; Boyle, "Oculos Sacerdotis," p. 89; Godfrey, *English Parish*, pp. 79–81.

over their social inferiors.[5] Such strictures against established group behaviors, often behaviors important to economic or broader social advancement, produced daily conflicts for parishioners between the church's ideals of abnegation and secular ideals of prosperity and success.

These conflicts originate in differences that oppose even the romances called "exemplary" to the claims of sermons and saints' lives. As a group the insular romances that pay close attention to Christianity are not as politically informed as the romances of English heroes, which defend baronial and mercantile values in the face of royal power and class disharmony. Generally, the pious romances attend less to conflicting secular powers than to the broad differences between religious and profane conceptions of the world. These romances do accept and incorporate Christian impulses from hagiography, but they temper their acceptance with clearly defined resistance to those implications of religious teaching that are incompatible with pursuing earthly well-being. The church's condemnation of the exemplary romances along with the others indicates that contemporary observers recognized the subordination of religious to worldly impulses in romance.

Veyn Carpyng

"There was once a king named Arthur!" cries Abbot Gevard, arousing his sleepy congregation to alertness. Immediately he reproaches them:

'Videte, fratres, miseriam magnam. Quando locutus sum de Deo, dormitastis; mox ut verba levitatis inserui, evigilantes erectis auribus omnes auscultare coepistis.'

'You see, my brothers, to how sad a pass we have come; when I was speaking to you about God, you fell asleep; but as soon as I began a secular story, you all woke up and began to listen with eager ears.'[6]

Again and again religious writers complain that secular tales, although less true, valuable, and important than the stories of Christ and the saints, are nonetheless more appealing to lay audiences. What is to be done with the man who listens impassively to the

---

5. E.g., lines 412–63, 647–53, 748–76.
6. Caesarius of Heisterbach, *Dialogus Miraculorum*, ed. Strange, I, 205; trans. Scott and Bland, I, 233.

Gospel account of Christ's Passion but weeps when he hears a reading of *Guy of Warwick*?[7] Many insular religious writers reproach their audience for enjoying tales that are "bot fantum o þis warld."[8] Denis Piramus begins the *Vie Seint Edmund* by admitting that *Partenopeus* has a fine dreamlike quality, that Marie's *Lais* are admirable, and that many such "cuntes, chanceuns e fables" [stories, songs, and fables] relieve sorrow and care. But, he continues,

> Jeo vus dirrai par dreite fei
> Un deduit, qui mielz valt asez
> Ke ces autres ke tant amez,
> E plus delitable a oïr.
> Si purrez les almes garir
> E les cors garantir de hunte.
> Mult deit hom bien oïr tel cunte.
> Hom deit mult mielz a sen entendre
> Ke en folie le tens despendre.[9]

I will tell you truly a pleasant tale that is worth much more than those others you love so much and is more delightful to hear. And it can cure souls and protect bodies from shame. One should surely listen well to such a story. Better that one should pay attention to sense than waste time on folly.

William of Nassington condemns *Guy of Warwick* and *Sir Ysumbras*, often considered exemplary romances, together with the rest:

I warne ʒow ferst ate benyngnyng,	
Y wyl make ʒow no veyn carpyng	chattering
Of dethes of armes, ne of amours,	
As doth menstrales and jestoures,	
That maketh carpyng in many place	
Of Octovyane and Ysambrace,	
And of many other gestes,	hero stories
Namely when they cum to festes;	
Ne of the lyf of Bewys of Hamptone,	
That was a knyʒt of gret renone,	
Ne of syre Gy of Werewyke,	
Alle ʒif hit myʒte some men lyke.[10]	Although / it might please

---

7. Owst, *Literature and Pulpit*, p. 14n. 2, citing MS Harley 7332, fol. 49.
8. *Cursor Mundi*, ed. Morris, line 91 (and lines 1–26, 85–100); see also Frère Angier, *Gregory the Great*, ed. Cloran, fols. 9.c.21–36, 10.a.9–14 (pp. 12, 14); and Robert Gretham, quoted in Aitken, *Etude sur le Miroir*, Prologue, lines 1–78.
9. *Vie Seint Edmund*, ed. Kjellman, lines 51, 60–68.
10. MS Bodleian 48, fol. 47, quoted in *Thornton Romances*, ed. Halliwell, p. xx. Owst, *Literature and Pulpit*, p. 13, quotes the corresponding passage from MS Royal 17. C. viii.

In these as in all the ecclesiastical protests, romance and religion are at odds. The religious writers' attitude counters the modern contention that, in the more seriously moral romances at least, secular and Christian values are successfully integrated.

Readers who seek to defend the religious integrity of particular romances must discount or ignore the substance of ecclesiastical comment. For example, Laurel Braswell finds "an essential irony" in the condemnation of *Sir Ysumbras* by Nassington and by the author of the *Cursor Mundi*—an irony because, she argues, *Ysumbras* teaches about faith and God's providence more successfully than either the *Speculum Vitae* or the *Cursor Mundi*.[11] We are to dismiss the religious authors as blind to literary merit and perhaps jealous of others' success. Similarly, G. W. Owst deems "somewhat strange" the avoidance of romance material in sermon literature, since the stories of romance often teach lessons effectively. Owst and M. D. Legge believe that the ecclesiastical condemnations of romance arise from professional competition, a rivalry between authors of sacred and secular literature for the attention of the same audience.[12]

But whatever the immediate motive for the ecclesiastical condemnations of romance, they have substantive importance. These attacks are comparable to the passages in chronicles that inveigh against the unrealities of romance, or to those in romance that condemn ribald tales for their baseness. Such attacks reflect not merely professional rivalry, but salient generic differences that set romance at odds with history and fabliau at odds with romance. Likewise, ecclesiastical animosity for romances is neither ironic nor strange, but rather openly recognizes that romances and religious literature are animated by different values and ultimately endorse separate truths.[13]

11. "'Sir Isumbras,'" p. 151. Another proposal is that *Sir Ysumbras* has allegorical significance that Nassington did not see—but if both he and the *Cursor Mundi* poet missed it, the allegorical reading is hardly relevant to *Ysumbras*'s reception (Blaicher, "*Sir Ysumbras*").

12. Owst, *Literature and Pulpit*, pp. 10–16 (quote at p. 14); Legge, "Anglo-Norman Hagiography." Mehl (*Middle English Romances*, pp. 18–19) proposes that the versions of certain romances to which moralists objected differed from the extant, morally exemplary versions—a doubtful proposition that again deflects attention from the substance of ecclesiastical objection.

13. Religious writers often claim their works are "truer" than romance: e.g., Angier, *Gregory the Great*, fols. 9.c.22–28, 10.a.9–14 (pp. 12, 14); Piramus, *Vie Seint Edmund*, lines 69–78; Gretham, in Aitken, *Etude sur le Miroir*, Prologue, lines 13–40; Strohm, "Middle English *Romaunce*," p. 5 ("s'avés oï asez souvent / Les romans de diverse gent, / Et des mençongez de cest monde"). On the hagiographical conception of "truth" in contrast to romance, see also Dembowski, "Literary Problems," pp. 120, 130n.7.

Even the most pious insular romances bear out ecclesiastical suspicions by redirecting the religious impulses they absorb. As the romances of English heroes confront a centralized royal power that challenges baronial independence, the pious romances confront a centralized and increasingly powerful religious institution that opposes secular values. The former romances discover an ideal resolution in which the hero's freedom sustains good kings and commons alike; the latter present a devotion to God that is compatible with pursuing earthly and secular well-being. The admixture of opposition and accommodation to Christian principles in the exemplary romances is less overt than the blend of political hostility and accommodation in the romances of English heroes, but the process is present nonetheless.

This analogy between political and religious awareness in romance echoes a well-known historical analogy. From the twelfth to the fourteenth century, the institutions of the state and of the Christian church developed similarly. King and pope sought to extend and regularize their power through the development of the Curia Regis and the Roman Curia, which were to become in the thirteenth century "two great centralized bureaucracies face to face."[14] Church and state frequently collided; conversely, each drew for its own ends on the other's sources of power. At his crown wearings Henry II had his royal chaplains chant the litany *Christus vincit, Christus regnat, Christus imperat*; an observer at one of William the Conqueror's crown wearings was so impressed as to cry out "Behold, I see God!"[15] The sacerdotal quality of kingship that such ceremonies nourished was an essential means of legitimating royal control. The church in turn increasingly claimed temporal powers and rights, owned and rented properties, fielded troops, and developed in further respects a corporate structure that made it a social institution of great importance.

In the thirteenth century, as the power of royal governments increased sufficiently to resist papal commands, the church directed its attention to the laity in general, asserting new control over each Christian's conduct and spiritual life. The English church promoted reforms with particular zeal,[16] perhaps in reaction against the pe-

14. Pantin, *English Church*, p. 3, also pp. 9–102; Southern, *Western Society*; Lagarde, *Esprit laïque*, I, 166 et passim.
15. Warren, *Henry II*, pp. 241–42; Morris, *Discovery of the Individual*, p. 25.
16. Legge, *Anglo-Norman Literature*, p. 206; Arnould, "Manuel des péchés," p. 2. On conditions during the Interdict, see Painter, *Reign of King John*, pp. 151–202; Warren, *King John*, pp. 170–73.

riod of King John's disputes with Innocent III. From 1208 until 1213 in England all rites of the church except for baptism and confession of the dying were suspended, and even these minimal ceremonies could not be performed in church buildings. There is little evidence of the Interdict's effect on the faithful, but Guillaume le Clerc expresses a moral discomfort that may have been widespread:

> Ceste ovraigne fu fete noeve
> El tens que Phelipe tint France,
> El tens de la grant mesestance
> Qu'Engleterre fu entredite,
> Si qu'il n'i aveit messe dite
> Ne cors mis en terre sacree.
> De l'entredit ne lui agree,
> Que a ceste feiz plus en die,
> Por ceo que dreiture mendie
> E lealte est povre e basse.
> Tote ceste chose trespasse
> Guillaume qui forment s'en doelt,
> Que n'ose dire ceo qu'il voelt
> De la tricherie qui cort
> E en l'une e en l'altre cort.
> Mais a plus halt dire se prent.

This work was translated in the time when Philip held France, in the time of the great unhappiness when England was under interdict, so that no mass was said nor any body placed in consecrated ground. He [who writes this] does not wish to say more of the Interdict at this time, for right goes begging and loyalty is poor and lowly. Guillaume, who laments it deeply, passes over all this, for he dares not say what he wishes of the falsehood that runs through the one and the other court. But he takes up a higher discourse.

From the abased conditions of the Interdict Guillaume takes refuge in the "plus halt dire" of his bestiary. Although excommunication and interdiction were relatively common tools of controversy in the thirteenth century, the Interdict of 1208–1213 probably intensified the need and the impulse for religious reform in England.[17]

Like the centralization of political power, the church's centralizing reforms both protected and constrained its subjects. Before this period, the laity participated little in the activity of the English church.[18] The faithful were members of a community that expressed

---

17. *Le Bestiaire*, ed. Reinsch, lines 10–24. On interdict and reform, see Arnould, "Manuel des péchés," pp. 8–9; Lang, *Bishops and Reform*, pp. 94–95.

18. Oakley, *Western Church*, pp. 82–84; Barlow, *English Church*, pp. 268–69; Owst, *Literature and Pulpit*, pp. 43–47.

its devotion in ceremonies performed on their behalf by the clergy alone. Some twelfth-century innovations, such as kneeling for prayer and contemplating the Host, derived from a new understanding of the relationship between Christian and God as a close and personal one.[19] The reforms of the thirteenth century were designed to regulate and enhance that relationship. Decrees of the Fourth Lateran Council (1215) sought to improve pastoral care, and required of all Christians annual confession to their parish priest and communion at Easter. The Council of Oxford (1222) extended the Lateran decrees; of the other councils of the century, Lambeth (1281) was particularly important for standards of clerical education and performance.[20] A tremendous outpouring of penitentials, manuals of instruction, and books of sermon *themata* responded from early in the thirteenth century to the councils' demands.[21] Sermons probably became common, even weekly, in parish churches during the century.[22] These developments together with the laity's access to churchwardenships, vestry associations, and charitable groups made the following century "the age of the devout layman, when it was becoming possible, more easily than before, for serious-minded laymen to have a deeper and more intelligent participation in the life of the Church."[23] However, where church reforms claimed authority over the daily life of parishioners, the result was conflict and evasion as well as grateful obedience.

Again, the analogy with royal systematization is telling. In the Middle Ages each person (with few and formal exceptions, as for the Jews) was just as surely and necessarily a member of the church as a citizen of the state. In an examination of the church's structure as it affected the faithful, R. W. Southern concludes: "In a word, the church was a compulsory society in precisely the same way as the modern state is a compulsory society. . . . [In an] extensive sense

---

19. Morris, *Discovery of the Individual*, pp. 139–57; Marie Dominique Chenu, *Eveil de la conscience*.
20. Powicke, *Thirteenth Century*, pp. 449–54; Moorman, *Church Life*; Cheyney, *English Synodalia*.
21. Boyle, "Oculos Sacerdotis," pp. 81–110; Pantin, *English Church*, pp. 189–243; Godfrey, *English Parish*, pp. 77–81; Arnould, "Manuel des péchés," pp. 1–59; Legge, *Anglo-Norman Literature*, pp. 206–42.
22. Moorman (*Church Life*) and Lang (*Bishops and Reform*) indicate a low frequency of preaching, but higher estimates are defended by Godfrey, *English Parish*, pp. 78–81; Boyle, "Oculos Sacerdotis," pp. 81–82, 90–91, 102; and Robertson, "Frequency of Preaching."
23. Pantin, *English Church*, p. 1. See also Mason, "English Parishioner," and Pantin, "Instructions."

the medieval church was a state."[24] The church was, in its statelike capacity, intrusive and coercive in handling its subjects' behavior. For example, the expansion of religious instruction was in part designed to combat heresy. The Lateran decree of 1215 requiring secular authorities to pursue and punish heretics complements the call to fuller religious instruction of the laity, for both decrees imply a stringent spirit of correct versus incorrect belief. That spirit soon led to the formal establishment of the Inquisition (1231) and the sanction of torture for extracting confessions from suspects (1252).[25] Although the church had long opposed heretical beliefs, the establishment of the Inquisition gave to the cause of orthodoxy institutional sanction, new importance and visibility, and great coercive force.

Similarly, the Lateran decree requiring annual confession to parish priests modified the church's earlier stand that contrition and faith were sufficient to win pardon and that a sinner should confess (to religious or even to lay persons) only if moved to do so. Enforced confession, in this context, was an extraordinary change—in E. J. Arnould's opinion "une innovation disciplinaire dont il serait difficile d'exagérer les conséquences"; in H. C. Lea's assessment, a reform that empowered "every parish priest to mould not only the internal but the external life of each member of his flock," assigning to the church "a spiritual domination without example in the history of mankind."[26] Manuals of instruction for priests and penitents further illustrate how extensive and concrete were the church's strictures on socializing, family relations, and economic transactions.[27]

The insistent pressure of these controls on daily conduct aroused considerable lay opposition to the institutional church. The Lateran decree requiring confession was evaded for some time.[28] Georges de Lagarde attributes the development of a "secular spirit" in the thirteenth century to conflicting secular and ecclesiastical interests

---

24. *Western Society*, pp. 17–18.
25. Lang, *Bishops and Reform*, pp. 96–98; Lagarde, *Esprit laïque*, I, 183–88.
26. Arnould, "*Manuel des péchés*," p. 42; Lea, *Auricular Confession*, I, 211–28 (quote at p. 228).
27. The church's institutional power and complexity reached their height in a climate of growing social diversity, secular identity, and individual self-awareness that could not fail to conflict in some ways with the authority claimed by the church. See Ullmann, *Medieval Foundations*, esp. pp. 53–88; Morris, *Discovery of the Individual*, pp. 47–48, 81, 121–22; Lagarde, *Esprit laïque*, I, 161.
28. Lea, *Auricular Confession*, pp. 233–36.

in the economic and judicial spheres. Disputes over clerical immunity, town liberties, and merchant practices are all facets of this secular spirit, "l'expression passionnée de l'effort tenté par les laïques pour reprendre un domaine que l'Eglise leur conteste."[29] The sharp decline of the church's authority in the later fourteenth and fifteenth centuries cannot be attributed to corruption or inadequate education among the clergy, since these problems also existed at the height of the church's power in the thirteenth century. Rather, Gordon Leff argues that the church's "corporate aspect," its hierarchical structure and statelike systems, of itself generated a revulsion in the laity of all classes, and in some ecclesiastical circles as well. This reaction encouraged people to seek spiritual fulfillment in extrainstitutional, often heretical movements stressing the imitation of Christ and the direct experience of God.[30]

The insular romances called "exemplary" align themselves not with the church's new supervision of secular life, but with lay resistance to the constraints that supervision imposed. In the broadest terms, the church's antipathy toward romance arises from the conceptual distinction between eternal and temporal on which the practical division between church and state was based. This distinction also informs the opposed conceptions of life's meaning that divide hagiography from romance.[31] It is not that romances speak for the state. Rather, they are concerned with the relations between personal autonomy and social engagement. Insular romances assess the uses and the limitations of a baronial ideology valuing control over heritable land along with actions which explain and extend that control. The exemplary romances provide a poetic ground on which this ideology can interact with religious claims, and they develop imaginative versions of the resulting conflict in which faith sustains baronial desires. These romances speak neither for the emerging state nor for the institutional church, but rather for the validity of private achievement within such structures. The saints of hagiography may seem also to exemplify a kind

29. Lagarde, *Esprit laïque*, I, 158 (see I, 157–88 et passim).
30. Leff, "Heresy," p. 47; Lagarde, *Esprit laïque*, I, 182–83; Southern, *Western Society*, pp. 45–48.
31. Commenting on Peter of Blois's comparison of true tears of repentance with the tears shed over stories of Tristan and Arthur, Erich Auerbach notes that Christianity "has concentrated all tragedy in the cardinal point of history, the divine sacrifice of Christ. This event has absorbed all the grief of the world; worldly grief has lost its independent value and has no further claim to tragedy in its own right" (*Literary Language*, p. 305).

of private achievement, but, as we shall see, their surrender of identity and of will to God as well as their transcendent goals divide them from heroes of romance.

The differences between hagiography and romance are the more intriguing for the extensive interaction between the two literatures. Many insular saints' lives of the later Middle Ages adopt the verse forms and the dramatic, event-centered narrative presentation of romance. Echoes of the sensibilities of *fine amor* animate Clemence of Barking's *Life of St. Catherine*: the heroine abandons her marriage to seek the superior love of God, while her desolate husband laments, "'Coment viveras tu sanz mei, / Et ge coment viverai sanz tei?'" ["How will you live without me, and I, how will I live without you?"].[32] In the *Anglo-Norman Voyage of St. Brendan* familiar structural elements of romance, the quest and cyclical design, are infused with religious purpose. Religious writers probably developed from a popular tale the legend of St. Eustace, which resembles the story of Bevis's second exile from England. And Derek Pearsall argues that John Capgrave's *Life of St. Katherine* is heavily influenced by Capgrave's familiarity with *Havelok the Dane*.[33] These brief examples indicate that although the authors of religious works condemned romance, they were sensitive to its sources of appeal. Hagiography and romance may hold conflicting ideal visions of what constitutes human achievement, but both genres seek to attract their audiences to their respective world views. Thus hagiography freely appropriates fabulous, affective, and dramatic elements from romance when they can make images of the holy life more compelling. While tacitly adopting these elements, religious literature overtly condemns the romances themselves.

Romances follow the inverse of this pattern. Openly and joyfully they adopt from religious writing the doctrine, the models of conduct, and the narrative patterns that can deepen their ultimately secular endeavor; tacitly they resist or subvert the full implications of the same religious material. This dual process is superficial and clearly discernible in many works, but in a few insular romances it

---

32. Ed. MacBain, lines 2175–76; similar echoes occur at lines 1633–60, 2165–214, 2281–96. Bloomfield points out that hagiography's adoption of some procedures typical of romance (marvels, motiveless episodes) predates the rise of romance and draws directly on folk tradition ("Episodic Motivation and Marvels in Epic and Romance," in *Essays and Explorations*, pp. 118–21).

33. Jones, "Precocity"; Heffernan, "Legend of St. Eustace"; Pearsall, "*Life of St. Katherine*." See also Strohm, "*Passioun*."

is not so facile or so easily explained—namely, in works that pay particular attention to moral conduct and Christian principle, the "exemplary romances" or "secular hagiography."

Ojars Kratins originated the concept of a work lying midway between hagiography and romance in his study of *Amis and Amiloun*. Several studies have since argued that the didactic and homiletic romances should be considered a separate genre. Although the boundaries of the genre are variously defined, proponents agree that the essential feature of the group is the subordination of all other concerns to moral ones, whether Christian or broadly ethical. Other more specific characteristics, such as the direct intervention of God in the course of events, a hero whose moral character develops or who undergoes trials patiently, and connections between the story material and saints' legends, also help to define the group.[34]

But can the exemplary romances really be distinguished from other romances in generic terms? Considerable disagreement over the canon of romances that should be counted as exemplary indicates the elusiveness of the proposed genre. Hanspeter Schelp and D. N. Klausner include *Guy of Warwick* while D. T. Childress excludes it; *Amis and Amiloun* fits the pattern for Kratins and Childress but not for Dieter Mehl or for Schelp; Childress and Mehl agree on *Athelston*'s exemplary status but Schelp excludes the work. As these differences of opinion indicate, the proposed genre shares so many characteristics with romance that in a given work, the degree—rather than the mere presence—of exemplarity, hagiographic connections, and divine intervention becomes decisive in different ways for different readers. Untidy as that "commodious bottom drawer" labeled romance may be,[35] to sort out the exemplary romances from the others is to misapprehend their deep allegiance to romance's generic norms and secular ideals. In generic terms, even highly moral and pious insular romances sustain the movements toward social integration and earthly apotheosis that are typical of romance and anathema to hagiography. In doctrinal

---

34. Kratins, "*Amis and Amiloun.*" Braswell writes of "that ambiguous genre between hagiography and romance," "'Sir Isumbras,'" p. 144; the proposed genre is directly defended and discussed by Schelp, *Exemplarische Romanzen*; Mehl, *Middle English Romances*, pp. 120–22; Klausner, "Didacticism," p. 117; and Childress, "Between Romance and Legend." Jones uses the designation "hagiographic romance" ("Precocity," p. 157).

35. Kratins, "*Amis and Amiloun*," p. 347.

terms, if these works did subordinate all to a Christian or moral purpose they would indeed differ from other romances, but instead they reconcile moral commitment to secular models of success and happiness.

This chapter concentrates on the pious romances that exist in both Anglo-Norman and Middle English versions: *Gui de Warewic* and *Guy of Warwick; Amis e Amilun* and *Amis and Amiloun*. These works offer contrasting images of heroic life. The story of Guy develops an ideal of knightly piety in which the hero actively seeks adventure; the story of Amis and Amiloun presents suffering heroes who must patiently accept sacrifices for each other. Both stories illustrate how insular poets adapt models of saintly life to new purposes.

Þe Kniȝt of Cristene Lawe

Several insular romances anticipate Guy's Christian knighthood in some respects. Well before the thirteenth- and fourteenth-century pious romances, religious devotion was a significant feature of heroic perfection. The most common gesture of knightly faith, in epic as in romance, was to oppose paganism. Most of Horn's military triumphs, while they serve his personal plan of vengeance and self-advancement, are also victories over pagan aggression. Heroes who are carried off to pagan lands oppose the religion they find there: Fulk Fitz Warin agrees to undertake the defense of Tunis only if its king and his followers will convert to Christianity; Bevis of Hampton, brought up in a pagan kingdom, refuses to convert from Christianity and frequently defeats pagan forces in his capacity as "cristene kniȝt."[36] Yet in all these cases, religious faith enhances a fundamentally political and military heroism, rather than subsuming knighthood within a Christian system of life.

The story of Bevis provides the fullest illustration of this kind of Christian heroism. The cause of religion is frequently invoked to justify Bevis's actions, but it provides only ancillary support for motivations that are centrally personal and political. Indeed, in his youth Bevis fights for pagans as often as against them. His imprisonment in Damascus, reminiscent of St. George's legend and

---

36. *Fouke le Fitz Waryn*, ed. Hathaway, 54.33–56.3; and *Beues of Hamtoun*, ed. Kölbing, quotation at line 1011; see also 555–76 and *Boeve de Haumtone*, ed. Stimming, lines 380–410.

sprinkled with references to God,[37] is actually brought about not by the hero's attack on a pagan idol but by the false accusation of sexual intimacy with Josian; the imprisonment is passed in planning vengeance as well as in prayer and is ended less by prayer than by clever ruses, single combats, and the wonderful strength of Bevis's horse.[38]

Sir Beues of Hamtoun expands from Anglo-Norman the number and importance of Christian elements in Bevis's adventures.[39] Almost as often as in *Boeve* Christianity is only a secondary justification for Bevis's adventures, but the hero himself gains the Christian awareness and solemnity of an ideal Crusader knight, "Þe kniȝt of cristene lawe" (A 4204). This sharply distinguishes him from the virtually uncharacterized man of adventures in *Boeve de Haumtone*. Bevis is naturally "hardi & of gode hert," but he is capable of fear and knows that he succeeds "'Þourȝ godes grace & min engyn [ingenuity]'" rather than by force alone.[40] But although religious faith deepens Bevis's character and increasingly colors his actions, no reader would be tempted to call *Sir Beues of Hamtoun* an exemplary romance. In both Anglo-Norman and Middle English, the story's affiliations to the legends of St. George and St. Eustace are marginal,[41] and Christian faith remains a subsidiary aspect of a knighthood whose goals are aggressively secular and political.

This model of knighthood resonates tellingly with the history of the church's efforts to incorporate knights into its service. Through its growing influence over the wording and trappings of investiture ceremonies and vows of knighthood, the church in the later Middle Ages won partial control of this military institution. However, the church's version of ideal knighthood "had to find its expression within the framework of a secular ideology that was founded on a Christianised version of heroic traditions, and that sacerdotal teaching and sacerdotal priorities could only modify, not transform." In promulgating an ideal standard for knighthood, the

---

37. Matzke, "Legend of Saint George," pp. 454–55.

38. *Boeve* 880–915, 954–65, 1035–1263; *Beues* A 1349–1410, 1603–14, 1655–1816. In the latter version a prayer breaks the hero's bonds (1645–49).

39. Bevis's first combat, which he undertakes on Christmas day, is inspired by his discovery of the festival's meaning (A 585–738); later he fights a dragon with divine aid, augmenting the correspondences to the legend of St. George (A 2597–910).

40. *Beues* A 2801, 2003; cf. "'Þourȝ godes help we scholle him slo'" (2724). References to God's help and prayers, absent in *Boeve*, are added to each of Bevis's battles.

41. On these relations see Matzke, "Contributions"; and Gerould, "Eustace Legend," pp. 444–45.

church had to sanction an institution whose violence and worldly designs it had previously condemned.⁴² Christian ideals came to embellish and justify secular motives, but rarely was secular gain truly subordinated to Christian principle. The romances of Bevis recognize this historical development: Bevis's career presents an ideal knighthood that is inspired by faith but that acts, in the final analysis, less for the advancement of faith than for political stasis and power.

The idea that knighthood should be transformed by faith fares even worse in *Richard Coer de Lyon*. This work survives only in a Middle English version that probably expands considerably the lost thirteenth-century Anglo-Norman source.⁴³ The English poem traces the whole course of Richard's life (with many historical inaccuracies), but the action concentrates on his captivity in Germany and on the Third Crusade. Richard's crusade and his own nature are far from exemplary in Christian terms. Rivalry between the French and English forces, especially between Richard and Philip Augustus, becomes as important to the exercise of Richard's greatness as the campaign against the Saracens. The English can find no courage in the French; the French insult the English in turn with the old fable that Englishmen have tails. When the Crusaders' rivalries erupt in armed conflict, Richard urges his men,

> 'Slee downe righte the Frensshe cowarde,
> And ken them in batayl   teach
> That ye haue no tayl.'
>
> (1958–60)

This current of vengeful prejudice sorely blurs the Christian-pagan dichotomy and contaminates the Crusade's ideal of Christian unity and superiority. Slurs on French and Saracens even lie side by side:

Ffrenssche men arn arwe and ffeynte,	cowardly / deceitful
And Sarezynys be war, and queynte,	sly / cunning
And off here dedes engynous;	of their / tricky
Þe Ffrenssche men be couaytous.⁴⁴	covetous

Further vitiating the moral justification for crusade is Richard's own thunderous violence. Viewed most favorably, he is a winner,

---

42. Keen, *Chivalry*, pp. 44–82 (quote at p. 81); M. Bloch, *Feudal Society* (trans. Manyon), II, 314–19.
43. *Richard Löwenherz*, ed. Brunner; Paris, "Roman de Richard Coeur de Lion."
44. *Richard* 3849–52; criticism of and rivalry with the French runs throughout the work, e.g., 1677–1748, 1769–2032, 3275–96, 3772–3865, 4633–4808, 5423–80, 5667–72, 5896–930.

"in dede lion, in thought lybarde [leopard]" (2194), always in control and always resourceful. But he is also a ferocious prodigy, child of a demon mother, who relishes a dish of roast Saracen and serves the Sultan's emissaries the boiled heads of the hostages whose release they have come to negotiate.[45] Scorning Philip's mercy on captured townspeople—"'To sloo men was me neuere leeff [never pleased me]'" (4687), explains the French king—Richard embraces any conduct that will advance the Christian forces.

In this frenzied world the occasional interventions of God and St. George on Richard's behalf do not raise the tone of Richard's exploits so much as they implicate divinity itself in the abasement of crusading ideals to human prejudice and bloodthirstiness.[46] The process is perfectly coherent in generic and thematic terms. The patterns of action and achievement typical of romance encourage knighthood's temporal significance at the expense of Christian ideals of transcendence. The design of St. George's legend, in which martyrdom demonstrates the futility of earthly power, is exchanged in these romances for Richard's bloody victories and Bevis's acquisition of crowns and queens for himself and his sons. The exchange negates the church's attempted appropriation of ideal knighthood and even recruits crusading zeal to the service of private success.

The pre-Christian Alexander cuts a somewhat better figure than Bevis or Richard. The Anglo-Norman *Alexander* and its Middle English descendant *Kyng Alisaunder*,[47] like other works on Alexander, have considerable moral appeal. Schelp classes some Alexander works with exemplary romances, and M. D. Legge characterizes the Anglo-Norman *Alexander* as an *"exemplum"* governed by a "moral purpose."[48] The maxim which begins the Middle English version, that "Oþere mannes lijf is oure shewer [teacher]" (18), directs the presentation of Alexander; as in the Anglo-Norman he is a bold strategist, generous and concerned for his men. Juxtaposed episodes develop his character: in Anglo-Norman he rejects a drink of water in the desert when his armies would go thirsty (4772–92), but later he insists on being the first to taste a potentially dangerous

---

45. *Richard* 197–234, 3077–226, 3363–669.
46. *Richard* 3061–68, 3749–50, 4883–900, 5530–77, 6961–80.
47. Thomas of Kent, *Alexander*, ed. Foster; *Alisaunder*, ed. Smithers. ME quotations are from MS Laud Misc. 622. The relation of AN and ME versions is surveyed by Smithers, edition, II, 15–28.
48. Schelp, *Exemplarische Romanzen*, pp. 31–53, 149–71; Legge, *Anglo-Norman Literature*, p. 105.

water supply (4823–36); he pardons an enemy soldier who attempted to assassinate him (AN 3166–296, ME 3886–4055), but he hunts down and executes the treacherous murderers of Darius, his enemy (AN 3658–769, ME 4547–718). Alexander's model leadership develops through such actions and through commentary on the moral issues raised by his deeds, issues such as human acquisitiveness, the transitoriness of earthly life, and God's power to chastise.[49]

This moral treatment also colors scientific (or pseudoscientific) information in the Anglo-Norman *Alexander* and *Kyng Alisaunder*, most fully illustrated in the campaign against Gog and Magog (AN 5951–6581, ME 5938–6287). The romances' quasi-anthropological perspective tolerates many cultures but establishes that the practices of Gog and Magog are "vers humeine nature" [against human nature] (5964). Alexander declares their people to be "'vile folk . . . / Þat ben of þe kynde [breed] of helle'" (5988–89) for their cannibalism, incestuousness, and consumption of raw meat and vermin. The campaign then gains an eschatological framework, in which "iceaux escomengez" [those excommunicated ones] (6335) are to be shut up "in-tyl domesday" (6235), when Antichrist will lead them out to harry the peoples of earth. The episode thus fuses moral commitment with learned curiosity about cultural differences.[50] Alexander judges that "dame nature" (AN 6352) is on his side in attacking the people of Gog and Magog, but he also prays for divine guidance. In response God reveals that the evil peoples may be enclosed by a dike of bitumen, a substance Alexander has learned about on his travels. Thus natural science and faith together overcome these people who are culturally marginal and morally "La racine de mal e tote trecherie" [the root of evil and all deception] (6115).

But Alexander's virtue is circumscribed by his drive to conquer: he risks lives needlessly (AN 4454–63, 4539–41), tricks adversaries into battle (AN 5237–310, ME 5457–538), and generally lives for victories and domination. Theologians and moralists of the period interpret Alexander negatively, as an example of pride, mad ambition, envy, dissolution, and even as a figure for the devil torment-

49. Examples of moral commentary are AN 1215–24, 2839–45, 3134–40, 5846–54; ME 235–41, 2889–96, 3880–85, 4717–24, 7820–32.
50. Examples of cultural diversity accepted in the Alexander works are the messenger, a hairy one-eyed monopod, who persuades Alexander to campaign against Gog and Magog; and the support of the Amazons, among other armies, in the campaign. See also Friedman, *Monstrous Races*; Anderson, *Alexander's Gate*.

ing the world before the advent of Christ.[51] Alexander is exemplary in the secular strengths of leadership and aggression rather than in Christian virtues; in this he resembles the conquering Bevis and Richard of other insular romances.

A subtler relationship between knighthood and morality develops when a hero not only undertakes military causes in God's name but also follows a course of action that closely recalls the legends of saints. Guy of Warwick's life after his marriage, in his rejection of social honors and family ties, his service to God, and particularly his anonymous and devout retirement just before death, parallels the legend of St. Alexis. West senses a "hagiographical spirit" in these episodes, and Mehl sees the spirit fully embodied as the "poem turns into a legend toward the end." Childress virtually concurs: "What began as a romance ends as a secular legend."[52] But the romances of Guy finally raise the expectations of hagiography only to frustrate their fulfillment. Guy's imitation of Alexis constitutes both a homage to saintly life and a secular corrective of its fundamental tenets.

In Alexis's legend the young Roman leaves home on his wedding night in order to avoid earthly ties.[53] He resigns his life to God, becoming for many years a poor anonymous beggar at the shrine of a sacred image. When the image miraculously reveals his holiness, he escapes again to anonymity. God directs his journey back to Rome, where he begs his own father for shelter, asking pity in the name of the lost son Alexis. He lives as a beggar for years in his father's household, mocked and insulted by the servants. Just before his death, he records his life story in writing; then a voice from heaven announces his presence in Rome and guides the Christian congregation to his obscure corpse. His amazed parents and wife lament his deliberate anonymity, while miracles demonstrate his saintliness.

---

51. Cary, *Medieval Alexander*, pp. 80–142: writers in England who give negative interpretations of Alexander include Giraldus Cambrensis, John of Salisbury, Ranulph Higden, Alexander Neckham, and Walter Burley.
52. West, *Courtoisie*, p. 61; Mehl, *Middle English Romances*, p. 224; Childress, "Between Romance and Legend," p. 317.
53. This summary and the following discussion reflect the most widely shared features of the main Latin, French, and English versions of the legend of Alexis. Quotations are from the ME version in Laud Misc. 622, ed. Horstmann, "Alexiuslieder," unless otherwise noted. Smithers describes Laud 622 in detail in his edition of *Alisaunder*, II, 1–3. Klausner, "Didacticism," discusses many relationships between the legend of St. Alexis and the romances of Guy of Warwick.

Similarly, Guy leaves Felice soon after their marriage (but not before conceiving a son), in order to expiate the wrongs of his youthful chivalry. Guy exercises his devotion in combat rather than in begging, but like Alexis his experiences deepen his spirituality. The people Guy saves feel his closeness to God, give thanks for his arrival, pray for him in battle, and celebrate his victories with religious processions.[54] Guy himself acquires an ability to make moral pronouncements about the situation he faces.[55] Like the Anglo-Norman *Horn*, Guy never accepts land or gifts from grateful lords; in his service of God he rejects in addition the comforts of baths, fine clothes, and traveling companions. His asceticism, his spirituality, and his avoidance of honors associate him with St. Alexis. At the same time, several features distinguish the lives of the two heroes. Centrally, whereas Alexis has no concern other than to serve God, Guy wishes as well to aid or avenge his friends, to defend baronial principles, and to protect England.[56] That Guy's inspirations to battle are both religious and secular is in accord with a wider difference between Guy's and Alexis's lives: Guy does not suffer the marginal social role of the beggar Alexis.

Alexis's voluntary isolation from the fine life that his parents envisioned for him demonstrates, like the martyrs' deaths, the essential incompatibility of secular and sacred goals. This incompatibility underlies the saints' claim to have discovered a life superior to ordinary secular life, and it calls worldly values into question. Martyrs, in accepting death gladly and at the same time foiling all attempts to execute them until God wills their deaths, demonstrate the inferiority of earthly life and temporal power in the face of God's power. Alexis recognizes the dichotomy of secular and sacred when he rejects family ties, marriage, and social standing as interferences with his devotion to God. Hagiography divides existence into opposing camps: spirituality versus secularity, service to God

---

54. *Gui de Warewic*, ed. Ewert, e.g., lines 9992–93, 10101–6, 10783–96, 11281–86, 11347; and *Guy of Warwick: The First or 14th-century Version*, ed. Zupitza, lines C 9579–81 and A 188.3–12, 209.11–12, 233.7–234.9, 270.1–9. King Athelstan is directed to Guy by an angel (AN 10931–45, ME A 242.4–243.12).

55. E.g., *Gui* 8217–26, 9717–24, 10743–56; *Guy* A 74.1–3, 160.1–9, 230.4–12.

56. A motive for Guy's second mature combat is "'Pur venger mun cher compaignun'" (9716) ["'To wreke Tirri, mi fere'" (A 159.12)], and one purpose of the third combat is to defend "Le dreit sun seignur" (11018) ["'for to make Inglond fre'" (A 248.5)]. In view of these explicitly secular motives, Klausner's assertion that Guy's mature adventures "are undertaken for God alone" ("Didacticism," p. 106) oversimplifies the situation.

versus service to Mammon. The saints of legend must reject the one camp for the other and must be prepared to defend their choice with their lives.

In contrast, *Gui de Warewic* and *Guy of Warwick* are typical of romance in attempting to integrate diverse interests through the hero's character and actions. What seems in tension comes to be resolved in harmony. This model of human possibility shapes Guy's mature life. His role as defender of secular justice, the public recognition he wins in that role, and the honors offered to him argue that spirituality is compatible with a variety of worldly interests. Although Guy chooses to evade honors and adulation, both his causes and the mass gratitude they attract unite hero and world in a way that, for Alexis, is out of the question.

The contrast between Guy's social integration and Alexis's abnegation extends to the way in which each hero claims anonymity. Both leave their high stations for humbler ways of life, and both hide their identities in the process. But Alexis, unlike Guy, sets about to destroy his old identity completely. Desiring to follow God rather than his earthly father, Alexis gives away all his goods, rejoices when his father's messengers do not recognize him begging at the shrine of the holy image, and speaks of himself as another person when asking his father for shelter: "'And of Alexius, þi son so fre, / Afterward I shal telle þee'" (664–65). He conquers his old identity through seventeen years of silence, seeing his family's sorrow but continuing to serve God rather than earthly forms:

. . . non hym knew,	no one recognized him
Noiþer by hide ne by hew:	(in any way)
Al chaunged was his lijf.	
His fader he seiȝ often grete,	saw / weep
And his moder teres lete. . . .	let fall
And he wolde hem nouȝth yknowe,	acknowledge
Bot bare hym boþe symple & lowe	
Þat had ben man of meyne.[57]	power

The radical rejection of an earthly for a heavenly father or spouse figures in the legends of other saints, such as Francis and Catherine, as well. A Christian maiden calls Queen Catherine to the faith with the instruction

---

57. Laud Misc. 622, lines 712–16, 802–4; cf. the similar reaction to the family's sorrow in *Alexis*, ed. Storey: "Alexis le met el consirrer; / Ne l'en est rien, si 'st a Deu aturnét" [Alexis puts it out of his thoughts; it means nothing to him, he is so turned toward God] (244–45).

'. . . bele amie,
Mun Deu a ses noces t'envie. . . .
Ne dutez cest mortel mari.
Sa poissance ne deis duter,
Ne s'amur guaires desirer.'⁵⁸

'Dear friend, my Lord invites you to his wedding. . . . Do not fear this mortal husband. You must not fear his power nor in any way desire his love.'

Often the families in saints' lives are left confused and sorrowful, unable to comprehend the superior life for which they have been deserted. When Alexis's name is revealed after his death, his grief-stricken family question his obduracy and his motives, blind to the incompatibility of Alexis's spiritual life and their family life (1009–92). It is illuminating that the posthumous discovery of Alexis's autobiography does not bring about the fusion of his identities as saint and as son. What is published at Alexis's deathbed is a record of the irreparable break in his identity. His family's inability to accept the break emphasizes in a new way the disjunction between saintly and secular life.

Guy's life as an anonymous pilgrim recalls Alexis's anonymity but does not entail a surrender of his previous identity. In the first place, Guy reveals his name to his closest friends after each of his combats. These scenes sustain a connection between the hero's identity as repentant pilgrim and his identity as earl of Warwick. Guy's old friend Tirri even reproaches himself for not having made the connection:

'Ben me deveie aparceveir
Par tes granz fez, par tun poeir,
Que eriez Gui le vaillant,
Le preuz, le hardi, le combatant.'
(10681–84)

'Well my3t I know a-ryght
That yt was Gye, the noble kny3te,
By the strength, and by the my3te,
And by the strokis so bold in fy3te.'⁵⁹
(C 10202–5)

---

58. Clemence of Barking, *St. Catherine* 1633–34, 1654–56. Alexis's two antithetical lives are discussed at length by Hatcher, "St. Alexis."

59. Guy's revelation of identity to Athelstan has a similarly integrating effect: "'A! sire *pelerin*, pur Deu, merci! / Estes vus dunc iço *Gui*?'" (11341–42) ["'*Pylgrym*,' seyd the kyng, 'mercy! / Art thow the noble kny3t sir *Gye*?'" (C 10834–35)]. (Italics mine.)

Rather than isolating him from society, Guy's pilgrim identity replenishes his knightly identity, replacing his youthful vainglory with sober dedication to Christianity but not at all shifting the theater of his involvement from earthly engagements. Guy seeks to amend his chivalric pursuit of renown, not to reject human society.

Nor does Guy ultimately deny his identity within his family or abandon its interests for the interests of God. Guy sends for Felice when death is near, although their reunion at his deathbed is only long enough for a glance, a kiss, or a gesture begging her pardon.[60] Still, the meeting reaffirms their union, and Felice's acceptance and understanding of Guy at his death contrasts with the prolonged complaints of Alexis's family. Guy's reconciliation to his family is more broadly illustrated when he reveals his identity to King Athelstan after defending England from Danish servitude in his last combat. Rejecting the honors proffered by the king, Guy asks instead that Athelstan's gratitude be commuted to the benefit of Reinbrun and his guardian Heralt:

>'Sire,' fait Gui, 'nel puis faire,
>Quite vus claim tote la tere.
>Mais si Deu doinst Heralt repairer
>E il puisse mun fiz ramener,
>Cels vus requer, sire, honorer;
>En els vus purrez ben afier.'
>(11353–58)

>'Sir king,' sayd Gij, 'y nil nouȝt so.
>Haue þou þi lond for euer-mo,
>   & god y þe bi-teche.   commend you to
>Ac, ȝif Herhaud to þis lond com,   But
>& bring wiþ him Reynbroun, mi sone,
>   Help him, y þe biseche;
>For þai er boþe hende & fre.'   skilled / noble
>(A 276.1–7)

The emotional and material well-being of his family are legitimate concerns for Guy,[61] so that Reinbrun's return and accession to his father's title make a fitting conclusion to the trials Guy endures.

Finally, whereas Alexis surrenders his freedom of action when

---

60. *Gui* 11559–63; *Guy* A 293.3–8, C 10937–42 (the latter includes a kiss); *Guy of Warwick: The Second or 15th-century Version*, ed. Zupitza, lines 10659–68 (includes a kiss, embrace, and gesture of pardon "hur mercy for to crye / Of þe sorowe, sche dud for him drye" [10663–64]).

61. Earlier, Guy also asks Tirri to help Reinbrun if he can: *Gui* 10713–16, *Guy* A 228.4–12.

he turns to God, Guy's will to act and determine events remains as strong as in his youth. The few choices Alexis makes are self-abnegating gestures that rid him of identity and free his will for God: leaving home, giving away goods, fleeing fame when the holy image speaks of him, and so on. Alexis is quintessentially "goddes kni3th" (745) in passivity, led to ship by the Holy Ghost (246), pointed out by the sacred image (445–68), brought back to Rome by Jesus (557–58), and finally revealed by a voice from heaven (817–73). God determines the course of events; Alexis frees himself to accept God's determination. In contrast, Guy maintains his autonomy. He chooses his route, his combats, when to obscure his identity and when to reveal it. He never suffers ostracism; he rejects honors by choice, while Alexis passively accepts insults and blows. At the end of his life, Guy determines for himself to return to Warwick, and he maintains a servant in his retirement through whom he announces his impending death to Felice and gives instructions for his burial.[62] So great is Guy's seignorial authority that he can even warn Felice that she will not live long after him; fittingly, she lives in prayer "Pur sun seignur qui tant ama" (11616) ["For Gye, her lord, that was so dere" (C 11047)] for just as many days after his death as he had lived in marriage with her.[63]

This contrast between Guy's heroic independence and Alexis's submissive dependence on God maintains Guy's status as temporal lord, master of his destiny, even during the time of his penance. Alexis's sharply reduced autonomy makes room for the powerful presence of God's will in the text. According to E. B. Vitz, God's role as an actively desiring presence (Subject) is an essential feature of hagiography:

> We need these two Subjects to understand the concept of a saint and the narrative structure of the hagiographical text. Without Alexis, without his will, his love for God, we would simply have a theophany, a manifestation of God's power. . . . And without God as Subject—with Alexis alone as Subject—we might have a hero, we can certainly have a glutton for punishment, but we cannot have a saint.[64]

---

62. *Gui* 11375–504; *Guy* A st. 278–88.
63. *Gui* 11505–6, 11543–44, and *Guy* A 288.10–11 (Felice warned of her own death); *Gui* 7557, 11626 (marriage and Felice's survival are fifty days each); *Guy* A 19.5–6, 297.8–9 (marriage and Felice's survival are fifteen days each). The addition in the Caius text of a funeral oration by King Athelstan emphasizes Guy's temporal nobility (10974–11022).
64. "*Vie de Saint Alexis,*" p. 400.

In the romances of Guy divine messages of warning or revelation are delivered, but the deity does not attain the status of a desiring presence who rivals the hero for control over events. Divine intervention is far outweighed by Guy's own power to determine events. The resultant narrative effect is double and even paradoxical: God's intervention brings to the text the high solemnity of a saint's legend, but the dominance of the hero as Subject places divine will in the service of a human agent.

In summary, the romances of Guy call on the legend of Alexis but deny its basic propositions. Hagiography models religious life on the rejection of worldly identity and family ties, and the surrender of personal will to God. Guy's heroism is exemplary, but it is based in a completely different image of Christianity's role in the world. This image denies the church's claim to supersede the claims of individual, family, and country.

The same denial opposes other pious romances to saints' legends. *Sir Ysumbras*, generally cited as an example of "secular hagiography,"[65] resembles the legend of St. Eustace quite closely. Eustace and Isumbras, both brave knights, learn from God that they are to undergo severe misfortunes, Eustace in consequence of his conversion to Christianity and Isumbras as a result of his proud life. Both suffer the loss of all their goods, then of their wives and children, who are abducted. The two men demonstrate their endurance and acceptance of God's will and, following their return to arms, they are reunited with their families.

This brief outline cannot indicate fully the striking parallels in incident that link the two stories.[66] But underlying these connections are essential differences. Most obviously, the reward of Eustace's search is the crown of martyrdom, while the reward of Sir Isumbras's is a temporal crown. Their different rewards culminate quite different struggles. From a course of similar misfortunes, Eustace learns to transcend worldly desires, while the sinner Isumbras rewins his right to fulfill those very desires.

Eustace, like Alexis, comes to understand that devotion to the

---

65. Braswell, "'Sir Isumbras,'" p. 144; Mehl, *Middle English Romances*, pp. 128–35; Schelp, *Exemplarische Romanzen*, pp. 53–69; Blaicher, "*Sir Isumbras*." Editions cited: "placidas" (Northern Homily Cycle), ed. Horstmann; *Ysumbras*, ed. Schleich.

66. These parallels are emphasized by Braswell, "'Sir Isumbras'"; Mehl, *Middle English Romances*, pp. 128–35; and Schelp, *Exemplarische Romanzen*, pp. 54–57; in addition, Heffernan, "Legend of St. Eustace," provides a fine study of the legend's narrative qualities.

world and devotion to God are mutually exclusive. His terrible trials wean him from earthly concerns:

> 'I seo þis world is so chaungable,   see
> þat nout þat is þer Inne is stable. . . .
> þerfore, world here I þe forsake
> And to Ihū crist I me take.
> Ihū Ihū, þou lene me grace   give
> To suwe in worldes wo þi trace!'   follow / path
> (435–36, 447–50)

Eustace's new passivity toward the world leads him to reject his knightly identity, a change signaled by the replacement of his old name, Placidas, with his new baptismal name. When messengers seeking their old commander Placidas describe him to Eustace, he answers their inquiries, "'I haue not herd of such a Man, / Of hym con I telle no tiþand [tiding], / ffor such mon is non in þis land'" (522–24). He returns to military life but only because his men recognize him; for he has become passive, directing his whole will to God and perceiving earthly and heavenly ambitions as antithetical.

Isumbras, in contrast, regards his penance almost as a bargain, a temporary disadvantage to be suffered in hope of future rewards:

> 'Lorde, ȝif it thi will bee,
> In ȝowthede pouerte þou send mee   youth / poverty
> And welthe in myn elde.'   old age
> (58–60)

> 'God, þat sent me alle this woo,
> Hase sent me joye and blys also,
> And ȝitt may send ynoghe.'   yet
> (94–96)

As these statements imply, Isumbras and Eustace draw strikingly different lessons from their experience of the world's instability. For Isumbras life's misfortunes generate an argument for persevering through bad times (good times will probably follow) rather than for rejecting the world altogether (better to trust in God, who is stable). Consequently, Isumbras strives to rewin his wealth and family by supplementing a humble acceptance of God's punishment with social initiative reminiscent of Havelok the Dane's. Reduced to utter poverty and isolated from his wife and children, Isumbras apprentices himself as a digger of iron ore, works his way up to salaried smith, forges weapons and armor for himself, and rides on the pit pony to battle with his wife's abductor. After extending his penance in years of pilgrimage, Isumbras in the end becomes ruler of the abductor's kingdom, which his own wife has inherited. Three more kingdoms are eventually won for the three sons Isumbras regains.

This dramatic ascent through the ranks of society to a final royal reward substantiates Isumbras's belief that Christian faith can support personal initiative and commitment to earthly goals. Like Guy of Warwick, Isumbras incorporates his faith successfully in a secular structure of values.

The romances of Guy and Isumbras call on the lives of saints, yet their heroes are clearly not saintly. What image of Christian life do Guy and Isumbras present? Certainly their faith is strong, and they experience the importance of devotion to God. At the same time, both Guy and Isumbras sustain earthly commitments throughout, maintain their autonomy of action as individuals, and use their faith to renew and validate their heroic identities. These transformations of legendary material are not of merely peripheral significance. Just as the adoption of patterns from hagiography in the romances demonstrates approval, so too their alteration of certain hagiographic elements demonstrates denial and resistance. The designation "secular hagiography" misapprehends the depth and importance of this resistance. The insular pious romances challenge the legendary ideal of Christian abnegation by proposing that heaven's favors are visited on heroes of worldly ambitions just as on saints.

Faithful Friends

Like the romances of Christian knighthood, romances that exalt brotherhood by drawing on Christianity also uphold nonreligious values. *Athelston* has no legendary analogue, but the Amis and Amiloun story exists in hagiographic versions.[67] The story origi-

---

67. *Amis and Amiloun*, ed. Leach; ME quotations are from this edition, hereafter cited as ME *Amis*. The three MSS of *Amis e Amilun*—K (Corpus Christi Coll. L), L (Royal 12. C. xii), and the much later C (Cod. Durlac 38, Carlsruhe)—are described by Kölbing, ed., *Amis e Amilun*, pp. lxxiii–lxxvi. AN quotations are from this edition, hereafter cited as AN *Amis*. Kölbing reproduces the Durlac fragments beneath the appropriate lines of K and L in his edition.

Durlac (C) is a late fourteenth-century MS, greatly expanded by narrative interpolations and by Carolingian context imitating the OF *Amis et Amiles*. These additions confuse the plot, and Mehl wrongly attributes to "the Anglo-Norman poem" two structural weaknesses unique to C (*Middle English Romances*, p. 108). The ME version is closer to KL in clarity and economy and even in narrative technique. Several passages in C, however, are closely parallel to the ME version (Leach, edition, pp. xx, xcvii; Kölbing, "Zu Amis and Amilloun," p. 307; Legge, *Anglo-Norman Literature*, p. 119).

nally was not religious, although its later medieval versions grow more and more cognizant of its spiritual possibilities. But sworn brotherhood remains at the heart of the romance versions, and that bond's strength, stability, and virtue rival the bond between saints and God in legend. Sworn brotherhood is well suited to demonstrating the worth of worldly allegiances, in that it unites the oath-keeping of feudal relations with the blood ties of kinship in one powerful, voluntary gesture. Little wonder that hagiographers sought to absorb this story of brotherhood into religious literature or that its worldly appeal continued to attract secular poets.

Amis e Amilun and *Amis and Amiloun* draw on saints' lives for elements of suffering and sacrifice, religious devotion, and divine intervention. But these elements are inverted, emptied of their legendary significance as signs of saintly life, and filled instead with new meaning as stages in the testing and development of a perfect friendship: Amis and Amiloun

> trew weren in al þing,   loyal, true
> And þerfore Ihesu, heuyn-king,
> Ful wel quyted her mede.   requited / kindness
> (34–36)

God tests and rewards friendship, validating it and conferring on it the sanction of the divine. Although this process honors Christian principles by finding a place for them in a secular tale, that place is finally defined and delimited by the capacity of Christian principles to support the tale's secular ideal of brotherhood.

MacEdward Leach and Kathryn Hume have explored the contrasting purposes of the hagiographic and the romance versions of Amis and Amiloun's story.[68] Disagreement still abounds on how to interpret the differences from legend in *Amis e Amilun* and *Amis and Amiloun*, but I take the differences themselves to be sufficiently established and discuss here only the Anglo-Norman and Middle English versions. These "must be considered as a unit, an important member of the romantic family of the *Amis and Amiloun* story."[69] They cannot be treated accurately as source and translation, but they are related versions whose divergences illustrate the

---

68. Leach, edition, pp. ix–lxxxix; Hume, "Structure and Perspective."
69. Leach, edition, p. xcvii. On manuscript filiation, see Kölbing, "Zu Amis and Amilloun," 295–310; Kölbing, edition, pp. cxxi–cxxxi; and Leach, edition, pp. xx, xciv–xcvii.

expanding influence of hagiography on romance from the twelfth century to the fourteenth.

The story's events are nearly the same in Anglo-Norman and Middle English. Amis and Amiloun, identical in appearance, swear eternal friendship while youths in service to a count (duke in Middle English). When the count's daughter Florie (Belisaunt in Middle English) seduces Amis, a seneschal betrays the lovers. Amiloun takes Amis's place in swearing to no fault against the count and thus by deception wins a judicial combat and the hand of Florie. Just before marrying her in Amis's stead, Amiloun hears a voice warning him that if he goes through with the ceremony he will be stricken with leprosy (this warning precedes the judicial combat in Middle English). He continues to hide his name and marries Florie for Amis, assuring his friend's happiness. Amiloun returns home but is soon cast out by his own wife when he becomes leprous. Helped only by Owein, a faithful young relative, Amiloun eventually arrives to beg at Amis's door. The friends are reunited by Owein's faithfulness and by recognition tokens, identical cups they exchanged at parting. Soon Amis hears from a voice in a dream that the blood of his two children would restore Amiloun to health. He kills the children, cures Amiloun, and finds the children miraculously restored. Amiloun takes vengeance on his wife and gives his land to Owein, then returns to live the rest of his life with Amis. The two lie buried together in Lombardy.

As it appears in the two complete manuscripts, *Amis e Amilun* is told with extraordinary simplicity. Its spareness throws into relief the reciprocity and equality of sacrifice in friendship that give this story its meaningful balance. Studies of the Middle English *Amis and Amiloun* contrast this characteristic linearity to the cohesive development and frequent foreshadowing of the Middle English redaction.[70] The earlier version accentuates the story's hyperbolic and exemplary quality, while the English version adds details and digressions that must then be brought under control by a heightened narrative intensity.[71] Often the later version strengthens a crucial scene's violent or pathetic possibilities so as to infuse its expanded

---

70. Kathryn Hume, "*Amis and Amiloun*," p. 21; Mehl, *Middle English Romances*, pp. 107–8; Leach, edition, p. xcvii.

71. I discuss style more fully in [Crane] Dannenbaum, "Insular Tradition"; see also Hume, "*Amis and Amiloun*," pp. 24–26; Kramer, "Structural Artistry," pp. 112–18.

concreteness with thematic meaning. Perhaps the finest example of such counterbalancing of naturalistic detail with new emotive intensity is the sacrifice of Amis's children (2257–322). A host of small circumstantial actions—sending the servants off to church, finding the nursery keys, taking a candle, relocking the nursery door, hiding the keys under a stone—surround a central passage in which Amis stands poised before his decision:

>   Alon him self, wiþ-outen mo,
>   Into þe chaumber he gan to go,
>   Þer þat his childer were,
>   & biheld hem boþe to,   two
>   Hou fair þai lay to-gider þo   there
>   & slepe boþe yfere.   together
>   Þan seyd him-selue, 'Bi Seyn Jon,   to himself
>   It were gret reweþe ȝou to slon,   great pity / slay
>   Þat god haþ bouȝt so dere!'   at such cost
>   His kniif he had drawen þat tide,   time
>   For sorwe he sleynt oway biside
>   & wepe wiþ reweful chere.   wept / countenance
>   (2281–92)

In this passage the physical evocation of the scene is subsumed in the universal pathos of the father's sorrow, the mythologizing analogy between the children and the sacrificial Christ, and the transcendent simplicity of the style. The event thereby overcomes its own specificity to achieve the absolute narrative necessity and merit that are more directly and simply achieved in the Anglo-Norman text (1086–106) through the hero's freedom from emotional conflict and an unspecific, emblematic approach to the story. The two scenes diverge in treatment but not in purpose.

The thematic development of *Amis and Amiloun* has appeared to literary critics to differ sharply from that of the Anglo-Norman version. Brotherhood is, in the asocial, minimally Christian atmosphere of *Amis e Amilun*, the unquestionable arbiter of right and wrong. In the more naturalistic and more sensitively Christian world of *Amis and Amiloun*, it has seemed that friendship becomes only a relative value. This, however, misstates the case. The differing social and religious content of the two poems necessitates divergent approaches to the theme of brotherhood, but the Middle English poet is scrupulously true to the sense of the Anglo-Norman version.

Characters in *Amis e Amilun* swear in God's name and the narrator prays for the heroes, establishing a Christian background for the story,[72] but only at two points do these appeals have a narrative function. Both are moments in the story that could be considered morally ambiguous, and the interjection of piety functions to remove any possible doubt of the heroes' righteousness. When Amilun impersonates Amis, he recognizes that Amis has wronged the count in acceding to Florie's demands (493–96), yet he can immediately pray for success (501–2), a prayer the narrator shares:

> Ore li seit deu en aie
> E doint, ke il puisse bien faire;
> Grant chose enprent pur son frere.
>   (522–24)

Now may God assist him and grant that he may do well; he is undertaking a great thing for his brother.

By associating the friends' loyalty to each other with the firm hope of God's support in these two prayers, Amis's fault against the count and the consequent need to trick the count and his court become morally irrelevant in the face of the exalted cause of friendship. A similar process associates piety with the sacrifice of Amis's children. Amis prays that his dream is true and that his brother may truly be cured (1086–96); after it proves true, Florie dismisses the children's deaths in giving thanks to God for Amilun's recovery (1126–34). The connection between Amis's act of friendship and Christian piety evades the claim that Amis's sons deserve his protection as much as does his friend. The moral issues inherent in both episodes are never confronted directly but are instead deflected by these perfunctory invocations of piety.

Thus religion in *Amis e Amilun* supports the plot without becoming important to it. The deity is a passive force at the disposal of the poet, to be invoked as necessary in support of friendship's demands. A more clearly present supernatural force and absolute arbiter of right in the poem is friendship itself. The perfection of the bond between Amis and Amilun confers upon them superhuman endurance of suffering, in their unhesitating acceptance of sacrifices for their friendship; prescience, in Amilun's warning against

---

72. Yet God has no clear part in the action: disembodied voices announcing the heroes' tests have no apparent source or commitment to the action, though the vaguely Christian background of the poem as a whole must suggest a heavenly origin; the miraculous restoration of the children is clearly a result of the heroes' total dedication to friendship, but not necessarily a reward from God.

the steward and in his dream of Amis's peril (74-92, 463-70); and an interdependent sympathy whereby vengeance on the seneschal becomes entirely mutual (501-3).

The uniquely exalted position friendship holds in *Amis e Amilun* makes Amis's failure to recognize the leper at his door the central crisis of the poem, because here alone the omniscient sympathy of friendship fails temporarily to unite them. The poor leper's possession of a gold cup which Amis recognizes as the friendship token leads to his ferocious physical attack on the supposed thief. Amilun has been too miserable in his affliction to entrust his need to Amis; he seems to realize his isolation fully when he hears Amis pronounce his name as if it belonged to another: "Kant Amilun s'oit nomer, / De dolur pout son quer crever" [when Amilun hears himself named, his heart could break for sorrow] (1017-18). Nor does Amis manage to sense his friend's presence. As he moves to kill the leper, Owein warns "'Si l'occiez, vus friez pecché'" ["If you kill him, you will commit a sin/terrible act"] (1042), but Amis then laments his deep sense of "pecché" simply for not having recognized his brother (1047-49). In Amilun's hopeless plea for death and in Amis's remorse, a sense of mutual shame, if not of mutual sinfulness in the full sense of the word, is essential. The Anglo-Norman poet not only makes Christianity a passive referent for the righteousness of friendship above other claims but even infuses friendship with a quasi-religious power and vocabulary. In this treatment of the story it is impossible to doubt the correctness of the friends' actions and therefore impossible to consider the consequences of these actions—leprosy and child sacrifice—as punishments in any sense, but rather only as tests of loyalty leading to reunion and happiness.

The author of *Amis and Amiloun* introduces complexities that make moral judgments more difficult for both characters and critics. God is more immanent and actively benevolent in this version; Christ rewards the heroes' *treupe* directly (34-36, 2362-64); the voices announcing tests are angel messengers of God (1250-54, 2200). These Christian intrusions, acting in the relatively detailed, rationalized world of *Amis and Amiloun*, produce moments of reflective doubt not found in the Anglo-Norman version. The heroes' oath to support each other "in wrong & riȝt" (149, 1451) even seems to place *treupe* at odds with morality. And indeed, Amis and Amiloun hesitate more profoundly before their actions, stressing the moral difficulties presented by Amis's false statements (940–47, 1099–102) and by the sacrifice of children (2245–47).

But the issues of crime and punishment that seem to be introduced in this heightened Christian context are suppressed by retaining the Anglo-Norman exaltation of friendship above all other values. The single change in plot from *Amis e Amilun* has often been seized upon as a sign of the Middle English poet's desire to show a morally wrong action punished. In *Amis and Amiloun* the warning that Amiloun will be stricken with leprosy if he continues his course of action comes not before his false marriage, as in Anglo-Norman, but before the judicial combat. From a purely narrative standpoint this change is a great improvement, since it consolidates Amiloun's sacrifice in one action: the friendly service leads from the first to leprosy, rather than only half the service (marriage but not duel) resulting in disease. It is tempting to see in the Middle English alteration not just a structural improvement but also an attempt to make leprosy a "punishment for false swearing" or for the "sin" of accepting the duel for Amis.[73] Yet this widely voiced explanation is tenable neither in terms of the nature of judicial combat nor in terms of the poem itself.

Numerous epics and romances represent judicial ordeals that verify not a whole human situation, but only the sworn statements made by participants. In the case of a literally true though functionally deceptive oath, it is not God and Justice who are being tricked, but simply the human onlookers. As a result, in medieval literature the equivocal oath is not inherently sinful but is rather a locus for resistance to social pressure in deference to personal allegiances.[74] *Amis e Amilun* follows this tradition. If the equivocal oath were punished in *Amis and Amiloun*, it would contradict the conventional understanding of judicial oaths and negate the Anglo-Norman exaltation of friendship above other values. It would also contradict the heroes' belief that, while Amis would indeed be "forsworn" if he maintained his own innocence, Amiloun is free

73. Quotations are from Leach, edition, p. 125 n.; and Mehl, *Middle English Romances*, p. 108. Cf. interpretations of leprosy as a punishment for the "sin of 'forswearing'" (Kramer, "Structural Artistry," p. 110); for "giving a false statement under oath" (Brody, *Disease*, p. 166; Krappe, "Amicus and Amelius," p. 155); and for sinfulness (Hume, "*Amis and Amiloun*," pp. 28–29; Childress, "Between Romance and Legend," p. 318).

74. Leach, edition, p. lxxxvi; for tricked ordeals as traditionally unpunished, see pp. lxiv, lxxxv–lxxxvi; Calin, *Epic Quest*, pp. 72, 84–87; Ménard, *Rire et le sourire*, pp. 362–63.

to "'swere so god me spede / As icham giltles of þat dede'" (1120–21).

In fact, there is no hint of wrong or punishment in the insular romances. Although the hagiographic versions treat Amiloun's choice as a sinful one, in *Amis and Amiloun* (as in Anglo-Norman) the warning angel avoids any suggestion of sin.[75] The right and wrong of Amiloun's decision turn on *treuþe*, the virtue central to sworn brotherhood, rather than on a Christian ideal of honesty. Amiloun must choose between *treuþe* and self-preservation: he reasons "'for drede of care / To hold mi treuþe schal y nouȝt spare'" (1282–83); the narrator recognizes the same basic choice in describing Amiloun's leprosy as "what sorwe he hadde for his treuþe" (1547). Only Amiloun's wife, a character so "wicked & schrewed [depraved]" (1561) that her accusations suggest their opposite, believes her husband's leprosy to be a punishment for falsifying the ordeal (1564–69). She refers to the medieval tradition that God could inflict leprosy to purge sins. In this tradition Henryson shows fallen Criseyde cleansed by the suffering of the illness, and Langland writes of poor lepers, "For loue of here lowe [humble] hertes · oure lord hath hem graunted / Here penaunce and here purgatorie · vp-on thys pure [very] erthe."[76] But Amiloun's leprosy is only a test, since the equivocal oath requires no repentance. His redemption draws on another medieval tradition: that bathing in the blood of children cures leprosy. Paul Remy has suggested that this treatment was so widely believed to be infallible that, in many medieval literary examples, the leper's physical condition is felt to be more horrifying than his longing for the cure.[77] Amiloun's restoration to health follows this tradition rather than one of purgation, despite the exemplary meekness with which he bears his dis-

---

75. Kratins notes the significance of the angel's wording: the voice "does not threaten Amiloun with punishment ('þou schalt haue an euentour strong' is a morally neutral statement); rather, he puts Amiloun's *treuþe* to the test by placing before him a choice" (*"Amis and Amiloun,"* p. 351). On the hagiographic versions, see Brody, *Disease*, pp. 164, 166–67; Hume, "Structure and Perspective," pp. 98–99. Baldwin, *"Amis and Amiloun,"* believes we are meant to see grace rather than *treuþe* resolving the trials, but he ignores the poem's contrary statement (lines 34–36).

76. *Piers Plowman*, ed. Skeat, Passus X, lines 184–85; see also Brody, *Disease*, passim; and Richards, *Medieval Leper*.

77. "Lèpre," pp. 195–242. Remy cites *Jaufre, Protheselaus, Gesta Romanorum*, and the *Queste del Saint-Graal* for examples of the blood-cure tradition (pp. 226–27); King Richard and Louis XI were advised to take this cure (pp. 222–3); see also Leach, edition, p. lxii.

ease. The means to his cure lie not within himself but in a second test, imposed on Amis by God to balance Amiloun's prior sacrifice.

Although Amis thinks to himself that "to slen his childer so ȝing, / It were [would be] a dedli sinne" (2246–47), Christian morality finally accommodates friendship's requirements. Quadruple repetition of the informing dream and its appearance to both Amiloun and Amis make its veracity unquestionable. This recurrence, the explicitly heavenly origin of the message, and a Christmas Eve setting that calls forth associations with Christ's sacrifice and its typological forebear, Abraham sacrificing Isaac (2289, 2325), all confer divine assurance and sanction on Amis's act.[78] The moral sensitivity that characterizes *Amis and Amiloun* serves ultimately to justify rather than condemn so apparently sinful a deed.

But religious awareness does slightly alter the handling of crises. The unique spiritual crisis of *Amis e Amilun*, the failure to recognize Amilun, takes its intensity from the limited importance of religion in the cause of sworn brotherhood. In the Middle English version Christianity provides not only support for friendship, but a general climate of moral awareness that requires deeper self-questioning and clearer self-justification before acting in the name of friendship. The resulting moments of hesitation and the expanded role of an active deity throughout *Amis and Amiloun* diffuse the single spiritual crisis of the Anglo-Norman version among several crises of decision. Still, these dramatic moments neither compromise nor qualify the ideal of friendship; they simply demonstrate in a more naturalistic mode the same complete dedication to friendship's demands as was conveyed in Anglo-Norman by the absence of all hesitation. The approach changes precisely so that the thematic meaning may remain constant. Both works make of friendship the only absolute value and require other values to arrange themselves subordinately as best they can.

Another romance of friendship, *Athelston*, echoes in a very different plot the hierarchy of values found in the insular *Amis* poems. *Athelston* seems particularly pious in that it depicts a vengeful king's repentant change of heart, brought about by a powerful archbishop of Canterbury, and a religious ordeal that reveals innocence and provides the context for St. Edmund's birth. As with the other

---

78. Hume, "*Amis and Amiloun*," pp. 29, 37.

romances discussed in this chapter, however, the action of *Athelston* supplies earthly problems and desires with earthly resolutions and rewards.

The four messengers of *Athelston* bind themselves "in trewþe trewely" with oaths of friendship "for euermare" (22–24), but the lie of one friend that another plots Athelston's death destroys reliability at all levels of the brothers' interaction. This work treats not the *treuþe* of Amis and Amiloun, but the *falsnesse* of broken friendship:

> Lystnes, lordyngys þat ben hende,
> Off falsnesse, hou it wil ende
> A man þat ledes him þerin.[79]

Because the betrayer works "þorw3 wurd" [through speech] (87), his falseness renders even language untrustworthy, so that truth becomes accessible only through direct appeal to God (see pp. 71–72). Yet the truth sought is a temporal one. Its recovery is a political event that restores a kingdom's justice and stability, rather than a transcendent event such as a martyr's death. And in his efforts to discover this political truth, the archbishop is concerned with sworn brotherhood, not faith:

> 'Blyþe schal I neuere be   Happy
> Tyl I my weddyd broþer see,   sworn
> To keuere hym out off care.'[80] recover

Through interdict and excommunication the archbishop begins to implement his threats of war and social dislocation as he strives to win control of the prisoners (465–530). In this temporal struggle the value of divine power is measured by its political effectiveness.

God's justice is indeed valuable by this measure, testing "þe treweþe" (776) of brotherhood in the fires of the ordeal. Peace returns, and the birth of St. Edmund reverses the wrong of Athelston's own son's death. Yet there is nothing hagiographic about this resolution, despite the saint's presence. No surrender of earthly for heavenly desires and values occurs; no martyrs die in this fire. Rather, the ordeal answers the temporal problem of the crown's succession:

---

79. Ed. Trounce, lines 7–9. Trounce translates "Listen, my courteous lords, (to a tale) of unfaithfulness, and to the fate it brings any man who concerns himself with it" (p. 93).

80. Lines 378–80; see also 399–404.

> Þey crystnyd þe chyld, þat men my3t see,
>   And callyd it Edemound.
> 'Halff my land,' [Athelston] sayde, 'I þe geue,   give
> Also longe as I may leue,   As / live
>   Wiþ markys and with pounde,
> And al afftyr my dede—   all of it / death
> Yngelond to wysse and rede.'   guide / direct
>   Now iblessyd be þat stounde!   hour
>   (655–62)

The hour of Edmund's birth is primarily "iblessyd" because of his future kingship, which signals the restoration of brotherhood, not because of his future saintliness. As in many other insular romances, the incorporation of faith and of God's sanction into the pursuit of secular destinies enhances the seriousness of the work without affecting its essential concerns. The ordeal re-creates temporal order and brotherhood; the birth of Edmund reestablishes the line of inheritance and the bond between friends; the archbishop's success restores the political balance between church and monarchy. The work's assertion that heaven's guidance is necessary to the pursuit of earthly ends is certainly a homage to Christian belief, but the pursuit of earthly ends remains aggressively the subject of interest.

Both *Amis and Amiloun* and *Athelston* have been called "homiletic romance" or "secular hagiography."[81] Yet to put the case most radically, both substitute human for divine salvation. In *Athelston* the bond of brotherhood motivates the archbishop to protect the innocent victims of a broken oath. The ordeal gives conviction to the archbishop's faith in his "weddyd broþer" (379), but the work's resolution is fully secular nonetheless. Similarly, Amiloun's redeemer is his friend Amis; the blood redeeming him is that of brotherly love, not of Christ. The evocation of Christ's sacrifice and the intervention of divine voices emphasize, because they sustain, devotion to brotherhood over devotion to any other value.

This analysis of the relation between divine and human love in *Athelston* and in the Amis poems contradicts analyses by those who believe that "homiletic romance" is a generically intermediate category. These romances are not in sympathy with hagiography's orientation. Brotherhood dominates; divine power aids in its development and provides validating analogies for acts of friendship.

---

81. Mehl, *Middle English Romances*, pp. 146–52; Childress, "Between Romance and Legend," pp. 316–19; Kratins, "*Amis and Amiloun*."

This structuring absorbs divine power into a secular framework of values. The wonders and miracles of these romances—the children laughing in the fires of the ordeal, Amiloun's deliverance from leprosy, the birth of St. Edmund and the rebirth of Amis's sons—all these joyful moments grant divine affirmation to the importance of friendship. If in so doing they imply an analogy between brotherhood and divine love, between earthly rewards and heavenly peace, the analogy redounds to the credit of the romances' primary concerns, those of the world, conferring exceptional value on the threatened and restored peace of brotherhood, family, and nation. In this we see not so much the fusing of romance and hagiography as romance's answer to hagiography's challenge.

Insularity and the Pious Romances

From *Amis e Amilun* in the twelfth century through *Athelston* late in the fourteenth, England's pious romances increasingly accept and incorporate religious impulses, but they do so with increasingly well-defined resistance to certain implications of religious teaching. The immediate context for the development of exemplary romances is the hagiographic *vitae*, which share many features with romance. In turn, many of the romances that show deep Christian influence have hagiographic analogues. Guy, like Alexis, leaves his family to follow a humble life of service to God; Isumbras, like Eustace, is rewarded for his acceptance of heaven-sent misfortunes; Amis and Amiloun in both romance and hagiography are visited by God and accept the tests heaven imposes upon them. Saints' legends influence the growth of new patterns of heroism in insular romance: the hero who seeks to glorify God through his chivalric exploits, the hero who knows God's part in his daily life and who accepts trials and tests imposed directly by God.

But the adoption of hagiographic patterns raises certain expectations that are thwarted in the exemplary romances. Acceptance of God leads a saint to understand existence as bipartite and to reject earthly concerns in favor of transcendent concerns, which are superior to and incompatible with those of the world. When a saint realizes God's power, he or she surrenders not only earthly identity but autonomy of action, allowing God as a desiring presence to counterbalance the saint's desire in the course of events. Finally, a saint's apotheosis in death rejects earthly desires and worldly power but brings the saint a heavenly reward.

Exemplary romances deny these consequences of faith. Rather than rejecting the world, their heroes integrate faith with involvement in profane affairs. Guy and Isumbras fight for personal vengeance as well as for God; Amis and Amiloun and the sworn brothers in *Athelston* value the *treupe* of their friendship above all else. They support their worldly concerns and their secular identities with a freedom of action that the saints do not wield. The heroes of pious romances even take initiatives or suffer dilemmas that are at odds with their religious commitment, giving them a substance and complexity that contrasts with saintly singlemindedness. Guy takes time out from anonymity to say goodbye to his friends and make provisions for his son; Isumbras supplements his humble acceptance of God's punishment with an economic aggressiveness that restores his social standing and avenges his wife. Amis knows the divine origin of the message announcing the cure for Amiloun's leprosy, yet he suffers great anguish in killing his children; Athelston's archbishop fights the pervasive corruption of *falsnesse* by calling on divine truth, but also by laying a deceitful trap for his untrue brother. The broad range of these characters' emotions and actions does not leave space in the works for God's actively determining presence. Divine intervention merely guides and supports the development of the hero's personal drama, a drama culminating in earthly adulation, success, and stasis—and perhaps in heavenly salvation as well.

In all these respects, the pious or exemplary works keep to the generic tendencies of romance rather than absorbing those of hagiography. Curiously, the restraints that romance poets place on religious elements are less immediately evident in moral romances that do not have hagiographic analogues. *Havelok the Dane* creates an immanent universe in which it is "mirácle fair and god [good]" that Godard spares young Havelok's life. Years later, when returning to his patrimony, Havelok asks Christ's assistance:

> 'And bringge me wel to þe lond
> Þat Godard haldes in his hond;
> Þat is mi riht, eueri del: birthright / every bit
> Iesu Crist, þou wost it wel!'[82]   knoweth

82. *Havelok the Dane*, ed. Skeat, lines 500, 1381–84.

Government and faith seem entirely compatible in Havelok's prayer as in Athelwold's ideal rule (27–247).[83] Because the romance has no hagiographic analogue, the harmonies it establishes are undisturbed by resonances with the conflicting standards of Christian life established in saints' legends.

Similarly, the Anglo-Norman *Alexander* and *Kyng Alisaunder* fuse moral and scientific impulses, indeed so successfully that the prologue to *Kyng Alisaunder* introduces the pre-Christian hero with conventional admonishments taken from religious works: many there are in the audience

Þat hadden leuer a ribaudye	Who would rather have a lewd tale
Þan here of God oiþer Seint Marie,	
Oiþer to drynk a copful ale	
Þan to heren any gode tale.	
Swiche Ich wolde weren out bishett,	I wish that such / shut
For certeynlich it were nett.	a good thing
(21–26)	

That the author admonishes his audience not just to listen seriously but to listen religiously, as to a tale of God or Mary, indicates how compatibly the Alexander story can coexist with a moral tone. Yet in the Alexander poems, even more than in *Havelok*, the dominant values and concerns are areligious ones; the appeals of heroic leadership, history, and scientific observation are more compelling than moral appeals.

The incompatibilities between romances and hagiographic *vitae* may be more evident in those insular works with hagiographic analogues, but other works classed as homiletic and briefly sampled here are also best understood as romances rather than as generically distinct from romance. Medieval romance is itself an exemplary form, which builds and animates varied ideals of self-realization, social harmony, and love. H. R. Jauss places the genre among the forms inspiring an "admirative Identifikation." This concept captures more precisely than that of exemplarity the nature and effect of romance: the genre presents not models for di-

---

83. Haskin examines the similar mutuality of a Christian ideal of generosity and the feudal virtue of *largesse* in "Food, Clothing and Kingship"; and Mills points out in "Havelok's Return" the importance of divine protection in Havelok's escape from and return to his patrimony. Nonetheless, social imperatives do conflict with Christian associations in HD, e.g., "as Havelok bowls down his fellow workers, we wonder what happened to the aura of Christian humility that surrounded his journey to Lincoln" (Ganim, *Style and Consciousness*, p. 24).

rect imitation but inspiring figures of ideal achievement that dignify a way of life, a history, or a standard of conduct.[84] Saints' legends, too, invite an admiring reaction, but as we have seen, their figures of achievement differ fundamentally from those of romance. Moreover, these generic incompatibilities express important cultural tensions between Christian and secular interests. The insular romances that draw on hagiography do not merely alter the model of sainthood to a model of Christian lay perfection. Rather, they absorb piety into a value system distinct from that of medieval Christianity.

As outlined in the first section of this chapter, church and state began to find themselves in strong conflict during the twelfth century. Henry II's disputes with Thomas Becket crystallized for contemporaries the opposition between new state coherence and the church's values and power.[85] As the church turned its attention to pastoral reform, the thirteenth century witnessed important expansions in the church's authority and role in the lives of Christians. These expansions produced wide-ranging improvements in spiritual care, and at the same time exacerbated oppositions between religious and secular demands on lay Christians. G. R. Owst borrows Courthope's image of "bulls in the china shop of Chivalry" to describe the "ruthless scorn which English preachers poured out unceasingly upon this [pride of ancestry] and every other ideal, which medieval men of the world sought after or held most dear . . . as successful members of feudal society."[86] The church's teachings on social behavior, cultural values, and economic restraint frequently conflicted with secular values and practices.

Resistance to hagiographic patterns in romance comments on these conflicts. By substituting worldly victories for legendary transcendence, the pious romances validate secular concerns. Political stability replaces heavenly rest, and sacrificial brotherhood stands in for martyrdom. Such substitutions assert the worth of pursuing security and prosperity and of respecting oaths and family ties. And in the romances' ideal vision, these goals lie within the

---

84. "Negativität und Identifikation"; see also Jauss, "Cinq modèles." Wehrli judges that exemplarity is insufficient to distinguish hagiography from romance (*Formen mittelalterlicher Erzählung*, p. 431).
85. Türk, *Nugae Curialium*.
86. *Literature and Pulpit*, p. 308.

reach of human power. Where the legend subordinates a saint's will to God's desire, these insular works give the hero center stage. Problems and their resolutions wait on his choices and actions, making him the prime mover of the poetic universe, the source of change and of order.

Establishing a correlation between the insular pious romances and the context of church reform raises one further issue. The impulse to religious reform in the thirteenth century may have been somewhat stronger in England than on the continent, but the reform movement was international and so followed in many countries the course established by the church in Rome and its councils. Why then should England have developed so many examples of morally committed romance, while in France the influence of religious writing on romance was so limited? Old French romance offers a few examples from the late twelfth and early thirteenth centuries of vital hagiographic influence, but in general the thirteenth century saw the triumph of hagiography over romance. Analyzing this continental development, Peter Dembowski concludes that religious reform gave impetus to the writing of hagiography in France, just as was the case in England, but that additionally Old French romance lost its vitality, its capacity to express important concerns, in the early thirteenth century: "Here lies the fundamental importance of hagiography for the history of Old French literature. When . . . romance becomes 'fluffy' and flippant, or allegorical and abstract, the function of the literary presentation of reality in a serious vein is taken over by the hagiographic narratives."[87] Yet during the same and the following century in England, romance retains its vitality, manifesting varied and increasingly subtle responses to hagiography.

This difference can be accounted for in both historical and literary terms. In addition to the striking changes of international religious reform, the thirteenth century saw the development of a Middle English literary culture that supplemented and later supplanted Anglo-Norman literary culture. The shift is related to England's increasing separation from the political and cultural patterns of the continent; the losses of Normandy in 1204 and of the

87. "Literary Problems," p. 122. Wehrli describes a parallel separation of romance and hagiography in Germany; and Hurley further describes differences between romance and hagiography in "Saints' Legends." Mehl also reviews this difference between insular and continental romance (*Middle English Romances*, pp. 17–20).

Angevin territories by 1243 are only the most prominent signs of isolation. The accompanying shift from Anglo-Norman to English as the dominant language of culture attenuated the patterns of literary development observable on the continent, prolonging the prominence of romance through the process of translation. And translation only partly describes the emergence of Middle English romance; as works move from French to English they find new meanings, voices, and audiences. Together, the change in language and the change in substance give romance an extended period of vitality in England.[88] At the same time hagiography achieves literary prominence in the wake of the church's pastoral reforms. In consequence the two genres are active—and interacting—over a considerable period in England.

At the intersection of generic pressure from the vital and popular saints' legends and ecclesiastical pressure toward fuller Christian commitment, romance in England stands confronted with a great challenge to its validity and its power to generate ideal images of human potential. Its response is in part adaptive, in accepting religious concerns more deeply and in proposing new models of conduct for morally sensitive heroes. However, the response of the insular works is at the same time resistant: in these works, religious sensibilities uphold fundamental commitments to the importance of worldly achievement, the value of earthly life, and the centrality of the hero's power.

88. The earliest ME romances all have AN or OF antecedents, but they postdate those antecedents by fifty to one hundred years: see Helaine Newstead's chart of dates in Severs, ed., *Manual*, I, 13–16.

Chapter Four

Measuring Conventions of Courtliness

The relation of baronial ideals to feudal, national, and religious principles is not the only concern of insular romance. A further subject of importance to insular as well as continental poets is ideal love and its relationship to noble life. The ascendancy of romances of love and chivalry in the later Middle Ages has disturbed some modern readers, because it seems to represent a rejection of historical and political concern. W. P. Ker complained that even in the finest twelfth-century romances "the glimpses of the real world are occasional and short . . . and then the heavy-laden, enchanted mists of rhetoric and obligatory sentiment come rolling down and shut out the view." Erich Auerbach found them "entirely without any basis in political reality" and concluded that "courtly romance is not reality shaped and set forth by art, but an escape into fable and fairy tale."[1]

The romances of love are indeed conventional, do use artful rhetoric, and do present characters who are idealized—clearly superior to real people in their personal attributes and in their ability to execute their purposes and achieve their desires. These characters, like the stories of their lives, have a perfect, polished wholeness that stimulates admiration and aesthetic pleasure. In contrast to the romances of English heroes and the pious romances, the

---

1. Ker, *Epic and Romance*, p. 353; Auerbach, *Mimesis*, pp. 133, 138.

Anglo-Norman romances of love have narrators who are strongly conscious of their status as fabricators. They make themselves interpreters of subtle visions of ideal behavior, mediators between their poetry and the audience their poetry fictionalizes. *Tristan* and *Ipomedon* exist as poetic objects at a considerable remove from historical reality, and their artfulness demands our attention.

Yet Ker's and Auerbach's analyses miss the distinctive and extensive relations these works have with their times. In attending to emotional development and individuality, romances of love engage issues fundamental to the twelfth-century renaissance.[2] Their concern with personal fulfillment in relation to public duty—with people as social beings—offers far more than mere "escape into fable and fairy tale." Like other romances in this study, the insular romances of love and chivalry assess ideal patterns of behavior (here the cultural formations of *courtoisie* and *fine amor*) in relation to conflicting images of conduct. But the historical situation of these romances changes more than that of other insular romances: the earlier poets of love and chivalry examine an ideal system that had far less importance to social behavior than did religion or feudal and national principles, but their Middle English successors saw literature's courtly ideals widely followed in social practice.

Courtly Literature and the Insular World

The cultures where the poetry of love and chivalry first flourished were distant from England, and twelfth-century poets responded to this literature with both enthusiasm and resistance. On the one hand, Anglo-Norman poets are quick, even precocious, in their acceptance of courtly procedures such as praise of ladies, depiction of rich clothing and objects, and delineation of fine manners and generous behavior.[3] Thomas of Britain's version of painful love recalls the troubadours, although transferring that love from lyric to narrative form distances his work from Provençal aesthetics and aligns it with northern French romances. But the insular poets are uneasy about their participation in the literature of love and chivalry. Thomas's *Tristan* and Hue de Rotelande's *Ipomedon* share a fun-

---

2. This aspect of romance is treated in different ways by Noltung-Hauff, *Liebeskasuistik*; Morris, *Discovery of the Individual*; Hanning, *Individual in Twelfth-Century Romance*.
3. See Legge, "'Courtoisie' en anglo-normand"; Press, "Precocious Courtesy."

damental objection to continental romance that is answered in the later *Amadas et Ydoine* and in Middle English romances. Rejecting the ideal play of reconciliation typical of Old French romances, Thomas and Hue hazard the most extreme tensions between private and public selves and between images of love's code and of human behavior. These Anglo-Norman poets establish an important line of questioning for later poets of love and chivalry in England. In a process similar to their compatriots' incorporation of Christian elements into romance, the insular poets of love at first resist much in courtly convention, then gradually accept it more fully while adapting it to suit insular literary purposes and social ideals.

In saying that these romances diverge from the norms of courtly romance, I do not endorse the widespread judgment that insular poetry often fails to be "courtly" altogether. Constance Birt West, for example, found much in Thomas "non-courtois" and declared of Hue that "though he is familiar with the language of courtoisie, he does not really express its point of view."[4] W. O. Evans extended to the Middle English romances West's conclusion that Anglo-Norman romances often abandon "*courtois* conventions"; and Gervase Mathew agreed that some English tendencies, such as making lovers equal and showing love in marriage, are "completely un-*courtois*."[5] These judgments assume that the literary tradition of noble love is monolithic and proscriptive, an assumption that can no longer be upheld. Andreas Capellanus was not an influential master for poets of love.[6] Even the strictest canon of Old French romances includes works with conflicting postulates, so that what is courtly cannot be narrowly defined: "There is not one courtly love but twenty or thirty of them."[7] This conclusion sounds almost paradoxical given the proscriptive history of the term *amour courtois*; thus the terms *fine amor*, *bone amor*, and *veraie amor*, which poets frequently used to describe varied manifestations of refined love, suit better our recognition that love in the romances is not one

---

4. *Courtoisie*, pp. 29 and 106. More recent critics also find Thomas uncourtly, e.g., Jonin, *Personnages féminins*, pp. 288–335, 452–57; Wind, "Eléments courtois."
5. Evans, "'Cortaysye,'" p. 149; Mathew, "*Amour Courtois*," p. 129. Gist likewise finds that the ME romances show "little understanding of the French concept of courtly love" (*Love and War*, p. 8).
6. Karnein, "Réception du *De Amore*"; Benton, "Court of Champagne" and "Andreas Capellanus"; Bowden, "Courtly Copulation."
7. Utley, "Courtly Love," p. 322. But Ferrante argues in "*Cortes' Amor*" that the term "courtly love" still has validity. The literature on the subject is enormous; surveys of controversies are Boase, *Courtly Love*; and Kelly, *Love and Marriage*, pp. 19–26.

thing but many.[8] *Fine amor* is especially evocative in its oxymoronic collapsing of "intense" and "refined" in the adjective *fine*. To describe a love (whether of a woman or of God) that is impassioned but also elevating, poets often choose the collocation *fine amor*.

The Anglo-Norman and Middle English romances have appeared "non-courtois" because they diverge energetically from supposedly rigid generic norms. But on the whole, insular detachment from continental romances of love is not best described as a failure to be courtly. Just as the nature of *veraie amor* is shaped and reshaped in various plots and poetic arguments but retains a general sense of refinement and intensity, so too *courtoisie* varies in specifics from text to text while generally signifying a complex of social and chivalric virtues instilled by noble education and the experience of noble love. Insular poets demonstrate in many ways that they are aware of courtly tradition and committed to producing idealized, inspiring visions of noble life.[9] In so doing, they resist certain elements of received continental literature and undertake a coherent revision of romance's generic norms.

Part of that revision, as we have seen, reduces tension between the hero and the political structures of his society. While Old French romances and *gestes de révoltés* discover important conflicts between noble aspirations and social restraints, the romances of English heroes tend to equate heroic desires with communal ones. The insular barony's experience of political systematization, particularly in the twelfth century, was less debilitating and contentious than was the continental experience. The romances of English heroes, in turn, could plausibly develop an ideal version of political heroism that located conflict in aberrant forces challenging hero and community together.

With regard to the role of cultural ideals in poetic depictions of noble behavior, the Old French and insular romances diverge again. In French romances dissonances between noble ambition and social restraint can be resolved within ideal chivalry and love. Internalizing the conflicts of violence versus pacification and passion versus control, protagonists work out emotional and behav-

---

8. Two studies on the limitations and uses of the term *fine amor* that do not appear in Boase's bibliography are Burnley, *"Fine Amor"*; and Reiss, *"Fin' Amors."*
9. Continental as well as insular romances can only be read consistently as a series of hypotheses on what *fine amor* and ideal chivalry might be and how they might manifest themselves in different narrative situations. For analyses of the genre from this perspective, see Sklute, "Ethical Norms"; Haidu, "Humor."

ioral equilibria that model resolutions for their society's turbulence. Early insular poets resist these inner resolutions, and later poets modify them extensively.

Fine amor, in continental narratives, tends to provide a positive experience of growth and integration. The fictional lovers are remarkable for the grace of their conduct and the sublimation of their sexual desires. Despite the French poets' tendency to ironize, *bone amor* typically guides its adepts toward perfect happiness and harmony with their world: "Il fallait embellir la vie, lui donner un rythme et des tonalités rares, mais aussi se soumettre à toutes les exigences propres à la rendre collectivement possible, agréable et utile."[10] This process is not primarily or centrally painful, but rather responds to sources of stress by dissolving them. Prowess serves love and quells rebellion, winning union and peace. Lovers engage primarily in self-discovery rather than in collective endeavors. In their high refinement, these works claim to initiate their audience into the "normes d'une manière parfaite d'aimer,"[11] and hermetic style expresses their restrictive impulse. The elevated rhetoric of the twelfth-century romances speaks only to "un auditoire initié" that can understand its ornaments and complexities of meaning: "Au 'trobar clus' répond un récit 'clos.'"[12]

Critics argue that these typical features of Old French romance work to validate the condition of the aristocracy and reconcile audiences to that condition. Eugene Vance analyzes the French romances, along with court ceremonies, as "a system of signs that would translate an ideology of supremacy into terms that would engage the acquiescence, if not the collaboration, of other sectors of society."[13] Reviewing much scholarship on the subject, R. Howard Bloch agrees that romances have "ideological effect" but argues that the effect is ultimately to undermine rather than to support the French aristocracy's desire for military power and class solidarity: through courtly literature, this class "came to embrace the very ideals which assured its own decline"—ideals of peace, individu-

---

10. Le Gentil, "La Légende de Tristan," p. 126; Le Gentil contrasts the Tristan story to this norm, which "s'accommode mal du tragique et de la violence, reste éminemment sociable" (p. 127).
11. Jauss, "Cinq modèles," p. 155.
12. Vance, "Combat érotique," pp. 553–54; see also Muscatine, *Chaucer and the French Tradition*, pp. 11–30.
13. "Signs of the City," p. 565; Boase's survey concludes similarly that "Courtly Love was a literary movement and an ideology with ethical implications" (*Courtly Love*, p. 128).

alism, and self-development guided by moral principle.[14] Even in their disagreements such analyses insist that Old French romances were not merely escapist entertainments; the pleasure of imagination these romances offered was locked to their ideological function in the world, as markers of class status and value or as agents of change in the aristocracy's gradual submission to monarchy.[15]

Insular poets draw unevenly on this literature. Thomas writes an orthodox "récit 'clos'" elevated far beyond simple discourse by its dense rhetorical ornamentation, its terms assigned special and unusual significance, and its doubled meaning in *conte* and *conjointure*. Yet he employs this exclusive style to resist the conventional idea that love is the key to reconciliation between desire and principle and between self and noble milieu. Thomas's lovers must accept their own fallibility and prepare themselves not for social integration but for death. Hue de Rotelande undermines his thoroughly conventional plot with a laughing, casual, often earthy commentary. *Ipomedon* simultaneously endorses and questions the principle that love and chivalry are mutually inspiring. *Amadas et Ydoine* and many Middle English romances tend to avoid high style and to reduce French heroism to something more accessible: in these works, love and chivalry are compatible with domesticity, economy, and good sense.

To some extent these departures from continental norms were invited by poetics. *Translatio studii*, proposing that literature continually reforms itself, encouraged poets to make each romance a new argument on the nature of love.[16] But the departures taken by the insular romances lead in one direction, suggesting that something more than poetic experimentation was guiding them. From Thomas's *Tristan* in the twelfth century through the Middle English romances of the fourteenth, insular romances of love gradually move from resisting courtly tradition's implausible claims about refinement and harmony to perceiving a stronger relationship between courtly literature and practice. The thread uniting all the

14. *Literature and Law*, pp. 215–38 (quote at pp. 223, 225); cf. Köhler, *Ideal und Wirklichkeit*, pp. 81–95.
15. Both functions are plausible and not incompatible; Georges Duby stresses the connection between rapid social change and the articulation of ideologies: "Ideological formations reveal themselves to the historian in periods of tumultuous change. In such grave times, the custodians of the word speak incessantly" (*Three Orders*, pp. 118–19; from *Trois ordres*, p. 151).
16. See below, n. 38. See also Freeman, "Translatio Studii"; Kelly, *Sens and Conjointure*; Vinaver, *Rise of Romance*, pp. 15–32.

insular poets is their preoccupation with the distance between received courtly ideals and perceived realities of individual and social behavior. Why did they recoil from courtly tradition, and how did they adapt the tradition to insular perceptions? This chapter and the following will attempt an answer in terms of literary and historical developments.

In historical terms French courtly literature was not tailored to English audiences. We have already surveyed the developments that produced in later twelfth-century England a relatively peaceful barony rather than a warring one, a society less rigidly divided by class than continental society, a nobility less threatened by the emergence of royal power, and not so concerned (or so able) to define itself as separate from humanity at large. The conflict between Henry II and his own heir, Henry the Younger, illustrates the differences between England and France in this period. The young Henry died at Martel in 1183, during his second rebellion against King Henry. While he lived he was the darling of northwest France's nobility, who scorned England as a dull place for gentleman farmers where tournaments were forbidden:

>   en Engletere . . .
>   . . . il n'i aveit nul bon sejor
>   Se ce n'esteit a vavasor
>   Ou a gent qui d'esrer n'ont cure,
>   Mais ki volt mettre peine & cure
>   En esrer ne en tornïer
>   Si le soleit l'om enveier
>   En Brutaingne ou en Normandie
>   Por hanter la chevalerie.[17]

There was no good to dwelling in England except for the gentle landholders and those who cared nothing for errantry; but whoever wanted to excel in errantry and tourneying used to be sent off to Brittany or Normandy in order to practice chivalry.

The younger Henry was an inspiration to the continental cult of chivalry, but also its victim. To maintain the extravagant largesse that followers such as Bertran de Born lauded as noble, Henry went so far as to make war on his father. In war as in his largesse he was encouraged by those who did not want to see Henry II's tight con-

---

17. *Guillaume le Maréchal*, ed. Meyer, lines 1527, 1537–44; on the *vavasor*, see Coss, "Social Terminology."

trol extended from England into France. Troubadours celebrated young Henry's aggression and his enrichment of small nobles, and greater nobles supported his frivolities and his rebellions insofar as they confounded Henry II's desire to impose "Angevin standards of law and order."[18]

Henry II, who was in closer contact with Anglo-Norman society than the rest of his family, was apparently uninterested in courtly fashion.[19] Walter Map's court commentary, *De Nugis Curialium*, contains only one story that might be associated with a lay and mentions nothing of courtly performances or literature in the daily life of the Anglo-Angevin court. Henry seems to have taken a political interest in Arthurian relics and history when they could justify his kingship or win prestige from the Capetian court.[20] But his zealous crusade to extend royal power over the barony could hardly endorse the *rois fainéants* of romance, Marc and Arthur, or approve the romances' images of knightly self-determination. He was the England to Henry the Younger's France, the more matured and settled kingdom confronting the rebellious turbulence of an adolescent continent.

From this historical perspective the French romances would have been only slightly more congenial to the insular barony than to Henry II. The crisis gripping the French aristocracy in the later twelfth century as Capetian and Angevin control began to tighten was past history in England, where royal power had been firmly entrenched since the Conquest. Insular audiences, aware that this particular struggle had long since been lost to the king, would have cast a somewhat jaundiced eye on the idealization of that struggle in Old French romances—whether they interpreted the romances as attempts to validate aristocratic claims to power or as attempts to reconcile aristocracy to a new ideal of peaceful order and self-

18. Warren, *Henry II*, pp. 577–93 (quote at p. 579); Moore, *Young King; Guillaume le Maréchal*, lines 2637–41, 5051–68.

19. Warren, *Henry II*, pp. 208, 360, 629; Bezzola, *Littérature courtoise*, part 3, pp. 13–20. But Schmolke-Hasselmann makes a case for the Angevin or Anglo-French appeal of Arthurian romances (legitimation of rule, glorification of a legendary king rivaling Charlemagne); see *Arthurische Versroman* and "Henry II Plantagenêt."

20. *De Nugis Curialium*, ed. James; the story of Sadius and Galo, 3.2, is reminiscent of the *Lai del Desiré* or Marie's *Lanval*. Like *Lanval*, *Desiré* is not Anglo-Norman in dialect. On Arthurian relics, see Fletcher, *Arthurian Material*, pp. 191–92; R. S. Loomis, "Tristram," p. 29. Political motives may have inspired some historical writing on Arthur, e.g., Rickard, *Britain in Medieval French Literature*, pp. 117–20; Zumthor, *Merlin le prophète*, pp. 49–114.

control. The Anglo-Norman barony, accustomed to royal systematization and to litigation as a means of protecting their families' interests, would have been disposed to dismiss romantic claims for the boundless rewards of individual responsibility and the ineffable joys of morally informed prowess. The skepticism of Thomas and Hue on these points is consonant with the peculiarities of England's situation in the twelfth century.

The early insular poets react to courtly conventions critically and even negatively, but later insular poets gradually develop alternate models of love and chivalry that are more in touch with romance's insular situation. Thus while Hue and Thomas find a troubling and preoccupying disjunction between romance ideals and their assessments of plausible reality, the later poets cheerfully assert a rapprochement of the plausible and the ideal. In part, the ideal was revised; in part, behavior was. What seemed a great gulf between literary model and contemporary practice in the twelfth century was no longer so great by the fourteenth.

In its presentation of ceremony, setting, and behavior, early courtly literature does not reflect but rather transforms noble practice. Courts in England, particularly, did not much resemble those of romance.[21] In this period tournaments were lethal melees for profit, outlawed where possible by church and state. Yet by the fourteenth century courtiers frequently composed love poems and engaged in such public formalizations of love as the parties of Leaf and Flower (Philippa of Lancaster seems to have been a Flower; Deschamps switched his allegiance from Flower to Leaf; Chaucer refused to take sides).[22] Likewise, the tournament changed in these centuries from "a graveyard of good fighters and a meeting-place for rebels" to a carefully controlled "round table" that was "made the occasion of much fantastic pageantry" drawn from romance.[23] Earlier romance poets invented glorious images that represented noble behavior in strictly imaginative terms, but later poets saw those images realized in actual practice—"a curious illustration of

21. See nn. 6 and 24, and Benton, "Clio and Venus"; Remy, "'Cours d'amour'"; Duby, *Medieval Marriage*, pp. 1–22, 83–110; Press, "Precocious Courtesy," pp. 269–70. The Angevin courts outside England were more sophisticated (Lejeune, "Rôle littéraire de la famille d'Aliénor").
22. Green, *Poets and Princepleasers*, pp. 109–11; *Oeuvres complètes de Eustache Deschamps*, ed. Queux de Saint-Hilaire, IV, 260, 262; Kittredge, "Chaucer"; *Works of Geoffrey Chaucer*, ed. Robinson, *The Legend of Good Women*, F 68–72 and G 61–78.
23. Barber, *Knight and Chivalry*, p. 291; Cline, "Tournaments," p. 206; McKisack, *Fourteenth Century*, p. 250.

Oscar Wilde's famous paradox that 'Literature always anticipates Life,' and that 'Life merely holds up the mirror to Art.'"[24]

The gap that the earlier poets, Thomas of Britain and Hue de Rotelande, perceive between literature and life is the greater for their double detachment from centers of courtly fashion: England's situation differed from those French ones that courtly romances addressed, and both Anglo-Norman poets seem to have written outside even the continentally oriented Angevin royal courts. Nor was there a strong lyric strain in twelfth-century Anglo-Norman poetry that might have supported the development of an insular courtly ethic. Because Thomas and Hue received continental romance stripped of some of its relevance, they turned its structures to new uses. They take the convention's very inappropriateness as raw material and build their poetic arguments in the space between the framework of received ideals and the substance of social conduct. Their approach to ideal and practice is necessarily indirect, since they can only represent aspiration and its failure through poetry's established verbal resources. Hue interrupts his letter-perfect pastiche of romance topoi in a voice that echoes the fabliaux; Thomas balances poetic traditions of *fine amor* against assessments of human nature that recall clerical writing. The poet works in verbal forms, but poetry's concerns are not thereby exclusively aesthetic. In questioning literary models of lovers' behavior, the insular poets simultaneously question the genre's relationship to personal and social experience in the world.

Thomas and Hue write in an Anglo-Norman of few dialectal peculiarities,[25] but Hue articulates his social detachment openly. Writing from a thoroughly provincial setting on the Welsh border, he

---

24. R. S. Loomis, "Imitations," p. 79. Benton is similarly moved to quotation when noting that "courts of love apparently did exist by the fifteenth century. As Valéry put it, *Imaginer, c'est se souvenir de ce qui va être*" ("Collaborative Approaches," p. 49).

25. Thomas, *Tristan*, ed. Wind; on dialect see pp. 17–23. A translation by A. T. Hatto is published in Gottfried von Strassburg, *Tristan*. Hue de Roteland, *Ipomedon*, ed. Holden; on dialect see pp. 25–35: "Nous tenons ici la preuve que, porté à son niveau le plus élevé, l'anglo-normand se distinguait à peine du français cultivé utilisé dans l'ouest de la France à la même époque" (p. 35).

Bouchard argues in "Nonexistence of Thomas" that the extant fragments of *Tristan*, except for MS C, represent a thirteenth-century poem not by Thomas; but Woledge and Short, "Manuscrits," reconfirm the twelfth-century date of MS Sneyd. Nor should Bouchard doubt Thomas's authorship of the extant fragments merely because later poets do not follow the fragments closely (see n. 38).

comments on local affairs, addresses *Protheselaus* to the local baron Gilbert FitzBaderon,[26] and in *Ipomedon* takes a tone of jocular familiarity with his Herefordshire neighbors. Hue's evident devotion to Credenhill and Herefordshire establishes his isolation from even the English royal court, to a degree consonant with his poetry's unconventionality. In contrast, many critics propose that Thomas's *Tristan* was written for the Angevin court, even specifically for Eleanor of Aquitaine. But it is unlikely that *Tristan* was written for this court.

Some critics find analogies between situations in *Tristan* and those of the royal family, and others argue that the Angevins' political use of Arthuriana makes their court a likely milieu for Thomas's romance. One passage in the extant fragments, Thomas's praise of London as a great trading port (D 1379–91), could be suitable flattery in a court work.[27] However, attributing the genesis of romances to specific political occasions is problematic,[28] and the proposed analogies are weak arguments indeed: Henry II would hardly have approved his equation to either a cuckolded king or an outcast lover, and Thomas's severity toward Isolt could not have been calculated to praise Eleanor's change of husbands.[29] Thomas's description of London suggests he wrote for an insular public but does not restrict his work to Henry's or Eleanor's patronage. A poet resident in England long enough to have acquired traits of Anglo-Norman dialect could obviously have visited London's harbor, heard Arthurian stories, and seen Henry's arms without being attached to the royal court.[30]

The situation of the royal family further undermines the patronage hypothesis. Although Henry II's political program involved

---

26. *Protheselaus*, ed. Kluckow, lines 12698–741. Hue's second romance will not be considered here since it is less concerned with love than *Ipomedon* and has no ME descendant.

27. E.g., R. S. Loomis, "Tristram"; Wind, edition, pp. 13, 16–17; Lejeune, "Rôle littéraire de la famille d'Aliénor," p. 334; Schirmer, *Patronat*, pp. 19–20. Tristan's coat of arms is not necessarily Henry's (Gay, "Heraldry").

28. For theories connecting political occasions to courtly romance, see Fourrier, *Courant réaliste*, pp. 22–27; Blumenfeld-Kosinski, "Narrative Genres"; Köhler, "Quelques observations," pp. 28–30. Such connections are widely rejected, however: see "Quelques observations," Discussion, pp. 31–36 for opinions of Jean Frappier, Aurelio Roncaglia, and Karl Ferdinand Werner.

29. See, e.g., Fourrier, *Courant réaliste*, pp. 43, 45, 54, 64, 95–98; a full argument against royal patronage of *Tristan* is Harris, "Cave of Lovers," pp. 483–500.

30. Many scholars argue for restraint when attributing patronage to Henry and especially to Eleanor: e.g., Brown, "Eleanor of Aquitaine," pp. 18–19; Richardson, "Letters and Charters"; Broich, *Patronat*, pp. 34–36; Haskins, "Henry II."

him closely in English affairs, his family's interests and many of his own were strongly continental. This royal family was not Anglo-Norman. At his coronation in 1154 Henry held not only the traditional Anglo-Norman lands of England and Normandy, which he claimed through his mother, but Anjou, Maine, and Touraine as well. Through his marriage to Eleanor he had acquired Aquitaine, Poitou, and Auvergne. To control these vast holdings the ruling family was obliged to expend far more energy and attention outside England than had the Anglo-Norman rulers. No longer part of a close-knit Anglo-Norman empire, England now had one of "five quite separate provincial administrations" in a "loose confederation of client states."[31] The ruling family was culturally and often physically separated from Anglo-Norman society. Henry II did spend nearly half his reign in England, but in the first twenty years of her marriage to him Eleanor paid just six visits to the island, only two of which were longer than a year (1157–58 and 1163–64).[32]

The Angevin family seems to have considered England less cultured and less interesting than its continental holdings. When Eleanor was imprisoned in England after her unsuccessful revolt against Henry in 1173, a sympathizer addressed her: "Plange cum rege Hierosolymitano [Ps. 120:5] et dic: Heu mihi! quia incolatus meus prolongatus est, habitavi cum gente ignota et inculta!" [Weep with the king of Jerusalem and say: Woe is me! for my sojourn is prolonged; I have lived among an obscure and uncultured people!].[33] It was under Angevin rule that Anglo-Norman speech and literature began to be ridiculed on the continent and that continental writers resident in England made a point of their noninsular origins.[34] The insular traits in Thomas's language, together with his work's substantial differences from Old French romance and the

---

31. Warren, *Henry II*, pp. 228, 230 (and "Federal Government," pp. 559–93); see also Intro., nn. 2–3.

32. Lejeune, "Rôle littéraire d'Aliénor," pp. 20–21, 50–57. Similarly, Richard patronized continental writers, tried his hand at Provençal poetry, and spent less than six months of his nine-year reign in England: see Appleby, *England Without Richard*; and Lejeune, "Rôle littéraire de la famille d'Aliénor," pp. 320–22.

33. Continuer of Richard le Poitevin, quoted by Labande, "Aliénor d'Aquitaine," pp. 213–14. On the Angevins' lesser interest in England, see Bossuard, "Institutions," pp. 35–36; and Poole, *Domesday Book*, p. 318. On England's isolation from the centers of love poetry, see Labande, "Aliénor d'Aquitaine," p. 208; Marc Bloch agrees that the social fashion of chivalry flourished only on the continent (*Société féodale*, II, 36–37).

34. Rickard, *Britain in Medieval French Literature*, pp. 163–205; see Intro., nn. 11–12.

Angevin family's continental orientation, argue that his *Tristan*'s origins lie outside the royal court.

Although we know much more about Henry II's court than about other centers of culture in England, it is clear that various cultural milieus did exist. Hereford was one center of learning,[35] and Hue de Rotelande writes a romance of great wit and elegance from this provincial setting. Sylvia Harris argues that Thomas composed *Tristan* "within the Earldom of Gloucester rather than at any of the courts of Henry II in England."[36] Although Thomas may have drawn some material from works composed for the Angevin court, and Hue may have owed his familiarity with romance motifs to the continental works introduced into England during Angevin rule, both poets write strongly against the grain of convention. Their extraordinary works establish a lineage of romances that measure literary models of love and chivalry against changing social practice in England.

Tristan: Love and Suffering

Thomas and Hue are so different in poetic temperament and approach that their romances sometimes read like opposites. Thomas argues, for example, that Tristan's desire to marry the second Isolt is shamefully false, even though the hero is far from his beloved, despairing of her love, and without any prospect of living near her again. For Thomas Tristan's desire exemplifies the inconstancy of humanity in general: "trop par aiment novelerie / Homes et femmes ensement" [both men and women love novelty too well] (Sn_1, 292–93).[37] Ipomedon similarly finds himself in a land far from his beloved, where a foreign queen gives him goodnight kisses and desires to do more. But when Ipomedon ignores her advances, Hue laughs that he himself, or better his friend Hugh de Hungrie

---

35. Russell, "Hereford and Arabic Science in England about 1175–1200," in *Twelfth Century Studies*, pp. 142–54 (rpt. from *Isis*, 18 [1932], 14–25); Orme, *Education in the West of England*, gives a general picture of well-developed educational systems in the region.

36. "Cave of Lovers," p. 498. Hunt argues in "Thomas' *Tristan*" that Thomas's alienation from conventional courtly literature may reflect opposition to Henry's quest for power and his relations with Eleanor.

37. The eight extant fragments of Thomas's *Tristan* are abbreviated as follows: Cambridge (C), first and second Sneyd (Sn_1, Sn_2), first and second Turin (T_1, T_2), first and second Strasburg (Str_1, Str_2), and Douce (D).

(5516–22), would have known how to handle that queen! While Thomas comments seriously and even ardently on the social and moral issues raised in his story, Hue treats those issues mockingly, sometimes seeming to parody Thomas's very text. Yet the two poets are alike in one respect: both are concerned above all with the distance separating principles of love and chivalry from less idealizing images of behavior.

In *Tristan* the disjunction between flawed and ideal behavior at first seems expressed in the opposition between the received, legendary *conte* and the artful, idealizing *conjointure*. Thomas speaks directly of the interacting forces of story and interpretation in two important passages on his compositional method. Analyzing the first of these passages, Douglas Kelly has shown that Thomas's guiding principle in handling inherited story material is to impose a logic determined by his understanding of the legend (D 835–40): the poet chooses among traditional episodes ("ne vol pas trop en uni dire") and gives the legend his own kind of coherence ("l'uni par mes vers").[38] Thomas declares his double allegiance to the legend and to his interpretation but does not discuss the nature of that interpretation. At the end of the poem, however, Thomas again addresses his audience and clarifies his intention in retelling this story:

> [Le] milz ai dit a mun poeir,
> [E dit ai] tute la verur,
> [Si cum] jo pramis al primur.
> E diz e vers i ai retrait:
> Pur essample issi ai fait
> Pur l'estorie embelir,
> Que as amanz deive plaisir.
> (Sn$_2$ 827–33)

I have spoken the best I could, and as I promised at the beginning, I have told the whole truth. I made a verse composition of it: this I did as an example, to embellish the story in such a way that it might please lovers.

Embellishing the story and directing it to lovers do not amount to "tute la verur" of *Tristan*: the legend has in addition its own pat-

---

38. "Lords, this story is very diversely told, and for this reason I have made it coherent in my verses, and tell as much of it as is right, and leave the rest aside. I do not wish to say too much in a unified work." In *"En uni dire"* Kelly discusses this passage in relation to numerous episodes altered or omitted by Thomas.

terns that have been truthfully exposed. Telling "the whole truth" is a separate compositional activity of the poet, his adherence to the received "estorie" as opposed to his imposition of the significance that makes the work exemplary. This opposition holds the central challenge to Thomas's art. His "essample" for lovers is not simply a negative one,[39] yet his material is only partly suited to the elaboration of a love that could be called *fine*—refined, intense, elevating.

The traditional Tristan episodes show no growth in the social or emotional lives of the characters that might have given Thomas's romance its dynamic. In many twelfth-century romances, love grows through the heroes' experience of noble life, as they discover ways to integrate their loving desire and their station in the world. The Tristan legend is not structured in this way: its love is permanent and unchanging; its events display unending conflict between love and society.[40]

To some extent Thomas can accommodate his material to conventional patterns. Certain episodes become knightly adventures; inexplicable marvels are replaced with psychological motivations; scenes of court society are decked out in fashionable details of luxury, gentle conversation, and chivalrous amusements.[41] Thomas's attention to richness of style, especially his endowment of particular words with profound significance and his long *question d'amor* appealing to the judgment of his audience of lovers, ally him to Provençal and Old French poets of love.[42] These modifications demonstrate Thomas's interest in conventional love poetry, but they are relatively superficial gestures that do not touch the fundamental difficulties of the story: Tristan and Isolt cannot be reconciled with

39. In arguing that *Tristan* is a "negative exemplum," Hunt takes *fine amor* to be a proscriptive term that cannot conceivably label a love encompassing jealousy, equality between lovers, physicality, or death. But there is strong evidence that the term *fine amor*, like the whole tradition of fictions of ideal love, was not proscriptive.

40. Thomas's work is closer to that of Marie de France in this respect (as in its geographic origin) than to courtly norms: on these see Frappier, "Conceptions courtoises," pp. 145–46; Hanning, "Social Significance." Frappier surveyed and analyzed work on the Tristan legend in "Structure et sens"; postdating Frappier's essay is Eisner's *Tristan Legend*. Beroul accepts the legend's permanent bond of love differently from Thomas, by limiting the duration of the potion's effect and yet continuing the lovers' clandestine relationship after their return to court from the forest.

41. E.g., Sn_1 377–84, 781–885; T_1 195–256; Str_1 25–68; D 797–805; see also Wind, "Eléments courtois."

42. T_1 71–183, D 1195–205; see also Frappier, "Structure et sens"; Wind, "Eléments courtois"; Lazar, *Amour courtois*, p. 166.

Marc; Tristan must marry in exile; the love of Tristan and Isolt must end in death. Repugnant behavior—subterfuge, murder, betrayal, faithlessness—suffuses this material. The lovers' behavior resists idealizing treatment, yet their legendary devotion to each other is striking in the sacrifices it induces, the power it holds over life and death, and the stretch of its influence over decades of the heroes' lives. This love invites poetic idealization. Thomas seeks to synthesize these two elements from the story, fallibility and superlative love, by forging a *fine amor* that recognizes and encompasses imperfection.

However Thomas may have dealt with his material in the lost portion of his text,[43] the extant fragments reveal a solution that he locates in the heroes' fatal love. The fragments begin with Marc's discovery of the sleeping lovers and Tristan's departure for exile, where he decides in a long monologue to marry Isolt of Brittany. Then, refusing to consummate the marriage, he spends secret hours in a cave where statues of Isolt and her maid Brangien make a shrine to love. To justify his love to his wife's brother Kaherdin, Tristan takes him secretly to England, where Brangien accepts Kaherdin as her lover. But the two men are slandered, leading Brangien to condemn Isolt, and Tristan suffers deeply before all are reconciled. In Brittany he receives a poisoned wound, sends for Queen Isolt to cure him, but dies when his vengeful wife lies that she has not come. Queen Isolt dies on his body.

In order to make these events more than just reversals and confusions afflicting a uniform devotion, Thomas first turns from the objective realm of events to the subjective, interior realm of thought and feeling. Here he builds a second plot line, parallel to the external structure of episodes. Then, through extended rhetorical analysis, he creates both a progressive development within the emotions of his lovers and a coherent connection between this inner world of significance and the external world of the inherited story material. Thomas becomes a rhetorician of the heart, building in his language a structure that links extremes of feeling and action.

His style is better suited to discussion and debate than to action and external description. He refuses the dramatic possibilities

---

43. I discuss only the surviving fragments of Thomas's text, in the conviction that reconstructions, including Bédier's, cannot be relied upon. See Gunnlaugsdóttir, *Tristán en el norte*; Cormier, "*Roman de Tristan*"; Shoaf, "Thomas' *Tristan*."

of allegorized interior monologue, of physical gesture that might heighten emotive appeal, even of the personification of *amor* into a force or a philosophy independent of the lovers' own sentiments.[44] The language of argument dominates the poem. Abstract terms, learned syntax, and syllogistic reasoning contribute to a general impression of detachment, of intellectual analysis. Multiple repetitions give almost pedantic emphasis to problems and conclusions. Thomas's *sententiae* are general observations, often clerical in origin, never proverbial in tone; his descriptions and explanations are technical, scrupulously ordered, and probing rather than visual or emotive.[45]

However rigorous Thomas's rhetoric may seem to modern eyes, it is eminently suited to the exposition of a love whose meaning lies in its own dialectic of pain against pleasure, asceticism against passion, jealous doubt against fanatical assurance. This is how the poet makes love the dramatic subject of the Tristan story—not through love's development or its testing, because it is born full-blown and unchangeable, but through an inner dynamic of perpetual conflict between joy and sorrow.

Tristan's decision to marry Isolt of Brittany (Sn_1, 1–648) illustrates how Thomas draws from his material a particular conception of *veraie amor*. The poet attributes a double motive to Tristan's act of marriage: his sexual need and his jealous doubt that Queen Isolt still loves him. The sexual pressure Tristan feels is reflected in the great variety of terms he applies to satisfaction—*fait, assembler, delit, naturel fait, ovre, faisance* (Sn_1, 165, 175, 515, 518, 523, 525)—but its source is his very love for Isolt as she is weakly mirrored in Isolt of Brittany, who shares her name and her beauty. These reflected traits and the maiden's desire for Tristan, echoing the queen's love, intensify unbearably Tristan's love-longing (Sn_1, 197–204, 28–34) and lead him to attempt to reduce his pain by marrying Queen Isolt's shadow. Thus his sexual motive for marrying is a function of his love for Queen Isolt; and only the marriage itself is "encontre

---

44. On conventional romance gestures (avoided by Thomas) see Lommatzsch, "Trauer und Schmerz"; on the widespread convention of allegorizing or personifying love see Frappier, "D'amors," and Muscatine, "Psychological Allegory."

45. I discuss Thomas's rhetorical procedure more fully in [Crane] Dannenbaum, "Doubling." On rhetorical devices see Bertolucci Pizzorusso, "Retorica"; see also the passages of general and abstract *sententiae*, Sn_1 755–64, D 1323–35. Thomas's love of analysis has been called "immodéré," "absurde," "pénible," "exagéré," "artificiel," "précieux" by Jodogne, "Amour de Tristan," p. 106; Lazar, *Amour courtois*, pp. 169–70; and Pauphilet, *Legs*, pp. 136–37.

amur" [against love], a kind of vengeance on his own love-suffering (Sn₁ 121-22, 160-64, 331-35). Sexual passion is necessary to love: "'ço est que plus alie / En amor amant e amie'" ["that is what most unites a lover and his friend in love"] (Sn₁ 539-40).

Tristan's longing for Queen Isolt would hardly result in marriage but for his second motive, his belief that the queen has forgotten him. For Thomas jealousy is as constant and integral to love as sexual passion. Both lovers experience jealous doubt in other situations (T₁ 6-24, 165; D 86-107, 1680-87), and Thomas argues that it is a natural feature of superlative love (T₁ 51-70). But the strong concentration of rhetorical devices in the argument preceding Tristan's marriage—*expolitio, adnominatio, correctio, sententia, dubitatio, ratiocinatio*[46]—suggests the particular difficulty that Thomas finds in this issue. Jealous doubt and the base marriage to which it leads challenge the ideal status of love in the poem. Nonetheless, that Thomas is able to motivate the marriage to Isolt of Brittany by the double intensity of Tristan's desire for and jealousy of Queen Isolt is a victory for the poet's concept of the legend: the marriage becomes not a forgetful abandonment of love, but a result of love's overwhelming power. In order to accomplish this both sexual need and jealous doubt must be accepted as features of *fine amor*, and Thomas accepts them wholeheartedly.

This incorporation of unattractive emotions into ideal love is consistent with other aspects of Thomas's treatment of the legend. Critics often stress that his approach throughout is rational, historicizing, and attentive to human behavior.[47] His artistic commitment to the rational and the plausible denies that love could be essentially inhuman—perfectly generous or completely fleshless. Indeed, the poet discovers in his lovers' behavior the truth that they (and all of us) are weak, changeable, pleasure-seeking; the creatures of "novelerie" and "errance" (Sn₁ 233-304, 345-52; T₁ 1-70).

Much in the legend is treated in terms of imperfection. Thomas acknowledges the conflicts between the heroes' love and social or moral obligations. Tristan's exile represents an isolation from society that both lovers experience: they must live far from their kin

---

46. Bertolucci Pizzorusso, "Retorica," pp. 41-42.
47. Fourrier, *Courant réaliste*, pp. 22-109; Vàrvaro, "Romanzi di Tristano," pp. 1063, 1068. Le Gentil writes of Thomas: "Réaliste et psychologue, il a le souci de rester en contact avec la vie et de scruter les consciences": ("Légende de Tristan," p. 128); Frappier similarly argues that Thomas seeks to make *raison* "signifier comme le verbe de la *fine amor*" ("'Raison,'" p. 176).

and in conflict with their spouses (D 86–92, 102–3, 1124–32). They recognize the legal injustices their spouses endure on their account, Marc by his wife's adultery and Isolt of Brittany by her husband's failure to consummate their marriage (Sn₁ 165–70, 413–16, 425–28). At times this recognition is colored with heartfelt guilt.[48] Under the great stress of these felt wrongs, the lovers sometimes regret their love or feel anger and despair over it (Sn₁ 39–46, 886–88; T₁ 5–32; D 99–101, 588–90, 604–14).

It can be argued that the tensions between love's demands and all others are merely stages in dialectic processes reemphasizing the supremacy of love.[49] Nonetheless, in Thomas's inner psychological drama, the lovers' moments of miserable guilt, their fits of anger, their jealousies, doubts, and ill-directed passions challenge ideal love with the ordinary vagaries of living souls. In response Thomas makes a radical attempt to reconcile ideal love with human frailty.[50] The bridge he builds between them is one of penance, suffering, and death, a bridge perfectly suited to his own sober morality and to the demands of the story material.

Many stories of love have tragic circumstances, but few celebrate a love that itself contains and embraces death. Thomas incorporates this element of the Tristan legend into his version of *fine amor* by extending the idea of ultimate fatality to a corollary idea of temporal suffering in love. A love both painful and fatal is better suited to conveying Thomas's interest in problematic weakness than the *fine amor* of most courtly romances, which tends to remain an optimistic, delicate conception of harmonious existence, "l'affirmation de la volonté, du désir de vivre en beauté; . . . l'*acquiescement de l'âme au bonheur*."[51] Even the Norman *Tristran* of Beroul denies that

---

48. Isolt accepts Brangien's accusation that in continuing to love Tristan after her judicial oath she is "Feimentie e parjuree" [oath-breaking and perjured] (D 233–39, 305–6). Tristan fears that if he fails to consummate his marriage, his fault will be moral as well as social: "'De ses parenz, des altres tuiz / Haïz e huniz en sereie, / E envers Deu me mesfreie'" ["I would be hated and shamed by her relatives and all others and would do wrong before God"] (Sn₁ 500–502, cf. 525–34).

49. See Frappier, "Structure et sens," pp. 451–54; but cf. Le Gentil, "Mariage de Tristan"; Ferrante, *Love and Honor*.

50. That is, Thomas does not simply stand back and let the legend play havoc with *fine amor*, the accusation of Cazenave, *Philtre*, p. 161; and Bédier, ed., *Tristan par Thomas*, II, 50–52, 318. Nor does he show a lack of concern for morality, as Payen accuses ("Lancelot contre Tristan," esp. p. 622). For Thomas's moral observations on narrative events, see Sn₁ 233–304, 345–52, 753–80; D 1323–35; also Vitz, "Desire," pp. 225–34.

51. Lot-Borodine, *Amour profane*, p. 31 (her italics).

the lovers suffer; their love easily erases the pain of exile and hardship:

> Aspre vie meinent et dure;
> Tant s'entraiment de bone amor,
> L'un por l'autre ne sent dolor.[52]

They lead a hard and bitter life, but they love together with such a true love that each feels no pain because of the other.

In contrast Thomas's *Tristan* is a deeply serious, even sorrowful presentation of love's cruelties as well as its joys. Pain is a mortal condition. As such it expresses for Thomas both the humanity of its victims and their desire to transcend themselves through suffering.

The contexts of the terms for love in *Tristan*, "grant amur," "ferm amur," "amur fine e veraie," "fine amur" (D 721, 1152, 1219, 1679), all picture a love that can tolerate great sorrow or pain. In contrast Tristan's act of marriage opposes "fin'amur" (Sn_1 319, 329), because it is an attempt to escape or resist love's pains (Sn_1 331–35). When Isolt acts as a "veire amie" (D 756, Sn_2 807) she accepts particularly great sacrifices, self-mortification and death. Pain is an inextricable part of the love experience,[53] and as the romance progresses pain becomes more important to love than pleasure.

A vast vocabulary of affliction records this development in the love affair: *tristur, peine, angoisse, travail, ahan, dolor, turment, ennui, pesance, destreit, mesaise, grevance*. Adjectives and verbs translate quiet, undemonstrative affliction: *chaitif, pensif, deshaité, soi doloir, souffrir, pleurer, plaindre, suspirer*.[54] This vocabulary suggests emotional states that are not pathetic or dramatic but private and almost devotional: they are states of love's refinement. Through this process Thomas reconciles the truth of his ideal to the fact of human

---

52. *Tristran*, ed. Ewert, lines 1364–66, further emphasized at lines 1649–55, 1783–87.

53. More than half the lines ending in *dolor* are coupled with lines ending in *amor*, a connection sustained through the poem's final couplet. When Kaherdin admonishes Isolt "'Ore vus membre des granz amurs / E des peines e des dolurs / Qu'entre vus dous avez suffert'" ["Now remember the great love and the troubles and sorrows that the two of you have suffered together"] (D 1465–67), the verb of suffering applies equally to love and to pains and sorrows. Isolt similarly animates all the joys and sorrows of love with the single verb *plaindre* (Sn_2 794–97).

54. Approximate equivalents for these terms are: sadness, suffering, anguish, toil, travail, pain, torment, trouble, affliction, difficulty, distress, grief; unhappy, pensive, disheartened; to lament, suffer, weep, complain, sigh. This vocabulary is collected and discussed by Johnson, "*Dolor*," pp. 546–54; see also Lavis, *Affectivité*.

weakness. Suffering becomes an ascetic discipline, the reverse face of love's pleasure. For the fault of his marriage, Tristan imposes upon himself the "penitance" of chaste contact with his wife, hoping that its double pain will permit Queen Isolt to pardon him (Sn$_1$ 570–88). When she comes to understand his state, Isolt "Partir volt a la penitance" [wishes to share the penance] (D 746): she foregoes many pleasures and wears an ascetic's leather corselet beneath her clothes (D 741–71). The religious terminology, the corselet, the physical torment on which the actions turn, and the greater spiritual happiness to which the lovers aspire associate their discipline of suffering to religious purification.[55] The devotional quality of the lovers' penances is further suggested by the strict secrecy with which they are performed. Through these penances Thomas unfolds his comprehensive *fine amor* into its exalting and debasing movements, and shows these movements achieving a higher plane of balance. "Partir volt" is repeated three times in presenting Isolt's action (D 746, 748, 751): the lovers' secret sharing of penance forms a bond of communication between them during their long separations. At this stage their love, by mortifying its weaknesses, begins to resist the physical in anticipation of its final state. Temporal suffering unites human nature to ideal love, but death is the form the fully realized union takes.

In Thomas's version of the Tristan story love and death are inextricable because Tristan and Isolt are unable to exist outside their relationship. Whether as cause or only by metonymy, the love drink gives form to their fatal interdependence as well as their devotion: "'El beivre fud la nostre mort, . . . / A nostre mort l'avum beü'" ["Our death was in that drink, . . . to our death we drank it"] (D 1223, 1226).[56] Waiting for Isolt, Tristan complains that without her he cannot survive and that he continues to live only in hope of her arrival (D 1544–53). Just as waiting for her keeps him alive, believing she will not come kills him: "'Quant a moi ne volez venir, / Pur vostre amur m'estuet murrir'" ["Since you do not wish to come to me, I must die for love of you"] (D 1761–62). Isolt's knowledge of healing arts is only an external manifestation of her vital role in

---

55. The Hall of Statues provides an earlier context for Tristan's demonstrations of devotion (perhaps modeled on devotions at a saint's shrine) and for his willing submission to the pain of love (see Ferrante, *Love and Honor*, pp. 82–83).

56. See also D 1219–26, 1440; T$_1$ 122; Sn$_2$ 805; Bédier, ed., I, 258 (Gottfried quotes two lines probably from Thomas, "Isolt ma drue, Isolt m'amie, / En vus ma mort, en vus ma vie").

love; Tristan's physical ailment is subsumed within his spiritual need for her presence.

How perfect a resolution does this love reach in death, since even their great suffering, their intense passion, and their awe-inspiring devotion cannot keep the lovers from dying, indeed from dying through their own incapacity? The two sails of the legend, one black and one white, symbolize for Thomas not so much the two possible answers of Queen Isolt as the double qualities of doubt and faith in Tristan's love that allow him to believe his wife's lie. There is throughout the fragments a sense of strain, of a great gap to be bridged between the lovers' humanity and their impulse toward perfect love. One example is the ironic episode of Tristan's death wound, in which Tristan le Nain asks the aid of "Tristran l'Amerus" (D 927) in rescuing his *bele amie* from seven giants. When Tristan accepts the adventure but asks for a delay in setting forth, Tristan le Nain denies that so hesitant a reply could come from the real Tristan: "'Jo sai que, si Tristran fuissét, / La dolur qu'ai sentissét'" ["I know that if you were Tristan, you would feel my suffering"] (D 979–80). Not only is pain the essential mark of love, but Tristan, already legendary in stature, is the one lover who above all others lives that truth. Tristan's apparent insensitivity to sorrow therefore negates his very identity, as he himself realizes: "'Par grant reisun mustré l'avez / Que jo dei aler ove vus, / Quant jo sui Tristran le Amerus'" ["You have shown most reasonably that I must go with you, since I am Tristan the Amorous"] (D 1012–14).[57]

As Tristan loses or only uneasily keeps contact with his epithet "l'Amerus," Thomas strains to hold the legend and his ideal of love together. Often his voice is his only recourse and only his words seem to argue, analyze, or gloss great love and natural frailty into harmony. The poet's own struggle is one source of the romance's power: "Cette insécurité latente, loin de nuire au texte de Thomas, l'enrichit au contraire de résonances humaines plus vraies et plus profondes."[58] Thomas does not find transcendence in the lovers'

---

57. Tristan's own myth similarly outstrips his present self in the *Folie Tristan d'Oxford* (ed. Hoepffner), where the hero's extended narration of his past fails to identify him. In this *lai*, even when Tristan is alone with Isolt and desires genuinely to achieve recognition through his stories, she refuses to believe that he is "Tristran l'Amerus" (712) until he dispenses with the past and uses only his voice and body to convince her. See the fine discussion of Haidu, "*Folie Tristan.*"

58. Le Gentil, "Interpretation," p. 179; see also Le Gentil, "Epilogue." Thomas's commitment to a love that is obviously troubled seems to inform the AN *Donnei des amants* (ca. 1180), ed. Paris. In this dialogue two lovers compare each other to Tristan

story, but he insists on its "verur" and "confort" (Sn₂ 828, 836). If the lovers' death is not the apotheosis of perfect love, it does mark the point at which fallible romantic love finds its absolute achievement. Tristan and Isolt are by this episode so entirely focused on each other, so perfectly free of impulses other than toward union in love, that the element of frail mortality in their love frees them from mortality itself.

During the last hours of their separation, Tristan's anguish is such that "A poi que del desir ne muert" [he nearly dies of his desire] (D 1738), echoing the anguish of Isolt who "A poi ne muert de sun desir" (D 1728). Their communion in suffering now expands to a final communion in death, as both die by choice, unable to tolerate their isolation from each other.[59] Isolt's last words declare that her death is an act of *veraie amor*—"'jo frai cum veraie amie: / Pur vos voil murir ensement'" ["I will behave like a true lover: I want to die likewise for you"] (Sn₂ 807–8). Their final embrace unites physical love to death:

> Embrace le, si s'estent,
> Baise la buche e la face
> E molt estreit a li l'enbrace,
> Cors a cors, buche a buche estent,
> Sun espirit a itant rent,
> E murt dejuste lui issi.
> (Sn₂ 809–14)

She embraces him and stretches herself out, kisses his mouth and face and draws him tightly to her, body to body, mouth to mouth she lies; now she gives up her soul and dies thus next to him.

The sober and even clinical precision of these verses gives great authenticity to a love so intense that Isolt seems physically to draw Tristan's death into herself.

That Thomas considers this version of *fine amor* to be a valid ideal is less clear in the death of the lovers, which is both attractive and frightening, than in the poet's final address to his audience, "As

---

and Isolt, "'Ke deit a essample estre treit'" ["who should be taken as an example"] (658, also 430). Yet the example they offer is of suffering and risk so great that the dialogue's lovers are not confident of living up to it. Is the lady willing to risk all for love (404–20)? Is her friend as long-suffering as Tristan, or false like Eneas (663–84)?

59. When Isolt arrives only moments after Tristan's death, she laments that he died because she could not arrive in time, "a tens" (D 1815; Sn₂ 790, 802, 817). But in fact Tristan died not from the delay but by conscious choice (D 1761–62).

pensis e as amerus, / As emvius, as desirus, / As enveisiez e as purvers" (Sn₂ 822–24): he writes for those who suffer, those who live in desire of love without possession, and those who wrongly seek only pleasure.[60] The very variety of lovers addressed, including those who sin against love, completes Thomas's demonstration that "amur fine e veraie" (D 1219) can comprehend human weaknesses and yet transcend them. Thomas insists in his closing address that his heroes are a consolation even for deeply flawed lovers and for those imprisoned in reality who will never achieve so perfect a union as Tristan and Isolt:

> Aveir em poissent grant confort,
> Encuntre change, encontre tort,
> Encuntre paine, encuntre dolur,
> Encuntre tuiz engins d'amur!
> (Sn₂ 836–39)

From this they may take great comfort against changeability, against error, against trouble, against sorrow, against all the vagaries of love!

These changes, wrongs, pains, and vagaries resonate in significance from legend to text to listeners. Retrospectively, these terms recall the external vagaries of fate that opposed the happiness of Tristan and Isolt in legend. With regard to Thomas's interpretation of the legend these terms retrace the lovers' own wrongs that have struggled against love's merits and the pains that have accomplished love's penitential purification. In addition, as Thomas directs these terms prospectively to his listeners' experience, their meaning extends to all sorrows as they oppose lovers' happiness in general. But in this final passage, they are no longer active forces; their power is checked in the face of, "encuntre," love's power to comprehend them. Thomas's *fine amor* now reaches its fullest expression, as it incorporates not simply joy but life's central difficulties—suffering, wrongdoing, mortality. In confronting these forces and subsuming them, the love of Tristan and Isolt reaches the heights of power: it is proof against the very changes, wrongs, pains, and vagaries that it has enclosed.

60. These interpretations of *enveisiez* and *purvers* are worked out by Baumgartner and Wagner, "'Enveisiez.'" Even if the passage is interpreted more strictly, the types enumerated are diverse: in A. T. Hatto's translation, "the sad and the amorous, the jealous and the desirous, the gay and the distraught, and all who will hear these lines" (p. 353).

Ipomedon: Love and Pleasure

While Thomas of Britain commits his poetic energies to bridging the gap between images of ideal love and earthly imperfection, Hue de Rotelande observes the same chasm like a casual sightseer and finds humor in the distance separating the realm of romance from his own Herefordshire. His irreverent, even parodic approach in *Ipomedon* differs from Thomas's serious and committed stance, but like Thomas, Hue contemplates the disparity between certain ideal conceptions of romance and his authorial conviction of human folly. Hue refuses until the last moment to synthesize these contradictory movements, juxtaposing romance conventions to an antagonistic vision of experience throughout his elaborate plot.

The date of Hue's *Ipomedon* accounts in part for its perspective on romance. Thomas's *Tristan*, difficult to date but perhaps quite early (ca. 1160), has the exploratory feel of a generative work. Hue's references to contemporary events place the composition of *Ipomedon* in the 1180s, more than two decades after *Tristan*, by which time the genre had accrued a stock of familiar motifs.[61] Some of Hue's episodes appear to be drawn from the romances of antiquity—*Thèbes*, *Troie*, and *Enéas*—but in part through intermediary romances such as *Partenopeus de Blois*. The three-day tournament could be imitated from *Cligès* but also occurs in other romances; Ipomedon's skill at hunting and his disguise as a fool recall *Tristan* and the two *Folies Tristan*.[62] Like his contemporaries, Hue uses traditional material in self-consciously new ways and takes pains to distinguish his production from the corpus of already successful works. Yet Hue is unique to his century in his profoundly ironic detachment from the very traditions he adopts.

Generally in continental romances of the twelfth century ironic perspectives and distancing laughter coexist with serious treatments of ideals of love and chivalry. Literary historians have traced

---

61. Legge dates *Tristan* in the 1150s (*Anglo-Norman Literature*, p. 49), disputing Fourrier's relatively late dating of 1172–74; the 1150s are also favored by Lejeune ("Rôle littéraire d'Aliénor," pp. 33–35) and by Wind (edition, pp. 14–17). Among the information leading Holden (edition, pp. 7–11) to date *Ipomedon* in the early 1180s are the siege of Rouen (1174), lines 5348–58; and the address to Gilbert Fitz-Baderon (died by 1191) in *Protheselaus*, 12699–741.

62. On *Ipomedon* and romances of antiquity, see Fisher, *Narrative Art*, pp. 69, 72, 76; Carter, "Ipomedon," pp. 239–63; Stengel, [Corrections], pp. 9–10; Kluckow, ed., *Protheselaus*, pp. 19–29; Kölbing, ed., *Hue de Rotelande's Ipomedon in drei englischen Bearbeitungen*, pp. xvi–xxx; Gay, "Ipomédon"; L. H. Loomis, *Mediaeval Romance*, pp. 226–29.

romance's ironic effects from their beginnings in rhetorical theory to their parodic inversion and denial of the genre in the thirteenth century.[63] Hue de Rotelande collapses this history by juxtaposing serious treatment and parodic inversion well before the turn of the century. Standing at the border of the genre's territory, Hue can endorse romance's power even as he questions its conventional assumptions.

Ipomedon's plot is remarkable for its familiar, even clichéd quality. Ipomedon, prince of Apulia, is attracted to the court of the Duchess of Calabria by its reputation for elegance and by the duchess's reputation for pride: her vow to marry only the best knight in the world has won her the nickname of "la Fière" (the Proud). During three years of anonymous service in Calabria, Ipomedon begins to fall in love with la Fière, but perceiving this, the lady communicates her displeasure that Ipomedon shows no interest at all in chivalric exploits. Ipomedon departs immediately, though both young people are now deeply in love. On a brief return home, he learns that he has a lost brother who will recognize a ring given to him by his mother. Ipomedon travels widely winning prizes at tournaments until he hears that la Fière, at the insistence of her barons, will take as husband the victor of a three-day tournament. In order to attend the tournament in secrecy, Ipomedon attaches himself to the court of Meleager of Sicily in the role of "dru la reïne" (3073), a knight who attends the queen and may kiss her once in the morning and once at night. Under the further cover of hunting parties, Ipomedon attends the tournament each day in different armor (white, red, and black) and each day is victorious. He lets la Fière know who he is through her squire each day but always departs without seeing her.

Rather than accepting the marriage he has won, Ipomedon chooses to pursue his life of chivalry, even rejecting his father's crown and the hand of a king's daughter won by his prowess. Finally, disguised as a fool from Meleager's court, he returns to Calabria to challenge la Fière's monstrous suitor Leonin d'Inde Majeur. He defeats Leonin and prepares to depart secretly again, now disguised as Leonin himself, but Meleager's nephew Capaneus attacks the presumed villain. The two fight until Capaneus recog-

---

63. E.g., Muscatine, *Chaucer and the French Tradition*; Haidu, *Aesthetic Distance* and "Humor"; Ménard, *Rire et le sourire*; D. H. Green, *Irony*. On *Ipomedon*'s precocity, see Legge, *Anglo-Norman Literature*, p. 85; Ménard, *Rire et le sourire*, pp. 352, 486.

nizes Ipomedon's ring. Ipomedon then reveals the history of his disguises to his new-found brother and to la Fière, and the lovers are married.

The assemblage of familiar motifs in *Ipomedon* has led critics to accuse Hue of writing a blindly derivative work, "sporadic" and "manufactured" rather than invented, "a patchwork of incidents and themes borrowed from or suggested by contemporary romance."[64] Readers who take the plot as the only subject of Hue's attention typically find the work "assez médiocre dans son ensemble" or even pointless and confusing. Of Ipomedon's departure after the tournament, Sarah Barrow protests that "the reader finds the hero's postponement of well-earned happiness almost as arbitrary as it seems to the less enlightened court of Meleager."[65]

Other readers, noting the frequent passages in which Hue seems not so much to imitate contemporary romances as to mock them, treat *Ipomedon* as a "roman burlesque" or a parody.[66] There are certainly some wonderful passages of parody in the work, for example in la Fière's stumbling revelation of her lover's identity, Hue's falsified claims to truth, and his obscene epilogue bidding farewell to all lovers. But these parodic moments do not fully account for the work as a whole. They are part of a wider response to romance made up not only of Hue's witty commentary, parodies, and obscenities but of the very conventionality of the plot itself. Hue, like Thomas, builds his romance on the dual levels of story and interpretation, but Hue provides two conflicting interpretations for his material. The plot, easily grasped and even banal, is the occasion for both a sophisticated conventional treatment and a critical reassessment of romance ideals.

This second perspective in *Ipomedon* reaches us primarily through the voice of the narrator, indistinguishable from that of the poet.[67] The narrating voice develops the story in traditional terms

---

64. Carter, "Ipomedon," p. 270; Wilson, *Early Middle English Literature*, p. 79.
65. J. H. Watkins in *Dictionnaire*, ed. Grente, p. 381; Barrow, *Medieval Society Romances*, p. 77.
66. Holden, edition, pp. 54–55 and line 7270 n.; Legge, *Anglo-Norman Literature*, pp. 85, 90; Ménard points out parodic passages but avoids calling the entire work a parody (*Rire et le sourire*, pp. 513–21).
67. The poet names himself at lines 33, 7270, 10552–53, and 10561. His poetic personality (laughing, sensual, etc.) may constitute a persona, but as is the case for Thomas, the poet/persona distinction is not as productive in treating his work as the assumption that the poet and audience considered the two functions inseparable: see Rowland, "Pronuntiatio."

and generates another poetic world, located in Hue's version of Herefordshire, which encloses and diminishes Ipomedon's world even as we are drawn into it.

The prologue first signals that Hue may be standing back from his material. Here the standard justification for writing poetry, that wisdom should not be hidden, is arrogantly inflated and concluded by an expansive sixteen-line passage on the importance of speaking briefly (33–48). Inflation also marks the poem's close, as Hue claims that the story he has just told is the source of the *Roman de Thèbes* (10541–50).[68] Hue takes on and puts off the mantle of authorial dignity more ostentatiously when he interrupts the narrative to declare that he always tells the truth—or almost always—or at least he is no worse a liar than Walter Map (7175–88). Because source-citing and assertions of truth establish validity in romance,[69] the poet's mockery of these practices shakes the foundations of his work.

The cheerful wit of this "lustiges Weltkind"[70] enlivens the narration of events and at the same time takes us out of the course of events and into the world of Herefordshire, Credenhill, and their contemporary incidents and personalities. Hue's glib fabulation, mockery, and profane sensuality are rooted in his provincial milieu, where Hereford locals sit around the market stalls all day hearing tall tales.[71] Hue's style often takes proverbial or colloquial turns that suit his informal rapport with story and audience. On la Fière's anxiety over the baronial demand that she marry, Hue comments,

> Ki chaut? Cument k'il seit alé,
> Ffemes n'unt pas tut ublïe
> De purveer lur point avant;
> Je qui k'el se purverrat tant
> K'el suffrerat la pudre as oilz
> E as jofnes e as plus veulz;
> Nel ferat pas del tut endart,
> K'el en avra mut bien sa part.

---

68. The prologue claims a Latin source in the same vein (25–39).
69. Von Ertzdorff, "Wahrheit." The same subtle devaluation of truth underlies Hue's "une fable orriez vus, / E cest est tut veir a estrus" [you would listen to a fabulous tale, and this one is entirely absolutely true] (5553–54). To Hue's procedure contrast Benoît de Sainte-Maure, *Troie*, ed. Constans, lines 1–41; *Thèbes*, ed. Constans, lines 1–12.
70. Kölbing and Koschwitz, eds., *Hue de Rotelande's Ipomedon*, p. vi.
71. See lines 5348–58, 5516–22, 7175–88, 8656–66, and 10551–80. Of Hue's technique Ménard observes: "Il faut attendre le XIIIᵉ siècle pour retrouver dans le roman courtois des questions plaisamment posées aux auditeurs, des allusions et des remarques souriantes" (*Rire et le sourire*, p. 486).

> L'un dit suvent en reprover,
> Ke teus quide autrë engingner
> Est engignez al chef de tur,
> De ren si suvent cum d'amur.
> (2139–50)

So what? Whatever may happen, women haven't entirely forgotten how to take care of their own interests; I think she'll manage so well that she'll blow dust in the eyes of both young and old. Nor will she do it without any punishment, for she will certainly have her part. They say in the proverb that the one who thinks to trick another is tricked in the end; in nothing so often as in love.

The nonchalant question, the generalization on women's wiles, the personal prediction, and the teasing *sententia* that at once summarizes la Fière's strategy and foreshadows Ipomedon's disguises typify Hue's manner of turning from story to audience and casually holding himself at a distance from his characters.

Although Hue sometimes excuses himself to women, he generally speaks of them almost as of another species and declares repeatedly that love is folly.[72] His answer to the love suffering of his characters is a resolutely cheerful, rather impersonal eroticism reminiscent of clerical humor or of the fabliaux. He enjoys the spectacle of men confused and agitated by desire (e.g., 2264–98); his female characters find Ipomedon irresistible. When Ismene creeps to Ipomedon's bed to beg his hand in marriage, Hue protests the hero's restraint:

> Ismeine l'ad regardé mut,
> Dehez ait il, se il ne la fut!
> Nu l'ait, a deu fei! ke il ne volt
> Pur la Fiere, dunt il se dolt.
> (8647–50)

Ismene kept looking at him: damn him if he doesn't fuck her! Or rather not damned, by God, for he didn't want to on account of la Fière, for whom he grieves.

As in many other passages, Hue's blunt expression of amoral sensuality coexists with his tolerant explanation of Ipomedon's principled self-denial.

Parodic episodes also juxtapose what we expect of romance with

---

72. Hue depicts women's cleverness or determination at 1911–24, 2139–46, 2576–82, 5956–60, 6937–40, 8793–804; women's changeability at 830–33, 5447–56, 8656–66. He excuses his attitude at 1916, 5961–66, 8802–4; connects love and folly at 763–68, 801–4, 4312–14, 9095–110, 9123–36.

another, reductive and humorous, approach. Ipomedon's disguise as a fool echoes Tristan's, but no secret suffering, no metaphoric identification of lover and outcast, no compelling need to reach the beloved enrich the disguise: Ipomedon simply keeps his own counsel and mocks the ignorance of all others. His role as the queen's *dru* similarly diminishes its prototypes, the hidden adulterous relationships of Tristan and Lancelot. These and other imitations locate the story of Ipomedon among the romances while also suggesting that its apparent orthodoxy conceals other possibilities.[73]

From one perspective *Ipomedon* is a handsome treatment of romance's most common subject, the relationship between love and chivalry—or more accurately, the young lovers' growing understanding of what they desire from both emotional experience and public standing in their courtly society.[74] At first both Ipomedon and la Fière respond to ideal standards of love and chivalry rather crudely, by swallowing them whole or revolting against them, but eventually the lovers find expressions for their desire that are consonant with the rigid codes of their noble world.

The powerful voice of court society establishes standards of merit in *Ipomedon*: men should engage in chivalry to be worthy of love, and women should accord their love only to the chivalrous. La Fière subscribes to these standards absolutely in making her proud vow, which even the court finds excessive (133–38), and in rebuking her anonymous *valet* for his lack of prowess (866–918). Refusing to give up the vow because "'Idunc s'en gabereient tuz; . . . A tuz dis serreie hunie'" ["then everyone would joke about it; I would be shamed forever"] (2480, 2484), she makes a second, contradictory vow in secret to marry none but the "vadlet estrange" (1524,

---

73. On *Ipomedon*'s reductive imitations of romance see Ménard, *Rire et le sourire*, pp. 348–49, 742–45; Holden, edition, pp. 46–57. Another romance from the twelfth century was probably Anglo-Norman, a *Lancelot* that survives only through Ulrich von Zatzikhoven's *Lanzelet*. It too seems distanced from conventions of love and chivalry: the young Lanzelet's paramour is a lady who has unsuccessfully tempted several other knights, and she is only the first of four lovers the hero takes in succession. Certain episodes mock courtiers' weaknesses, and the plot as a whole is reminiscent of *Ipomedon*'s in its assemblage of familiar motifs and its ironic potential. One episode resembles the *Lai du Cor*, which survives in an insular manuscript but cannot be definitely classified as Anglo-Norman (Bell, "*Lai du Cor*").

74. Haidu writes in *Aesthetic Distance*: "The essential conflict is not between the individual and the world, but in what the individual himself desires" (p. 106). Muscatine makes the same point in *Chaucer and the French Tradition*, p. 13. Hanning, *Individual in Twelfth-Century Romance*, pp. 123–35, provides a sensitive reading of *Ipomedon* in these terms, stressing the challenge that society's ideal codes make to individuality: "As all men are judged by the same external touchstone, private identity is in effect lost" (p. 132).

1555–58). Both vows are exaggerated reactions to the code of love and prowess, the first as completely accepting as the second is rebellious. But subsequently, by manipulating her barons and providing Ipomedon with opportunities to prove himself, she encourages the events that bring her two vows into harmony, allowing her to sustain both her secret love and (after some confusion) her public dignity.

Ipomedon, in response to la Fière, confronts courtiers' standards of judgment for knights. Stricken with self-reproach for not having shown his prowess (1173–82), the hero withdraws from himself into disguises until his inner conviction of merit matches his record of chivalric successes. But he also asserts his superiority by reproaching noble society even as he fulfills its rigid code. The court's censure, as befits a society of manners, always takes the form of ridicule: its weapons are *ris, suzris, gabs*; words spoken *en deduit, par eschar, en ramposnant*.[75] Ipomedon chooses a response appropriate to this society's own tactic of censure through mockery. Although he accepts the justice of la Fière's rebuke (1154–55), his life of chivalry turns the courtiers' ridicule—and la Fière's—back upon themselves. As the queen's *dru* who seems too foppish to risk his skin but in fact wins the three-day tournament, and as the laughable fool-knight who turns out to be the only courtier willing to fight Leonin for la Fière, the hero continually demonstrates the superficiality of society's judgment: "Teus tent suvent pur fol autrui / Ke asez est plus fol de lui" [often one who holds another foolish is far more foolish himself] (7923–24).[76]

Although *Ipomedon* can be read as a conventional story of two lovers asserting their personal worth while complying with the standards of court society, every turn in this apparently orthodox plot is subverted by misappropriation of stock patterns, parody, and ironic commentary. A rich conventional picture of the young lovers' emotions and symptoms establishes their relationship,[77] but

---

75. Laughs, smiles, jokes; speaking humorously, mockingly, insultingly: e.g., 490, 528, 1149–51, 3123–30, 3281–83, 3540–41, 4320; see Ménard, *Rire et le sourire*, pp. 420–54.

76. Similar conclusions are drawn from Ipomedon's encounters at 5485–86 ("Cil s'en rient e il dit veir / Mes nul nel sout aparceveir" [they laughed at it and he spoke truly, but none could perceive it]) and 3067–72.

77. E.g., 807–10, 939–1172, 5231–58, 10421–36. Many poets treat young love with some irony (see Frappier, "Conceptions courtoises," p. 150; Susskind, "Love and Laughter," p. 654), but the kind of detachment Hue establishes from his lovers is extraordinary.

Hue's personal, colloquial voice is at odds with the lovers' impassioned flights of rhetoric:

> De penser la color lui mue,
> Mes qe chaud? Mult par esteit sage
> E se combat od son corage.
> Dehez eit ore sun granz senz!
> (670–73)

Her color changed with her thoughts, but so what? She was very sensible and fought her feelings. Damn her fine good sense!

> Tost est l'oil la ou est l'amur,
> Le dei la ou l'en sent dolur.
> (799–800)

The eye goes quickly where love is, the finger where it hurts.

> Ceo say mult bien, de trop amer
> Ne vint for mal . . .
> (notes to 1111–12)

This I know for certain, only bad ever came from loving strongly.

Hue's description of la Fière's beauty extends a scrupulously ordered *effictio* to an indecorous extreme, inviting his audience to speculate on her hidden attractions: "K'en dites vus de cel desuz / Ke nus apelum le cunet? / Je quit qe asez fut petitet." [What would you say of that part beneath, which we call the cuntlet? I think it was tiny enough] (2268–70). Comments like these are pervasive; as Philippe Ménard documents, "aucun conteur n'aime autant dire *je cuit* que Huon de Rotelande."[78] Nor are these simply the comments of a wiser narrator on the ignorance of young lovers. Hue counters the heroes' high seriousness with casual laughter and their dignity with pure sensuality.

At times the lovers are even put at odds with their own voices. La Fière recalls other lovesick heroines when she tries to reveal in sighing syllables that she loves her *valet*. But whereas Lavinia's stammered "E—ne—as" works magnificently, la Fière must interrupt her sighing to explain to her maid Ismene that she hasn't finished yet, and then that "Va—ha—let," the syllables plus the sigh, is not a proper name: "'Nai, ostez le suspir en mi, / Dunc l'avrez vus bien entendu'" ["No, take out the sigh in the middle, then you'll understand it"] (1518–19). Ismene's comical misappre-

---

78. *Rire et le sourire*, p. 471; see pp. 471–77.

hension and la Fière's technical explanations undercut the emotional intensity that such scenes achieve in other romances.[79]

During the three-day tournament, la Fière is similarly vexed. Although she repeatedly and properly speaks of her devotion to Ipomedon and her hope that he will be the victor, she is nonetheless attracted to each of the three anonymous victor knights (who are in fact Ipomedon) and on each day persuades herself that one or the other would be a good substitute for her beloved:

> En sun quer mut se cumforta
> E mut suvent se purpensa,
> Se ele ad sun dreit ami perdu
> Del neir vassal ferat sun dru.
> (6159–62)

In her heart she comforted herself well and thought often to herself that if she has lost her true friend, she would make the black knight her lover.[80]

Her fickle confusion coexists with her love for Ipomedon, and Hue ironically endorses both her purposefulness (2576–82) and her vacillation (5961–74). Even Ipomedon plays on her shifting affections, by leading her to believe each day that she has lost her beloved and should devote herself instead to the new day's victor.

In all, Hue's romance provides a disorienting set of assertions about love and chivalry. *Fine amor* does operate as a traditionally inspiring and perfecting force in *Ipomedon* (e.g., 7931–36, 8293–96, 10385–404), yet Hue insists that the sentiment is more passionate than refined, more violent than ennobling:

> Mut ad grant valur amur fine
> Ki set danter rei e reïne. . . .
> Quant force ne vaut ne beauté,
> Sens ne coïntise ne bunté,
> E qe vaudra dunc cuntre amur?
> Certes, ren nule al chef de tur.
> (9095–96, 9107–10)

Great is the power of *amur fine*, which can overcome kings and queens. . . . When strength cannot prevail, nor beauty, wisdom nor prudence nor goodness, what then can prevail against love? Surely, in the end, nothing at all.

---

79. *Enéas, Partenopeus de Blois,* and *Yder* take seriously the topos that Hue undermines here (Holden, edition, pp. 55–56; Fourrier, *Courant réaliste,* p. 335; Legge, *Anglo-Norman Literature,* pp. 92–93).

80. With this passage compare 3755–72, 3865–78 (la Fière's attraction to the white knight) and 4793–806 (attraction to the red knight).

The consistent mark of love's power is that it cannot be manipulated as a reward for merit, even when women seek consciously to do so. Like la Fière, the queen of Sicily and Ismene are determined not to love the hero in his disguises as coward and fool, but they are unable to resist.[81] Both their courtships belie models of women's aloofness in love, of love as a pervasively refining principle, and of reciprocity between male chivalry and female mercy. J. D. Burnley observes that for Hue "*fine amor* has the intensificatory significance which is found in the *fabliaux*," manifesting "the wryly humorous, gently cynical, treatment of consuming sexual passion."[82] This effect moves from minor to major characters: the queen's inability to dose her love according to chivalric merit parallels la Fière's inability to resist the appeal of nameless knights, and Ismene's essentially physical desire foreshadows the lovers' happy marriage, in which Ipomedon and la Fière "se entreaiment tant par amur / Ke il se entrefoutent tute jur" [love each other so truly that they fuck all day long] (10515–16).

The three female characters, unable to make faithful love consonant with proofs of valor, act out a dislocation between love and chivalry. Male characters, for their part, experience the relation of love and chivalry as annihilating—perpetually violent rather than constructive. Grisly carnage at the tournament for la Fière's hand in marriage is the ironic fulfillment of the knights' sensual desire (2264–66, 2555–62):

> N'i ad si membré ne si sage
> Ki gueres penst de mariage . . .
> Teus quidout espuser la Fere
> Ke l'um d'eloc porte en sun bere;
> Unc noces si cher achatees
> Ne furent ne tant cumperees.
> (4935–36, 4941–44)

---

81. The queen's unfortunate love is a source of much humor for Hue, who often describes her desire bluntly (3277–80, 3337–38, 4305–14, 5451–56, 5509–22). Her initial aloofness, when she cannot love her servant because he is not valorous (3085–86), only emphasizes her love's irrational disregard for the reciprocity of prowess and esteem; in the end she adores the hero "Coment k'il fut de hardement. . . . Amur ne quert fors sun delit, / Mult valt le juster enz el lit" [regardless of how brave he was. . . . Love seeks only its own pleasure; jousting in bed is what counts] (4308, 4313–14). Similarly, Ismene is ashamed of loving a fool and afraid he will kill her, but she creeps up to his bed in spite of herself, obliging Ipomedon to drive her off by pretending to want to eat her hand or to cut it off when she touches him (8837–56, 9149–72).

82. "*Fine Amor*," p. 140.

There was none, however wise or prudent, who gave any more thought to marriage. . . . Some who had thought to marry la Fière were carried from there on their biers; never was a wedding bought or paid for so dearly.

The knights' violence and in particular Ipomedon's death-dealing answer la Fière's demand that love spring from evidence of valor, but expose the destructiveness latent in such an ideal of love. For Ipomedon submission to the ideal is isolating rather than integrative. He refuses to claim la Fière as prize of the tournament because he believes it would interfere with his prowess (6650–52); soon after, he even refuses to claim his patrimony because he prefers to wander "cume soldeer / Ke pris e los vult purchacer" [like a professional soldier eager to win renown and praise] (7239–40). For Ipomedon to choose the life of a mercenary at this point is an alienated, aggressive rejection of his properly won place in society.

Readers who consider the romance to be traditional argue that Ipomedon's departure after the tournament shows him "making amends for his earlier unsatisfactory conduct" or "compensating for his initial lack of fulfillment" of the vow.[83] A conventional and pleasing whole inheres in this distention of the plot only to the extent that Ipomedon and la Fière achieve subsequently a better understanding of their love and a fuller concord between emotional life and action. The second half of the romance, in Ipomedon's chivalric progress from tournaments to war to defense of la Fière's people, who pray for him (9415–20) and for whom he feels "mut grant pité" (9625), is reminiscent of how Chrétien gives Yvain a course of greater service to good causes.

But again, despite the plot's fully orthodox possibilities, Hue's presentation offers a second, fully ironic reading as well. Ipomedon's good causes are oddly subverted. To succeed the carnage of tournaments, he joins a war against Daire of Lombardy—who was apparently already killed by the hero himself during the three-day tournament, a striking instance of Hue's "attitude désinvolte" for narrative integrity (note to line 7270). His next cause, the defense of la Fière and her people against Leonin d'Inde Majeur, is functional and meritorious. Yet despite his pity for the people as he fights, Ipomedon conceals his victory and even teases the citizens and la

---

83. Spensley, "Ipomedon," p. 351; Bruckner, *Narrative Invention*, p. 165; see also Hanning, *Individual in Twelfth-Century Romance*, pp. 126, 134, and 268 n.38, on the growth of Ipomedon and la Fière through their experiences.

Fière cruelly by pretending to be Leonin himself and to have vanquished their champion:

> As portes vent de la cité,
> A haute voiz ad apelé
> E sovent a la Fiere escrie:
> 'Bele, or vus avrai a amie,
> N'en poez mes fere danger,
> Vencu ai vostre chevaler;
> Ffetes tost si vus aprestez,
> En Inde ensemble od mei irrez!'
> (9931–38)

He came to the gates of the city and called loudly, crying often to la Fière: 'Beauty, now I will have you for my lover, you can't put me off any longer— I have conquered your knight. Hurry and get yourself ready: you'll go with me to India!'

The citizens are left weeping, tearing their hair, falling in faints, crying and groaning (9939–54)—hardly the responses an orthodox protector would strive to inspire in his beneficiaries.

La Fière is similarly shaken by her encounters with Ipomedon. She does abandon her heritage rather than marry the supposed Leonin, but she appears more to be fleeing Leonin's monstrousness (7701–12) than affirming her love for the hero. Were it not for Hue's assurance that she, like all women, is more than capable of looking after her own interests (1911–24, 2139–46, 2576–82), the course of events would seem to reduce her to a powerless walking irony, a mere antiphrasis, as she continues to be known only as "the Proud" even after reforming this quality in herself (4584–614, 5237–58, 6359–72). Like the condition of her people, la Fière's total humiliation hardly seems the objective of a benevolent hero.

What, then, is the relation of Ipomedon's love to his actions? With great artfulness the poet has given us two answers at once, two readings of Ipomedon's life. In one reading, Ipomedon is motivated by love for la Fière and a need to fulfill her vow,[84] and he is so consumed by those desires that only the rediscovery of his own blood (when Capaneus reveals they are half-brothers) can bring him to awareness of his achieved identity as perfect chivalric lover. But in another reading, Ipomedon is a detached manipulator of literary ideals and of the public that propounds them. This is the hero

---

84. E.g., 1173–91, 6712–24, 7624–30, 7931–36, 9473–76, 10385–91.

who controls multiple disguises, makes la Fière believe over and over that she has lost him, and warns Leonin that "'De parfunt sens ad cil petit / Ke creit quanke femme li dit'" ["he has little wisdom who believes everything a woman tells him"] (9489–90). The double capacity of Ipomedon to act as faith-holding lover and as disabused educator makes him an elusive, even paradoxical hero.

Ipomedon's doubleness dramatizes the work's two narrative stances as well as connecting the story's two meanings. The protagonist is a vehicle for Hue's serious commitment to his material, but also for Hue's detached manipulation of traditional patterns. The poet, like the hero, is elusive. That Hue invents multiple disguises and evasions for Ipomedon expresses in the plot his own relationship to courtly material as outsider, mocker, and dissembler. Yet despite his air of nonchalance Hue says much about human weakness that Thomas of Britain says too: that people are by nature changeable, self-ignorant, weak of will, and sensual. The resonances between humor and insight, and between the coherent image of noble ideals and the vivid depiction of foolish conduct, enrich the work just as the hero is enriched by the confluence in his character of starry-eyed dedication and informed disenchantment.[85] There is no separating these paradoxical elements in *Ipomedon*. They coexist throughout, and Hue finally constructs between them a rapprochement of sorts, though hardly on Thomas's model.

In part Hue's portrayal of selfishness and folly within a conventional scheme of ideals seems to please him just for its incongruity, its feast-of-fools confounding of system and order. But in part as well Hue may acknowledge the power of natural impulses so cheerfully, rather than somberly as Thomas does, simply because he finds the fulfillment of those human impulses adumbrated in the ideal. Perhaps, Hue suggests, traditional *fine amor* and ordinary

---

85. Ménard refuses to believe in Ipomedon's dedication to love, regarding his justifications as false: "en fait, Ipomedon n'a rien du parfait amant qui pense par la souffrance mériter la *merci* de sa Dame" (*Rire et le sourire*, p. 354). Hanning, on the contrary, refuses to believe in Ipomedon's free manipulation of roles: Ipomedon suffers "victimization by prowess," from which he is unable to release himself (*Individual in Twelfth-Century Romance*, pp. 133, 134–35). The two forces (engagement/detachment) in Ipomedon's character can seem mutually exclusive, but both are genuinely present. Hue uses both to explain the hero's behavior, e.g., "Mut aime lealment sa amie" [he loves his lady very loyally] (7932) as against "Mut esteit vecïez e sage, / Asez covre ben sun curage" [he was very wary and wise; he covers his thoughts very well] (5335–36).

selfish desire are not contradictory forces. Perhaps they share a secret kinship. R. Howard Bloch finds the same connection in the thirteenth-century fabliaux, *Roman de Renart*, and Jean de Meun's *Roman de la Rose*: despite the elements that distinguish these works from courtly literature, "the selfish individualism of rapacious animals, promiscuous wives, luxurious priests, and deceptive suitors is nonetheless latent in the alienation of the chivalric hero and lyric lover."[86] Hue anticipates the discoveries of his successors without abandoning the structures of romance. He reforms romance's typical premise that the lover's search for selfhood is essentially a journey toward responsible maturity and social integration.[87] For Hue the full discovery of selfhood invites the freeing of love's energy in purely autonomous gratification. This is what Hue's epilogue states more directly than the work as a whole. Rather than urging on us, as Thomas does, lovers who scourge the fallen soul to make it ready and clean for love, Hue reveals that promiscuous enjoyment is the lesson of Ipomedon's story.

In what appears to be an imitation of Thomas's parting words to lovers,[88] *Ipomedon* concludes:

> Ipomedon a tuz amanz
> Mande saluz en cest romanz,
> Par cest Hue de Rotelande;
> De part le deu d'amur cumande
> Des or mes lealment amer. . . .
> (10559–63)

Ipomedon sends greetings in this work to all lovers, through this Hue of Rhuddlan, and commands them on behalf of the God of Love to love loyally from now on.

The God of Love, excommunication, and absolution make of the epilogue a little allegory of love that recalls Thomas's congregation of devout listeners. Thomas avoids openly religious analogies but does invite his audience to absorb his work as proof against love's wrongs and changes, as if his text could be distributed like the Host to renew both faithful and faltering lovers. *Ipomedon* closes with a similar claim, but the soaring desire for purification in *Tris-*

---

86. *Literature and Law*, p. 227.
87. *Ille et Galeron* and *Partonopeus* can illustrate the convention as well as Chrétien's romances; see n. 74 above.
88. Cf. "Tumas fine ci sun escrit: / A tuz amanz saluz i dit . . ." [Thomas ends his work here; now he says farewell to all lovers] (Sn_2 820–21ff). Holden argues that Hue consciously imitates this passage (edition, pp. 51, 56).

tan dives now toward insouciant sensuality; Thomas's congregation of lovers re-forms into a sequential line of sexual partners. In Hue's allegory timid lovers are to be excommunicated until promiscuity absolves them,[89] or in the case of ladies, until Hue himself pardons them. This private pardon for women replaces Thomas's text as Host with a text as phallus:

> A Credehulle a ma meisun
> Chartre ai de l'absoluciun;
> Se il i ad dame u pucele
> U riche vedve u dameisele
> Ne voille creire ke jo l'ai,
> Venge la, jo li musterai;
> Ainz ke d'iloc s'en seit turné
> La chartre li ert enbrevé,
> E ço n'ert pas trop grant damages
> Se li seaus li pent as nages.
> (10571–80)

At Credenhill in my house I have a license to give absolution; if there is any lady or virgin or fine widow or maiden who does not want to believe that I have it, let her come there, and I'll show it to her: before she turns from there the document will be pressed upon her, and it won't be too bad if the seal hangs from her ass.[90]

This boisterous conclusion derives from the premise that the romance hero is self-determining. The miniature allegory of love's God, excommunication, and absolution that closes Hue's work recalls the rigid social code to which Ipomedon and la Fière gradually accommodate their desires, like many other romance heroes facing constructs of ideal love and chivalry. But Hue is convinced that ro-

---

89. "And if anyone withdraws from loving before achieving his goal, then such a one will be excommunicated and will have full permission to take his pleasure where he can; he who gets the most will be absolved" (10565–70). Holden notes the apparent illogic of these verses (edition, p. 571), which is surely part of Hue's joke: in this religion of love, promiscuous abandon is the man's atonement for living with restraint. See also Susskind, "Love and Laughter," p. 657.

90. The document in this phallic metaphor is a letter patent with bishop's or pope's seal granting power of absolution, such as Chaucer's Pardoner carries: "'Oure lige lordes seel on my patente, / That shewe I first, my body to warente'" (*Works*, ed. Robinson, *Pardoner's Prologue*, lines 337–38). Such documents were rolled to the seal, as shown in the Reims cathedral fresco reproduced by Jadart ("Peinture murale," pl. VII, p. 38: a scribe holds a rolled letter with pendent seal). The phallic sense of the passage as a whole is clearer than the sense of *enbrever* (10578), which Holden takes as *embriever* (to inscribe), resulting in some obscurity; but which Godefroy's *Dictionnaire* interprets also as *embriver* (to rush into, cast upon). The second interpretation offers a more consistent "métaphore scabreuse" (Holden, edition, p. 572n.) than does *embriever*.

mance's versions of achievement disguise or evade the true character of personal desire. Thus his final allegory refuses to elevate the envisioned reconciliation between desiring individual and demanding social code. Instead, his machinery of idealization merely facilitates the self-determined sensual fulfillment that his lovers truly seek.

Thomas of Britain and Hue de Rotelande adopt conventional romance patterns but question and reform them. Jean-Charles Payen even sees Thomas's work as a provocative challenge to courtly literature in general. Subsequent romance writing, he argues, must be understood as a series of attempts to exorcise the Tristan story, to demystify it and to substitute for it more satisfactory courtly models of behavior.[91] M. D. Legge attributes *Ipomedon*'s popularity with Middle English adapters to the fact that it "is a parody of the courtly romance" and thus well suited to the general English detachment from French romance.[92] Both assessments exaggerate Thomas's and Hue's resistance to courtly convention, but both perceive that the Anglo-Norman poets are significantly isolated from that convention.

To be sure, the clerical milieu that accounts for both Thomas's moral sensitivity and Hue's goliardic laughter is shared by continental poets, and that milieu affects twelfth-century romance in general: D. H. Green concludes in his wide-ranging study that the "hero's distance from the court, implying his ability to transcend it, thus reflects the poet's critical aloofness from courtly values." Clerics of this period constitute an international community vital to cultural development, yet their ecclesiastical training and relatively low social status encourage their literary stances of self-conscious detachment and reflectiveness.[93] In their learned romances, images of refined sentiment and behavior may be undermined by authorial comment, or interrupted by "comically realistic passages," or even vitiated by characters' inabilities to meet the standards they set for

---

91. "Lancelot contre Tristan"; Le Gentil answers this article persuasively in "Epilogue." Köhler, *Ideal und Wirklichkeit*, p. 85, and Ferrante, *Love and Honor*, p. 16, believe the Tristan story is inherently anticourtly; see also n.4. But for evidence of the story's acceptance, see Sudre, "Allusions."
92. "Rise and Fall," p. 4.
93. D. H. Green, *Irony*, p. 363; Auerbach, *Literary Language*, pp. 237–338; Gallais, "Mentalité des romanciers" (1970), pp. 333–38; Uitti, "Clerkly Narrator"; Köhler, "Sistema sociologico."

themselves.[94] In the end most critics see continental romances balancing these inner conflicts and affirming the value of their ideals for their audience, but some critics insist on the romances' simultaneous awareness that the opposition between individual and community is not fully resolvable and that the lover's desire for resolution is thus troubling and isolating.[95]

These features ally *Tristan* and *Ipomedon* to romance tradition but are greatly extended and modified in the two insular works. Thomas makes an inescapable contradiction of the latent tension between public and private loyalties, refusing optimistic harmony for a tragic vision of love refined by inner torment. His strained but magisterial union of humanity to absolute love recognizes an opposition deeper than the typical interplay of courtly code and adventuring knight. Hue's treatment of the interdependence of love and chivalry strikes at the motif's heart by reading the plot doubly and by giving the alternate reading a world of its own, a local milieu that engulfs the traditional reading. There is nothing in twelfth-century romance to match Hue's full context of anecdotes and attitudes enclosing and commenting on the characters' world.

Yet Thomas and Hue remain committed to the principle of heroic self-determination and to the process of confronting heroes with challenges raised by their own aspirations. That commitment allies them with the deepest impulses of romance, making their doubts about the means and processes of heroic achievement the more striking. While *courtoisie* and *fine amor* may have functioned metaphorically as cultural ideals or as social resolutions in the continental provinces of their origin, they did not carry immediate conviction for Anglo-Norman poets. Soon, however, Thomas's doubt and Hue's laughter were to fade from the insular poetic repertoire, as poets gradually turned from resisting courtly tradition to reforming it.

---

94. Susskind, "Love and Laughter," p. 657; see also n.63 above and Hanning, *Individual in Twelfth-Century Romance*, p. 135.
95. Muscatine (*Chaucer and the French Tradition*, pp. 14, 42–57) and D. H. Green (*Irony*, pp. 389–93) regard irony as subordinate to the acceptance of courtly ideals; Köhler (*Ideal und Wirklichkeit*, pp. 66–128) and R. H. Bloch (*Literature and Law*, pp. 215–48) posit that romance's oppositions are not fully resolvable.

Chapter Five

Adapting Conventions of Courtliness

Two young men seeking brides illustrate what happens to ideas of love and chivalry between the twelfth and the fourteenth centuries. The first, Arnulf of Guines, pursued a very wealthy widow, Countess Ida of Boulogne. The Guines family chronicler recounts baldly that Arnulf either loved Ida—or only pretended to love her "virili prudentia et cautela" ["in his masculine sagacity and cunning"] because "ad terram tamen et Boloniensis Comitatus dignitatem, veri vel simulati amoris objectu recuperata ejusdem Comitissae gratia, aspiravit" ["in seeking the favors of the countess by this true or pretended love, he aspired to the land and the dignity of the county of Boulogne"].[1] Arnulf's conventional gestures (exchanging secret love-messages with Ida) are merely implements of his calculated acquisitiveness.

Substantially different is the conduct of William Marmion just over a century later, during Edward II's Scottish wars. While this Lincolnshire knight sat feasting, "un damoisel faye" [a fairy damsel] presented him with a golden helmet and "vn lettre de comaundement de sa dame qil alast en la plus perillous place de la graunt Bretaigne et qil feist cel healme estre conuz" [a letter of

---

1. Lambert of Ardres, *Chronicon Ghisnense et Ardense*, ed. Ménilglaise, pp. 205–7; trans. in Duby, *Medieval Marriage*, p. 108. Duby comments, "All the posturing ultimately served only as a cover for the ruthless pursuit of a policy strictly designed to further the interests of the lineage" (p. 109).

commandment from his lady that he go to the most dangerous place in Great Britain and that he make this helmet known]. Those at the feast decided that Norham Castle on the Scottish border was presently the most dangerous place, so Marmion went there, agreed with the garrison commander that he would face the enemy alone, and rode into a crush of knights who wounded and unhorsed him before the garrison came to his rescue.[2] At mortal risk, Marmion submits to his lady's command in an obvious imitation of romance heroics. Yet the chronicler does not condemn Marmion's fanciful escapade, whereas the Guines chronicler found Arnulf's detachment and even falseness entirely suitable.

These two courtships trace a change in the relation of literary ideals and historical practice, from superficial imitation to serious and life-risking engagement. Critics have attributed the change itself to royal programs of control and to increasing economic constraints on the barony, as well as to the stimulus of chivalric literature.[3] During the thirteenth and fourteenth centuries the landholding class lost economic ground to the expanding mercantile sector and later to labor, and yielded political terrain to the crown. France's nobility resembled England's in these losses, for the turbulent relations between king and nobles that characterized France's twelfth century settled into firmer royal control in the thirteenth, while in England the exceptional wealth and security of the earlier barony gave way to harder economic times and greater pressure for rights and power from competing social groups.[4] In adopting the pageantries and the principled behaviors of literary knights, the barons affirmed their original status as *bellatores* but also established a more sophisticated and less refutable claim to superiority than simple military rights—which they had never enjoyed freely in England anyway. The prestige of a complex courtly ethos seemed to replace the barony's eroded economic and political power with cultural power. In France the process benefited king and commons

---

2. Sir Thomas Gray, *Scalacronica*, ed. Stevenson, pp. 145–46. The two accounts are nearly contemporary with the events: Gray's father was the garrison commander whom Marmion approached; Lambert writes in the hope of pleasing Arnulf and his father (pp. 3, 363–67).

3. R. S. Loomis, "Edward I"; McKisack, *Fourteenth Century*, pp. 248–53; Muscatine, *Poetry and Crisis*, pp. 1–25. Some similar changes occur in French chivalric society and literature during these centuries; see Dembowski, *Froissart*, and M. Vale, *War and Chivalry*.

4. Pp. 8, 22, 48. See also Duby, *Three Orders*, pp. 346–53; Coleman, *Medieval Readers*, pp. 43–57 et passim.

as well, by encouraging the aristocracy to curb and reform its violent tendencies. In England the barony's increasingly cultural identity similarly facilitated royal control and in addition provided the higher strata of commoners with a ground they could share in some ways with the nobility. England's fluid social categories permitted the literature and history of courtly ideals to reach beyond the barony itself.

This marked change in the social context of courtly writing allowed later insular poets to express fuller confidence in the practical meaning of literary ideals. *Melior et Ydoine*, an Anglo-Norman poetic debate of the thirteenth century,[5] argues that the clerk is a superior "fyn amaunt" (235, 337–38) not only for his virtues but for the social value of his writing:

> '. . . de clers vient tuit nostre bien:
> Trestout le sen de nostre vie,
> Queintise e curtoisie,
> Valour e amur e druerie,
> C'est escrit de clergie.'
>
> (330–34)

All our good comes from clerks: all the sense of our life—prudence and courtliness, worthiness and love and romancing—is written by clerks.

During the thirteenth and fourteenth centuries, insular poets of love, like the *Melior* poet, came to represent writing about "curtoisie" as writing in valuable relation to social activity. They were no longer aloof and critical observers, but engaged and useful members of an important movement.

A courtly ethos had begun to develop in the twelfth century, as nobles divided themselves from commoners by claiming superior military standards, uncalculating generosity, and finer emotional sensitivity. These claims were soon greatly elaborated. Prowess unfolded in practices of dedication, honor, loyalty, and fairness that were as visible during peace as in war. Increasingly complex social standards of grace, spiritual generosity, education, and relations between men and women further distinguished the aristocracy. For English and French barons alike, this system of virtues associated with knighthood and courts provided an ideology pertinent to their losses of power. This ideology countered the barons' dimin-

---

5. Ed. Meyer; see also Vising, *Anglo-Norman Language*, p. 64.

ished status by locating merit within character and personal conduct, and it explained their remaining rights over commoners by pointing to behaviors that continued to distinguish noble from common life in many respects. Literature's idealized representations of courtly virtues became one source for these claims to value. In the later Middle Ages courtly literature provided scripts for noble endeavor—for behavior between lovers, among knights, to prisoners, and to enemies in war. By the fourteenth century, "the Arthurian Oath was a living reality that governed behavior more strictly than any precept in the Bible."[6]

A rich culture grew around knighthood in these centuries. Tournaments imitated those of romance, as did feasts and pageants and Edward I's vow on his roasted swans. Secular chivalric orders such as the "chevaliers du Bleu Gertier," the Round Table built by Edward III for his knights, and the badge of the White Hart awarded to knights by Richard II at a Smithfield tournament united barons and king in bonds of honor and ritual rather than mere obligation.[7] The pomp and the literary cast of these new practices should not mislead us into thinking they were only games or poses.[8] Their political function was genuine, as was their cultural function in demonstrating noble merit. Their idealism took conduct beyond the merely practical into principled service, sacrifice, and even death. William Marmion survived his adventure, but at Mauron in 1352, eighty-nine knights of the new Order of the Star were massacred only because they held to an oath of the Order that they would never retreat in battle.[9] Such oaths, adventures, fairy messengers, and round tables derived from imaginative writing and were adopted in these centuries as regular and serious expressions of committed chivalric life.

6. Harvey, *Black Prince*, pp. 118–20, 148 (quote at p. 119). Barnie (*War*, pp. 56–96) examines some relations and some differences between chivalric ideals in romance and in practice. On the early development of these ideals, see Duby, *European Economy*, pp. 257–70; Hunt surveys recent work in "Emergence of the Knight."

7. Whiting, "Vows of the Heron"; Barber, *Edward*, pp. 43–44, 83–93; Prestwich, *Three Edwards*, pp. 203–9; Keen, "Chivalrous Culture." Froissart recounts the founding of the Order of the Garter, connecting it to Arthur's Round Table (*Oeuvres*, ed. Lettenhove, IV, 203–6).

8. This essential point is argued strongly and at length by Barnie, *War*; Keen, "Chivalrous Culture"; M. Vale, *War and Chivalry*, and Benson, "*Morte Darthur*," pp. 137–201. It modifies earlier treatments such as Huizinga's *Waning of the Middle Ages* and Kilgour's *Decline of Chivalry*.

9. Jean le Bel, *Chronique*, ed. Viard and Déprez, II, 206–7. For examples of similar conduct, see Prestwich, *Three Edwards*, pp. 203–9; Barnie, *War*, pp. 79–91; Keen, *Chivalry*, pp. 179–99, 212–16.

In England two changes in the later courtly romances accompany these social changes. The earlier poets' ironic detachment from literary ideals diminishes, and later poets adapt those ideals to extant social standards. For example, heroic love is less often adulterous and marriage more often emphasized. The God of Love in a thirteenth-century Anglo-Norman *Art d'aimer* instructs the "fine amaunt" in the traditional virtues of courtesy, loyalty, and modesty but stresses above all that "bone amour ne qwert peché" [true love does not seek to sin]. Consequently lovers will serve God and do no more than kiss their ladies until marriage.[10] The *Art d'aimer* could be a program for *Amadas et Ydoine*, so compatible are their versions of good love.

Some literary historians hold that such changes reject the literary tradition of courtliness. So believing, C. B. West repeatedly opposes the "human" to the "courtois": *Amadas et Ydoine*, integrating love with social virtues and marriage, is "an account of human rather than courtois relations."[11] In Old French romances the "human" and the "courtois" are often in tension but are not antithetical; Thomas of Britain and Hue de Rotelande are particularly concerned with that tension, which later insular poets seek to reduce. Courtly ideals do not constitute a static code. They rather epitomize, through various formal strategies, strong cultural convictions about the value of noble life. Adulterous love could well stand for self-determined, aspiring desire in formal metaphoric terms, but when life began to draw actively on literature, forbidden models gave way to socially acceptable models. It is inaccurate to label Amadas and Ydoine's concern for propriety "un-courtois" or to call the Middle English *Ipomadon* and *Sir Degrevant* bourgeois because they end in marriage.[12] Much of the difference between earlier and later insular romances springs from the changing relation of romances to social practice, rather than a changing class of audience.

Some change did occur in that audience, although in the case of those romances with Anglo-Norman roots it is more accurate to imagine the audience broadening downward in rank than shifting downward and away from the barony. It is important to remember,

10. Ed. Södergård (lines 652, 1115; see 658–83 et passim).
11. *Courtoisie*, pp. 118–20 (quote at p. 120).
12. See Chap. 4, n. 5, and "Définition d'amour" (ed. Studer), p. 434: counsels on love "s'adaptent à la moralité bourgeoise plutôt qu'à l'idéalisme chevaleresque." On adultery in literature and practice, see Benton, "Clio and Venus," pp. 24–29, 36; Benson, "*Morte Darthur*," pp. 156–62.

as for the romances of English heroes, that considerable mobility linked England's barony to professional and mercantile circles. And, once chivalry was no longer a strictly military matter, chivalric society no longer began and ended with those who engaged in military activity. To his great Windsor tournament of 1344 Edward III invited "omnes dominas australium partium Angliae et uxores burgensium Londoniensium" [all the ladies from the southern part of England and the wives of London burgesses]. Esquires and even non-knightly landowners began in the fourteenth century to use heraldic arms on their seals, and by the end of the century "the esquires had inherited some of the chivalric aura that had long surrounded knighthood."[13] Powerful merchants also used armorial bearings; their presence at the royal court may explain why Edward III, his sons, and nineteen other nobles found it appropriate to disguise themselves as the Mayor and aldermen of London for a tournament in the week following John of Gaunt's marriage. Indeed, leading burgesses often achieved knighthood under Edward III and his successors.[14] Geoffrey Chaucer, despite his identifications with trade and civil service, testified in the 1386 "Court of Chivalry" to the Scropes' true coat of arms; the proceedings describe him as "armeez pour xxvii ans" [having been armed for twenty-seven years].[15] In sum, England's chivalrous society encompassed people of diverse background and station. Better than trying to fix a narrow audience for the Anglo-Norman and related Middle English romances of love and chivalry is to recognize that these works expressive of court values could appeal as well to groups outside baronial courts.[16]

The later courtly poets enjoy a new and strikingly privileged position. They need not concoct elaborate (and ironic) confections

13. Adae Murimuth, *Continuatio Chronicarum*, ed. Thompson, p. 155; Saul, *Knights and Esquires*, pp. 6–29 (quote at p. 23); see also Bennett, *Community*.
14. Thrupp, *Merchant Class*, pp. 249, 286–87 et passim on class fluidity; *Chronica Johannis de Reading*, ed. Tait, pp. 131–32; McFarlane, *Nobility*, pp. 161–67.
15. *De Controversia in Curia Militari inter Ricardum le Scrope et Robertum Grosvenor*, ed. Nicolas, I, 178. In the preceding century London merchants had a poetry-writing fraternity whose chief inspiration was to be "honeste pleisaunce de bone dame" [the virtuous pleasure of good ladies]: *Liber Custumarum*, ed. Riley, Vol. II, Pt. 1, pp. 216–28 (quote at p. 224); Vol. II, Pt. 2, pp. 579–94.
16. Pearsall concludes that *courtly* poetry, "that is, poetry expressive of the values associated with court society, may seem a better term than 'court poetry' since it does not insist on a direct social relationship" (*Middle English Poetry*, p. 189); see also R. F. Green, *Poets and Princepleasers*, pp. 8–10; Doyle, "English Books"; Keen, "Chivalrous Culture," pp. 10, 23. But Coleman generally opposes court to merchant circles (*Medieval Readers*, pp. 13–57).

to dignify, or criticize, or disguise harsh aristocratic realities, for they find themselves in "a golden age of chivalry, a time when men at least tried to be chivalric knights" as never before.[17] After the twelfth century, insular romances of love and chivalry continue to present images of remarkable achievement, but instructive tones supplant ironic ones, homely naturalism tempers fanciful disconcern for plausibility, and authorial claims about courtly exclusivity yield to claims that the heroes are imitable and useful models. These claims are perplexing in that the scale of heroic accomplishments remains enormous in the later romances. But the changes in authorial treatment and tone, far from signaling a lack of sympathy for literary ideals, speak to a society assimilating literary ideals into practice. The romances' changing voice speaks especially clearly in those works that respond to or descend from Anglo-Norman works.

Tristan Revised

Two insular works from the thirteenth century, *Amadas et Ydoine* and *Sir Tristrem*, respond directly to *Tristan*'s vision of love. Both works are dependent on *Tristan* for plot motifs and for images of noble love, but both react against Thomas's argument that sin and isolation lie at the heart of love's self-discovery. *Amadas et Ydoine* responds with a model of virtuous, socially integrated love, while *Sir Tristrem* unselfconsciously resists Thomas's ideal through its misapprehensions and faltering reformations. These revisionary tendencies reach their full expression only in the fourteenth century.

Like *Ipomedon*, *Amadas et Ydoine* places itself in a tradition of similar stories, building a composite but generally familiar plot and referring to other heroes to help define and distinguish the story of Amadas and Ydoine.[18] But these references go beyond Hue's ironic mockery: *Amadas et Ydoine* confronts the tradition directly in order to revise and correct it. As she falls in love, Ydoine regrets having

---

17. Benson, "*Morte Darthur*," p. 141, on the fourteenth to sixteenth centuries; also Keen's description of the fourteenth: "If ever there was in England a golden age of chivalry, surely this was it" ("Chivalrous Culture," p. 2). On this chivalry and literature, see R. S. Loomis, "Imitations"; Ferris, "Chronicle."

18. Ed. Reinhard. Three AN fragments (V, G_1, G_2) and a complete Picard version survive (edition, pp. iii–v). The Picard MS is reasonably close to the AN version; see Le Gentil, "*Amadas et Ydoine*"; Paris, "Sur *Amadas et Ydoine*." Reinhard places the composition of *Amadas* between 1190 and 1220 (edition, pp. v–vii). Legge proposes that the wool trade may be responsible for Picard versions of several Anglo-Norman works ("Significance of Anglo-Norman," pp. 10–11).

been extremely harsh to Amadas, "'Plus que unc mes ne fut meschine'" ["more than any other maiden ever was"] (G₁ 28), and Amadas accepts her love with the same consciousness of a romantic community: "'Tuz amanz vus en rendent grez'" ["All lovers give you thanks"] (G₁ 104). Neither of these generalizing comments is carried into the complete Picard version; the few Anglo-Norman fragments reveal a strong preoccupation with the difference and superiority of Amadas and Ydoine's love that the continental redactor has toned down but not effaced. In their devotion these lovers

> Sormontent tous autres amans
> Qui sont et qui or ont esté,
> Dont on avra dit et conté
> Ne en estoire n'en cançon.
> (4686–89)

exceed all other lovers who are or who have been, those of whom people will speak and recount whether in stories or in songs.

The *Amadas* poet both emulates and strives to surpass the Tristan story in particular. Young Amadas falls in love with the daughter of his lord, suffering "tel dolur quo unches Tristran / Ne sufri pur Isoude la bloie" [such sorrow as Tristan never suffered for fair Isolt] (V 430–31). The pain of love recalls Thomas's conception and sometimes his wording. Amadas pleads, "'Ma vie est en vus et ma mort'" ["My life is in you and my death"] (V 799); his love is "Duce dolur mellé a ire, / A volenté fine martire" [sweet sorrow mixed with rage, complete and tender martyrdom] (V 285–86).[19] When Ydoine takes pity on him, their first embrace gives rise to a natural love superior to that of the Tristan story:

> Naturalment lur est creü
> L'amur es os, ne l'unt beuu
> Par baivres, par manger, par fruit . . .
> Cum de Tristran dunt vus avez
> Oï, et des autres asez.
> (G₁ 73–75, 79–80)

Love grew naturally in them from the bones; they didn't swallow it from a drink, from food, from fruit, like Tristan and so many others of whom you've heard.

Ydoine, like Isolt, must marry another. She preserves her virginity nonetheless and sickens for love "plus . . . / Que ne fist Tristran

---

19. Further echoes of Thomas are suggested by Adams, "*Amadas et Ydoine.*"

pour Yseut, / N'ele pour lui quant l'ama plus" [more than Tristan did for Isolt, or her for him when she loved him most] (2883–87).

With exemplary loyalty, Ydoine seeks out and cures Amadas, whose thwarted love has made him insane. A magical knight then tests Amadas's loyalty by making it appear that Ydoine has died and that she was unfaithful in life. Deeply shaken, Amadas first reflects that his plight unites him with other deceived lovers, of whom "li cortois Tristans" (5833) heads the list, but then he denies the evidence and defends Ydoine's body from the magical knight. This knight declares Amadas to be more loyal than "'tous les amans / Qui sont et qui aront este'" ["all the lovers who are and who will be"] (6356–57). Ydoine awakes, arranges to divorce her husband, and marries Amadas; "Leur amors fu tos jors estavle / Et fine et vraie et bien duravle" [their love was always stable, refined and true and very lasting] (7873–74).

The suggestive parallels in plot reinforce the direct references to Tristan's story. Virgin marriage, divorce and remarriage correct adultery and tragic death; the lovers' unshakable loyalty ("fine loial amour" [1177]) contrasts with Thomas's image of a *fine amor* suffering from weaknesses and inconstancies. In addition, the plot of *Amadas et Ydoine* proposes madness and death as responses to love's pain, only to reject both. Satisfied by these revisions, the poet endorses the lovers and shuns the ironic perspectives characteristic of Hue's and Thomas's narration.

When Ydoine appears to be dying, Amadas plans to share death "'a grant dolor / Ensemble o vous par grant amor'" ["in great sorrow with you, for great love"] (5209–10). So strong is his desire that Ydoine must go beyond merely urging him to marry another (4920–49): she invents a tremendous sin in her past that she begs Amadas to help her expiate through his lifelong prayers (5015–170). Amadas resembles Tristan in his longing for death and his discovery of *dolor* in acts of *amor*, but Ydoine's lie makes her superior to all history's lovers (4961–64) by protecting Amadas from death or insanity (5232–36). As we have seen, Tristan's death results from his failure of faith in Isolt: he believes his wife's report that Queen Isolt has not come to save him. But even the magical knight does not break Amadas's faith in Ydoine's love, despite what seems to be evidence of her betrayal.

Ydoine's loyalty passes a similar test when Amadas loses his mind for her love. Many poets of *fine amor* use madness to represent the social marginality of love: frustrated lovers whose fulfillment seems impossible, criminal, or merely offensive may go mad. At first Amadas's love has this potential, when his unreciprocated feeling tortures him with "la fine rage d'amours" [the perfect madness of love] (1044).[20] But the romance changes its initial direction by reacting again to the Tristan story—this time not so directly to Thomas's interpretation, however, since his ideal of *fine amor* excludes *folie* and encompasses *raison*.[21] Nonetheless, the fated, death-enclosing love of Tristan and Isolt can easily express itself in madness, a condition the *Folies Tristan* explore.

The Anglo-Norman *Folie Tristan d'Oxford* identifies madness with Tristan's access to Isolt.[22] "Prueisse ne lu pot valer, / Sen ne cuintise ne saver" [prowess cannot help him, nor wisdom nor trickery nor knowledge] (161–62), because his love opposes Marc's marriage and sovereignty. Tristan concludes that his best recourse is *folie*, which thus becomes the metaphor for this love's social exile. "'Pur vostre amur sui afolez'" ["For your love I am maddened"] (175), Tristan recognizes as he adopts the identity of fool.[23] This madness opposes the lovers to Marc and disrupts their own interactions. Tristan's public discourse emphasizes that his love offends Isolt in her status as Queen and as Marc's beloved; then, alone with her, Tristan desires recognition and reunion with her yet fears her "desdein" and "feintise" [scorn, deception] (690–700; 854–56, 938). The *Folie Tristan d'Oxford*'s brief representations make up a "table des matières" for Thomas's version,[24] with Tristan's *folie* expressing the pain of dislocated identity and social ostracism. Even alone with Isolt, Tristan cannot easily shake free of his disguise, as if he finds it all too appropriate to their relationship.[25]

Tristan's figurative madness expresses his love's impossibility, while Amadas's literal madness is only an early stage in his love for

20. See also MS V 381–91, 846–47, 870–75, and 1040; and Ménard, "Fous."
21. Burnley, "*Fine Amor*," pp. 143–44; Adams, "*Folie*," pp. 88–90; and Chap. 4, n. 47.
22. Ed. Hoepffner. According to Hoepffner, Thomas may have composed the Oxford *Folie* (edition, pp. 34–39).
23. Hoepffner notes the double sense of *afolez*, "injured" as well as "maddened" (edition, p. 97). Tristan also uses intoxication as a metaphor for his state: "'d'itel baivre sui ivre, / Dunt je ne quid estre delivre'" ["I am intoxicated by a drink from which I do not think to be freed"] (461–62); see also lines 475–76.
24. Delbouille, "'Folies Tristan,'" p. 127. Delbouille argues for the influence of Thomas on the Oxford *Folie*, as does Legge, "*Folies*."
25. It appears that Tristan controls his disguise at lines 969–75 but not in earlier passages: he is hurt when Isolt rebuffs his embrace (681–88), he seems to use his own voice without winning recognition (840, 922), and even his love token and Husdent's acceptance do not convince Isolt that the madman is Tristan (901–68).

Ydoine. When the "fol volair" [mad desire] (V 1040) of his youthful passion changes to insanity, Ydoine cures him with loving words, especially her own name: "Pur le nom d'Ydoine s'amie / Li trespasse la derverie" [his insanity leaves him because of his friend Ydoine's name] (3347–48). The repeated insistence that Ydoine's name is restorative (3318–414), like the emphasis on her *loiauté* when she seems to be dying, also resonates suggestively with the Tristan story. Tristan was partly misled, partly tempted by the recurrence of Isolt's name in Brittany. In *Amadas et Ydoine* the beloved's name is no longer a cause for pain and transgression, but a cure and a blessing "Com uns des nons Nostre Signour" [like one of the names of Our Lord] (3399). Ydoine stretches her body along Amadas's to cure him, but she inverts Isolt's death embrace by recalling Amadas to sanity. He, in turn, recalls her to life after proving his loyalty to the magic knight, rather than sharing death with her.

Amadas and Ydoine refuse madness and death for reason, life—and marriage. Ydoine prays to God after curing Amadas that her love may be fulfilled "Sans reparlance de folie" [without any more talk of madness] (3711):

> raisnavlement
> Quide aciever tot son talent
> D'Amadas et de son signour,
> Qu'ele ne doit dou Creatour
> Ne de la gent mal gré avoir.
>   (3715–19)

She hopes reasonably to achieve all she desires from Amadas and from her husband, in such a way that neither her Creator nor her people should find fault with her.

Raison, throughout the romance, signals moderation, foresight, and especially accommodation to the extant social order. Lovers' conduct ought not offend the church, nor their parents, nor "la gent" in general. After rescuing her Amadas proposes that they run away together and live in adultery, but Ydoine "li moustre raisnavlement / Raison" [reasonably shows him the reason] (6678–79) that they should rather work to be united "'sans pecié . . . Que nus n'i puisse vilounie / Noter, ne mal, ne felonnie'" ["without sin . . . such that no one can find baseness in it, or wrong, or crime"] (6727, 6729–30). Ydoine's divorce strikes the poet as "raisnavle" (7326) since Ydoine and the count of Nevers are not happy together (7317–35); the church complies by finding some grounds for divorce "Soit par parentage u par el" [whether for consanguinity or for some other cause] (7347).²⁶ Ydoine, "Par grant raison et par savoir" [with great reason and wisdom] (7585), allows her father's barons to believe they are choosing her next husband.

The poet's laudatory, unironic attitude reinforces the happy development of all these plans. In *Tristan* and *Ipomedon*, characters' follies and sins often oppose the ideal principles they strive toward, and the poets' comments emphasize that disparity. Such irony is vestigial in *Amadas et Ydoine* at a few points where, like Thomas, the poet reflects on women's behavior in connection with the heroine's. But Ydoine disproves the rule that Tristan and Isolt illustrate: rescuing Amadas sets her apart from women's falseness and frivolity (3568–652); her divorce tactics provoke an antifeminist passage ending in a laudatory about-face, that a few women still seek to do good (7037–97). Similarly, the poet's summary of the plot in terms of Fortune's power and vagaries (7407–36) is at odds with the overall presentation of Amadas and Ydoine as effective agents of their own destiny, making choices that determine their success.²⁷ In these passages *Amadas et Ydoine* hovers transitionally between the rejected ironies of Thomas and its own new vision of exemplary love.

In general these lovers conduct themselves in perfect consonance with their principles, and the poet takes pains to protect those principles from the taint of blasphemy or disrespect. Ydoine's falsehood on her deathbed, for example, is justified for saving Amadas's soul and is followed by her private contrition to God (5260–71).²⁸ Many other episodes suggest that this story of love is superior to others precisely because it does not betray church, family, or social proprieties.²⁹

---

26. The reading "parage" is corrected to "parentage" by Labande, [Corrections], p. 435.

27. This emphasis on the lovers' active determination even functions in the episodes involving magic: the sorcery Ydoine arranges to preserve her virginity does not work, but because of her own pleas and her extreme lovesickness she and her husband sleep apart (2380–448); the magical knight proves to be a tester of Amadas's loyalty, sent by God, rather than an insurmountable adversary (5713–20, 6430–35). Here we have the supernatural "used psychologically, rather than magically . . . to measure and define the human" (Cooper, "Magic," p. 134).

28. With reference to this scene, Riedel cites Thomas Aquinas's judgment that a falsehood may be justifiable "'if the end intended be not contrary to charity'" (*Crime and Punishment*, pp. 103, 173n.20).

29. E.g., 1075–84, 1224–61, 3395–403, 3708–19, 3768–74, 4679–702, 4978–80, 5139–42, 6744–64, 6947–63, 7317–35.

Here the contrast to *Cligès* is inescapable. Both *Cligès* and *Amadas et Ydoine* set out to revise the Tristan story of adulterous and fatal love,[30] but Chrétien de Troyes presents his lovers with consistent irony: Fénice's feigned death parodies the Crucifixion; Cligès's knightly prowess has little to do with the lovers' escape, which is extraordinary for its bold rejection of all that is holy, matrimonial, and even sociable.[31] *Amadas et Ydoine* differs from *Cligès* in endorsing the lovers' problem-solving as exemplary and successful. In this respect it is closer to *Tristan* than to *Cligès*. Thomas's irony expresses the difficulty of establishing a harmonious poetic union between ideal love and human nature, yet Thomas does believe that his *fine amor* forged in the extremities of suffering can encompass the problems of folly, weakness, and sin. *Amadas et Ydoine* seeks to establish that harmonious union with more assurance, by significantly revising literary convention. But *Amadas*'s revisions move in the opposite direction from the revisions of earlier insular poets.

Thomas and Hue, questioning received courtly ideology, exaggerate two conventional structures to reveal their difficulties. Thomas chooses a story of absolutely irreconcilable adultery, and Hue fabricates as his hero's object a lady so haughty her only name is la Fière. The Anglo-Norman poets' radical versions of adultery and love-service clarify that these conventional structures associate love with alienation and violence. This association expresses the abductive impulse endemic to the continental aristocracy. For that audience, writes Georges Duby, the poetry of adultery translates "profound hostility to marriage," that state of achievement which was often refused to young nobles except by theft and abduction. The later continental poetry of chivalric service winning a proud lady merely disguises the "fundamentally misogynous" character of the old abduction pattern: "Woman was an object and, as such, contemptible."[32] Eugene Vance corroborates Duby's historical de-

---

30. Since *Amadas* effectively corrects difficulties raised by *Cligès* as well as by *Tristan*, the common hypothesis is that the *Amadas* poet knew Chrétien's poem: see A. Micha in *Grundriss*, ed. Frappier et al., p. 455; Reinhard, *Old French Romance of Amadas*, pp. 27–30, 175. But while *Amadas* refers freely to surpassed heroes (notably Tristan and Isolt but also Eneas and Lavinia, Gawain, Floris, etc.), there is no mention of Cligès or Fénice.

31. Haidu, *Aesthetic Distance*, pp. 25–112; Owen, "Profanity," pp. 37–48; Adams, "*Amadas et Ydoine*," p. 253. The lovers', especially Ydoine's, power to solve problems contrasts with thirteenth-century OF romances such as *L'Escoufle* and *Galeran de Bretagne*.

32. *Medieval Marriage*, pp. 12–15, 105–10 (quotes at pp. 14, 108).

coding by connecting early lyrics of adultery to romances of love-service: throughout, love's poetic expression is typically "le combat érotique," an aesthetic of antithesis recognizing the violence that is veiled by the mystified perfection of *fine amor*.[33] Thomas is troubled, Hue bemused, by the latent sexual conflict and social alienation in courtly poetry, and their structural exaggerations prepare for their detached assessments of continental norms. The *Amadas* poet, in contrast, seeks to resolve those problems by adjusting the norm toward moderation and inner harmony.

First, in *Amadas et Ydoine*, *fine amor* is considerably tamed. These lovers are not locked in metaphorical combat; they are allies in complicity to get married. Even in *Cligès* the lovers' complicity is antisocial, and Chrétien favors plots that drive the sexes into fuller "combat érotique." Love in *Amadas et Ydoine*, however, resembles other kinds of relationships. Not mad or antisocial, this love can be actively, overtly integrated with familial and feudal allegiances.

The socializing of *fine amor* is complemented in *Amadas et Ydoine* by a gentler assessment of human nature. The moral profundity Thomas and Hue share, their awareness of the subtle contradictions between self-interested indulgence and ideal principle, has no place in the simple permanence of a love that grows "Naturalment . . . es os" [naturally from the bones] (G_1, 73–74). Unlike la Fière, Ydoine is capable of unshakable *loiauté*; unlike Tristan, Amadas trusts his beloved even in the face of evidence that she is false. The answers are simpler for this romance because the problems are simpler: the ideal is more accessible, and the characters more empowered to try for it. This solution to the challenge of romance convention becomes widespread and is essential to Middle English romance in the fourteenth century. *Sir Tristrem*, perhaps because of its early date, fails to find this way out of Thomas's dilemma.

"Tout est dit sur l'étrangeté et l'incohérence du poème anglais. A quoi bon les décrire?"[34] Joseph Bédier's frustration typifies modern reactions to *Sir Tristrem* (ca. 1280). This is a dismaying poem, but its

---

33. "Combat érotique," p. 548; see also R. H. Bloch, *Literature and Law*, pp. 153–56.
34. *Tristan par Thomas*, ed. Bédier, II, 86. Kölbing edits *Sir Tristrem* in *Tristansage*, vol. II; also *Sir Tristrem*, ed. McNeill. Quotations are from McNeill (hereafter cited as *ST*); quotations from Thomas are from *Les Fragments du roman de Tristan*, ed. Wind.

odd misapprehensions and omissions help to map the direction of insular reactions to twelfth-century courtly ideology.

Sir Tristrem's incoherence is the more surprising for the poem's close relationship to Thomas of Britain's Tristan. Eugen Kölbing proposed that Sir Tristrem was written from memory of Thomas's work, thus explaining many of the English poet's confusions, but Bédier argued that it could equally well have been written with direct reference to a copy of Thomas's poem.³⁵ Probably there was between the Anglo-Norman Tristan and the Auchinleck Sir Tristrem a thirteenth-century intermediary, a Northern Tristan poem by an English Thomas:

> I was at Erþeldoun,
> Wiþ tomas spak y þare;   I spoke there
> Þer herd y rede in roune   read from writing
> Who tristrem gat and bare. . . .   begot
> Tomas telles in toun
> Þis auentours as þai ware.   they were
> (1–4, 10–11)

This "Tomas" has been diversely identified as the author of Sir Tristrem's English source, the author of Sir Tristrem speaking about himself in the third person, and a confusion of the author's contemporary, Thomas of Erceldoune, with his actual source, Thomas of Britain.³⁶ Sir Tristrem does follow Thomas of Britain's Tristan closely, but the English poem treats this cited "Tomas" (2, 397, 412, 2787) as a contemporary and as the immediate source of Sir Tristrem. Another contemporary writer, Robert Manning of Brunne, substantiates this association between the Tristan story and Erceldoune, in addition to lamenting the story's degenerate form.³⁷

---

35. Kölbing, ed., Tristansage, I, cxlvii; Bédier, ed., Tristan, II, 87–88; also on the relation to Thomas's poem, see Remigereau, "Tristan"; and Bossert, Légende chevaleresque, pp. 131–32, 136–43.

36. Pickford, "Sir Tristrem," surveys these opinions. Historical and literary references to Thomas of Erceldoune are collected in The Romance and Prophecies of Thomas of Erceldoune, ed. Murray, pp. ix–xxiii.

37. The Chronicle of Robert Manning of Brunne, ed. Furnivall, lines 93–100:

> I see in song, in sedgeyng tale
> of Erceldoun and of Kendale,
> Non þam says as þai þam wroght,
> And in þer sayng it semes noght;
> þat may þou here in sir Tristrem;
> ouer gestes it has þe steem,
> Ouer alle that is or was,
> if men it sayd as made Thomas.

Sir Tristrem condenses faithfully, if not intelligibly, the events and sometimes the rationalizations of Thomas's text. The whole of Tristan's debate on whether or not to marry Isolt of Brittany (Sn₁ 1-364) is distilled into one stanza:

Tristrem a wil is inne,	feels a desire
Has founden in his þou3t:	which he has
'Mark, mi nem, haþ sinne,	my uncle
Wrong he haþ wro3t;	
Icham in sorwe and pine,	
Þer to hye haþ me bro3t.	she
Hir loue, y say, is mine,	
Þe boke seyt it is nou3t	Bible says
Wiþ ri3t.'	rightly
Þe maiden more he sou3t,	
For sche ysonde hi3t.	Because / was named
(2663-73)	

These lines proffer tiny souvenirs of Thomas's monumental conceptions: that *voleir* ("wil") opposes Tristan to his own love,[38] that social and even religious fault is the inescapable condition of this *fine amor*, and yet that love's own ascetic discipline can reverse social right so that it is truly Marc who sins against love. But in the English stanza, outside the dialectic structure of Thomas's long debate, these conceptions pass by too quickly to make sense: "wil" has no place in an analysis of Tristrem's state of mind; Mark's "sinne" and the rights of marriage are simply contradictory. As the awkward turn of the first two lines suggests, inner debates and authorial dissertations are of no interest to the poet of *Sir Tristrem*. This vestigial monologue simply introduces action, rather than analyzing its meaning or its motivation.

Meaning and motivation often disappear in the English account. Since Ysonde expresses no anger at Tristrem's flight from her tent (3147-57), his return as a leper makes no sense as a gesture of supplication, nor does his "sorwe" (3180) make sense in the absence of

---

Kölbing discusses the passage, *Tristansage*, II, xxvii–xxxi. Also supportive of a Northern background is *ST*'s unusual stanza (ababababcbc, ninth line bob): its three-stress lines, bob-line, alliteration, and stanza linking all associate it with Northern alliterative verse, whereas its syllabic line structure, rhyme, and the tail-rhyme stanza itself associate it with other Southern poems in the Auchinleck manuscript. *ST*'s dialect seems to be that of London but with some Northern features; see Vogel, "Sir Tristrem." Pearsall agrees that the author was Southern, his source Northern ("Development," p. 107).

38. Bédier, edition, I, 287n; Jodogne, "Amour de Tristan," pp. 104-6.

Ysonde's censure. The eponymous Tristrem (3296–344) provides the circumstance for the hero's fatal wound, but the encounter no longer vibrates with Thomas's implications of psychological doubling and identity-questioning.[39] Occasionally, flashes of Thomas's interpretation do seem to appear. Tristrem's sudden and unique statement when wounded by Moraunt, "'In sorwe ich haue ben ay / Seþþen [since] ich aliue haue ben'" (1138–39), may translate Thomas's idea that an ultimately fatal love should express itself in temporal suffering. A few more passages seem to draw on Thomas's pain-encompassing love:

Þai wende haue ioie anouȝ,	thought to have
Certes, it nas nouȝt so.	
Her wening was al wouȝ	Their hope / false
Vntroweand til hem to;	Untrue to them
Aiþer in langour drouȝ,	Each fell into sorrow
And token rede to go;	decided
And seþþen ysonde louȝ	then
When tristrem was in wo	
Wiþ wille.	
(1728–36)	

This dramatization of feelings alternating between joy and sorrow, hope and disappointment nearly captures Thomas's idea that love's contrary movements are reciprocal and inseparable. But the English poet does not pursue the interpretation consistently. Often *Sir Tristrem* just drifts with the narrative current; often both narrative and interpretation have a cursory evasiveness that Bédier labeled "le logographe du conteur anglais."[40]

This is the kind of Middle English romance that critics shrug off as popular oral composition or as a crowd-pleaser for an excessively simple audience. Neither explanation is plausible for *Sir Tristrem*. The work does appear to imitate or descend from minstrel recitation, although its calls for attention, rhetorical questions, and vacuous line fillers are entirely characteristic of Middle English written style.[41] One unusual stanza describes listeners questioning

---

39. Kunstmann, "Tristan," pp. 173–86; [Crane] Dannenbaum, "Doubling," pp. 8–9.
40. *Tristan*, I, 338; Mehl (*Middle English Romances*, p. 177) believes the ruling conception of *ST* to be "the history of a fatal error, by which a noble and promising knight is brought to misery," but I find no clues that the poet was aware of this possible structuring.
41. On *ST* and ME style see Kölbing's introduction and notes; Baugh, "Authorship," argues against the minstrel composition hypothesis.

"Tomas" about his story and then takes up a reciter's attitude, challenging the interrupting listeners to do better:

> Þo tomas asked ay
> Of tristrem, trewe fere,
> To wite þe riȝt way
> Þe styes for to lere.
> Of a prince proude in play
> Listneþ, lordinges dere.
> Who so better can say,
> His owhen he may here
> As hende.
> Of þing þat is him dere
> Ich man preise at ende.[42]

So complete an evocation of oral delivery is rare in Middle English romance. However, *Sir Tristrem*'s close relationship to a lengthy written source makes oral composition unlikely. Oral recitation may well be part of *Sir Tristrem*'s history, but the poem's lapses of sense and losses of significance cannot be explained away by presuming even a highly dramatic performance. "The gesture, the facial expression, the vocal cadences and modulations of a skilled reciter"[43] could hardly supply deleted motivations or untangle mistakenly ordered episodes.

Nor is it satisfactory to propose that *Sir Tristrem*'s audience was ignorant or coarse. This argument is dangerously fluid: no sooner have we explained a poem's awkwardness by hypothesizing an "uncultured" audience than we find ourselves demonstrating the existence of the uncultured audience by using the poem's awkwardness as evidence![44] The circularity of the argument is in any case broken by *Sir Tristrem*'s preservation in the Auchinleck manuscript, in company with other adaptations from Anglo-Norman. An audience ca-

---

42. Lines 397–407; the sense is: "They used to ask Thomas about Tristrem the true friend, to know the right way of the story and learn its steps (episodes?). Listen, lords, about a prince proud in play. Whoever can tell it better, can tell his own version like a courteous man. But let each man praise what pleases him at the end" (see McNeill, edition, pp. 104–5nn.).

43. McNeill, edition, p. xlvii.

44. Rumble invents without historical basis a "relatively uncultured audience" which "accounts for" this poem's characteristics ("*Sir Tristrem*," p. 223); then Pearsall argues on the basis of Rumble's article that the poem's characteristics "presuppose" the same audience ("Development," p. 107). Pickford also uses this argument ("*Sir Tristrem*," pp. 224–28). The Auchinleck MS's plainness argues that its designer "did not intend it to be a treasured addition to a library," but not necessarily that its buyer was ignoble (Shonk, "Auchinleck Manuscript," p. 81).

pable of enjoying the length and thematic complexity of *Beues of Hamtoun*, *Guy of Warwick*, and *Amis and Amiloun* cannot be invoked to explain the extraordinary reductions and simplifications of *Sir Tristrem*.

Robert Manning of Brunne provides a more likely explanation. He blames corruption of a Northern "sir Tristrem" on its "strange Inglis," its difficult verse and language. He, Robert, will write "In symple speche . . . for þe luf of symple men"; too difficult for his listeners is the Tristrem poem "in so quante Inglis / þat many one wate not what it is [many do not understand it]." He claims that the original "sir Tristrem" was excellent, but that those who disseminate it refuse to simplify its language "for pride & nobleye, / þat non were suylk as þei" [out of pride and haughtiness, as if none were such as they are], leading to many errors of transmission. We see that Robert does not think of this Tristrem poem as a popular work and contrasts its intended audience to his own intended audience of "lewed men."[45] His account of ambitious retellers who are not quite able to handle difficult English versification or Thomas's subtle treatment of the legend can explain both the clumsiness of the extant *Sir Tristrem* and its niche among more sophisticated poems in the Auchinleck manuscript.

This erratic text does share certain revisionary tendencies with other romances of its period. Most important, *Sir Tristrem* does not conceive of the heroes' love as Thomas of Britain does. Indeed, the poet has so little affinity for Thomas's *fine amor* that he reduces the lovers' encounters to entirely physical "playing,"[46] and he even allows Tristrem's dog Hodain to lap a bit of the love drink and share the passions resulting from it:

> Þe coupe he licked þat tide   time
> Þo doun it sett bringwain;   When
> Þai loued al in lide   all together
> And þer of were þai fain. . . .   glad
> Þai loued wiþ al her miȝt,   their
> And hodain dede al so.
> (1675–78, 1693–94)

It is possible that Brengwain joins the loving couple here and certain that Hodain does. This startling equation of human and animal sen-

---

45. *Chronicle*, lines 71–128 (quotations at lines 97, 79, 73, 77, 109–10, 105–6, 84).
46. ST 1686, 1690, 1744, 1808, 1931, 2061, 2170, 2439, 2617, 3225.

timent is hardly justifiable as "an obvious attempt to give some rational explanation for the unusual faithfulness of Tristrem's dog."[47] The English poet evades a problem central to the story, the lovers' fatal interdependence, by treating the episode as if mere affection were its subject.

Strange as Hodain's participation is, it reflects a late insular tendency to portray lovers' commitment coexisting easily with other kinds of devotion. Another animal friend, the lion in *Yvain*, shares the lovers' joy in *Ywain and Gawain*. In his conclusion Chrétien de Troyes distinguishes between Yvain's "joie" and Lunete's "eise" at having helped; the heroine Laudine's reaction, perhaps ironically, goes unrecorded. The English version makes all three principals, and the lion, share an apparently equal happiness ever after:

> And so Sir Ywain and his wive
> In joy and blis þai led þaire live.
> So did Lunet and þe liown
> Until þat ded haves dreven þam down.[48]   Until death

Similarly, *Amadas et Ydoine* replaces *Tristan*'s isolating, antisocial love with a love encompassing family and social proprieties. The Anglo-Norman *Horn* gives a ring in token of love to Rigmel, whereas his English counterpart gives one ring to Rimenhild and one to his friend Aþulf. *Gui de Warewic* integrates romantic love with marriage, nurturance of a hero-son, lifelong friendship for Terri, and devoted service to God as well. Admirable love, for these later romances, does not exclude lovers from any other relationships, but rather facilitates complete engagement in life.

This context illuminates why *Sir Tristrem* avoids Thomas's emphases on how at odds with society or how laden with inner tensions the love of Tristan and Isolt is. Often these elements lose their sense in Middle English. The hall of statues in *Tristan* is the theater (or shrine) for a ceremony of anguished suspicion played against repentant faith—the lovers' "estrange amor" [strange love] (T, 71) ritualized. *Sir Tristrem* stops short of this ceremony, narrating only the construction of the hall and statues (2804–49). Brangien's anger and her threat to reveal the truth to Marc, another locus of great tension over the wrongs of love for Thomas, is reduced from more than three hundred lines to only two lines in English (D 1–344 ver-

47. Rumble, "*Sir Tristrem,*" p. 225.
48. *Ywain and Gawain*, ed. Friedman and Harrington, lines 4023–26; cf. Chrétien's *Yvain*, ed. Foerster, lines 6799–813.

sus 3182–83), with the point of the episode turned from Iseut's "malvesté" and "huntage" [wickedness, shame] (D 149, 277) to Ysonde's pleasure over the banishing of her enemy Canados (3208–12). Both these alterations retain the event (construction of the hall, revelations of Brangien) while omitting the sense given by Thomas (wrongful, painful love). Similarly, Tristrem's epithet throughout is "þe trewe," accepting the issue of faith in love but evading Thomas's emphasis on failures of faith: his Tristan is "l'Amerus" but hardly "þe trewe." In each case, as in the love-drink episode, *Sir Tristrem* avoids Thomas's preoccupation with the problems of love. What was central for Thomas is peripheral for the English poet.

Strengthening this tendency in *Sir Tristrem* are some gestures toward giving positive interpretations to the story's episodes. Not only do Brengwain's revelations to Mark somehow signify a victory for Ysonde, but Tristrem becomes something more of an adventuring hero, one who succeeds at whatever he attempts. His wife's brother feels shamed by the unconsummated marriage to Ysonde, but upon seeing the hall of statues he declares, "'Tristrem, we ar wode [crazy] / To speken oʒain þi [against your] wille'" (2991–92). Tristrem's tangible success over his detractors replaces the Anglo-Norman examination of "estrange amor." Tristrem is also a hero of English custom and history, as the originator of hunting and gaming practices (484, 1273–74) and the defender of England against Ireland (1033–34). His gaming skill is matched by his generosity (320–41 and notes); he bears himself nobly (1222) and stands in contrast to those who butcher deer like common "husbond men" (455). In these passages exemplary ability or breeding or bearing substitute for Thomas's exploration of fatal love as the significance of the Tristan story.[49]

But the English poet does not consistently accommodate the story's central love affair to these interpretations of Tristrem's heroism. Nor can the poet's gestures toward revising Thomas's *fine amor* convince us that the heroes' love is natural and untroubled. The Tristan story has lost the significance developed for it by Thomas, and it has not gained a new one.

---

49. Tristrem also shows he "honour can" [understands honor] in his treatment of guests (696); he prays for aid or in thanks (390–96, 1462–63, 2351–52, 2780–81). Rumble would have it that the prayers show "character development" ("*Sir Tristrem*," p. 227) since they occur in three of Tristrem's four combats and not in the first. But since Tristrem's longest prayer for aid (390–96) predates his first combat, he is never a godless youth.

Yet *Sir Tristrem*'s half-articulated penchants for ingenuous and integrating love are precisely those of thirteenth-century insular romances as a whole. In *Floris and Blancheflur*, another very early English romance about love, Floris's affection grows in him like a plant, developing as naturally as his sense of taste:

> Loue is at his hert roote
> Þat no þing is so soote: sweet
> Galyngale ne lycorys   (spice)
> Is not so soote as hur loue is.⁵⁰

This natural love, in contrast to Tristan's, faces surmountable obstacles and reaches a happy, sociable resolution.

Gui de Warewic, from the earlier thirteenth century, resists in a more general way than *Sir Tristrem* the romance structures that troubled Thomas and Hue de Rotelande. The poet of *Gui* is interested enough in conventions of love to depict at length the young heroes' developing feelings and courtship, with Guy's pain echoing Tristan's: "'beu ai ore itel beivre, / Que mielz aim la mort que la vie'" ["'suche a drinke me is yive, / That y ne kepe noo lenger lyve'"].⁵¹ Further analogies with Tristan's situation emphasize the problems love brings, as Guy must oppose his parents' wishes and see his friends die in order to fulfill Felice's command that he become the best knight in the world. Guy's regrets and his protest against the isolating tendency of love (see pp. 62–63) call to mind Tristan's laments and prepare for a central episode in which, like Tristan, Guy remembers his beloved just as he is marrying a foreign lady (AN 4225–50, ME A 4193–216). But in Guy's case the ceremony is not quite over, so he can escape unmarried; the strong family context of his subsequent marriage to Felice reverses the ostracism and tragic wrong of Tristan and Isolt's love. Next, the self-interested violence latent in serving a proud lady, which Hue exposed in *Ipomedon*, is revised when Guy repudiates his youthful adventures and undertakes new adventures in God's service.

This plot carefully modifies romance patterns that Thomas and Hue explored: Guy experiences absolute, self-risking love without ultimately suffering Tristan's isolation, then transforms the pleasure-

---

50. Ed. McKnight, lines 117–20. Amadas and Ydoine's love also grows as if physically (see p. 182 above; cf. the continental manuscript's more metaphysical image at lines 1181–82: "Natureument leur est venus / Cis dous fus es cuers et creüs" [this sweet fire came and increased naturally in their hearts]).

51. *Gui de Warewic*, ed. Ewert, lines 598–99 (also II, 191n.); *Guy of Warwick: The First or 14th-century Version*, ed. Zupitza, A 643–44.

seeking triviality Hue finds in love-service into the principled service of God. Not all the implications of these patterns are faced in the presentation of Guy, who remains a powerful, self-determining hero (see pp. 109–15). And precisely because some implications are refused, Guy's story, like *Amadas et Ydoine*, can propose that the pursuit of love is ideally compatible with feudal achievement, and feudal achievement with Christian principle.

Guy's story corroborates the revisionary directions of *Amadas et Ydoine* and *Sir Tristrem* and returns us to the historical situation that nurtured such revisions. The thirteenth century shows growing acceptance of romance fictions as substantial guides for life. Although the Anglo-Norman *Gui de Warewic* was probably not commissioned by the family with title to Warwick, that family did soon claim Guy as their ancestor. In 1298 his first namesake, Guy Beauchamp, acceded to the title of earl of Warwick, and this Guy's grandson is said by the family chronicler to have built a mansion called Gyclif "in remembrans of sir Gy" his distant ancestor. The fourteenth-century *Speculum Gy de Warewyke* takes Guy's religious contrition as the starting point for an instructive work on repentance.[52] In these ways Guy begins to have tangible influence on behavior around the turn of the century, stimulating gestures of vanity, respect, and faith.

In wider terms as well, conscious imitation of literature characterizes this period. The tournament developed from a "miniature war" of profit-taking chaos into the ceremonial "round table" with its blunted weapons, judges and regulations, and Arthurian pageantry. Participants began to disguise themselves as literary characters.[53] Edward III rode incognito in a Dunstable tournament of 1334, identified in its records only as Sir Lyonel, a cousin of Lancelot. He seems to have extended the connection by transferring the arms he used there to his son Lionel of Antwerp, born four years later. In such actions Edward perpetuated his grandfather's close and practical engagement with Arthurian legend: responding to Boniface VIII's charge that he had violated Scotland's liberties, Edward I defended his actions by invoking King Arthur's subju-

---

52. John Rous, *Rous Roll*, ed. Ross, pp. 19–23 (on characters from Guy story), 46 (on Guy Beauchamp), 48 (on Gyclif); *Dictionary of National Biography*, S.V. "Guy Beauchamp"; *Gy de Warewyke*, ed. Morrill.

53. See Chap. 4, nn. 23–24, and Denholm-Young, "Tournament"; Keeler, *Geoffrey of Monmouth*, pp. 131–37; Barber, *Knight and Chivalry*, pp. 159–82 ("miniature war" at p. 167).

gation of the Scots, in a letter sealed by one hundred of his barons.[54] As literature gradually affected behavior more extensively, romances became more fully imitable, even didactic. Later insular poets amended what was unseemly in conventional courtly romance without surrendering what was instructive and entertaining. *Sir Tristrem* stumbles in this direction, burdened by recalcitrant material; *Amadas et Ydoine* and *Gui de Warewic* move ahead with more assurance.

Ipomedon Revised

By the time an English poet adapted Hue de Rotelande's *Ipomedon* into the tail-rhyme *Ipomadon* (ca. 1375), the pageantry of literature was entering more fully into English baronial life. The middle and later fourteenth century saw extensive interactions between chivalric literature and social behavior, and the nature of these interactions is important to assessing the claims to exemplarity so often made by fourteenth-century poets.

Imitating romance topoi, knights of this period took vows, accomplished adventures, and proclaimed *pas d'armes* in which they faced challengers for a fixed number of days. Elaborate tournaments celebrated festivals and military successes.[55] In an English diplomatic mission of 1337 several young men wore patches over one eye,

> et disoit on qu'ilz avoient voé entre les dames de leur pays que jamaiz ne verroient que d'un oeul, jusques à tant qu'ilz avroient fait aucunes proesses d'armes ou royaume de France, laquelle chose ilz ne vouloient pas confesser à ceulx qui leur demandoient.

and it was said that they had vowed to the ladies of their country that they would see with only one eye until such time as they had performed feats of arms in France, and this they did not wish to reveal to those who inquired about it.

Like Guy and Amadas, these young knights test themselves through the service of ladies, and the congruence of their personal oaths

---

54. J. Vale, *Edward III*, pp. 68–69; Keeler, *Geoffrey of Monmouth*, pp. 52–54. The contemporary chronicler Peter of Langtoft several times compares Edward I to Arthur, e.g.: "De chevalerye, après ly reis Arthure, / Estait ly reis Edward des Cristiens la flure" [in chivalry, except for King Arthur, King Edward was the flower of Christendom] (*Chronicle*, ed. Wright, II, 380; cf. II, 264, 296, 368).

55. John of Reading, *Chronica*, ed. Tait, pp. 129–30; *Chronica monasterii de Melsa*, ed. Bond, III, 52, 69. See also n. 7 above.

creates a fraternal body that shares in chivalric experience. The young men's reticence signals that their motive is serious and not vainglorious, yet it is also essential that their vow become known, to be held a "grande merveille" and recorded by Jean le Bel.[56] This process imitates the characteristic romance sequence in which a hero's isolated self-improvement is finally published to the court, reintegrating heroic individuality into a noble community.

Fourteenth-century knights were linked to literature by their imitations, and further by their elevation to literary record in the work of chroniclers and poets. The great 1358 festival of the Knights of the Garter was said to be "invisa a tempore regis Arthuri," of a kind unseen since the reign of Arthur.[57] A combat of 1351, arranged between thirty knights on the English side and thirty on the French during a truce in the general hostilities, was celebrated in verse and prose as "ung moult merveilleux fait d'armes que on ne doibt pas oublier" [a most wonderful feat of arms that should not be forgotten]. Far from breaking off the encounter when one of the participants was killed, the knights "se maintinrent noblement d'une part et d'aultre aussy bien que tous fussent Rolant ou Olivier" [carried on as nobly on both sides as if they had all been Roland or Oliver]. As the Chandos Herald asserts in his *Life of the Black Prince*, of such lives as these "homme en purroit faire un livre / Bien auxi grant come d'Artus, / D'Alisandre ou de Clarus" [one could make a book as long as that of Arthur, Alexander, or Clarus].[58] Literature in this period commemorated as well as inspired chivalric behavior.

Some historians claim that such behavior was empty show, but these knights did risk their lives to act on principle. Even in the newly controlled tournament, fought for honor rather than gain, men were killed with some regularity. Honor was also important to conduct in war and sometimes led men to death where military strategy would have dictated restraint or retreat. The knights who swore oaths over roast pheasants and swans were risking their lives

---

56. *Chronique*, I, 124; a famous *pas d'armes* appears in Froissart's chronicle (*Oeuvres*, XIV, 55–58, 105–51).

57. *Eulogium, Historiarum sive Temporis*, ed. Haydon, III, 227. The Chandos Herald describes the period after the victory of Poitiers as Arthurian: "Dauncier et chacier et voler, / Faire grantz festes et juster, / Faisoit [com] en regne d'Artus / L'espace de quatre ans ou plus" [for four years or more, they danced and hunted and hawked, held great feasts and jousted, as in the reign of Arthur] (*Vie du Prince Noir*, ed. Tyson, lines 1513–16).

58. Jean le Bel, *Chronique*, II, 194, 196 (cf. *Bataille de trente Anglois*, ed. Brush); Chandos Herald, lines 4098–101.

to imitate literature, and the captains who arranged the Combat of the Thirty are said to have chosen combat over jousting in order to win greater "onneur" and "pris" from their deaths. It was not for mere show that knights were willing to die, but for a chivalric honor of which public ceremony and literary celebration were part.[59]

Defining knighthood as a complex of social and military virtues was largely new to social practice, but not to literature. The concept's sources were religious writings about ideal knighthood, chronicle accounts of legendary heroes, and romance visions of self-discovery through the service of love. Like William Marmion, Eustace d'Aubrichecourt imitated love service from literature. According to Jean Froissart, this Garter knight loved the niece of Queen Philippa,

> pour quoy il en valloit mieux en armes et en touttes mannières, et la dame ossi l'amoit si loyaument et si enterinement que mieux ne pooit, et souvent lettres, salus et segnefianches li envoioit, par quoi li chevaliers en estoit plus gais et plus jolis, plus larges et plus courtois et plus preux as armes.[60]

> such that he was worthier in arms and in every way, and the lady loved him also, so loyally and perfectly that it could not be better; and often she sent him letters, greetings, and tokens, which made the knight more gay and ardent, more generous and more courteous and braver in arms.

The transactions between these lovers copy the kind of courtship Amadas and Ydoine enjoy while Amadas is a knight errant. Undoubtedly, Eustace's courtship looks so much like one from ro-

---

59. Quotations are from Jean le Bel, *Chronique*, II, 195. See pp. 175–79 above; Barber, *Knight and Chivalry*, pp. 136–49; Barnie, *War*, pp. 70–91. Keen, "Chaucer's Knight," and Orme, "Courtier," discuss courtly literature's influence on education of the aristocracy.

60. *Oeuvres*, VI, 153; cf. *Amadas et Ydoine*, lines 1420–23 and 1459–64:

> . . . as autres exemplaire estoit
> De sens et de cevalerie,
> D'ensegnement, de courtoisie
> Et de francise et de largece. . . .
> Souvent li tramet ses messages,
> Et les proueces que il fait,
> Dont Ydoine maint souspir trait
> De la joie qu'a des nouveles.
> Ses rices drüeries beles
> Li renvoie souventes fois.

To other knights he was an example of wisdom and chivalry, of learning and courtesy, of nobility and generosity. . . . He often sent her messages about his acts of prowess, over which Ydoine drew many a sigh for the joy she took in his news. Many times she sent in return her fine love tokens.

mance because Froissart assists in the imitation. The vocabulary of virtues and the syntax of love's relation to prowess are drawn straight from literature; in his second version Froissart adds the thoroughly romantic hyperbole, "ne nuls ne duroit devant lui, car il estoit jones et amoureus durement" [nor could anyone withstand him, for he was young and deeply in love].[61] Froissart and Eustace strive in their different ways to demonstrate that life can fulfill literature's ideal of self-improving service to love.

In contrast the twelfth-century chronicler Lambert of Ardres and his subjects do not seem to take courtly behavior seriously. According to Lambert, Arnulf courted Ida unscathed because of his wise detachment. Arnulf's ancestor Sigfried also behaved opportunistically rather than humbly: he exchanged some secret messages with a certain Elstrude and then "nolenti velle, immo nolle volenti, sine vi ludendo vim intulit, et eam clanculo impregnavit" [she unwilling to be willing, indeed willing to be unwilling, in sport he attacked her by force without violence and secretly impregnated her].[62] Lambert treats Sigfried's courtship, like Arnulf's, as calculating and manipulative rather than idealizing. In the later Middle Ages, however, both the sympathy of the cultural record and the deeper engagement of knights with courtly ideology mark a shift from accepting the distance between literature and life to seeking to unite the two.

In this union writers come to associate the transforming power of love closely and regularly with marriage. Sir Thomas Gray attributes David of Scotland's marriage with Margaret de Logy to love alone—"cest matrimoigne fust fait soulement per force damours, qe toutz veint" [this marriage was accomplished only by the power of love, which conquers all].[63] Praise of love in marriage was the subject of many lyrics written by courtiers; Eustache Deschamps involves several of his friends in a ballade asking whether it is

---

61. *Oeuvres*, VI, 154. Further examples of imitating lovers from literature are given in Benson, "Morte Darthur," pp. 153–56; Prestwich, *Three Edwards*, p. 207; R. F. Green, *Poets and Princepleasers*, pp. 101–34. Froissart's *Meliador* has some similarities to later ME romances with respect to exemplarity (Dembowski, *Froissart*).

62. Lambert of Ardres, *Chronicon*, p. 35. Lambert says Sigfried's love for Elstrude was intemperate and morbid and brought him to a miserable death "alterum Andream exhibens Parisiensem" [like another Andrew of Paris] (p. 37). If this refers to Andreas Capellanus, it indicates that contemporaries understood his treatise to be cautionary and satirical rather than exemplary of good love; see Karnein, "Autor."

63. *Scalacronica*, p. 203. Gray's assessment disregards David's pressing need for an heir, a motive made clearer by David's later estrangement from the childless Margaret and his plans for another marriage; see Dickinson, *Scotland*, pp. 182–84.

better to marry a young or an older lady. His refrain makes Sir Lewis Clifford the authority on this *question d'amour*: "m'escripvez vostre accort; / Et s'avisez n'estes de la partie, / Demandez ent a l'amoureux Cliffort" [write me your decision; and if you aren't informed on the question, ask the lover Clifford about it].[64] Deschamps's strategy asserts that literary topoi (the young versus the older woman, the *question d'amour*) can be illuminated by Clifford's personal experience as a lover. Similarly, Chaucer's elegy for Blanche of Lancaster treats her husband John of Gaunt as the living embodiment of literary love-conventions; and the Chandos Herald presents the Black Prince's wife complaining to a literary fabrication, "la dieuesse d'amours" [goddess of love], when her husband goes overseas.[65] Blurring the distinction between literature and life becomes itself a literary convention in the fourteenth century, one that recognizes and encourages the contemporary practice of imitating literature.

It is quite true, as historians like Huizinga and Kilgour demonstrate, that in many instances noble behavior did not live up to the standards proclaimed by the age. However, the issue is not whether nobles invariably based their actions on literary ideals, but whether on the whole they believed that these were worthy ideals whose pursuit was valid in life.[66] This they did believe. Commemorated by writers, praised by society, rewarded with status, the imitation of literary love and chivalry became an important feature of fourteenth-century experience.

Romances were part of this world of literary imitations. The English romances of love and chivalry vary widely, but *Ipomadon* illustrates a dominant tendency for the more accomplished works of the century. These works revise earlier literary ideals of behavior to make them more accessible in many ways. Continuing in the directions

---

64. *Oeuvres complètes*, ed. Queux de Saint-Hilaire, III, 375; Gower's "Cinkante Balades" and "Traité pour essampler les amantz marietz" also exemplify the century's tendency to link love with marriage (*The Complete Works of John Gower*, ed. Macaulay, I, 335–92).

65. *The Works of Geoffrey Chaucer*, ed. Robinson, pp. 267–79; *Vie du Prince Noir*, lines 2052–53. The Chevalier de la Tour Landry describes his courtship of his wife in literary terms—he served love devotedly and was rewarded with a beautiful and virtuous lady to whom he wrote many lyrics (*Chevalier de la Tour Landry*, ed. Montaiglon, pp. 1–2). Barnie's contention (*War*, p. 66) that romances could not guide life because their view of love was counter to marriage seems to refer to OF rather than ME works.

66. See n.8 above.

established by *Amadas et Ydoine*'s and *Sir Tristrem*'s revisions of *Tristan*, *Ipomadon* and similar romances alter their sources sufficiently to permit an authorial stance of endorsement rather than ironic distance. Their revisions reduce tension and increase exemplarity, move style toward naturalism, and in general assert that romance heroes are understandable and that we can learn from them.

These alterations align poetry with the growing impulse toward imitation. Yet the late romances' naturalism is highly selective, and their didacticism is couched in hyperbole and fantasy. They expand their claims to practical value at a time when the barony's economic and political power was actually diminishing. These developments are not so paradoxical as they seem. Rather than attempting a direct correlation between represented and real noble behavior, the assertions of the later poets confer a metaphoric and cultural value on the barony that fills in for its losses in concrete power. The experience provided by these English works is quite different from that of early romances, but that experience continues to relate ideals about courtliness to perceptions about noble status and behavior.

Ipomadon provides a striking example of the process because it adheres so closely to its source, Hue de Rotelande's *Ipomedon*, and yet revises that source so consistently.[67] In general *Ipomadon* reproduces Hue's text sympathetically.

> 'Alez?—Oÿl!—Pur quey?—Ne say!
> —Ky li mefist?—Nuls—Si fist!—Nay!
> Eins est son songe k'ad songé.'
> (1423–25)

'Gone?' 'Yes!' 'Why?' 'I don't know!' 'Who did him wrong?' 'No one.' 'Someone did!' 'No! Rather it's because of a dream he dreamed.'

> 'Ys he goone?' 'Madame, yea!'
> 'Whotte thow oghte, why?' 'Madame, na,   Do you know
> As haue I joye or blis!'
> 'Dyd anny man hym aught but righte?'
> 'Nay, but a dreme, he dremyd to night.'[68]
> (1364–67)

---

67. *Hue de Rotelande's Ipomedon in drei englischen Bearbeitungen*, ed. Kölbing. Kölbing's date of composition (1350) is modified to ca. 1375 by Trounce, "Tail-Rhyme Romances" (1934), p. 42. Kölbing also edits the fifteenth-century *Lyfe of Ipomydon* and prose *Ipomedon*, both of which are not so close to Hue's work as *Ipomadon*. The tail-rhyme version appears in a large collection MS (Chetham 8009) in company with *Beues of Hamtoun*.

68. For technical studies of the ME adapter's methods, see Kölbing, edition, pp. lxv–cxlvii; Blessing, "Antecedents," pp. 296–335; Wadsworth, "Historical Romance," pp. 257–78; and Bjorklund, "*Ipomadon*."

This is a faithful rendering, but its slowed tempo deflects the extravagant, even comical impact of Hue's chopped dialogue. The English poet tends to revise any element of style, commentary, or plot that could undermine the story's validity.

The most obvious change, since it involves many deletions through the whole work, is that Hue's bantering asides, pointed ironies, and insouciant sensuality virtually disappear from *Ipomadon*. Gone are Hue's speculations on la Fière's hidden beauties, on the queen's secret desires, on his lovers' virginity, and on how he himself would pardon ladies hesitant to love. Other reductions move in the same direction. Lovers' monologues, especially the more tortured and hopeless ones, shrink or become calmer. Exotic love-symptoms such as turning black and livid largely disappear from the English text.[69] These reductions all contribute to the English poet's effort to alter fundamentally the tone and thematic focus of *Ipomedon*.

When Hue's ironic commentary does move into English, it can be so transformed that blame becomes praise:

> Celui ke plus femme harra,
> Quant sun quer li rechangera
> Pus ert cil de li amez plus;
> E si runt eles un autre us:
> Celui ke eles plus amerunt
> Pur poi de achesun plus harrunt,
> Si ke plus tost recovereit
> L'estrange, ke cil ne fereit
> Ki a poer l'avreit servi,
> Jo en sai le veir, pur ço le di.
> (8657–66)

When a woman's heart changes on her, the man she hates most becomes the one she loves most; and they have another habit too: the man they love most, they'll hate most with little justification, such that they become distant more quickly than would he who wished to serve her as best he could. I know the truth of this, that's why I'm saying it.

> A womon is bothe warre & wyse,   perceptive
> Grette loue & lykyng in them lyse,

---

69. Some love symptoms are deleted from *Ipomedon* (ed. Holden): lines 785 (trembling), 934–35 (heart leaving body), 1100–1101 (yawning and changing color), 1464 (turning black and livid), and 8733–48 (various; vs. ME 7122–26). Reduced monologues are AN 955–1098 vs. ME 911–1034, AN 4584–614 vs. ME 3414–17, AN 5237–58 vs. ME 3993–95. A few of Hue's comments appear almost unchanged in ME: 389–90, 512–13, 750–54, 797–808, 2786–88, 6468–71, 7346–54.

Who lyste, to lere at there lore;	For those who desire to learn
There they haue byn most straunge,	distant
All att onys then will they chaunge,	
Yff they be not sought ouer-sore,	too insistently
And love twyse so herttly syne:	deeply thereafter
Godes dere blessyng and myne	
Muste they have therefore!	
(7088–96)	

The Anglo-Norman passage typifies Hue's attitude: women are imponderable, consistent only in their inconsistency, and this he knows from his own experience. In the English version women's behavior becomes generous, subtle rather than irrational, and praiseworthy rather than vacillating. The economical but thorough change worked on Hue's passage gives some idea of the English poet's remarkable talent for revision.

To dismantle Hue's ironic perspective might seem simply naive, were this poet not simultaneously engaged in altering Hue's material sufficiently to convince us that irony is not an appropriate response to Ipomadon's career. Hue revels in the inadequacies of conventional courtly formulas by raising contradictions and difficulties in his narrative. But the English poet forges Hue's plot into a smoothly finished model of noble behavior. Virtually every troubling situation that Hue invents is altered or answered in the English poem. In Hue's poem the three-day tournament organized to find a husband for la Fière (AN 3911–14, 4935–44) is a grisly illustration of the folly of fighting for love; in English it becomes a chivalric exercise, through eliminating Hue's critical commentary, the knights' regrets, and many deaths. Watching the tournament strengthens rather than weakens the Fere's dedication to Ipomadon (AN 6159–62): she resolves that if Ipomadon is lost to her, she will never love another (4370–75).[70] And Ipomadon leaves the tournament not because he believes that marriage ruins good knights (AN 6648–52), but rather because he feels too young to marry (4962–65) and too green to claim that he fulfills the Fere's vow (5098–101). This treatment turns Hue's examination of conflict between love and prowess into an exemplary illustration of chivalric devotion to love.

Because Hue questions convention not just in commentary but

---

70. Other examples of la Fière's vacillation are AN 3765–66, 5087–94; of the Fere's devotion strengthened by adversity, ME 4546–52 (vs. AN 6157–62), 8168–73.

through the plot itself, sometimes Middle English reformations coexist with original versions of episodes in a confusing way. The Anglo-Norman hero, wary of women and ready for adventures, tricks la Fière into believing that her monstrous suitor Leonin has won her kingdom—a surprisingly cold-hearted deception. The English poet explains that Ipomadon wore armor like Leonin's not to hurt the Fere but to spare her pain if he should be defeated (7698–700); the hero leaves for further adventures after his successful combat because "euermore in his hert he thought: / 'Till [to] her vowe corde [accord] I novght, / Therefore I will wythdrawe'" (8159–61). Unfortunately these justifications sit oddly with a passage retained from Anglo-Norman in which the disguised Ipomadon taunts the Fere "'To morowe in to Yndde ye shall wyth me, / For I haue slayne youre knyght!'" (8151–52). Usually the translator's revisions are more coherent, but occasionally Hue's subversions still trouble the English text.[71]

Most effective in establishing a new coherence for *Ipomadon* is the English poet's use of a central motif from *Ipomedon*, la Fière's proud vow to marry only the best knight in the world. In Hue's poem Ipomedon's absences appear to be alienated reactions to the wrongful pride inspiring the vow; the English poet reappraises the vow so that it explains these absences in terms of love's duty. Although he does translate the Fere's own feeling that her conduct was too proud (938–46), several new passages stress that Ipomadon's respect for the vow is so strong that it inhibits him, against the wishes of his heart, from ending his search for "losse and price" [praise and merit]:

> But euer more in his herte he þought,
> Yet till her avow cordede he nowght,   did not accord to
> Here husbond for to bee;
> That made hym oftyn tymes fro her fare.   go from her
> (5098–101)

The English poet praises Ipomadon's dedication (5092–97), and even the Fere's courtiers, who first condemn the vow as in Hue's

---

71. Ipomadon's behavior in disguise as the red knight is also still harsh in ME (4334–54). Modifications to make the English hero more orthodox than Hue's outweigh the vestigial outrages to la Fière's dignity, a fact important to assessing the English poet's intentions. Schroeder, unaware of Hue's work, finds the conjunction of Ipomadon's respect and vengeance in ME "weird" and argues from it that the English poet was not interested in portraying character ("Hidden Depths," p. 381). This conclusion needs to be measured against the adaptive challenges the poet faced.

work (AN 134–38, ME 121–26), later are so impressed by the heroine that they concede, "'No wounder, yf she be daungerus [hesitant] / To take an onworthy spowsse'" (2058–59).⁷² Poet, court, and hero all respect the vow, encouraging us to understand Ipomadon's adventures only as expressions of love for the Fere, rather than as punishments for her pride.

The direction of the English poet's revisions is unmistakable. Indeed, the adapter conducts a rescue operation, freeing characters from Hue's manifold ironies and restoring integrity to their actions and motivations. This twofold process of deletion and revision is characteristic of Middle English adapters who stay relatively close to their twelfth-century sources. In reworking *Yvain*, the *Ywain and Gawain* poet deletes precisely those passages that call into question the social value of love and the dignity of lovers: gone are Chrétien's reflections that Laudine is paradoxically both Yvain's beloved and his mortal enemy and that a lover has a body but no heart; gone is Lunete's casuistry persuading her mistress to love a better man than her husband by loving the man who was able to kill her husband. Further ironies of word and deed also disappear in the English version.⁷³

Ywain and Gawain's reductions complement revisions that strengthen the harmony between prowess and love. In Chrétien's *Yvain*, Gawain exhorts the hero to "break free of the bridle and halter" of Laudine in order to pursue chivalry and warns Yvain to "take care that our companionship does not fail on account of you."⁷⁴ The *Ywain* poet revises Gawain's speech to remove these implications that marriage imprisons knights and unties chivalric allegiances (1463–65), and he adds lines to emphasize the spouses' mutual respect as they accommodate their love to Gawain's request (1482, 1499). Surely the English work—which has been called "bowdlerized" and "as wholesome as porridge"⁷⁵—cannot be said

---

72. Their respect usefully replaces Hue's account of the lust la Fière inspires in her barons and Hue's own sensual speculations (AN 2267–94). Similar passages not in AN on the vow as Ipomadon's motivation are 5621–29, 8159–61, 8541–43, and 8565–67; other references to the vow not in AN are 548–50, 706, 1128–31, and 2258–66.

73. For a comprehensive list of alterations to *Yvain*, see *Ywain and Gawain*, pp. xvi–xxxiv. Stevens attributes ME reductions in irony to the poets' naïveté or lack of aesthetic sophistication (*Medieval Romance*, pp. 208–26); however, ME alterations so carefully excise and revise irony that authorial ignorance is not a satisfying explanation.

74. "'Ronpez le frain et le chevoistre. . . . Gardez, que an vos ne remaigne, / Biaus conpainz! nostre conpaignie'" (2500, 2510–11).

75. Stevens, *Medieval Romance*, p. 72; Pearsall, *Middle English*, p. 146.

to be *more* sensitive to romance ideals than *Yvain* simply because it rejects irony and conflict in those ideals. But English romances are *differently* sensitive, committed to reducing the extravagances and relaxing the tensions that aroused the irony of earlier poets.

Even in *Guy of Warwick*, which follows closely an Anglo-Norman romance attuned to later insular developments, some changes smooth over conflicts between ideals of life. When Gui determines to use his prowess to serve God rather than to serve Félice, she protests, "'Avez mei vus dunc en despit?'" ["Do you scorn me then?"] (7636), and Gui explains, "'Pur vus ai fait maint grant pecché'" ["For you I have sinned greatly"] (7674). The Middle English poem reshapes the encounter so that Guy's new life seems more to improve on than to conflict openly with his past life. Guy's explanation, "'Y schal walk for mi sinne'" (A 29.8), displaces the wrong from the love relationship to Guy's own soul, and Felice no longer feels scorned. Most striking, the poor Anglo-Norman wife sees herself as God's rival when Gui departs: "'Cest anel d'or od vus portez, / Pensez de mei quant le verrez, / Que vus pur Deu ne me ubliez'" ["Take this gold ring with you; think of me when you see it, so that you don't forget me for God"] (7722–24). But the English Felice understands Guy's departure as a new stage of self-improvement that does not deny his past: of her gold ring she says "'When þou ert in fer cuntre / Loke heron, & þenk on me, / & god y þe biteche [commend you to God]'" (A 33.7–9). Felice remarkably extends the convention that love improves knights when she connects Guy's love for her to service of God.

Felice's acquiescence erases the conflict her Anglo-Norman counterpart experienced between love and faith by revising her own role as proud heroine (she, like la Fière, had demanded that her lover become the best knight in the world).[76] Hue questioned the validity of that role through his rough treatment of la Fière, and the later insular romances prefer to show lovers in sympathy with each other, working productively to achieve their happiness. The English Ipomadon's willing acceptance of the Fere's vow eliminates the tension Hue builds between the lovers, and the English poet further declares (despite the plot's dependence on the convention of

---

76. Earlier in Guy's courtship, an added ME passage (A 621–24) explains that Felice's demands are principled rather than cold, preparing for her submission to Guy's new life. Camargo, "Metamorphosis," finds similar alterations of the AN *Alexander* in *Alisaunder* (pp. 101–11).

serving a proud lady) that the Fere's suffering makes this love one of mutual sacrifice:

> 'She [the Fere] is more worthy, hym to haue,
> Then euer were ye, Imayne!
> For her love he hathe suffyrd woo,
> And, sertus, she for hym also,   certainly
> Bothe they hadde full mekyll payne.'   great
>   (8704–8)

All these revisions illustrate consistent English responses to twelfth-century hesitations about courtly ideology in romance. Hue's *Ipomedon* questions the fundamental premises that love improves lovers and that prowess can fruitfully serve love. The English poets of this study endorse those very premises by redefining the terms. Love is more natural for English poets, less dramatic in its expressions and less imperious in its demands. It improves lovers not so much by refining their sensibilities as by encouraging their progress toward a full, varied experience of life. The prowess that serves love tends to facilitate worldly success, to be less ambiguously directed and less lethal except in war.[77]

These alterations make English romances more exemplary than their sources, but also more natural. Representations of ideal behavior become immediate and material in Middle English. Ipomadon explains his long course of adventures by describing love as a branch that grows and bends: "'lovers shold well leynand be, / For mekyll [greatly] I preyse that wande / That brekes not and will well bowe'" (2334–36).[78] A kind of emotional synecdoche represents feeling through physical manifestation. "Bothe there chekys [their cheeks] was wete" (8315) translates sorrow, while the development of love makes the heart an actor as "A thynge in her hert gan ryse" (424); "Wyth hyr owne hertt þis [thus] she strave" (1037). The Fere's

---

77. Examples from *Ipomadon* of expanded emphasis on the merit of chivalry and its relation to love are lines 1–12, 1556–86, 2492–503, and 8876–84; conflict with the Fere's suitor is over love rather than defense of her country (7952–75). Ipomedon willingly fights his friend Capaneus over love (AN 6183–202), but Ipomadon is sad to be forced into doing so (ME 8394–411). Daire, whom Ipomedon kills in the three-day tournament but who reappears in France (see p. 168), is not killed in ME (3315–20, 4071–76).

78. Compare "Betwene them burgenyd such a bravnche, / That in þer lyves schall neuer stavnche, / Tille they on bere [bier] be brought" (1268–70), which replaces the less natural image of hearts uniting outside their bodies (AN 1297–1300). Other examples of concrete images not in AN are lines 522–23, 1022, 1106–11, 5138–39, and 8682.

collapse from love, "She tombyled doun upon her bedde" (1406), does translate "Vent a son lit si chet enverse" [she comes to her bed and falls backward on it] (1463), but the English gesture is less histrionic, requires no premeditation, and therefore seems more heartfelt as well as more plausible. Critics often remark the shift from a mannered and even hermetic style to a natural and even colloquial style in the Middle English romances; *William of Palerne*, *Ywain and Gawain*, and *Floris and Blancheflur* are other obvious illustrations. But the shift does not imply a loss of idealism despite the changed understanding of love and chivalry. Rather, in the later insular romances, principled love and chivalry come to be presented as natural practices rather than held at a distance through the twin and opposed motions of irony and elevation. The naturalness of *Ipomadon*'s presentation is part of its argument that these lovers are understandable even in their excellence—they are the ideal made accessible.

Part of the English romances' accessibility lies in their didacticism, their gestures toward helping the audience step from admiration to imitation. *Ipomadon* begins, "Off love were lykynge of to lere" [it would be pleasant to learn about love], and executes its teaching almost programmatically by transforming many of *Ipomedon*'s episodes into lessons. Where Hue mocks women's incomprehensibility, the English poet invites us "to lere at there lore" [learn from their wisdom] (7090). Where Hue exposes chivalrous society's pretensions through Ipomedon's disguise as a coward, the English poet finds a lesson in manners verbalized by the chastised mockers themselves:

> All that euer to skorne hym lovgh,
> Off them selff thought skorne inovgh
> And sayden on ther avyce: admonished themselves
> 'Off a straunge man in uncovthe place,
> In them, that moste skornyng mas,   who scorn him most
> Leste off norture lyse!'
>   (5230–35)

The concern for "norture" is characteristic of the later romances, where "cortaysye" has become a matter of social education in a broad sense.[79] To instruct us, the poetic world strives to make itself

---

79. Evans, "'Cortaysye'"; Mathew, "Knighthood"; *Ipomadon*, lines 151–52; *Gui*, lines 63, 85, 118, 149; *Amadas*, line 1422. An important facet of ME exemplarity is respect for marriage and sexual propriety (nn. 12, 63–65 above). Poets go to great lengths to emphasize chastity: in *Degrevant* the lovers cuddle in bed while courting,

like our own world and not difficult to understand. Thomas and Hue find human nature more perplexing and draw from continental tradition their sense that romances are poetic artifacts existing separately from daily life. The English romances, without claiming to be realistic in plot, introduce this new kind of practical admonishing.

And yet the exemplary quality of the English romances, striking as it is, cannot account convincingly for their success. Only when we take exemplarity as one manifestation of what is more fully and forcefully implicit in their natural style, their revised ideals, and their refusal of ironic distance can we see how these romances worked for their audience.

Middle English romances deny to traditional Old French courtliness something essential: its elitism, its hermetic reserve. Twelfth-century courtliness functioned ideologically by exclusion. Its love and chivalry were worthy of celebration in part because of their distance from and superiority to life. This literature did not strive to be accessible. It was *récit clos* and as such was emblematic of the aristocracy's claim, however futile, to economic and political autonomy. But in England in the fourteenth century, literature itself provided a means of demonstrating superiority. Barons sought to take hold of literature's cultural status by imitating art in life and by generating new texts out of their exploits. English romances facilitate the barony's claim to status by their very openness, by advertising the naturalness and imitability of their new courtly love and chivalry.

In Few Wordes Ys Curtesye

This shift in the function of courtly literature is the culmination of literary and social changes that began with Anglo-Norman responses to Old French romance. Thomas of Britain's *Tristan* and Hue de Rotelande's *Ipomedon* establish an approach to continental convention that is continued in the Anglo-Norman and Middle English romances of the thirteenth and fourteenth centuries. The later works tend to concentrate, like their predecessors, on the degree of reconciliation possible between ideal models and observed realities

---

but "or þei wer wed, / Þei synnyd nat þare" (ed. Casson, lines 1559–60); and *Knight of Curtesy* turns the adulterous tragedy of the OF *Châtelain de Couci* into an entirely chaste love affair, "'Fro luste our bodyes to kepe clene'" (ed. McCausland, line 92). See also *Courtesy and Nurture*, ed. Parsons.

of human behavior. Despite the differences in temperament that separate Thomas from Hue, this concern unites their convictions that, on Thomas's side, "unc ne sot que fud amur, / Ne put saver que est dolur" [one who has never known love cannot know what sorrow is] (D 991–92), and on Hue's side that "Amur ne quert fors sun delit" [love seeks only its own pleasure] (4313). To argue that *fine amor* is shot through with pain or that it is above all sensual and selfish is in both cases to recognize the contingency of refined love upon lovers' merely physical being. The recognition anchors disembodied courtly ideals firmly in mortal clay, resisting conventional hermeticism and hyperbole.

Thomas and Hue handle their powerful images of noble extremists of love with skeptical detachment, while thirteenth- and fourteenth-century poets are able to handle their less problematic versions of courtliness with glad confidence. They make literary principles more compatible with ordinary social conviction, associating ideal love to many other fulfillments and chivalric ideals to military practice, sensible moderation, and politeness. This adaptation greatly reduces the tension between courtly image and ordinary humanity that troubled the earlier Anglo-Norman poets. From *Amadas et Ydoine* on, a strong current in insular romance finds a solution to love's antisocial potential in the natural sympathy of lovers and their complicity in seeking a good life. In *Sir Tristrem* as well, love becomes a simpler, more accessible good (unfortunately accessible even to a dog), and the heroes grow more able to control events. *Ipomadon* revises its source's ironic discord between love and lengthy adventures into a delicate symbiosis that requires separation and adventure to nurture the natural slow growth of love.

In terms of literary history, then, the later insular poets answer their Anglo-Norman predecessors coherently and purposefully. The course of generic development also makes sense in terms of the barony's growing social engagement with patterns of behavior from literature. Fourteenth-century poets' assertions that their heroes are explicable and imitable are not naive; these poets "wrote about chivalrous ideals that were neither a pose nor the exclusive property of a narrow caste, but rather about ideals which they knew as a living and powerful force or ethos."[80] In this context it is

---

80. Keen, "Chivalrous Culture," p. 10; see also Benson, "*Morte Darthur*," pp. 197–201.

not surprising that romance should begin to look almost nonfictional. Ipomadon's explanation for his disguises might apply directly to the English knights who wore eyepatches abroad but would not discuss their vows:

> 'In few wordes ys curtesye:
> Lette his dedes bere wittenes, why
> He shuld be louyde agayne! . . .   in return
> And ay the moste man of price   of greatest worth
> The leyste of them selff wille sayne!'
>   (2339–41, 2346–47)

Hue and Thomas attempt poetic connections between ideal systems and their authorial perceptions of human nature, but this English passage even moves toward linking poetry and history. The many words of romance, superfluous to behavior, make themselves mere vehicles for a lesson that demands "few wordes" and many deeds. In this period living knights treated literature as a guide to behavior, and literature actively provided them with instruction.

Readers may lament, for poetry, that cultural history moved in this direction. The later romances of love and chivalry work changes on courtly ideology that are more aesthetically troubling than the changes worked on religious and national ideology in other romances, because these changes are to some degree at odds with the literary project itself. The English adapters' refusal of difficulties in the *fine amor* of their sources may strike us as a refusal of imagination. Consistently smoothing over a source's thematic tensions often gives the Middle English redactions a flat, riskless quality. Hardly any problems are left to be resolved, and those remaining have solutions that are taught to us as if they were simple matters. Even in the context of what has been called a golden age of chivalry, this teaching may seem facile. To provide exempla of politeness is one thing, but these romances even assert that the enormous deeds and extraordinary careers of their sources are not distant in their perfection but are instead open lessons for the attentive. It is puzzling that the romances changed at the cost of aesthetic subtlety, even when revisions were undertaken carefully and consistently as in *Ipomadon*.[81]

That the English romances of love and chivalry so often reflect

---

81. The traditional explanation, that the audience for ME romances was "popular," is not convincing in terms of these works' social situation and often becomes a circular evasion of aesthetic problems (see n.44 above). Ganim rejects this kind of argument in "History and Consciousness."

historical practices and so often take a stance of exemplarity is misleading, however. They ignore reality too persistently to be considered mirrors of their time and simplify life's problems too drastically to be satisfying as exemplary texts.[82] They deliberately evade the tough issues of their sources and ignore the turbulent age around them. Rather, the consistent revisions that these works perform—their naturalism and exemplarity, their release of tensions and problems within plots, their refusal of ironic detachment and mystifying elevation—attempt to provide the audience with access to the ideals the text encloses. The later poets maintain not that there is no difference between the world of romance and the historical world, but that poetic ideals can be possessed and used. This claim, imaginative as it may be, breaks down the hermetic exclusiveness that was essential to twelfth-century French romances' defense of the aristocracy's specialness. That exclusiveness was alien to Anglo-Norman romancers and quickly attacked by thirteenth- and fourteenth-century poets.

Poetic resistance to the hermeticism that made twelfth-century French courtly ideology powerful is consonant with the insular barons' social position in the later Middle Ages. From the Conquest, England's was a relatively open nobility, quite firmly controlled by the crown. By the fourteenth century the class was even less exclusive and its economic and political power were steadily declining.[83] One source of status that the barony could still call on was cultural, and the proliferation of tournaments, orders of chivalry, courtiers' lyrics, and chivalric biographies in this period exercised the barony's claim to be the living embodiment of courtly and chivalric ideals. Literature provided support for the claim to cultural importance partly by altering *courtoisie* in ways compatible with social behavior, but more pervasively by simply taking a stance of imitability, however fanciful or inimitable its plots and characters actually were. This stance implies that cultural importance can flow from poetic fabrications to an absorbing audience.

---

82. Even the more aesthetically sophisticated works of this century tend not to "link up with the age's deeper currents of social unrest" (Muscatine, *Poetry and Crisis*, pp. 1–35 [quote at p. 25]). Coleman notes similarly that the romances are "far from depicting a confrontation with any specific element of the present reality" (*Medieval Readers*, p. 92). Their pervasive refusal of confrontation must be recognized as a real issue. To take these romances as transparently exemplary diminishes their merit by the degree to which they mismeasure the real conditions which their advice purports to address.

83. Intro., nn. 16–23; Chap. 1, nn. 75–77. See also Russell, "The Triumph of Dignity over Order in England," in *Twelfth Century Studies*, pp. 137–50.

The barons' victory over decline was only partial, however, for displacing their merit from concrete toward cultural grounds made something of their merit available to all who had access to culture. Emphasizing their cultural superiority distinguished them from those merchants and professionals who could match barons in wealth and influence, yet that emphasis was itself vulnerable to middle-class ambition. Merchants who adopted coats of arms, attended tournaments, formed poetry-writing fraternities, and even achieved knighthood were encroaching on new territory in the fourteenth century, the very territory barons were attempting to occupy as their political and economic dominance gradually faded. And the audience for later courtly romances broadened just as participation in courtly behaviors expanded in the fourteenth century. Indeed, the attempt in the late romances to confer courtly standing on listeners served competitive commoners better than it served the barony, insofar as it freely offered them a kind of status previously closed to them.

Although congenial to the middle class, the late romances of love and chivalry address primarily the aristocracy's deteriorating situation. Their naturalism, like their exemplarity, associates ideal to practice, endorsing the single change that seemed to improve the barony's position in this period—active imitation of literature in life. Their images of resolved tensions and easy victories are escapist but also laudatory and optimistic. More significantly, these elements taken globally provide a wellspring of renewed merit for the barony.

For in the later Middle Ages, knights in disguise at tournaments, ladies sending them tokens and fairy messengers, and nobles joining quasi-Arthurian orders of chivalry profess the same thing the late romances profess: that living persons can lay claim to the dignity of courtly ideology. When Froissart treats Eustace d'Aubrichecourt as if he were a figure from romance, or when *Ipomadon*'s final lesson for lovers is "That for a littill lette ye noughte [you don't give up]: / Sertes, no more dyd hee" (8883–84), we need not conclude that Froissart was a crazy dreamer or that the *Ipomadon* poet was hopelessly simplistic. Rather, such claims that romance and life are at one establish a new topos for courtly writing, a figurative assertion that life takes courtly ideals seriously and has absorbed the value of romance. This new topos is part of a historical process that allowed England's courtly society to reshape its identity and reaffirm its dominance in troubled and changing times.

Conclusion

Over two centuries the Anglo-Norman and related Middle English romances were insular in their divergences from continental romances, their distance from the royal court, and their specific engagements in English baronial milieus. Even the earliest Anglo-Norman romance poets expressed their separateness from France by resisting its literary conventions, by choosing English heroes, or by directly distinguishing themselves from the French as does the *Alexander* poet: "Ces sunt les esteilles qe nos Charle Wain nomon. / Char l'apellent Franceis" [these are the stars we call Charles's Wain; the French call them the Cart].[1] In the later twelfth century, "Normans in England were ceasing to call themselves Normans. . . . If they had to be described by a collective or national name, it was not 'Norman' but 'English.' The change was universal because from 1154 even the king of England was not a Norman."[2] The Anglo-Norman poets' insular identity was consolidated as Henry II's reign gradually changed England's cultural and administrative relationship to Normandy and other Angevin territories. The local affiliations of many Anglo-Norman romances—Lincoln for *Haveloc*, Hereford for *Ipomedon*—extend to their Middle English adaptations, whose origins read like an itinerary of the realm, from Lan-

---

1. Thomas of Kent, *Alexander*, ed. Foster and Short, lines 4674–75; cf. "Fort est a translater; suffreite ay de romanz" [this is difficult to translate; my French is insufficient] (4662).
2. R. H. C. Davis, *Normans and Their Myth*, p. 131.

cashire and Yorkshire to Dorset, from East Anglia to Erceldoune. Works often made their way to London, but this is first of all a provincial literature, and stylish urbanity is not one of its identifying features.

Nonetheless, this is an aristocratic literature. The Anglo-Norman works addressed England's briefly bilingual elite in the language of their superiority. English adaptations spoke to a broadened but still largely baronial public. By the later thirteenth century, many nobles were not at ease with French, while the mercantile sector began to share some baronial interests. The two groups were in significant contact and competition during the fourteenth century, but the English descendants of Anglo-Norman romances continued primarily to examine baronial preoccupations and ideas about the world. The English works' aesthetic level, too, is consistent with a baronial public. *Guy of Warwick, Amis and Amiloun,* and *Beues of Hamtoun* may be unsophisticated in comparison to some court productions, but we have seen that they are in sympathy with and often polish Anglo-Norman sources of narrower aristocratic milieu.

These romances do not treat their subjects as if they had no correlatives in life. On the contrary, insular poets seem as interested in their ability to comment on the world as in their capacity to escape life's necessities or to idealize life's processes through the transformations of poetry. They are sharply aware of contemporary political, religious, and cultural principles, and they examine as well a set of convictions important to the barony: that noble power rests in the land and its heritability, so that noble merit inheres in perpetuating the patrimony and the family; furthermore, that the behaviors fostered by this system—courageous initiative in war, respect for law and custom in peace, cultivation of social graces through wealth—are virtues that justify and expand the dominance brought by landholding. The insular romances give poetic form to this ideology and to other beliefs, dramatizing their confrontations and finally picturing all of them contributing to baronial advancement.

The romances of English heroes tell of political crises resolved by military and legal action. Usually the hero loses his inheritance and wins it back; typically the hero's community loses and gains with him. Horn and Havelok go into exile accompanied by loyal followers and restore the rights of those followers by overthrowing wicked usurpers. As Fulk and Horn demand justice for themselves, they correct royal injustice toward their fellow vassals. Bevis and Guy defend Christians from pagans and barons from rapacious lords, altering social conditions for the general good. The external and political crises, the national scale, and the heroic support of whole communities are so marked in these works that some of them (*Boeve*, *Fouke*, the Anglo-Norman *Horn*) are occasionally called epics rather than romances. But it is the hero's program of landed and lineal fulfillment, not the nation's need, that determines the course of events, no matter how closely the two are allied in these plots.

That baronial and national interests do appear to coincide in these works is significant in relation to the historical tension between barony and king. Centralization was in many ways congenial to England's landholders, yet the gradual subordination of feudal rights to royal control, and of family fortunes to national well-being, demanded that the barony accept a new political ideology. Feudal custom must bend to the king's will; private rights must accommodate themselves to the national good. John of Salisbury's *Policraticus* expressed this ideology in the Anglo-Norman period, invoking the metaphor of head and body for king and subjects and urging on knights a full acceptance of authoritative rule. Two centuries later Walter Burley was still claiming that a virtuous king's subordinate social order was a good one in which "quilibet est contentus de gradu suo sub rege" [everyone is content with his station beneath the king].[3]

The romances of English heroes acknowledge the dominance of national ideology by recognizing the right and power of kings, placing high value on communal stability, and representing the legal system as a legitimate source of redress for the barony. But at the same time, these romances reinterpret nationalism to the advantage of the newly constrained barony. The desires of the noble hero subsume the desires of his community, so that the hero's impulse toward personal achievement is in harmony with a broader, impersonal impulse toward national stability. Through this pattern the romances of English heroes consistently subvert the political principle that royal and national interests must come before those of landed barons. Indeed, these romances stand the ideal on its

---

3. Thomson, "Walter Burley's Commentary," p. 578; *Policraticus*, ed. Webb, 5.2 and 6.29.

head by proposing that baronial interests are the key to the public good. This confident cohesiveness diminishes in the later romances, but generally the desires of a noble hero and of the people at large are inseparable and are to be realized concurrently through the hero's struggle to recover his patrimony and establish his lineage. King John's insistence on controlling Fulk and his fellow barons is thus misguided; King Edgar's desire to punish Bevis for the death of the heir to the throne is doomed to failure—because only when the desires of kings and commons follow those of the dispossessed hero will harmony be achieved.

A similar literary refraction turns Christian models of abnegation to the purpose of private, worldly advancement. Particularly during and after the great thirteenth-century institutional reforms directed at expanding the church's role in the lives of the faithful, religious content infused romances written in England. The most pious romances seem to construct so symbiotic an interrelation of religious and secular impulses that some critics coin new generic designations for them—"homiletic romance," "exemplary romance," "secular hagiography." For these critics the pious romances express perfectly the church's new emphasis on lay piety and on the instruction of the laity through sermons and saints' legends. But as with the move toward governmental centralization, the church's extended and regularized control benefited its members only at the price of their reduced autonomy and increased compliance with institutional standards. The pious romances resist these implications of Christian teaching as they revise hagiography's ideal models of surrender to God, transcendent faith, and heavenly apotheosis.

The stories of Guy of Warwick and Amis and Amiloun illustrate the tendency most fully. Guy's conversion to God's service and his wandering life recall the legend of St. Alexis, while Amis and Amiloun demonstrate their constancy in willing submission to tests from God. But piety is subordinate to profane achievement and happiness in these romances. St. Alexis effaces his identity, abdicates control of his life to God, and rejects his family and all worldly ties. In contrast, Guy retains control of his life of service to God, acts on secular (as well as religious) motives, and attends to the well-being of his family. His mature pattern of life is a deliberate reversal in the secular sphere of his earlier proud actions, rather than an irrevocable surrender of will and identity to God. Amis and Amiloun's story also bears strong resemblances to religious literature in the heroes' submission to divinely imposed trials and in the rewards sent from God. Indeed, the story exists in hagiographic versions. But the source of the friends' trials in legend—God's chastening of those he truly loves—shifts in Anglo-Norman and Middle English to the testing of an oath of brotherhood. Heaven rewards earthly friendship, not Christian faith. In keeping with this substitution of the flesh for the spirit, an earthly apotheosis replaces the hagiographic translation of saints to heaven with the restoration of domestic happiness and years of brotherly companionship.

Despite the deep moral commitment of these romances, their ultimate refusal of hagiography's vision compromises their religious element and finally makes it contingent on impulses opposed to Christian teaching. Preachers' objections to the "veyn carpyng" [foolish chatter] of *Guy, Sir Ysumbras,* and other romances are well taken from this perspective.[4] Religious faith, like nationalism, cannot alienate the insular hero from his freedom of action or his private and profane concerns. Even the devout romances build an ideal of worldly achievement in which piety contributes to political and economic success, and divinity supports baronial causes.

As Christian principles fail to dominate secular allegiances in some insular romances, so too the cultural ideal of *courtoisie* does not disguise for Anglo-Norman poets the capricious and irrational ambitions of lovers. *Tristan* and *Ipomedon* take such detached attitudes to *courtoisie* that some critics deny them generic status as romance. These critics emphasize the typical continental presentation of noble characters refined by a sublimating love that generates numerous virtues and complements morally informed prowess. Thomas of Britain and Hue de Rotelande write of this ideal with full consciousness of its aspiration to perfecting sentiment and behavior, but both poets hesitate to discover in their heroes or in humanity at large the ability to fulfill that aspiration. In *Tristan* penance and suffering acknowledge the rift between *fine amor* and human frailty. Rigorous self-denial counterbalances the sexual passion of love, and violent devotions oppose love's violent jealousies. Hue approaches the problem differently, narrating a conventional story of noble courtship from a conflicting stance on so-

---

4. The phrase is used by William of Nassington, MS Bodleian 48, fol. 47; quoted in *Thornton Romances,* ed. Halliwell.

cial and emotional behavior that questions the plot's model of ideal love, troubles the relationship of love and chivalry, and diminishes the characters' stature.

For the early insular poets Old French *courtoisie* is alien and implausible, but later poets embrace it as a source of heroic value by rejecting its claims to exclusivity and high refinement. Amadas and Ydoine are mutually supportive partners whose loyalty is powered by pragmatic watchfulness, restraint, and cleverness. Similarly, the English poets complement their removal of ironic perspectives with alterations designed to make their material less troubling and more open to understanding. In their works love is natural and productive; *curtesye* is a straightforward set of teachable virtues.

State and church theorists contributed to the formation of courtly and chivalric ideals, as did literature, but the practical use for *courtoisie* as an ideology lay with the aristocracy's claims to superiority and special rights. In twelfth-century France the claim through *courtoisie* was largely an imaginative one not connected to operative principles of conduct, a disjunction observed with particular irony by Anglo-Norman poets. But by the later Middle Ages the English barony's claims to status located value in a range of behaviors that qualified and supplemented their landed and more distant military character. Here the late medieval nobility found a prestige that seemed to make up for its losses in economic and political status. Later insular poets adapt *courtoisie* in ways that enhance its usefulness for the English barony. They deny the ideology's first and deepest claims by developing a courtliness that is facilitating and imitable rather than exclusive. The *fine amor* that rejects madness and isolation for a carefully arranged marriage in *Amadas et Ydoine* and the links Guy's career establishes between marriage, chivalric excellence, and faith draw literary ideals closer to didactic exemplarity and imply that courtliness is directly accessible to the audience.

In summary, insular romances resist the political principle that national or royal interests must come before baronial ambition, the Christian teaching that religious values are superior to concern for the world, and the cultural principle that courtliness transforms its adepts beyond the merely human. To be sure, these dominant ideologies deeply affect the romances, providing them with important measures of value. Guy of Warwick's enormous popularity may be due to the conjunction of ideals called upon in his story: Guy is a national figure who defends England from foreign threats, he strives for years to answer his lady's command to become the best of all knights, and he serves God during lonely years of pilgrimage. At the same time Guy like other heroes of this study evades the very ideals that nurture him. His defense of the nation is only a function of his private commitments, first to love and then to God. His love, though intense and aspiring, occasions regrets in his youth and repentance in age. And in serving God he does not surrender his identity, worldly motives, or concern for his family. The Guy poems, and other insular romances, seem to invoke dominant ideologies precisely in order to examine the telling differences between them and the hero's contrary program of fulfillment. By this process the romances answer generic and historical challenges together.

Insular romances often draw on epic, hagiography, and courtly romance, yet they take pains to distance themselves from these strong influences. To epic's heroic sacrifice and national commitment the English heroes respond that self-advancement guarantees the community's good and that the family's perpetuation can stand for the nation's security. In opposition to hagiography's polarizing of earthly and heavenly preoccupations, pious romances integrate faith into worldly identities and secular pursuits. Without becoming simply parodic, insular works reject continental versions of self-transformation through love for images of courtliness more natural, plausible, and even imitable. Their generic interactions are so marked that insular romances often seem to be themselves generically marginal. Yet their interactions usually sustain broadly characteristic features of romance: a successful hero who forges his own destiny; a world that defines and measures heroism but is at last controlled and made subject to heroic will. The insular poets' sensitivity to the strength of other literatures thus leads them not to exclude so much as to suggest and then engulf their generic opposition, consolidating their allegiance to a particular version of romance.

Generic interactions resonate with the insular romances' investigation of ideal systems in relation to baronial desire. The three ideologies that can be associated with epic, hagiography, and courtly romance aspire to direct the barony away from autonomous action and private gain, and toward behaviors that serve the wider interests of nation, church, and peacetime society. Insular romances recognize the growing power of these systems of conduct, in English even adopting them more fully into the noble hero's presentation. Yet one indication of the romances' baronial milieu is their resistance to all in these ideologies that would check baronial achievement. The insular heroes are eminently principled, but their principles finally support rather than check their pursuit of titles, property, lineage, and status. The move would seem to return the barony to a golden age of free autonomy when warriors dominated unquestioned, but the evocation of current social issues in the works denies that they are escaping to an imagined past. Resisting the dreams of ideological system and nostalgic class desire alike, the insular romances offer the barony nothing less than its future.

Insular romances are indeed nostalgic in that they draw material from tradition and distant history, and conservatively endorse hierarchy and feudal custom. Yet their nostalgia is only a first expression of their poetic liberation from time, and they are more importantly visionary than reactionary. They move beyond class identity, in that the noble hero's successes are primarily personal and only secondarily of broader significance. Attending to the heritage sustains the nation—not the reverse. Religious commitment is not to crusading solidarity with the church, but to personal faiths that support private goals. Courtliness, too, makes self-improvement the center of value, and public estimation only one of its results. These solutions to ideological tension do respect baronial ideals, yet they disperse class interest by insisting that success lies in private pursuits. The insistence stretches the insular romances beyond the specifics of their baronial milieu and addresses any listener for whom the manipulation of social constraints could have meaning. In these works baronial values become contiguous with many ambitions, and private action becomes stronger than communal commitment. And when private action is imagined to succeed at everything from defending the nation to achieving salvation to finding a wife, we are on the threshold of the competitive mercantile world that displaced feudalism. In celebrating the noble hero's ability to make every social ideal serve personal ends, the insular romances reinforce the barony's image even as they intimate that the barony's time is passing.

Abbreviations

AnM	*Annuale Mediaevale*
Annales ESC	*Annales: Economies, Sociétés, Civilisations*
ANTS	Anglo-Norman Text Society
Archiv	*Archiv für das Studium der neueren Sprachen und Literaturen*
BBSIA	*Bulletin Bibliographique de la Société Internationale Arthurienne*
BJRL	*Bulletin of the John Rylands University Library*
CCM	*Cahiers de Civilisation Médiévale*
CFMA	Classiques Français du Moyen Age
ChauR	*The Chaucer Review*
CL	*Comparative Literature*
CN	*Cultura Neolatina*
EETS	Early English Text Society
e.s.	extra series
o.s.	original series
FMLS	*Forum for Modern Language Studies*
FR	*French Review*
FS	*French Studies*

GRM	Germanisch-romanische Monatsschrift
JEGP	Journal of English and Germanic Philology
LR	Les Lettres Romanes
MA	Le Moyen Age
MÆ	Medium Ævum
M&H	Medievalia et Humanistica
MedR	Medioevo Romanzo
MHRA	Modern Humanities Research Association
MLR	Modern Language Review
MP	Modern Philology
MS	Mediaeval Studies
N&Q	Notes and Queries
Neophil	Neophilologus
NLH	New Literary History
NM	Neuphilologische Mitteilungen
PAPS	Proceedings of the American Philosophical Society
PLL	Papers on Language and Literature
PQ	Philological Quarterly
RES	Review of English Studies
RF	Romanische Forschungen
RMSt	Reading Medieval Studies
RPh	Romance Philology
RR	Romanic Review
SAC	Studies in the Age of Chaucer
SATF	Société des Anciens Textes Français
SP	Studies in Philology
TLF	Textes Littéraires Français
TLL	Travaux de Linguistique et de Littérature
TRHS	Transactions of the Royal Historical Society

YFS	Yale French Studies
ZAA	Zeitschrift für Anglistik und Amerikanistik
ZDP	Zeitschrift für deutsche Philologie
ZFSL	Zeitschrift für französische Sprache und Literatur
ZRP	Zeitschrift für romanische Philologie

Bibliography

Primary Sources

Primary sources are listed alphabetically by author, if known, or by the key word in the title. Phrases preceding the key word are bracketed.

Adae Murimuth. *Continuatio Chronicarum Robertus de Avesbury.* Ed. Edward M. Thompson. Rolls Ser., 93. London, 1889.
[*La Vie de Saint*] *Alexis.* Ed. Christopher Storey. TLF, 148. Geneva, 1968.
"Alexiuslieder." Ed. Carl Horstmann. *Archiv,* 59 (1878), 71–90.
[*Kyng*] *Alisaunder.* Ed. G. V. Smithers. 2 vols. EETS, o.s. 227, 237. London, 1952, 1957.
Amadas et Ydoine. Ed. John R. Reinhard. CFMA, 51. Paris, 1926.
Amis and Amiloun. Ed. MacEdward Leach. EETS, o.s. 203. London, 1937.
Amis e Amilun. In *Amis and Amiloun.* Ed. Eugen Kölbing. Heilbronn, 1884.
Angier, Frère. *The Dialogues of Gregory the Great, Translated into Anglo-Norman French by Angier.* Ed. Timothy Cloran. Diss. Strasbourg, 1901.
"Un Art d'aimer anglo-normand." Ed. Östen Södergård. *Romania,* 77 (1956), 289–330.
Arthour and Merlin. Ed. Eugen Kölbing. Altenglische Bibliothek, No. 4. Leipzig, 1890.
Athelston. Ed. Allan McI. Trounce. EETS, o.s. 224. London, 1951.
La Bataille de trente Anglois et de trente Bretons. Ed. Henry Raymond Brush. MP, 9 (1911–12), 511–44; 10 (1912–13), 82–136.
Benoît de Sainte-Maure. *Le Roman de Troie.* Ed. Léopold Constans. 6 vols. SATF, 51. Paris, 1904–12.
Beroul. *The Romance of Tristran.* Ed. Alfred Ewert. 2 vols. Oxford, 1939, 1970.

[*The Romance of Sir*] *Beues of Hamtoun*. Ed. Eugen Kölbing. EETS, e.s. 46, 48, 65. London, 1885, 1886, 1894.
Bodel, Jean. *Saxenlied [Les Saisnes]*. Ed. F. Menzel and E. Stengel. 2 vols. Marburg, 1906, 1909.
[*Der anglonormannische*] *Boeve de Haumtone*. Ed. Albert Stimming. Bibliotheca normannica, No. 7. Halle, 1899.
[*Der festländische*] *Bueve de Hantone*. Ed. Albert Stimming. 5 vols. Gesellschaft für romanische Literatur, Nos. 25, 30, 34, 41, 42. Göttingen, 1911–20.
Caesarius of Heisterbach. *Dialogus Miraculorum*. Ed. Joseph Strange. 2 vols. Cologne, 1851. (Trans. H. von E. Scott and C. C. Swinton Bland. *The Dialogue on Miracles*. 2 vols. London, 1929.)
Chandos Herald. *La Vie du Prince Noir*. Ed. Diana B. Tyson. Tübingen, 1975.
Chaucer, Geoffrey. *The Works of Geoffrey Chaucer*. Ed. F. N. Robinson. 2nd ed. Boston, 1957.
[*Le Livre du*] *Chevalier de la Tour Landry*, ed. Anatole de Montaiglon. Paris, 1854.
Chrétien de Troyes. *Yvain*. Ed. Wendelin Foerster, rev. T. B. W. Reid. Manchester, 1942.
Chronica Monasterii de Melsa. Ed. Edward A. Bond. 3 vols. Rolls Ser., 43. London, 1866–68.
Clemence of Barking. *The Life of St. Catherine*. Ed. William MacBain. ANTS, 18. Oxford, 1964.
[*Anglo-Norman Books of*] *Courtesy and Nurture*. Ed. H. Rosamond Parsons. MLA Publications, No. 44 (1929). Rpt. New York, 1967.
Cursor Mundi. Ed. Richard Morris. Vol. I. EETS, o.s. 57. London, 1874.
De Controversia in Curia Militari inter Ricardum le Scrope et Robertum Grosvenor. Ed. Nicholas H. Nicolas. 2 vols. London, 1832.
"Une Définition d'amour en prose anglo-normande." Ed. Paul Studer. In *Mélanges de philologie et d'histoire offerts à M. Antoine Thomas*. Paris, 1927, pp. 433–36.
[*The Romance of Sir*] *Degrevant*. Ed. L. F. Casson. EETS, o.s. 221. London, 1949.
Deschamps, Eustache. *Oeuvres complètes*. Ed. Marquis de Queux de Saint-Hilaire et al. 11 vols. SATF, 9. Paris, 1878–1903.
Le Donnei des amants. Ed. Gaston Paris. *Romania*, 25 (1896), 497–541.
[*La Vie d'*] *Edouard le Confesseur*. Ed. Östen Södergård. Uppsala, 1948.
Eulogium, Historiarum sive Temporis. Ed. Frank Scott Haydon. 3 vols. Rolls Ser., 9. London, 1858, 1860, 1863.
Floris and Blancheflur. Ed. George H. McKnight. EETS, o.s. 14. London, 1901.
La Folie Tristan d'Oxford. Ed. Ernest Hoepffner. Publications de la Faculté des Lettres de l'Université de Strasbourg. Textes d'étude, No. 8. 1938.
Fouke le Fitz Waryn. Ed. E. J. Hathaway et al. ANTS, 26–28. Oxford, 1975.
Froissart, Jean. *Oeuvres de Froissart*. Ed. Kervyn de Lettenhove. 25 vols. Brussels, 1867–77.

[*The History of*] *Fulk Fitz Warine*. Ed. Thomas Wright. London, 1885.
Gaimar, Geoffrey. *L'Estoire des Engleis*. Ed. Alexander Bell. ANTS, 14–16. Oxford, 1960.
———. See [*Le Lai d'*] *Haveloc*.
[*The Tale of*] *Gamelyn*. Ed. W. W. Skeat. 2nd ed. Oxford, 1893.
Gottfried von Strassburg. *Tristan, with the Surviving Fragments of the "Tristan" of Thomas*. Trans. A. T. Hatto. Harmondsworth, 1960.
Gower, John. *The Complete Works of John Gower*. Ed. G. C. Macaulay. 4 vols. Oxford, 1899–1902.
Gray, Sir Thomas. *Scalacronica*. Ed. Joseph Stevenson. Edinburgh, 1836.
Gui de Warewic. Ed. Alfred Ewert. 2 vols. CFMA, 74, 75. Paris, 1932, 1933.
Guillaume le Clerc. *Le Bestiaire*. Ed. Robert Reinsch. Leipzig, 1890.
[*L'Histoire de*] *Guillaume le Maréchal*. Ed. Paul Meyer. 3 vols. Paris, 1891–1901.
[*The Romance of*] *Guy of Warwick: The First or 14th-century Version*. Ed. Julius Zupitza. EETS, e.s. 42, 49, 59. London, 1883, 1887, 1891.
[*The Romance of*] *Guy of Warwick: The Second or 15th-century Version*. Ed. Julius Zupitza. EETS, e.s. 25, 26. London, 1875, 1876.
[*Speculum*] *Gy de Warewyke*. Ed. Georgiana Lea Morrill. EETS, e.s. 75. London, 1898.
[*Le Lai d'*] *Haveloc and Gaimar's Haveloc Episode*. Ed. Alexander Bell. Manchester, 1925.
[*The Lay of*] *Havelok the Dane*. Ed. W. W. Skeat. 2nd ed. rev. Kenneth Sisam. Oxford, 1915.
Henry of Huntingdon. *Historia Anglorum*. Ed. Thomas Arnold. Rolls Ser., 74. London, 1879.
[*King*] *Horn*. Ed. Joseph Hall. Oxford, 1901.
[*King*] *Horn*. Ed. Rosamund Allen. Garland Medieval Texts, No. 7. New York, 1984.
Horn Childe and Maiden Rimnild. Ed. J. Caro. *Englische Studien*, 12 (1889), 323–66.
Hue de Rotelande. *Hue de Rotelande's Ipomedon*. Ed. Eugen Kölbing and Eduard Koschwitz. Breslau, 1889.
———. *Hue de Rotelande's Ipomedon in drei englischen Bearbeitungen*. Ed. Eugen Kölbing. Breslau, 1889.
———. *Ipomedon*. Ed. A. J. Holden. Paris, 1979.
———. *Protheselaus*. Ed. Franz Kluckow. Gesellschaft für romanische Literatur, No. 45. Göttingen, 1924.
Jean le Bel. *Chronique de Jean le Bel*. Ed. Jules Viard and Eugène Déprez. 2 vols. Paris, 1904, 1905.
Johannes Bramis' Historia Regis Waldei. Ed. Rudolf Imelmann. Bonner Studien zur englischen Philologie, No. 4. Bonn, 1912.
John of Reading. *Chronica Johannis de Reading et Anonymi Cantuariensis*. Ed. James Tait. Manchester, 1914.
John of Salisbury. *Policraticus*. Ed. C. C. J. Webb. 2 vols. Oxford, 1909. (Trans. John Dickinson. *The Statesman's Book of John of Salisbury*. New York, 1927.)

The Knight of Curtesy and the Fair Lady of Faguell. Ed. Elizabeth McCausland. Smith College Studies in Modern Languages, Vol. 4, No. 1. Northampton, Mass., 1922.
Lambert of Ardres. *Chronicon Ghisnense et Ardense.* Ed. Godefroy Ménilglaise. Paris, 1855.
Langland, William. *The Vision of William Concerning Piers Plowman.* Ed. W. W. Skeat. EETS, o.s. 54. London, 1873.
Liber Custumarum. Ed. Henry Thomas Riley. Rolls Ser., 12. 3 vols. in 4. London, 1859-62.
Map, Walter. *De Nugis Curialium.* Ed. Montague Rhodes James. Oxford, 1914. (Trans. Frederick Tupper and Marbury Bladen Ogle. *Courtiers' Trifles.* London, 1924.)
Marie de France. *Lais.* Ed. Alfred Ewert. Oxford, 1969.
Melior et Ydoine. Ed. Paul Meyer. *Romania,* 37 (1908), 236-44.
Peter of Langtoft. *The Chronicle of Pierre de Langtoft.* Ed. Thomas Wright. 2 vols. Rolls Ser., 47. London, 1866, 1868.
Piramus, Denis. *La Vie Seint Edmund le Rei.* Ed. Hilding Kjellman. Göteborg, 1935.
"[þe story off] placidas." Ed. Carl Horstmann. In "Die EvangelienGeschichten der Homiliensammlung des Ms. Vernon." *Archiv,* 57 (1877), 262-72.
Reinbrun. See *Guy of Warwick: The First or 14th-century Version.*
[*Der mittelenglische Versroman über*] *Richard Löwenherz.* Ed. Karl Brunner. Wiener Beiträge zur englischen Philologie, No. 42. Vienna, 1913.
Richard, Son of Nigel [Richard FitzNeale]. *Dialogus de Scaccario.* Ed. and trans. Charles Johnson. London, 1950.
Robert Manning of Brunne. *The Chronicle of Robert Manning of Brunne.* Ed. Frederick J. Furnivall. 2 vols. Rolls Ser., 87. London, 1887.
Ross, John. *Historical Account of the Earls of Warwick.* Ed. Thomas Hearne. Oxford, 1729.
Rous, John [John Ross]. *The Rous Roll.* Ed. Charles Ross. Gloucester, 1980.
[*Le Roman de*] *Thèbes.* Ed. Léopold Constans. 2 vols. SATF, 31. Paris, 1890.
Thomas. *The Romance of Horn.* Ed. Mildred K. Pope and T. B. W. Reid. 2 vols. ANTS, 9-10, 12-13. Oxford, 1955, 1964.
Thomas of Britain. *Les Fragments du roman de Tristan.* Ed. Bartina H. Wind. 2nd ed. TLF, 92. Geneva, 1960.
———. *Le Roman de Tristan par Thomas.* Ed. Joseph Bédier. 2 vols. SATF, 46. Paris, 1902, 1905.
Thomas of Erceldoune. *The Romance and Prophecies of Thomas of Erceldoune.* Ed. James A. H. Murray. EETS, o.s. 61. London, 1875.
Thomas of Kent. *The Anglo-Norman "Alexander."* Ed. Brian Foster with Ian Short. 2 vols. ANTS, 29-33. London, 1976, 1977.
The Thornton Romances. Ed. James O. Halliwell. Camden Society, No. 30. London, 1844.
[*Die nordische und die englische Version der*] *Tristansage.* Ed. Eugen Kölbing. 2 vols. Heilbronn, 1882.

[Sir] *Tristrem*. Ed. George P. McNeill. Publications of the Scottish Text Society, No. 8. Edinburgh, 1886.
Ulrich von Zatzikhoven. *Lanzelet*. Ed. K. A. Hahn, rev. Frederick Norman. Berlin, 1965. (Trans. Kenneth G. T. Webster, rev. R. S. Loomis. *Lanzelet: A Romance of Lancelot*. New York, 1951.)
Wace, Robert. *Maistre Wace's roman de Rou*. Ed. Hugo Andresen. 2 vols. Heilbronn, 1877, 1879.
[*Le Roman de*] *Waldef*. Ed. A. J. Holden. Bibliotheca Bodmeriana. Textes, No. 5. Geneva, 1984.
William of Malmesbury. *Gesta Regum Anglorum*. Ed. William Stubbs. 2 vols. Rolls Ser., 90. London, 1887, 1889.
[*Sir*] *Ysumbras*. Ed. Gustav Schleich. Palaestra, No. 15. Berlin, 1901.
Ywain and Gawain. Ed. Albert B. Friedman and Norman T. Harrington. EETS, o.s. 254. London, 1964.

Secondary Sources

Adams, Alison. "*Amadas et Ydoine* and Thomas' *Tristan*." *FMLS*, 14 (1978), 247–54.
———. "The Metaphor of *Folie* in Thomas' *Tristan*." *FMLS*, 17 (1981), 88–90.
Aitken, Marion Y. H. *Etude sur le Miroir ou les Evangiles des domnées de Robert de Gretham*. Diss. Univ. of Paris, 1922.
Anderson, Andrew R. *Alexander's Gate, Gog and Magog, and the Inclosed Nations*. Monographs of the Mediaeval Academy of America, No. 5. Cambridge, Mass., 1932.
Appleby, John T. *England Without Richard, 1189–1199*. London, 1965.
Arens, Werner. *Die anglonormannische und die englischen Fassungen des Hornstoffes*. Studien zur Anglistik, Studienreihe Humanitas. Frankfurt am Main, 1973.
Arnould, E. J. *Le "Manuel des péchés": étude de littérature religieuse anglo-normande*. Paris, 1940.
Auerbach, Erich. *Literary Language and Its Public in Late Latin Antiquity and in the Middle Ages*. Trans. Ralph Manheim. Princeton, 1965.
———. *Mimesis: The Representation of Reality in Western Literature*. Trans. Willard Trask. Princeton, 1953.
Baechler, Jean. *Qu'est-ce que l'idéologie?* Paris, 1976.
Baldwin, Dean R. "*Amis and Amiloun*: The Testing of *Treupe*," *PLL*, 16 (1980), 353–65.
Barber, Richard. *Edward, Prince of Wales and Aquitaine*. New York, 1978.
———. *The Knight and Chivalry*. Totowa, N.J., 1975.
Barlow, Frank. "The Effects of the Norman Conquest." In *The Norman Conquest*. London, 1966, pp. 125–61.
———. *The English Church 1066–1154: A History of the Anglo-Norman Church*. London, 1979.
Barnie, John. *War in Medieval English Society: Social Values in the Hundred Years War, 1337–99*. Ithaca, 1974.

Barrow, Sarah F. *The Medieval Society Romances*. New York, 1924.
Barteau, Françoise. *Les Romans de Tristan et Iseut. Introduction à une lecture plurielle*. Paris, 1972.
Baugh, Albert Croll. "The Authorship of the Middle English Romances." *Annual Bulletin of the MHRA*, 22 (1950), 13–28.
———. "Convention and Individuality in the Middle English Romance." In *Medieval Literature and Folklore Studies: Essays in Honor of Francis Lee Utley*. Ed. Jerome Mandel and Bruce Rosenberg. New Brunswick, N.J., 1970, pp. 123–46.
———. "Improvisation in the Middle English Romance." *PAPS*, 103 (1959), 418–54.
———. "The Middle English Romance: Some Questions of Creation, Presentation, and Preservation." *Speculum*, 42 (1967), 1–31.
Baumgartner, E., and R.-L. Wagner. "'As enveisiez e as purvers.' Commentaire sur les vers 3125–3129 du *Roman de Tristan* de Thomas." *Romania*, 88 (1967), 527–37.
Bell, Alexander. "Comments on the *Lai du Cor*." *MÆ*, 45 (1976), 265–68.
Bennett, Michael J. *Community, Class and Careerism: Cheshire and Lancashire Society in the Age of "Sir Gawain and the Green Knight"*. Cambridge, 1983.
Benson, Larry D. *Malory's "Morte Darthur"*. Cambridge, Mass., 1976.
Benton, John F. "Clio and Venus: An Historical View of Medieval Love." In *The Meaning of Courtly Love*. Ed. F. X. Newman. Albany, N.Y., 1968, pp. 19–42.
———. "Collaborative Approaches to Fantasy and Reality in the Literature of Champagne." In *Court and Poet*, ed. Glyn S. Burgess. Liverpool, 1981, pp. 43–57.
———. "The Court of Champagne as a Literary Center." *Speculum*, 36 (1961), 551–91.
———. "The Evidence for Andreas Capellanus Re-examined Again." *SP*, 59 (1962), 471–78.
Bertolucci Pizzorusso, Valeria. "La retorica nel Tristano di Thomas." *Studi mediolatini e volgari*, 6–7 (1958–59), 25–61.
Bezzola, Reto. *Les Origines et la formation de la littérature courtoise en Occident (500–1200)*. 5 vols. Paris, 1944–63.
Bisson, Thomas N. "The Problem of Feudal Monarchy: Aragon, Catalonia, and France." *Speculum*, 53 (1978), 460–78.
Bjorklund, Victoria A. "The Art of Translation in *Ipomadon*: From Anglo-Norman to Middle English." Diss. Yale, 1977.
Blaess, Madeline. "L'Abbaye de Bordesley et les livres de Guy de Beauchamp." *Romania*, 78 (1957), 511–18.
Blaicher, Günther. "Zur Interpretation der mittelenglischen Romanze *Sir Ysumbras*." *GRM*, n.s. 21 (1971), 135–44.
Blessing, James Hartman. "A Comparison of Some Middle English Romances with the Old French Antecedents." Diss. Stanford, 1959.
Bliss, A. J. "Notes on the Auchinleck Manuscript." *Speculum*, 26 (1951), 652–58.

Bloch, Marc. *La Société féodale.* 2 vols. Paris, 1939, 1940. (Trans. L. A. Manyon. *Feudal Society.* 2 vols. Chicago, 1961.)
Bloch, R. Howard. *Medieval French Literature and Law.* Berkeley and Los Angeles, 1977.
Bloomfield, Morton W. *Essays and Explorations.* Cambridge, Mass., 1970.
Blumenfeld-Kosinski, Renate. "Old French Narrative Genres: Towards the Definition of the *Roman Antique*." *RPh,* 34 (1980–81), 143–59.
Boase, Roger. *The Origin and Meaning of Courtly Love: A Critical Study of European Scholarship.* Manchester, 1977.
Bolton, Whitney F. "The Conditions of Literary Composition in Medieval England." *History of Literature in the English Language.* Vol. I, *The Middle Ages.* London, 1970, pp. ix–xxxvi.
Borst, Arno. "Das Rittertum im Hochmittelalter: Idee und Wirklichkeit." *Saeculum,* 10 (1959), 213–31.
Bossert, A. *La Légende chevaleresque de Tristan et Iseult.* Paris, 1902.
Bossuard, Jacques. "Les Institutions de l'empire Plantagenêt." In *Histoire des institutions françaises au moyen âge.* Ed. Ferdinand Lot and Robert Fawtier. Vol. I. Paris, 1957, pp. 35–69.
Bouchard, Constance B. "The Possible Nonexistence of Thomas, Author of *Tristan and Isolde*." *MP,* 79 (1981–82), 66–72.
Bowden, Betsy. "The Art of Courtly Copulation." *M&H,* n.s. 9 (1979), 67–85.
Boyle, L. E. "The *Oculos Sacerdotis* and Some Other Works of William of Pagula." *TRHS,* 5th ser., 5 (1955), 81–110.
Braswell, Laura. "'Sir Isumbras' and the Legend of Saint Eustace." *MS,* 27 (1965), 128–51.
Brody, Saul Nathaniel. *The Disease of the Soul: Leprosy in Medieval Literature.* Ithaca, 1974.
Broich, Ulrich. *See* Schirmer, Walter Franz.
Brown, Elizabeth A. R. "Eleanor of Aquitaine: Parent, Queen, and Duchess." In *Eleanor of Aquitaine: Patron and Politician.* Ed. William W. Kibler. Austin, 1976, pp. 9–34.
———. "The Tyranny of a Construct: Feudalism and Historians of Medieval Europe." *American Historical Review,* 79 (1974), 1063–88.
Bruckner, Matilda Tomaryn. *Narrative Invention in Twelfth-Century French Romance.* French Forum Monographs, No. 17. Lexington, Ky., 1980.
Burnley, J. D. "*Fine Amor*: Its Meaning and Context." *RES,* n.s. 31 (1980), 129–48.
———. "The 'Roman de Horn': Its Hero and Its Ethos." *FS,* 32 (1978), 385–97.
Calin, Françoise, and William Calin. "Medieval Fiction and New Novel. Some Polemical Remarks on the Subject of Narrative." *YFS,* 51 (1974), 235–50.
Calin, William. *The Epic Quest.* Baltimore, 1966.
———. *The Old French Epic of Revolt.* Geneva, 1962.
Camargo, Martin. "The Metamorphosis of Candace and the Earliest En-

glish Love Epistle." In *Court and Poet*. Ed. Glyn S. Burgess. Liverpool, 1981, pp. 101–11.

Carter, Charles Henry. "Ipomedon, An Illustration of Romance Origin." *Haverford Essays*. Haverford, Pennsylvania, 1909, pp. 235–70.

Cary, George. *The Medieval Alexander*. Ed. D.J.A. Ross. Cambridge, 1956.

Cazelles, R. "La Réglementation royale de la guerre privée de Saint Louis à Charles V et la précarité des ordonnances." *Revue historique de droit français et étranger*, 4th ser., 38 (1960), 530–48.

Cazenave, Michel. *Le Philtre et l'amour*. Paris, 1969.

Chenu, Marie Dominique. *L'Eveil de la conscience dans la civilisation médiévale*. Conférence Albert-le-Grand, 1968. Montreal, 1969.

Cheyney, C. R. *English Synodalia of the Thirteenth Century*. London, 1941.

Childress, Diana T. "Between Romance and Legend: 'Secular Hagiography' in Middle English Literature." *PQ*, 57 (1978), 311–22.

Christmann, Hans Helmut. "Über das Verhältnis zwischen dem anglonormannischen und dem mittelenglischen 'Horn.'" *ZFSL*, 70 (1960), 166–81.

Clark, Cecily. "Women's Names in Post-Conquest England: Observations and Speculations." *Speculum*, 53 (1978), 223–51.

Cline, Ruth Huff. "The Influence of Romances on Tournaments of the Middle Ages." *Speculum*, 20 (1945), 204–11.

Coleman, Janet. *Medieval Readers and Writers, 1350–1400*. New York, 1981.

Cooper, Helen. "Magic that Does Not Work." *M&H*, n.s. 7 (1976), 131–46.

Cormier, Raymond J. "Bédier, Brother Robert and the *Roman de Tristan*." In *Etudes de philologie romane et d'histoire littéraire offertes à Jules Horrent*. Ed. Jean Marie d'Heur and Nicoletta Cherubini. Liège, 1980, pp. 69–75.

Coss, P. R. "Literature and Social Terminology: The Vavasour in England." In *Social Relations and Ideas: Essays in Honour of R. H. Hilton*. Ed. T. H. Ashton et al. Cambridge, 1983, pp. 109–50.

———. "Sir Geoffrey de Langley and the Crisis of the Knightly Class in Thirteenth-Century England." *Past and Present*, No. 68 (August 1975), pp. 3–34.

Crane, Ronald S. "The Vogue of *Guy of Warwick* from the Close of the Middle Ages to the Romantic Revival." *PMLA*, 30 (1915), 125–94.

Creek, Herbert LeSourd. "The Author of *Havelok the Dane*." *Englische Studien*, 48 (1914–15), 193–212.

Curtius, Ernst Robert. *European Literature and the Latin Middle Ages*. Trans. Willard Trask. London, 1953.

Dannenbaum, Susan [Crane]. "Anglo-Norman Romances of English Heroes: 'Ancestral Romance'?" *RPh*, 35 (1981–82), 601–8.

———. "Doubling and *Fine Amor* in Thomas' *Tristan*." *Tristania*, 5:1 (1979), 1–14.

———. "'Fairer bi one ribbe / þane eni Man þat libbe' (*King Horn* C 315–16)." *N&Q*, n.s. 28 (1981), 116–17.

———. "Guy of Warwick and the Question of Exemplary Romance." *Genre*, 17 (1984), 351–74.

---. "Insular Tradition in the Story of Amis and Amiloun." *Neophil*, 67 (1983), 611–22.
Davies, R. R. *Lordship and Society in the March of Wales, 1282–1400*. Oxford, 1978.
Davis, H.W.C. *England under the Normans and Angevins, 1066–1272*. London, 1905.
Davis, Ralph H. C. *The Normans and Their Myth*. London, 1976.
Dean, Ruth J. "A Fair Field Needing Folk: Anglo-Norman." *PMLA*, 69 (1954), 965–78.
Delany, Sheila, and Vahan Ishkanian. "Theocratic and Contractual Kingship in *Havelok the Dane*." *ZAA*, 22 (1974), 290–302.
Delbouille, Maurice. "Le Fragment de Cambridge et la genèse des 'Folies Tristan.'" *TLL*, 16:1 (1978), 117–129.
Dembowski, Peter F. *Jean Froissart and His "Meliador": Context, Craft, and Sense*. Edward C. Armstrong Monographs on Medieval Literature, No. 2. Lexington, Ky., 1983.
---. "Literary Problems of Hagiography in Old French." *M&H*, n.s. 7 (1976), 117–30.
Denholm-Young, Noël. "The Tournament in the Thirteenth Century." In *Studies in Medieval History Presented to Frederick Maurice Powicke*. Ed. R. W. Hunt et al. Oxford, 1948, pp. 240–68.
Dickinson, W. Croft. *Scotland from the Earliest Times to 1603*. 3rd ed. rev. Archibald A. M. Duncan. Oxford, 1977.
Douglas, David C. *The Norman Achievement, 1050–1100*. London, 1969.
Doyle, A. I. "English Books In and Out of Court from Edward III to Henry VII." In *English Court Culture in the Later Middle Ages*. Ed. V. J. Scattergood and J. W. Sherborne. New York, 1983, pp. 163–81.
Dronke, Peter. "Peter of Blois and Poetry at the Court of Henry II." *MS*, 38 (1976), 185–235.
Duby, Georges. "The Culture of the Knightly Class: Audience and Patronage." In *Renaissance and Renewal in the Twelfth Century*. Ed. Robert L. Benson and Giles Constable. Cambridge, Mass., 1982, pp. 248–62.
---. "Dans la France du Nord-Ouest au XIIe siècle: les 'Jeunes' dans la société aristocratique." *Annales ESC*, 19 (1964), 835–46.
---. "The Diffusion of Cultural Patterns in Feudal Society." *Past and Present*, No. 39 (1968), pp. 3–10.
---. *The Early Growth of the European Economy*. Trans. Howard B. Clarke. Ithaca, 1974.
---. *L'Economie rurale et la vie des campagnes dans l'occident médiéval*. 2 vols. Paris, 1962. (Trans. Cynthia Postan. *Rural Economy and Country Life in the Medieval West*. Columbia, S.C., 1968.)
---. "Une Enquête à poursuivre: la noblesse dans la France médiévale." *Revue historique*, No. 226 (July 1961), pp. 1–22.
---. "La Féodalité? Une mentalité médiévale." *Annales ESC*, 13 (1958), 765–71.
---. *Medieval Marriage: Two Models from Twelfth-Century France*. Trans.

Elborg Forster. The Johns Hopkins Symposia in Comparative History, No. 11. Baltimore, 1978.

———. *La Société aux XIe et XIIe siècles dans la région mâconnaise*. Paris, 1953.

———. *Les Trois ordres ou l'imaginaire du féodalisme*. Paris, 1978. (Trans. Arthur Goldhammer. *The Three Orders: Feudal Society Imagined*. Chicago, 1980.)

Dyer, Christopher. *Lords and Peasants in a Changing Society: The Estates of the Bishopric of Worcester, 680–1540*. Cambridge, 1980.

Eisner, Sigmund. *The Tristan Legend: A Study in Sources*. Evanston, 1969.

Ernle, R.E.P. *The Light Reading of Our Ancestors: Chapters in the Growth of the English Novel*. London, 1927.

Evans, W. O. "'Cortaysye' in Middle English." *MS*, 29 (1967), 143–57.

Everett, Dorothy. *Essays on Middle English Literature*. Ed. Patricia Kean. Oxford, 1955.

Ferrante, Joan M. *The Conflict of Love and Honor: The Medieval Tristan Legend in France, Germany and Italy*. The Hague, 1973.

———. "*Cortes' Amor* in Medieval Texts." *Speculum*, 55 (1980), 686–95.

Ferris, Sumner. "Chronicle, Chivalric Biography, and Family Tradition in Fourteenth-Century England." In *Chivalric Literature: Essays on Relations Between Literature and Life in the Later Middle Ages*. Ed. Larry D. Benson and John Leyerle. Studies in Medieval Culture, No. 14. Kalamazoo, 1980, pp. 25–38.

Fisher, Fay. *Narrative Art in Medieval Romances*. Cleveland, 1938.

Fletcher, Robert Huntington. *The Arthurian Material in the Chronicles*. 2nd ed. New York, 1966.

Foreville, Raymonde. "La Typologie du roi dans la littérature historiographique anglo-normande aux XIe et XIIe siècles." In *Etudes de civilisation médiévale (IXe–XIIe siècles): Mélanges offerts à Edmond-René Labande*. Poitiers, 1974, pp. 275–92.

Fourrier, Anthime. *Le Courant réaliste dans le roman courtois en France au moyen âge*. Vol. I, *Les Débuts (XIIe siècle)*. Paris, 1960.

Frappier, Jean. "D'amors, par amors." *Romania*, 88 (1967), 433–74.

———. "Structure et sens du *Tristan*: version commune, version courtoise." *CCM*, 6 (1963), 255–80, 441–54.

———. "Sur le mot 'raison' dans le *Tristan* de Thomas d'Angleterre." In *Linguistic and Literary Studies in Honor of Helmut A. Hatzfeld*. Ed. Alessandro S. Crisafulli. Washington, D.C., 1964, pp. 163–76.

———. "Vues sur les conceptions courtoises dans les littératures d'oc et d'oïl au XIIe siècle." *CCM*, 2 (1959), 135–56.

Frappier, Jean, et al., eds. *Grundriss der romanischen Literaturen des Mittelalters*. Vol. IV:1, *Le Roman jusqu'à la fin du XIIe siècle*. Heidelberg, 1978.

Freeman, Michelle A. *The Poetics of "Translatio Studii" and "Conjointure": Chrétien de Troyes's "Cligés"*. French Forum Monographs, No. 12. Lexington, Ky., 1979.

Friedman, John Block. *The Monstrous Races in Medieval Art and Thought*. Cambridge, Mass., 1981.

Galbraith, V. H. "Nationality and Language in Medieval England." *TRHS*, 4th ser., 23 (1941), 113–28.
Gallais, Pierre. "Recherches sur la mentalité des romanciers français du moyen âge." *CCM*, 7 (1964), 479–93; 13 (1970), 333–47.
Ganim, John. "History and Consciousness in Middle English Romance." *Literary Review*, 23 (1979–80), 481–96.
―――. *Style and Consciousness in Middle English Narrative.* Princeton, 1983.
Gay, Lucy M. "Heraldry and the 'Tristan' of Thomas." *MLR*, 23 (1928), 472–75.
―――. "Hue de Rotelande's *Ipomédon* and Chrétien de Troyes." *PMLA*, 32 (1917), 468–91.
Gerould, Gordon Hall. "Forerunners, Congeners, and Derivatives of the Eustace Legend." *PMLA*, 19 (1904), 335–448.
Gist, Margaret Adlum. *Love and War in the Middle English Romances.* Philadelphia, 1947.
Godfrey, John. *The English Parish, 600–1300.* London, 1969.
Gouttebroze, Jean-Gui. "Henri II Plantagenêt, patron des historiographes anglo-normands de langue d'oïl." In *La Littérature angevine médiévale: Actes du colloque du samedi 22 mars 1980.* Ed. Georges Cesbron. Paris, 1981, pp. 91–109.
Gombrich, Ernst. Rev. of *The Social History of Art*, by Arnold Hauser. *The Art Bulletin*, 35 (1953), 79–84. Rpt. in *Meditations on a Hobby Horse.* 2nd ed. London, 1971, pp. 86–94.
Gradon, Pamela. *Form and Style in Early English Literature.* London, 1971.
Gransden, Antonia. *Historical Writing in England c. 550 to c. 1307.* Ithaca, 1974.
Green, Dennis Howard. *Irony in the Medieval Romance.* Cambridge, 1979.
Green, Richard Firth. "King Richard II's Books Revisited." *Library*, 5th ser., 31 (1976), 235–39.
―――. *Poets and Princepleasers: Literature and the English Court in the Late Middle Ages.* Toronto, 1980.
Grente, Georges, ed. *Dictionnaire des lettres françaises.* Vol. IV, *Le Moyen Age.* Paris, 1964.
Gunnlaugsdóttir, Álfrún. *Tristán en el norte.* Reykjavik, 1978.
Haidu, Peter. *Aesthetic Distance in Chrétien de Troyes: Irony and Comedy in "Cligès" and "Perceval."* Geneva, 1968.
―――. "Humor and the Aesthetics of Medieval Romance." *RR*, 64 (1973), 54–68.
―――. "Text, Pretextuality and Myth in the *Folie Tristan d'Oxford.*" *MLN*, 88 (1973), 712–17.
Halverson, John. "*Havelok the Dane* and Society." *ChauR*, 6 (1971–72), 142–51.
Hanning, Robert W. "Beowulf as Heroic History." *M&H*, n.s. 5 (1974), 77–102.
―――. "*Havelok the Dane*: Structure, Symbols, Meaning." *SP*, 64 (1967), 586–605.

———. *The Individual in Twelfth-Century Romance*. New Haven, 1977.

———. "The Social Significance of Twelfth-Century Chivalric Romance." *M&H*, n.s. 3 (1972), 3–29.

Harris, Sylvia C. "The Cave of Lovers in the 'Tristramssaga' and Related Tristan Romances." *Romania*, 98 (1977), 306–30, 460–500.

Hart, Cyril. "Hereward 'the Wake.'" *Proceedings of the Cambridge Antiquarian Society*, 65:2 (1974), 28–40.

Hartenstein, Otto. *Studien zur Hornsage*. Kieler Studien zur englischen Philologie, No. 4. Heidelberg, 1902.

Harvey, John. *The Black Prince and His Age*. Totowa, N.J., 1976.

Haskin, Dayton. "Food, Clothing and Kingship in *Havelok the Dane*." *American Benedictine Review*, 24 (1973), 204–13.

Haskins, Charles Homer. "Henry II. as a Patron of Literature." In *Essays in Medieval History Presented to Thomas Frederick Tout*. Ed. A. G. Little and F. M. Powicke. Manchester, 1925, pp. 71–77.

Hatcher, Anna Granville. "The Old-French Poem St. Alexis: A Mathematical Demonstration." *Traditio*, 8 (1952), 111–58.

Heffernan, Thomas J. "An Analysis of the Narrative Motifs in the Legend of St. Eustace." *M&H*, n.s. 6 (1975), 63–89.

———. "A Middle English Poem on Lovedays." *ChauR*, 10 (1975–76), 172–85.

Heyman, Harald E. *Studies on the Havelok-tale*. Uppsala, 1903.

Hilton, Rodney. *Bond Men Made Free: Medieval Peasant Movements and the English Rising of 1381*. New York, 1973.

Hirsh, John C. "*Havelok* 2933: A Problem in Medieval Literary History." *NM*, 78 (1977), 339–49.

Hofer, Stefan. "Horn et Rimel, ein Beitrag zur Diskussion über die Ursprungsfrage." *RF*, 70 (1958), 278–322.

Hollister, C. Warren. "Normandy, France and the Anglo-Norman *Regnum*," *Speculum*, 51 (1976), 202–42.

Holt, J. C. *Magna Carta*. Cambridge, 1965.

Hopper, Vincent Foster. *Medieval Number Symbolism*. New York, 1938.

Huizinga, Johan. *The Waning of the Middle Ages*. Trans. F. Hopman. London, 1924.

Hume, Kathryn. "*Amis and Amiloun* and the Aesthetics of Middle English Romance." *SP*, 70 (1973), 19–41.

———. "Structure and Perspective: Romance and Hagiographic Features in the Amicus and Amelius Story." *JEGP*, 69 (1970), 89–107.

Hunt, Tony. "The Emergence of the Knight in France and England, 1000–1200." *FMLS*, 17 (1981), 93–114.

———. "The Significance of Thomas's *Tristan*." *RMSt*, 7 (1981), 41–61.

Hurley, Margaret. "Saints' Legends and Romance Again: Secularization of Structure and Motif." *Genre*, 8 (1975), 60–73.

Hynes-Berry, Mary. "Cohesion in *King Horn* and *Sir Orfeo*." *Speculum*, 50 (1975), 652–70.

Jack, George B. "The Date of *Havelok*." *Anglia*, 95 (1977), 20–33.

Jadart, Henri. "Une peinture murale du XIIIe siècle à la cathédrale de Reims." *Bulletin archéologique du comité des travaux historiques* (1901), pp. 36–43.
Jameson, Frederic. *The Political Unconscious: Narrative as a Socially Symbolic Act*. Ithaca, N.Y., 1981.
Jauss, Hans Robert. "Cinq modèles d'identification esthétique: Complément à la théorie des genres littéraires au moyen âge." In *XIV congresso internazionale di linguistica e filologia romanza, Napoli, 15–20 aprile 1974. Atti,* I. Ed. Alberto Varvaro. Naples, 1978, pp. 145–64.
―――. "Negativität und Identifikation: Versuch zur Theorie der ästhetischen Erfahrung." In *Positionen der Negativität*. Ed. Harald Weinrich. Poetik und Hermeneutik, No. 6. Munich, 1975, pp. 263–339.
―――. "Theorie der Gattungen und Literatur des Mittelalters." In *Grundriss der romanischen Literaturen des Mittelalters*. Vol. I, *Généralités*. Ed. Maurice Delbouille et al. Heidelberg, 1972, pp. 107–38.
Jefferies, P. J. "Social Mobility in the Fourteenth Century: The Example of the Chelreys of Berkshire." *Oxoniensia*, 41 (1976), 324–36.
Jodogne, Omer. "Comment Thomas d'Angleterre a compris l'amour de Tristan et d'Iseut." *LR*, 19 (1965), 103–19.
Johnson, Phyllis. "*Dolor, dolent* et *soi doloir*: le vocabulaire de la douleur et la conception de l'amour selon Béroul et Thomas." *RPh*, 26 (1972–73), 546–54.
Jolliffe, John Edward Austin. *Angevin Kingship*. 2nd ed. London, 1963.
Jones, Robin F. "The Precocity of Anglo-Norman and the *Voyage of Saint Brendan*." In *The Nature of Medieval Narrative*. Ed. Minnette Grunmann-Gaudet and Robin F. Jones. French Forum Monographs, No. 22. Lexington, Ky., 1980, pp. 145–58.
Jonin, Pierre. *Les Personnages féminins dans les romans français de Tristan au XIIe siècle*. Annales de la Faculté des Lettres, Aix-en-Provence, n.s. 22. Gap, 1958.
Kaeuper, Richard W. "An Historian's Reading of *The Tale of Gamelyn*." *MÆ*, 52 (1983), 51–62.
Kane, George. "Outstanding Problems of Middle English Scholarship." In *The Fourteenth Century*. Ed. Paul E. Szarmach and Bernard S. Levy. *Acta*, 4 (1977), 1–17.
Kantorowicz, Ernst. *The King's Two Bodies: A Study in Mediaeval Political Theology*. Princeton, 1957.
Karnein, Alfred. "Auf der Suche nach einem Autor: Andreas, Verfasser von *De Amore*." *GRM*, 28 (1978), 1–20.
―――. "La Réception du *De Amore* d'André Le Chapelain au XIIIe siècle." *Romania*, 102 (1981), 324–51, 501–42.
Keeler, Laura. *Geoffrey of Monmouth and the Late Latin Chroniclers, 1300–1500*. University of California Publications in English, Vol. 17, No. 1. Berkeley, 1946.
Keen, Maurice. "Chaucer's Knight, the English Aristocracy and the Crusade." In *English Court Culture in the Later Middle Ages*. Ed. V. J. Scattergood and J. W. Sherborne. New York, 1983, pp. 45–61.

———. "Chivalrous Culture in Fourteenth-Century England." *Historical Studies*, 10 (1976), 1-24.

———. *Chivalry*. New Haven, 1984.

Keeney, Barnaby C. "Military Service and the Development of Nationalism in England, 1272-1327." *Speculum*, 22 (1947), 534-49.

Kelly, Douglas. "*En uni dire* (*Tristan* Douce 839) and the Composition of Thomas's *Tristan*." *MP*, 67 (1969-1970), 9-17.

———. *Sens and Conjointure in the "Chevalier de la Charrette."* The Hague, 1966.

Kelly, Henry Ansgar. *Love and Marriage in the Age of Chaucer*. Ithaca, 1975.

Ker, William Paton. *Epic and Romance. Essays on Medieval Literature*. 2nd ed. London, 1908.

Kilgour, Raymond Lincoln. *The Decline of Chivalry*. Cambridge, Mass., 1937.

Kittredge, George Lyman. "Chaucer and Some of His Friends." *MP*, 1 (1903-4), 1-18.

Klausner, David N. "Didacticism and Drama in Guy of Warwick." *M&H*, n.s. 6 (1975), 103-19.

Köhler, Erich. *Ideal und Wirklichkeit in der höfischen Epik*. Tübingen, 1956.

———. "Quelques observations d'ordre historico-sociologique sur les rapports entre la chanson de geste et le roman courtois." In *Chanson de geste und höfischer Roman: Heidelberger Kolloquium, 30 Januar 1961*. Heidelberg, 1963, pp. 21-30 and 31-36 (discussion).

———. "Il sistema sociologico del romanzo francese medievale." *MedR*, 3 (1976), 321-44.

Kölbing, Eugen. "Die Alliteration in Sir Beues of Hamtoun." *Englische Studien*, 19 (1894), 441-53.

———. "Zu Amis and Amilloun." *Englische Studien*, 2 (1879), 295-310.

Kramer, Dale. "Structural Artistry in *Amis and Amiloun*." *AnM*, 9 (1968), 103-22.

Krappe, A. H. "The Legend of Amicus and Amelius." *MLR*, 18 (1923), 152-61.

Kratins, Ojars. "Middle English *Amis and Amiloun*: Chivalric Romance or Secular Hagiography?" *PMLA*, 81 (1966), 347-54.

Kunstmann, Pierre. "Texte, intertexte et autotexte dans le *Tristan* de Thomas d'Angleterre." In *The Nature of Medieval Narrative*. Ed. Minnette Grunmann-Gaudet and Robin F. Jones. French Forum Monographs, No. 22. Lexington, Ky., 1980, pp. 173-86.

Labande, Edmond-René. "Pour une image véridique d'Aliénor d'Aquitaine." *Bulletin de la Société des antiquaires de l'Ouest*, 4th ser., 2 (1952), 175-234.

———. [Corrections to *Amadas et Ydoine*.] *Romania*, 56 (1930), 433-36.

Lagarde, Georges de. *La Naissance de l'esprit laïque au déclin du moyen âge*. New ed., 5 vols. Louvain, 1956-63.

Landsberger, Henry A., ed. *Rural Protest: Peasant Movements and Social Change*. London, 1974.

Lang, Jane, and Marion Gibbs. *Bishops and Reform 1215-1272, with Special Reference to the Lateran Council of 1215*. London, 1934.
Langlois, Ch.-V. "Les Anglais du moyen âge d'après les sources françaises." *Revue historique*, 52 (1893), 298-315.
Lavis, Georges. *L'Expression de l'affectivité dans la poésie lyrique française du moyen âge (XIIe-XIIIe s.): Etude sémantique et stylistique du réseau lexical "joie-dolor"*. Bibliothèque de la Faculté de Philosophie et Lettres de l'Université de Liège, No. 200. Paris, 1972.
Lawton, David, ed. *Middle English Alliterative Poetry and Its Literary Background: Seven Essays*. Cambridge, 1982.
Lazar, Moshé. *Amour courtois et "Fin'Amors" dans la littérature du XIIe siècle*. Paris, 1964.
Lea, Henry Charles. *A History of Auricular Confession and Indulgences in the Latin Church*. 3 vols. Philadelphia, 1896.
Leach, Henry Goddard. *Angevin Britain and Scandinavia*. Harvard Studies in Comparative Literature, No. 6. Cambridge, Mass, 1921.
Lefèvre, Y. "De l'usage du français en Grande-Bretagne à la fin du XIIe siècle." In *Etudes de langue et de littérature du moyen âge offerts à Félix Lecoy*. Paris, 1973, pp. 301-5.
Leff, Gordon. "Heresy and the Decline of the Medieval Church." *Past and Present*, No. 20 (November 1961), pp. 36-51.
Le Gentil, Pierre. "A propos d'*Amadas et Ydoine*." *Romania*, 71 (1950), 359-73.
———. "A propos du mariage de Tristan et de la colère de Brangain dans le roman de Thomas." In *Mélanges de philologie romane offerts à Charles Camproux*. Vol. I. Montpellier, 1978, pp. 401-5.
———. "La Légende de Tristan vue par Béroul et Thomas." *RPh*, 7 (1953-54), 111-29.
———. "Pour l'interprétation du *Tristan* de Thomas." *BBSIA*, 18 (1966), 178-79.
———. "Sur l'épilogue du *Tristan* de Thomas." In *Mélanges de littérature du moyen âge au XXe siècle offerts à Jeanne Lods*. Vol. I. Paris, 1978, pp. 365-70.
Legge, Maria Dominica. "Anglo-Norman Hagiography and the Romances." *M&H*, n.s. 6 (1975), 41-49.
———. *Anglo-Norman Literature and Its Background*. Oxford, 1963; corr. repr. 1971.
———. "Archaism and the Conquest." *MLR*, 51 (1956), 227-29.
———. "La 'Courtoisie' en anglo-normand." In *Orbis Mediaevalis: Mélanges de langue et de littérature médiévales offerts à Reto Raduolf Bezzola*. Ed. Georges Güntert et al. Berne, 1978, pp. 235-39.
———. "The Influence of Patronage on Form in Medieval French Literature." In *Stil- und Formprobleme in der Literatur*. Ed. Paul Böckmann. Heidelberg, 1959, pp. 136-41.
———. "La Précocité de la littérature anglo-normande." *CCM*, 8 (1965), 327-49.

———. "Le Problème des *Folies* aujourd'hui." In *Mélanges de littérature du moyen âge au XXe siècle offerts à Jeanne Lods.* Vol. I. Paris, 1978, pp. 371–77.
———. "The Rise and Fall of Anglo-Norman Literature." *Mosaic,* 8:4 (1974–75), 1–6.
———. "The Significance of Anglo-Norman." University of Edinburgh Inaugural Lecture, No. 38. Edinburgh, 1968.
Lejeune, Rita. "Rôle littéraire d'Aliénor d'Aquitaine et de sa famille." *CN,* 14 (1954), 5–57.
———. "Rôle littéraire de la famille d'Aliénor d'Aquitaine." *CCM,* 1 (1958), 319–37.
Le Patourel, John. *The Norman Empire.* Oxford, 1976.
Levy, Bernard S., and Paul E. Szarmach, eds. *The Alliterative Tradition in the Fourteenth Century.* Kent, Ohio, 1981.
Levy, Brian Joseph. "The Ancestral Romance in Mediaeval French with Special Reference to Anglo-Norman Literature." Diss. Univ. of Edinburgh, 1966.
———. "Waltheof 'Earl' de Huntingdon et de Northampton: la naissance d'un héros anglo-normand." *CCM,* 18 (1975), 183–96.
Livingston, Charles H. "Manuscript Fragments of a Continental French Version of the *Roman d'Ipomedon.*" *MP,* 40 (1942), 117–30.
Lommatzsch, Erhard. "Darstellung von Trauer und Schmerz in der altfranzösischen Literatur." *ZRP,* 43 (1923), 20–67.
Loomis, Laura Hibbard. "The Auchinleck Manuscript and a Possible London Bookshop of 1330–1340." *PMLA,* 57 (1942), 595–627.
———. *Mediaeval Romance in England.* New ed. New York, 1963.
Loomis, Roger Sherman. "Chivalric and Dramatic Imitations of Arthurian Romance." In *Medieval Studies in Memory of A. Kingsley Porter.* Ed. Wilhelm R. W. Koehler. Vol. I. Cambridge, Mass., 1939, pp. 79–97.
———. "Edward I, Arthurian Enthusiast." *Speculum,* 28 (1953), 114–27.
———. "Tristram and the House of Anjou." *MLR,* 17 (1922), 24–30.
Lot-Borodine, Myrrha. *De l'amour profane à l'amour sacré.* Paris, 1961.
McFarlane, K. B. *The Nobility of Later Medieval England.* Oxford, 1973.
McIntosh, Angus. "Early Middle English Alliterative Verse." In *Middle English Alliterative Poetry and Its Literary Background: Seven Essays.* Ed. David Lawton. Cambridge, 1982, pp. 20–33.
McKeehan, Irene P. "*Guillaume de Palerne*: A Medieval 'Best Seller.'" *PMLA,* 41 (1926), 785–809.
McKisack, May. *The Fourteenth Century, 1307–1399.* The Oxford History of England, Vol. 5. Oxford, 1959.
McKnight, George H. "The Germanic Elements in the Story of King Horn." *PMLA,* 15 (1900), 221–32.
Maddicott, J. R. *The English Peasantry and the Demands of the Crown, 1294–1341.* Past and Present Suppl., No. 1. Oxford, 1975.
Martin, E. M. "A Shropshire Lad of the Middle Ages." *Fortnightly Review,* 113 (January 1923), 966–76; 114 (July 1923), 81–94.

Martin [Weiss], Judith Elizabeth. "Studies in Some Early Middle English Romances." Diss. Cambridge, 1967.
Mason, Emma. "Legends of the Beauchamps' Ancestors: The Use of Baronial Propaganda in Medieval England." *Journal of Medieval History*, 10 (1984), 25–40.
———. "The Resources of the Earldom of Warwick in the Thirteenth Century." *Midland History*, 3 (1975–76), 67–76.
———. "The Role of the English Parishioner, 1100–1500." *Journal of Ecclesiastical History*, 27 (1976), 17–29.
Mathew, Gervase. "Ideals of Knighthood in Late-Fourteenth-Century England." In *Studies in Medieval History Presented to Frederick Maurice Powicke*. Ed. R. W. Hunt et al. Oxford, 1948, pp. 354–62.
———. "Marriage and *Amour Courtois* in Late Fourteenth-Century England." In *Essays Presented to Charles Williams*. London, 1947, pp. 128–35.
Matzke, John E. "Contributions to the History of the Legend of Saint George, with Special Reference to the Sources of the French, German, and Anglo-Saxon Metrical Versions." *PMLA*, 18 (1903), 99–171.
———. "The Legend of Saint George: Its Development into a *Roman d'Aventure*." *PMLA*, 19 (1904), 449–78.
———. "The Oldest Form of the Beves Legend." *MP*, 10 (1912), 19–36.
Mehl, Dieter. *The Middle English Romances of the Thirteenth and Fourteenth Centuries*. London, 1968.
Meisel, Janet. *Barons of the Welsh Frontier: The Corbet, Pantulf, and Fitz Warin Families, 1066–1272*. Lincoln, Nebraska, 1980.
Ménard, Philippe. "Les Fous dans la société médiévale: le témoignage de la littérature au XIIe et au XIIIe siècle." *Romania*, 98 (1977), 433–59.
———. *Le Rire et le sourire dans le roman courtois en France au moyen âge (1150–1250)*. Publications Romanes et Françaises, No. 105. Geneva, 1969.
Meneghetti, Maria Luisa. "'L'Estoire des Engleis' di Geffrei Gaimar fra cronaca genealogica e romanzo cortese." *MedR*, 2 (1975), 232–46.
Meyer-Lindenberg, Herlint. "Zur Datierung des *Havelok*." *Anglia*, 86 (1968), 89–112.
Mills, Maldwyn. "Havelok's Return." *MÆ*, 45 (1976), 20–35.
Mollat, Michel, and Philippe Wolff. *The Popular Revolutions of the Late Middle Ages*. Trans. A. L. Lytton-Sells. London, 1973.
Moore, Olin Harris. *The Young King Henry Plantagenet (1155–1183) in History, Literature and Tradition*. Columbus, 1925.
Moorman, John R. H. *Church Life in England in the Thirteenth Century*. Cambridge, 1945.
Morris, Colin. *The Discovery of the Individual, 1050–1200*. New York, 1972.
Muscatine, Charles. *Chaucer and the French Tradition*. Berkeley and Los Angeles, 1957.
———. "The Emergence of Psychological Allegory in Old French Romance." *PMLA*, 68 (1953), 1160–82.

———. *Poetry and Crisis in the Age of Chaucer*. Notre Dame, 1972.

———. "The Social Background of the Old French Fabliaux." *Genre*, 9 (1976), 1–19.

Nichols, Stephen G., Jr. "A Poetics of Historicism? Recent Trends in Medieval Literary Study." *M&H*, n.s. 8 (1977), 77–101.

Noltung-Hauff, Ilse. *Die Stellung der Liebeskasuistik im höfischen Roman*. Heidelberg, 1959.

Oakley, Francis. *The Western Church in the Later Middle Ages*. Ithaca, 1979.

Orme, Nicholas. *Education in the West of England, 1066–1548*. Exeter, 1976.

———. "The Education of the Courtier." In *English Court Culture in the Later Middle Ages*. Ed. V. J. Scattergood and J. W. Sherborne. New York, 1983, pp. 63–85.

Owen, D. D. R. "The Craft of Guillaume le Clerc's *Fergus*." In *The Craft of Fiction: Essays in Medieval Poetics*. Ed. Leigh A. Arrathoon. Rochester, Mich., 1984, pp. 47–81.

———. "Profanity and Its Purpose in Chrétien's *Cligès* and *Lancelot*." *FMLS*, 6 (1970), 37–48.

Owst, Gerald R. *Literature and Pulpit in Medieval England*. 2nd ed. Oxford, 1961.

Painter, Sidney. "The Family and the Feudal System in Twelfth-Century England." *Speculum*, 35 (1960), 1–16.

———. *The Reign of King John*. Baltimore, 1949.

———. "The Sources of *Fouke Fitz Warin*." *MLN*, 50 (1935), 13–15.

———. *Studies in the History of the English Feudal Barony*. The Johns Hopkins University Studies in Historical and Political Science, Ser. 61, No. 3. Baltimore, 1943.

Pantin, William A. *The English Church in the Fourteenth Century*. Cambridge, 1955.

———. "Instructions for a Devout and Literate Layman." In *Medieval Learning and Literature: Essays Presented to Richard William Hunt*. Ed. J. J. G. Alexander and M. T. Gibson. Oxford, 1976, pp. 398–422.

Paris, Gaston. "Le Roman de Richard Coeur de Lion." *Romania*, 26 (1897), 353–93.

———. "Sur *Amadas et Ydoine*." In *An English Miscellany: Presented to Dr. Furnivall*. Oxford, 1901, pp. 386–94.

Partner, Nancy F. *Serious Entertainments: The Writing of History in Twelfth-Century England*. Chicago, 1977.

Pauphilet, Albert. *Le Legs du moyen âge*. Melun, 1950.

Payen, Jean-Charles. "Lancelot contre Tristan: la conjuration d'un mythe subversif (réflexions sur l'idéologie romanesque au moyen âge)." In *Mélanges de langue et de littérature médiévales offerts à Pierre le Gentil*. Paris, 1973, pp. 617–32.

Pearsall, Derek. "The Alliterative Revival: Origins and Social Backgrounds." In *Middle English Alliterative Poetry and Its Literary Background: Seven Essays*. Ed. David Lawton. Cambridge, 1982, pp. 34–53.

———. "The Development of Middle English Romance." *MS*, 27 (1965), 91–116.

———. "John Capgrave's *Life of St. Katherine* and Popular Romance Style." *M&H*, n.s. 6 (1975), 121–37.
———. *Old English and Middle English Poetry*. London, 1977.
———. "Understanding Middle English Romance." *Review*, 2 (1980), 105–25.
Pensom, Roger. "The Lexical Field of 'Fiers' in Old French." *Archivum Linguisticum*, n.s. 1 (1970), 49–66.
Perroy, Edouard. "Social Mobility Among the French *Noblesse* in the Later Middle Ages." *Past and Present*, No. 21 (April 1962), pp. 25–38.
Petit, Herbert H. "A Wood Needing—Clearing, Desiderata in Anglo-Norman—English Linguistics." *AnM*, 1 (1960), 102–7.
Petit-Dutaillis, Charles. *La Monarchie féodale en France et en Angleterre, X^e–XIIIe siècle*. Paris, 1933.
Pickford, Cedric E. "*Sir Tristrem*, Sir Walter Scott and Thomas." In *Studies in Medieval Literature and Languages in Memory of Frederick Whitehead*. Ed. W. Rothwell et al. Manchester, 1973, pp. 219–28.
Poole, Austin Lane. *From Domesday Book to Magna Carta, 1087–1216*. 2nd ed. Oxford, 1955.
Pope, Mildred K. *From Latin to Modern French with Especial Consideration of Anglo-Norman*. Rev. ed. London, 1952.
———. "Further Notes on the Vocabulary of the Romance of Horn and Rimel and Some Queries." In *Studia romanica: Gedenkschrift für Eugen Lerch*. Ed. Charles Bruneau and P. M. Schon. Stuttgart, 1955, pp. 339–47.
———. "The *Romance of Horn* and *King Horn*." *MÆ*, 25 (1956), 164–67.
Postan, M. M. *The Mediaeval Economy and Society*. London, 1972.
Powicke, Maurice. *The Thirteenth Century, 1216–1307*. 2nd ed. Oxford, 1962.
Press, A. R. "The Precocious Courtesy of Geoffrey Gaimar." In *Court and Poet*. Ed. Glyn S. Burgess. Liverpool, 1981, pp. 267–76.
Prestwich, Michael. *The Three Edwards: War and State in England, 1272–1377*. New York, 1980.
Quinn, William A., and Audley S. Hall. *Jongleur: A Modified Theory of Oral Improvisation and Its Effects on the Performance and Transmission of Middle English Romance*. Washington, D.C., 1982.
Ramsey, Lee C. *Chivalric Romances: Popular Literature in Medieval England*. Bloomington, 1983.
Reinhard, J. R. *The Old French Romance of Amadas et Ydoine: An Historical Study*. Durham, N.C., 1927.
Reiss, Edmund. "*Fin' Amors*: Its History and Meaning in Medieval Literature." *Journal of Medieval and Renaissance Studies*, 8 (1979), 74–99.
Remigereau, François. "Tristan 'maître de vénerie' dans la tradition anglaise et dans le roman de Thomas." *Romania*, 58 (1932), 218–37.
Remy, Paul. "Les 'cours d'amour': légende et réalité." *Revue de l'Université de Bruxelles*, n.s. 7 (1954–55), 179–97.
———. "La Lèpre, thème littéraire au moyen âge." *MA*, 52 (1946), 195–242.
Richards, Peter. *The Medieval Leper and his Northern Heirs*. Cambridge, 1977.

Richardson, H. G. "The Letters and Charters of Eleanor of Aquitaine." *English Historical Review*, 74 (1959), 193–213.
Richmond, Velma Bourgeois. "*Guy of Warwick*: A Medieval Thriller." *South Atlantic Quarterly*, 73 (1974), 554–63.
———. *The Popularity of Middle English Romance*. Bowling Green, Ohio, 1975.
Rickard, Peter. *Britain in Medieval French Literature, 1100–1500*. Cambridge, 1956.
Riedel, Frederick Carl. *Crime and Punishment in the Old French Romances*. New York, 1938.
Robertson, D. W., Jr. "Frequency of Preaching in Thirteenth-Century England." *Speculum*, 24 (1949), 376–88.
Rothwell, William. "Anglo-Norman Perspectives." *MLR*, 70 (1975), 41–49.
———. "A quelle époque a-t-on cessé de parler français en Angleterre?" In *Mélanges de philologie romane offerts à Charles Camproux*. Vol. II. Montpellier, 1978, pp. 1075–89.
———. "The Role of French in Thirteenth-Century England." *BJRL*, 58 (1975–76), 445–66.
Rowland, Beryl. "*Pronuntiatio* and Its Effect on Chaucer's Audience." *SAC*, 4 (1982), 33–51.
Rumble, Thomas C. "The Middle English *Sir Tristrem*: Toward a Reappraisal." *CL*, 11 (1959), 221–28.
Russell, Josiah C. *Twelfth Century Studies*. New York, 1978.
Salter, Elizabeth. "The Alliterative Revival I., II." *MP*, 64 (1966–67), 146–50, 233–37.
Saul, Nigel. *Knights and Esquires: The Gloucestershire Gentry in the Fourteenth Century*. Oxford, 1981.
Scattergood, V. J. "Literary Culture at the Court of Richard II." In *English Court Culture in the Later Middle Ages*. Ed. V. J. Scattergood and J. W. Sherborne. New York, 1983, pp. 29–43.
Schelp, Hanspeter. *Exemplarische Romanzen im Mittelenglischen*. Palaestra, No. 246. Göttingen, 1967.
Schirmer, Walter Franz, and Ulrich Broich. *Studien zum literarischen Patronat im England des 12. Jahrhunderts*. Cologne, 1962.
Schlight, John. *Monarchs and Mercenaries: A Reappraisal of the Importance of Knight Service in Norman and Early Angevin England*. Studies in British History and Culture, No. 1. Bridgeport, Conn., 1968.
Schmolke-Hasselmann, Beate. *Der arthurische Versroman von Chrestien bis Froissart*. Tübingen, 1980.
———. "Henry II Plantagenêt, roi d'Angleterre, et la genèse d'*Erec et Enide*." *CCM*, 24 (1981), 241–46.
Schroeder, Peter R. "Hidden Depths: Dialogue and Characterization in Chaucer and Malory." *PMLA*, 98 (1983), 374–87.
Severs, J. Burke. *A Manual of the Writings in Middle English, 1050–1500*. Vol. I, *Romances*. New Haven, 1967.
———, ed. *Recent Middle English Scholarship and Criticism: Survey and Desiderata*. Pittsburgh, 1971.

Shannon, Edgar F., Jr. "Mediaeval Law in *The Tale of Gamelyn*." *Speculum*, 26 (1951), 458–64.
Shelly, Percy Van Dyke. *English and French in England, 1066–1100*. Philadelphia, 1921.
Shoaf, Judith P. "Thomas' *Tristan* and *Tristrams Saga*: Versions and Themes." Diss. Cornell, 1978.
Shonk, Timothy A. "A Study of the Auchinleck Manuscript: Bookmen and Bookmaking in the Early Fourteenth Century." *Speculum*, 60 (1985), 71–91.
Short, Ian. "On Bilingualism in Anglo-Norman England." *RPh*, 23 (1979–80), 467–79.
Sklute, Larry M. "The Ambiguity of Ethical Norms in Courtly Romance." *Genre*, 11 (1978), 315–32.
Southern, Richard W. *The Making of the Middle Ages*. London, 1953.
———. "The Place of England in the Twelfth-Century Renaissance." *History*, 45 (1960), 201–16.
———. *Western Society and the Church in the Middle Ages*. Harmondsworth, 1970.
Spensley, Ronald M. "The Structure of Hue de Rotelande's *Ipomedon*." *Romania*, 95 (1974), 341–51.
Staines, David. "Havelok the Dane: A Thirteenth-Century Handbook for Princes." *Speculum*, 51 (1976), 602–23.
Starkey, David. "The Age of the Household: Politics, Society and the Arts c. 1350–c. 1550." In *The Later Middle Ages*. Ed. Stephen Medcalf. New York, 1981, pp. 225–90.
Stengel, Edmund. [Corrections to *Ipomedon*.] *ZFSL*, 13:2 (1891), 9–27.
Stevens, John. *Medieval Romance: Themes and Approaches*. London, 1973.
Strohm, Paul. "Chaucer's Audience." *L&H*, No. 5 (Spring 1977), 26–41.
———. "The Origin and Meaning of Middle English *Romaunce*." *Genre*, 10 (1977), 1–28.
———. "*Passioun, Lyf, Miracle, Legende*: Some Generic Terms in Middle English Hagiographical Narrative." *ChauR*, 10 (1975–76), 62–75, 154–71.
Sudre, Léopold. "Les Allusions à la légende de Tristan dans la littérature du moyen âge." *Romania*, 15 (1886), 534–57.
Susskind, Norman. "Love and Laughter in the Romans Courtois." *FR*, 37 (1963–64), 651–57.
Tanquerey, F. J. *L'Evolution du verbe en anglo-français, XIIIe–XIVe siècles*. Paris, 1915.
Thomson, S. Harrison. "Walter Burley's Commentary on the *Politics* of Aristotle." In *Mélanges Auguste Pelzer*. Louvain, 1947, pp. 557–78.
Thrupp, Sylvia. *The Merchant Class of Medieval London*. Chicago, 1948.
Tierney, Mark Aloysius. *The History and Antiquities of the Castle and Town of Arundel*. 2 vols. London, 1834.
Timmins, Samuel. *A History of Warwickshire*. London, 1889.
Treharne, Reginald Francis. *The Baronial Plan of Reform, 1258–1263*. Manchester, 1932.
Trounce, Allan McIntyre. "The English Tail-Rhyme Romances." *MÆ*, 1 (1932), 87–108, 168–82; 2 (1933), 34–57, 189–98; 3 (1934), 30–50.

Türk, Egbert. *Nugae Curialium: Le Règne d'Henri II Plantegenêt (1145–1189) et l'éthique politique*. Geneva, 1977.

Turner, Ralph V. "The Judges of King John: Their Background and Training." *Speculum*, 51 (1976), 447–61.

Ullmann, Walter. *Medieval Foundations of Renaissance Humanism*. Ithaca, 1977.

Uitti, Karl D. "The Clerkly Narrator Figure in Old French Hagiography and Romance." *MedR*, 2 (1975), 394–408.

Utley, Francis Lee. "Must We Abandon the Concept of Courtly Love?" *M&H*, n.s. 3 (1972), 299–324.

Vale, Juliet. *Edward III and Chivalry: Chivalric Society and Its Context 1270–1350*. Bury St. Edmunds, 1982.

Vale, Malcolm. *War and Chivalry: Warfare and Aristocratic Culture in England, France and Burgundy at the End of the Middle Ages*. London, 1981.

Vance, Eugene. "Le Combat érotique chez Chrétien de Troyes." *Poétique*, 12 (1972), 544–71.

———. "Signs of the City: Medieval Poetry as Detour." *NLH*, 4 (1973), 557–74.

van der Gaaf, W. "Parliaments Held at Lincoln (Havelok l. 1006)." *Englische Studien*, 32 (1903), 319–20.

Vàrvaro, Alberto. "L'utilizzazione letteraria di motivi della narrativa popolare nei romanzi di Tristano." In *Mélanges de langue et de littérature du moyen-âge et de la renaissance offerts à Jean Frappier*. Vol. II. Geneva, 1970, pp. 1057–75.

Vinaver, Eugène. *The Rise of Romance*. Oxford, 1971.

Vising, Johan. *Anglo-Norman Language and Literature*. London, 1923.

———. *Etude sur le dialecte anglo-normand du XIIe siècle*. Uppsala, 1882.

Vitz, Evelyn Birge. "Desire and Causality in Medieval Narrative." *RR*, 71 (1980), 213–43.

———. "*La Vie de Saint Alexis*: Narrative Analysis and the Quest for the Sacred Subject." *PMLA*, 93 (1978), 396–408.

Vogel, Bertram. "The Dialect of *Sir Tristrem*." *JEGP*, 40 (1941), 538–44.

von Ertzdorff, Xenja. "Die Wahrheit der höfischen Romane des Mittelalters." *ZDP*, 86 (1967), 375–89.

Wadsworth, Rosalind. "Historical Romance in England: Studies in Anglo-Norman and Middle English Romance." Diss. York, 1972.

Wallerstein, Immanuel. *The Modern World-System*. New York, 1974.

Warren, Wilfred Lewis. *Henry II*. Berkeley and Los Angeles, 1973.

———. *King John*. London, 1961.

Wathelet-Willem, Jeanne. *Recherches sur la Chanson de Guillaume*. Vol. I. Paris, 1975.

Watson, George, ed. *The New Cambridge Bibliography of English Literature*. Vol. I. Cambridge, 1974.

Waugh, S. L. "The Profits of Violence: The Minor Gentry in the Rebellion of 1321–1322 in Gloucestershire and Herefordshire." *Speculum*, 52 (1977), 843–69.

Wehrli, Max. *Formen mittelalterlicher Erzählung: Aufsätze*. Zurich, 1969.

Weiss, Judith. "The Major Interpolations in *Sir Beues of Hamtoun*." *MÆ*, 48 (1979), 71–76.

———. "Structure and Characterisation in *Havelok the Dane*." *Speculum*, 44 (1969), 247–57.

West, Constance Birt. *Courtoisie in Anglo-Norman Literature*. Oxford, 1938.

West, Henry S. *The Versification of King Horn*. Baltimore, 1907.

Weyrauch, Max. "Die mittelenglischen Fassungen der Sage Guy of Warwick und ihre altfranzösische Vorlage." Diss. Breslau, 1899.

White, Hayden. *Metahistory: The Historical Imagination in Nineteenth-Century Europe*. Baltimore, 1973.

Whiting, B. J. "The Vows of the Heron." *Speculum*, 20 (1945), 261–78.

Wilson, Richard Middlewood. *Early Middle English Literature*. 2nd ed. London, 1951.

———. "English and French in England 1100–1300." *History*, n.s. 28 (1943), 37–60.

———. *The Lost Literature of Medieval England*. Rev. ed. London, 1970.

Wind, Bartina. "Eléments courtois dans Béroul et dans Thomas." *RPh*, 14 (1960–61), 1–13.

———. "Nos incertitudes au sujet du 'Tristan' de Thomas." In *Mélanges de langue et de littérature du moyen-âge et de la renaissance offerts à Jean Frappier*. Vol. II. Geneva, 1970, pp. 1129–38.

Wittig, Susan. *Stylistic and Narrative Structures in the Middle English Romances*. Austin, 1978.

Woledge, Brian, and Ian Short. "Liste provisoire de manuscrits du XIIe siècle contenant des textes en langue française." *Romania*, 102 (1981), 1–18.

Wood, Charles T. *The Age of Chivalry. Manners and Morals, 1000–1450*. London, 1970.

Zaddy, Z. P. *Chrétien Studies*. Glasgow, 1973.

Zumthor, Paul. *Essai de poétique médiévale*. Paris, 1972.

———. *Langue, texte, énigme*. Paris, 1975.

———. *Merlin le prophète. Un thème de la littérature polémique, de l'historiographie et des romans*. Lausanne, 1943.

Index

Aälof, in Horn Romances, 24, 85; in *Romance of Horn*, 25–26
Abnegation, Christian, 12, 94, 109–17, 128–29, 162, 219–20
Achievement, personal, 2, 25, 37, 104, 135; barony and, 44, 83, 217, 223; religious values and, 101–2, 219, 222; society and, 12, 13–14, 84
Adultery, 179, 183, 187–88, 211 n
Ailmar, in *King Horn*, 24
Albini family, 16–17
Alexander, 107–8. See also *Anglo-Norman "Alexander," The*; *Kyng Alisaunder*
Alexandrines, in *Romance of Horn*, 28, 30
Alexis, Saint, 109–15, 128, 219
Alienation in love, 151–52, 168, 171, 184, 187–88, 194–97
Alliterative verse, 76, 190 n
Allof, in *King Horn*, 33
Amadas, in *Amadas et Ydoine*, 179, 198–99, 221; love and, 181–86, 188, 196 n, 200
Amadas et Ydoine, 6, 136, 139; exemplarity in, 203, 221; knighthood in, 198–99, 200; ideal love in, 179, 181–87, 188, 194, 196 n, 212
Amiloun (Amilun), in Amis and Amiloun romances, 92–93, 117–19, 121–24, 127–28, 129
Amis, in Amis and Amiloun romances, 92–93, 117–20, 121–25, 127–28, 129
Amis, in *Guy of Warwick*, 65
Amis and Amiloun (ME), 103, 104, 117–28, 193, 217, 219–20

Amis e Amilun (AN), 6, 104, 117–28
Anarchy, 19 n
Ancestors, English, 15, 23, 55, 67, 76, 85, 197
"Ancestral romance," theory of, 12, 16–18, 41 n, 86
Andreas Capellanus, 136, 210 n
Angevin court, 2, 28 n, 142 n; centralization under, 7–8, 19, 21, 59, 141; influence on romance, 2–3, 11, 133, 144–46, 216
Anglo-Norman "Alexander," The (Thomas of Kent), 92, 107–8, 130, 216
Anglo-Norman literature, 2–3, 12, 28 n, 92, 132, 145
Anglonormannische Boeve de Haumtone, Der (AN), 6, 13, 105; ancestral theory and, 16–17; heritage in, 55–61, 218; style of, 75, 76, 78, 80–81
Anglo-Norman romances, 3, 9–18, 83, 135, 180; baronial issues and, 19–24, 76, 85–86; courtliness and, 136–37, 211–12, 214, 221; insularity and, 1, 6, 216–17; religious influences on, 92, 220. See also specific romances
Anglo-Norman Voyage of St. Brendan, The, 102
Anjou, 145
Anonymity, 109, 111–13, 129. See also Disguise
Aquinas, Thomas, 186 n
Aquitaine, 145
Archbishop of Canterbury, in *Athelston*, 71, 72, 93, 125–27, 129

253

Argentille, in *Lai d'Haveloc*, 40, 41, 46, 52n
Aristocracy. *See* Barony, English; Nobility, French
Arnould, E. J., 100
Arnulf of Guines, 175, 176, 201
"*Art d'aimer* Anglo-normand, Un," 179
Arthour and Merlin, 10
Arthur, 141, 197–98, 199
Arthurian legend, 141, 144, 197–98
Arthurian Oath, 178
Arundel (horse), in *Beues of Hamtoun*, 59, 61, 67, 105
Arundel (place), in *Boeve de Haumtone*, 16, 17, 56
Athelstan, King, in *Gui de Warewic*, 65–66; in *Guy of Warwick*, 85, 113
Athelston, 13, 85, 87n, 90, 103; justice in, 54, 69, 71–72, 74; religious values in, 93, 117, 125–28, 129
Athelston, King, in *Athelston*, 69, 71–72, 85, 93, 126–27
Athelwold, in *Havelok the Dane*, 44, 46n, 48n, 130
Aþulf, in *King Horn*, 34, 194
Auchinleck manuscript, 21, 74, 75, 189, 190n, 192–93
Auerbach, Erich, 101n, 134, 135
Authorial comment, 27, 80, 147, 173, 186, 213; in *Ipomedon*, 139, 160–62, 165, 174, 203
Autonomy, 61, 83, 163n; baronial, 18, 60, 142, 222–23; destiny and, 32, 52, 93, 172, 174, 186; religious values and, 114, 117, 128, 129, 219; society and, 101, 119
Auvergne, 145

Baltof, in *Romance of Horn*, 28
Barlow, Frank, 7n
Barnie, John, 202n
Baronial reform movement (1258–67), 22, 48, 61n
Barony, English, 6–10, 75, 85–86, 90, 140, 216–17; centralization and, 97, 137, 141–42; class consciousness and, 43–46, 47, 179–80; ideals of, 11–12, 32, 39–40, 52, 101, 214–15, 222–23; legality and, 36–38, 48–50, 69; national feeling and, 59–62, 65–67, 74, 83, 218–19; rights of, 13–23, 58; social behavior and, 176–78, 198, 202–3, 211, 212, 221
Barrow, Sarah, 160
Baugh, Albert Croll, 10n, 75n, 191n
Beauchamp, Guy, 197
Becket, Thomas, 131

Bédier, Joseph, 188–89, 191
Belisaunt, in *Amis and Amiloun*, 119, 121
Bellatores, 6, 176
Benoît de Sainte-Maure, 3, 161n
Benton, John F., 143n
Bernart de Ventadorn, 3
Beroul, 148n, 152
Bevis, in *Beues of Hamtoun*, 53, 82–83; exile and return theme and, 55n, 76–78, 87–88; justice and, 54, 58–59; nationalism and, 60, 61–62, 67, 86; society and, 84, 218, 219; religious values and, 63–64, 68, 102, 104–6, 107, 109. *See also Romance of Sir Beues of Hamtoun, The*
Bigod family, 16n
Bilingualism, 4–5, 10, 217. *See also* Language
Blanche of Lancaster, 202
Bloch, R. Howard, 7n, 90, 138, 171, 174n
Bloomfield, Morton W., 102n
Boase, Roger, 138n
Bodel, Jean, 13
Boeve, in *Boeve de Haumtone*, 55–57, 60, 80–81, 89. *See also Anglonormannische Boeve de Haumtone, Der*
Bone amor, 136–37, 138. *See also* Courtly convention; *Fine amor*
Boniface VIII, 197–98
Born, Bertran de, 3, 54–55, 140
Bouchard, Constance B., 143n
Bourgeoisie, English, 15, 176, 179, 217; mobility and, 44, 180, 215; values of, 47, 52, 83
Bradmund, in *Beues of Hamtoun*, 68
Brangien, in *Tristan*, 149, 152n
Braswell, Laurel, 96, 103n
Brengwain, in *Sir Tristrem*, 193–94, 195
Brotherhood, in romances, 93, 117–28, 129, 131, 220
Bueve de Hantone (OF), 55–56
Bureaucracy, state, 19–20. *See also* Centralization, of government
Burley, Walter, 109n, 218
Burnley, J. D., 167

Calabria, 159
Capaneus, in *Ipomedon*, 159–60, 169, 209n
Capetian court, 141
Capgrave, John, 102
Catherine, Saint, 111–12
Centralization, of government, 7–8, 19–22, 90, 218–19. *See also* National feeling
Champenois literature, 3

Index

Chandos Herald, 199, 202
Chastity, 210–11 n
Châtelain de Couci, 211 n
Chaucer, Geoffrey, 93–94, 142, 180, 202
Chelrey, Edmund, 22–23 n
Chevalier de la Tour Landry, Le, 202 n
Children, 65, 124–25, 128; continuity and, 26–27, 42, 46, 56–57, 89; killing of, 51, 119, 120, 121, 123, 129
Childress, Diana T., 103, 109
Chivalry. See Knighthood
Chrétien de Troyes, 3, 89 n; on love, 168, 187, 188, 194, 207
Christ, parallels to, 38, 120, 125, 187
Christian church, 92, 94–96; reform in, 11, 12, 93, 97–100, 131–33, 219; secular values and, 15, 51 n, 71, 72, 105–6
Christian principles, 135, 136, 197, 217, 219; brotherhood and, 117–18, 124–25; secular values and, 96–97, 103–4, 105–7, 131, 221
Chronicles, 11, 12, 14–16, 43, 85, 96, 145, 175–76, 178, 180, 197–202, 215
Class consciousness, 46–47, 52, 66, 88, 223; mobility and, 8–9, 22–23, 43–45, 90, 177, 180. See also Barony, English; Bourgeoisie, English; Nobility, French
Clemence of Barking, 102
Clifford, Sir Lewis, 202
Cligès (Chrétien de Troyes), 158, 187, 188
Coleman, Janet, 180 n, 214 n
Combat of the Thirty, 199, 200
Confession, in church, 93, 99, 100
Conjointure, 139, 147
Conte, 139, 147
Council of Lambeth (1281), 99
Council of Oxford (1222), 99
Courtly convention (courtliness), 9, 35, 66, 135–37, 189, 215; accommodation to, 163, 172; adaptation of, 12, 142, 176–78, 202–6, 209–14, 221–23; ideal vs. practice, 135–36, 173–74, 179, 187, 201, 220
"Court of Chivalry" (1386), 180
Credenhill, 144
Criseyde, in Testament of Cresseid, 124
Crusades, 59, 60, 93, 106–7
Curia Regis, 97
Cursor Mundi, 96
Custom, 14, 19, 38–39, 74, 87; justice and, 23, 64, 69. See also Legality

Daire of Lombardy, in Ipomedon, 168, 209 n
Dame de Civile, in Boeve de Haumtone, 57 n
Daniel, Arnaut, 3
David of Scotland, 201
Death, 51 n, 139, 152, 154–56, 183, 185, 199
Degrevant, Sir, 66 n, 67, 179, 210–11 n
Delbouille, Maurice, 184 n
Dembowski, Peter F., 132
Denmark, 41, 45, 47, 49, 84, 87
Deschamps, Eustache, 142, 201–2
Disguise, 25, 76, 184; in Ipomedon, 158, 159–60, 162–63, 164, 169–70; knights in, 197, 213
Divine intervention, 103, 107, 118, 220; as guide, 108, 114–15, 122–23, 125, 129
Divine power. See Providence
Divorce, 185–86, 201 n
Donnei des amants, Le, 155–56 n
Doubling, in thematic development: examples of, 24–27, 41 n, 62, 170, 174; heritage and, 42, 54, 87–88
Dreams, 59 n, 87; in Amis and Amiloun romances, 119, 122, 125; in Romance of Horn, 26 n, 34 n
Dru la reïne, 159, 163, 164
Duby, Georges, 8 n, 32, 89, 139 n, 175 n, 187–88
Duchess of Calabria. See Fere, in Ipomedon; Fiere, la, in Ipomedon
Duel, judicial, 37, 65, 72, 123
Dunn, Charles W., 53 n
Durlac (C) manuscript, 117 n

Edelsi, in Lai d'Havelok, 41, 49 n, 58
Edgar, King, in Beues of Hamtoun: justice and, 58, 61, 69, 87; society and, 83, 84, 219
Edgar, King, in Boeve de Haumtone, 56, 57 n, 60–61
Edmund, Saint, 125, 126–27, 128
Edward I, 48 n, 60, 197–98
Edward III, 178, 180, 197
Edward the Confessor, 15
Eleanor of Aquitaine, 2–3, 144, 145, 146 n
Elstrude, in Chronicon Ghisnense, 201
Emotion, 51, 78–81, 119–20, 191; in Ipomedon, 164–66, 168, 169; in King Horn, 30, 33; in Tristan, 151, 153
Eneas, 187 n
Enéas, 3, 158, 166 n
England, 11–12, 15, 140–41, 145, 211; linguistic development in, 1–6, 9, 216–17; national feeling in, 60, 65, 84, 222; religious values in, 132–33, 219; social order in, 45, 90, 176–77, 214. See also Barony, English; Feudal system, in England

Epic, 11, 12, 14, 28n, 89, 218, 222
Ernle, R. E. P., 53
Estoire des Engleis, L' (Gaimar), 15, 40, 43
Eustace, Saint, 102, 105, 115–16, 128
Eustace d'Aubrichecourt, 200–201, 214
Evans, W. O., 136
Everett, Dorothy, 76
Exemplarity, 81–82, 103, 119, 130–31, 221; naturalism and, 203, 209–11, 214, 215; secular ideals and, 109, 186, 198
Exemplary romances, 92, 94–96, 105, 107, 214n; secular values and, 101–4, 128–31, 219
Expulsion and return, motif of, 24–25, 40–42, 54, 62, 87–88; baronial concerns and, 18, 23, 74, 76–77

Fabliaux, 9, 96, 143, 162, 167, 171
Faith, 100; divine sanction and, 125–30, 223; exemplarity and, 133, 221–22; heroic identity and, 76, 77n, 104, 117, 196–97; love and, 179, 186, 195, 208; secular values and, 12, 74, 101, 105–6, 118, 125–26; service and, 62, 92, 110–11, 219–20
Family, 88, 218; defense of, 24, 37, 59–61, 142; love and, 63, 188, 194; religious values and, 112–13, 115, 131, 219, 222; stability of, 18, 25, 38, 74, 93. *See also* Lineage
Fealty, 37, 54–55, 58, 65, 188; oath of, 7, 18, 41, 84
Felice, in *Gui de Warewic*, 208; in *Guy of Warwick*, 62, 113, 114, 196, 208
Fénice, in *Cligès*, 187
Fere, in *Ipomadon*, 205–7, 208–10
Festländische Bueve de Hantone, Der (OF), 55–56
Feudal system, in England, 2, 11, 16, 74, 87, 135, 223; baronial power and, 13, 32–35, 37, 40, 74; heritage and, 41, 54–55, 57; love and, 188, 197; royal control and, 7, 18–22, 58–61, 64–65, 84, 218
Feudal system, in France, 2, 18, 140–41, 176–77. *See also* France
Fière, la, in *Ipomedon*, 159–72, 187, 188, 204–6, 207n, 208
Fikenhild, in *King Horn*, 24, 32, 34n, 38
Fine amor, 102, 136–38, 213; behavior and, 135, 143, 149, 179; passion and, 12, 151–54, 166–67, 170–71; skepticism about, 148, 174, 188, 193; social order and, 58–59, 63, 183–84, 190, 221; suffering and, 156–57, 187, 195, 212, 220

FitzBaderon, Gilbert, 144
FitzGilbert, Constance, 43
Fitz Warin family, 17, 58, 68, 70
Florie, in *Amis e Amilun*, 119, 121
Floris, in *Floris and Blancheflur*, 187n, 196
Floris and Blancheflur, 196, 210
Folie Tristan d'Oxford, La, 155n, 158, 184
Fouke le Fitz Waryn, 6n, 13, 16–17, 21, 218; ancestry in, 54, 57–58, 59
Fourth Lateran Council (1215), 99, 100
France, 18, 132, 140–41, 176–77; elitism in, 211, 216, 221; linguistic development in, 1–2, 5–6. *See also* Nobility, French
Francis, Saint, 111
Frappier, Jean, 151n
Froissart, Jean, 178n, 200–201, 215
Fulk Fitz Warin, in *Fouke le Fitz Waryn*, 74, 77n; heritage and, 55, 57–58, 83, 219; justice and, 54, 68, 69–70, 87, 217–18; nation and, 60, 67, 84, 86; religious values and, 63–64, 104
Fulk romances. See *Fouke le Fitz Waryn*; *History of Fulk Fitz Warine, The*

Gaimar, Geoffrey, 15, 40, 43
Gamelyn, in *Tale of Gamelyn*, 73–74
Ganim, John, 213n
Gawain, 187n; in *Yvain* and *Ywain and Gawain*, 207
Generosity, 130n, 195
George, Saint, 59, 60, 104, 105, 107
Germany, 106, 132n
Gesta Romanorum, 124n
Gestes des révoltés, 14, 137
Gevard, Abbot, 94
Gilimot, son of Thomas, 27
Giraldus Cambrensis, 109n
Gist, Margaret Adlum, 136n
Gloucester, Earldom of, 146
Godard, in *Havelok the Dane*, 48, 50, 51, 58, 84, 129
God of Love, 62, 171–72, 179, 202
Godrich, in *Havelok the Dane*, 46n, 48, 51n
Gog, 108
Goldeboru, in *Havelok the Dane*, 40, 42, 46
Gower, John, 202n
Gradon, Pamela, 10n
Gray, Sir Thomas, 201
Green, Dennis Howard, 173–74
Grim: in *Lai d'Haveloc*, 40, 41, 45, 52n; in *Havelok the Dane*, 50
Grimsby, 85
Gudreche, King, in *Romance of Horn*, 25
Guernes de Pont-Sainte-Maxence, 5

Gui, in *Gui de Warewic*, 65–66, 78–79, 208
Gui de Warewic (AN), 13, 21, 75, 104, 198; ancestral theory and, 16, 17, 197; love in, 194, 196, 208; secular themes in, 62, 65–66, 78–79, 111
Guillaume d'Angleterre, 92n
Guillaume le Clerc, 98
Guy, in *Guy of Warwick*, 53, 62–67, 77n, 85, 221–22; justice and, 54, 69, 79–80, 87; love and, 58, 196–97, 208; nationalism and, 59, 60; religious values and, 104, 109–15, 117, 128–29, 219; secular values and, 74, 83, 84, 92–93, 218; self-development of, 81–82, 198–99. See also *Romance of Guy of Warwick*
Gyclif, 197

Hadermod, in *Romance of Horn*, 27, 34n
Haderof, in *Romance of Horn*, 26
Hagiography, 12, 92–94, 107, 222; nationalism and, 59, 60; secular values and, 101–5, 109–19, 126–33, 219–20
Haidu, Peter, 163n
Hall of statues, in *Tristan*, 149, 154n, 194–95
Halverson, John, 43n
Hanning, Robert W., 163n, 170n
Harris, Sylvia, 146
Haskin, Dayton, 130n
Havelock, in *Lai d'Havelock*, 41, 45–46, 49–50, 87
Havelok, in Havelok romances, 52, 54, 85, 88, 89; justice and, 58, 59, 83, 217
Havelok, in *Havelok the Dane*, 42, 44–45, 46–47, 49; heritage and, 51, 84; religious values and, 116, 129–30. See also *Lay of Havelok the Dane, The*
Henry II, 2–3, 131, 140–41, 216; baronial concerns and, 7, 19–20, 68; patronage and, 17–18, 28n, 144–46
Henry III, 17
Henry de Newburgh, 16, 17
Henry of Bracton, 48
Henry of Huntingdon, 15
Henryson, Robert, 124
Henry the Younger, 17, 28n, 140–41
Hereford, 146, 161, 216
Herefordshire, 144, 161
Heresy, 100, 101
Hereward the Wake, 15
Heritage. See Inheritance, right to
Herland, in *King Horn*, 34n
Heroes, insular, 18, 80–83, 199, 216–23; exemplarity and, 133, 181, 203, 212–13; secular values and, 58–59, 70, 128–29, 172. See also specific heroes
Higden, Ranulph, 109n

Hirsh, John C., 45
History of Fulk Fitz Warine, The, 6n, 13
Hodain, in *Sir Tristrem*, 193–94
Hoepffner, Ernest, 184n
Holden, A. J., 41n, 172n
"Homiletic romance," 127, 130, 219
Honor, chivalric, 110, 177, 199–200
Horn, in Horn romances, 24–25, 52, 76, 88, 104; heritage and, 41, 55, 82, 83, 84; justice and, 40, 54, 59, 217–18
Horn, in *King Horn*, 27–34, 38–40, 88
Horn, in *Romance of Horn*, 25–27, 31, 34–38, 87, 110, 194
Hue de Rotelande, 139, 181, 183, 203–7; literary tradition and, 135–36, 142, 187–88; on ideal vs. practice, 146–47, 158–62, 170–73, 179, 208–13, 220–21; insularity and, 143–44, 174; on violence, 166–69, 196–97
Hugh de Hungrie, 146–47
Huizinga, Johan, 178n, 202
Hume, Kathryn, 118
Humor, in romances, 28, 158–59, 162
Hunlaf, in *Romance of Horn*, 24, 25, 26, 36, 87
Hunt, Tony, 146n
Hurley, Margaret, 132n
Hynes-Berry, Mary, 30
Hyperbole, 31, 119, 201, 203

Ida of Boulogne, Countess, 175, 201
Identity, personal, 11, 13, 184; religious values and, 102, 111–15, 128–29, 219, 222
Individuality, 142, 163n, 199. See also Autonomy
Inheritance, right to, 54, 61, 64, 74, 87–89, 168; baronial concerns and, 18–20, 23, 55–57, 83, 101, 219; external threats to, 27, 32–35, 73, 84; legality and, 14, 37, 40–42, 48–50, 68–69; nation and, 39, 67, 86, 223
Injustice, 68–69, 84, 85, 152, 218
Innocent III, 98
Inquisition, 100
Interdict of 1208–1213, 98
Ipomadon, 205–7, 209, 213
Ipomadon, 198, 202–6, 212, 213, 215
Ipomedon, 146, 158–60, 162–72, 206, 210
Ipomedon (Hue de Rotelande), 158–74, 203–4, 216; authorial attitude in, 135–36, 139, 144, 186; love in, 6, 181, 196, 204–6, 209–12, 220; social behavior in, 179, 198
Ireland, 37, 39
Irony, 28, 96, 174n, 187, 221; *Amadas et Ydoine* and, 179, 181, 183, 186;

Irony (continued)
　Ipomadon and, 203, 207, 212; in *Ipomedon*, 158–59, 169, 204–5
Ismene, in *Ipomedon*, 162, 165–66, 167
Isolt, Queen, in *Tristan*, 144, 148–52, 186, 187n, 196; suffering and, 153–57, 182–85, 194
Isolt of Brittany, in *Tristan*, 146, 149, 150, 151, 152, 190
Iseut, in *Sir Tristrem*, 195
Isumbras, in *Sir Ysumbras*, 115, 116–17, 128, 129

Jaufre, 124n
Jauss, Hans Robert, 11, 130
Jealousy, 76, 151, 220
Jean de Meun, 171
Jean le Bel, 199
John, king of England (historical), 17, 58, 98
John, King, in Fulk romances, 57–58, 219; justice and, 68, 70, 84, 87; centralization and, 60, 86
John du Plessis, 17
John of Gaunt, 202
John of Salisbury, 109n, 218
Josian, in *Boeve de Haumtone* and *Beues of Hamtoun*, 55n, 58–59, 105
Justice, 14, 23, 67–74, 88; inheritance and, 36–37, 54, 89; providence and, 41, 42, 48, 111, 126; royal control and, 20, 38, 84, 217–18. *See also* Legality

Kaherdin, in *Tristan*, 149
Kantorowicz, Ernst, 48–49
Keen, Maurice, 181n, 200n
Kelly, Douglas, 147
Ker, William Paton, 134, 135
Kilgour, Raymond Lincoln, 178n, 202
King Horn (ME), 21, 24–25, 38–40, 84; style in, 27–35, 82
Kingship, 49, 68–69, 90
Klausner, David N., 103, 110n
Knighthood, 32, 137, 158–59, 210; baronial status and, 6–7, 9, 12, 140–42, 177–81; ideal vs. practice in, 146, 147, 198–202, 213–15; love and, 139, 163–67, 172–74, 175, 207, 221; orders of, 9, 178, 199, 214; religious values and, 104–9, 113, 116–17
Knight of Curtesy and the Fair Lady of Faguell, The, 211n
Köhler, Erich, 89, 174n, 189, 203n
Kratins, Ojars, 103
Kyng Alisaunder, 107–8, 130

Lagarde, Georges de, 100–101
Lai del Desiré, 141n

Lai d'Haveloc, Le (AN), 3n, 13, 18; inheritance and, 40–42, 43, 45–46; society and, 49–52, 87
Lai du Cor, 163n
Lai of Baltof, in *Romance of Horn* (2782–844), 28
Lais (Marie de France), 95, 141n
Laisse, 27–28, 75, 78
Laity, in church, 93, 94, 98–101, 131, 219
Lambert of Ardres, 176n, 201
Lancelot, 163
Land, 25, 63, 83, 90, 218; baronial concerns and, 6–9, 20, 49n, 53, 64–65, 101, 217; heritage and, 27, 32–33, 37–38; royal control and, 14, 18–19, 23, 56, 68, 85; stability and, 39, 52, 87–88
Landholders. *See* Barony, English
Langland, William, 124
Language, 5, 70–74, 126; Anglo-Norman dialect, 1–6, 9, 23, 30, 133, 145; English, 2, 5, 9–10, 23, 133; French, 1–6, 9–10, 23, 43, 133, 217
Lanzelet (Ulrich von Zatzikhoven), 163n
Largesse, 130, 140–41
Laudine, in *Yvain*, 194, 207
Lavinia, in *Enéas*, 165, 187n
Lay of Havelok the Dane, The (ME), 21, 216; emotion in, 78, 80n; religious values in, 102, 129–30; secular themes in, 40–52, 73, 84
Lea, Henry Charles, 100
Leach, MacEdward, 118
Leaf and Flower, parties of, 142
Lef, Gordon, 101
Legality, 16, 67–74, 79, 119, 121, 142; class consciousness and, 44, 52, 83; fealty and, 16, 54–55, 58; inheritance and, 23, 40–41, 48, 87; prosperity and, 7–8, 14, 90; royal control and, 18–21, 36–37, 84, 85, 217–18
Legge, Maria Dominica, 7n, 28n, 96, 107, 173, 181n
Legibus et Consuetudinis Angliae, De (Henry of Bracton), 48
Leonin d'Inde Majeur, in *Ipomedon*, 159, 164, 168–69, 170, 206
Leprosy, 119, 122, 123, 124–25, 128, 129, 190
Levy, Brian Joseph, 41
Life of the Black Prince, The (Chandos Herald), 199, 202
Life of St. Catherine, The (Clemence of Barking), 102
Life of St. Katherine, The (Capgrave), 102
Lincoln, 41, 45–46, 216
Lindsey, 41

Lineage, 22, 36, 41–42, 53, 84–85; continuity of, 18, 26–27, 32–34, 55–57, 88–89, 217; heroic purpose and, 12, 218, 219, 223
Llewelyn, Prince, in *Fouke le Fitz Waryn*, 69–70
Lombardy, 119
London, 144, 217
Lorraine, 16
Louis XI, 124n
Love, 12, 13–14, 43n, 76, 175–76, 200–202; in *Amadas et Ydoine*, 179, 182–88, 221; in Guy romances, 62–63, 77n, 208, 221–22; in Horn romances, 25–27, 30, 34–35, 39; in Ipomedon romances, 139, 162–72, 174, 204–10, 212; in *Tristan*, 139, 147–57, 174, 181, 220; in *Sir Tristrem*, 190–91, 194–97, 212. *See also* Courtly convention; *Fine amor*
Loyalty, 30, 121, 177, 183, 185, 188, 221. *See also* Brotherhood, in romances
Lunete, in *Yvain* and *Ywain and Gawain*, 194, 207

McFarlane, K. B., 8n
Madness, 183–85, 221
Magna Carta, 20n, 21–22, 58, 90
Magog, 108
Maine, 145
Maistre Wace's Roman de Rou (Wace), 15
Manuals of instruction, Christian, 93–94, 99, 100
Map, Walter, 5, 141, 161
Marc, in *Tristan*, 141, 149, 152, 184, 190
Marcher lords, 58
Margaret de Logy, 201
Margery d'Oilly, 16, 17
Marie de France, 3, 5, 95, 148n
Mark, in *Sir Tristrem*, 190, 195
Marmion, William, 175–76, 178, 200
Marriage, 5, 25, 38, 63, 210n; barony and, 19, 40, 63; chivalry and, 159, 167–68, 205, 207; love and, 136, 149–54, 179, 201–2, 221; religious values and, 41, 102; women and, 34, 46, 187–88
Marshal, William, 20
Martin [Weiss], Judith Elizabeth, 56n
Mason, Emma, 17n
Mathew, Gervase, 136
Matilda, in *Fouke le Fitz Waryn*, 58
Mauron, 178
Mehl, Dieter, 50–51, 61n, 85n, 117n, 132n, 191n; on exemplary romances, 96n, 103, 109
Meisel, Janet, 17n
Meleager of Sicily, in *Ipomedon*, 159

Melior et Ydoine, 177
Ménard, Philippe, 160n, 161n, 165, 170n
Merchant class, English. *See* Bourgeoisie, English
Meyer-Lindenberg, Herlint, 40n
Middle English literature, 3, 12, 75–76, 92, 132
Middle English romances, 4, 13–14, 83, 133; baronial issues and, 9–12, 21–24, 76, 86, 180; idealism and, 136–37, 139, 188, 202n, 211–12; insularity and, 1, 6, 216; religious influence on, 92, 220; style in, 28–30, 43, 191–92, 206–7, 210, 213. *See also specific romances*
Military power, 8, 32, 34, 138, 180, 217–18; barony and, 20, 85, 176; as heroic combat, 25, 58, 83, 200; religious values and, 104, 109
Mills, Maldwyn, 130n
Misogyny, 187–88
Morality, 38, 92; inheritance and, 27, 33, 48, 51–52, 65; love and, 152, 188; religious values and, 12, 103–4, 107–9, 120–25, 220
Mortimers of Attleborough, 16n
Muscatine, Charles, 163n, 174n

Narrators. *See* Authorial comment
National feeling, in romances, 12, 14, 48–49, 74–75, 86, 87, 135; romance heroes and, 39, 59–62, 65–67, 82–83, 221–22
Naturalism, in style, 9, 50–51, 203, 209–11, 212, 214–15
Neckham, Alexander, 109n
Newburgh family, 16, 17
Nobility, English. *See* Barony, English
Nobility, French, 7–8, 89–90, 176–78, 187; idealism of, 138–42, 214, 221
Norfolk, 41
Norham Castle, 176
Norman Conquest, 1–2, 15
Normandy, 2, 59, 132, 145, 216
Norman literature, 3
Normans, 2, 15–16, 216
Nugis Curialium, De (Map), 141

Oaths, 41, 131, 178, 198–99; in Amis and Amiloun romances, 123, 124; in *Athelston*, 71, 126–27, 129
Oilly family, 16, 17
Old French romances, 1, 3–4, 132, 141–42, 158–59; courtliness and, 173–74, 179, 211, 221; divergences from, 83, 136–39, 145–46, 173, 187, 216; love and, 13, 148, 187, 202n, 211;

Old French romances (*continued*)
  nobility and, 89–90, 214. *See also* Romances, courtly
Order of the Garter, 178, 199
Order of the Star, 178
Orme, Nicholas, 200n
Osney, 16
Otes de Pavie, in *Guy of Warwick*, 70
Owein, in Amis and Amiloun romances, 119, 122
Owst, Gerald R., 96, 131

Paganism, 25–27, 33, 35n, 104
Painter, Sidney, 17n
Parody, 159, 160, 162–63, 173
Parson's Tale (Chaucer), 93–94
Partenopeus de Blois, 95, 158, 166n
Pathos. *See* Emotion
Patrimony. *See* Inheritance, right to
Patronage, 16–18, 144–45, 197
Payen, Jean-Charles, 75, 173
Pearsall, Derek, 102, 180n, 190n, 192n
Peasantry, 43, 44–46
Penances, 152, 154, 220
Perroy, Edouard, 8n
Peter of Blois, 101n
Peter of Langtoft, 198n
Petit Brut d'Angleterre, 85
Phallic metaphor, 172
Philip Augustus, 106–7
Philip IV (the Fair), 37n
Philippa of Lancaster, 142
Pickford, Cedric E., 192n
Piety, 121, 125, 131, 219, 220; heroic action and, 63–64, 92–93, 104
Piramus, Denis, 95
Placidas (St. Eustace), 102, 105, 115–16, 128
Poitou, 145
Policraticus (John of Salisbury), 218
Political power, 11, 25, 80n, 88, 104, 217; centralization and, 7–8, 22–23, 60–61, 97, 137, 218; claims to, 14, 19–20, 48–52, 56–57, 67–69, 141; courtliness and, 176–79, 221
Poole, Austin Lane, 19n
Pope, Mildred K., 28n, 34n
Powicke, Maurice, 60
Primogeniture, 8, 23
Property, rights of, 14, 44, 65, 223
Protheselaus (Hue de Rotelande), 6n, 124n, 144
Provençal literature, 3, 135, 148
Providence, 103, 118, 121, 130n; confidence in, 23, 35–36, 48; as guide, 108, 125, 129; justification through, 38, 40, 41, 72, 107, 126, 220; power of, 114–15, 122–23, 127–28

Provisions of Westminster, 22
Prowess, 32; barony and, 142, 172; heroic service and, 76, 80, 83, 164, 168–70, 196, 209; love's effect on, 12, 138, 187, 201, 220
Pseudo-Turpin MS (ca. 1214), 17n

Queen of Sicily, in *Ipomedon*, 146–47, 159, 167
Question d'amor, 148, 202

Raison, 184, 185–86
Ramsey, Lee C., 10n
Reforms, political, 19–22, 37, 48–49, 61n
Reinbrun, in *Guy of Warwick*, 62, 65, 75n, 113
Reinhard, J. R., 181n
Religious commitment. *See* Faith
Remy, Paul, 124
Repetition, 26, 29–30, 50n, 78, 125, 150
Revenge, theme of, 18, 35, 41n, 64, 73–74; in Bevis romances, 76–77, 105; in Horn romances, 25–27, 32–33, 37, 104
Richard I (Coeur de Lion), 19, 124n, 145n; in romances, 68, 106–7, 109
Richard II, 178
Richard Coer de Lyon, 106–7
Riedel, Frederick Carl, 186n
Rigmel, in *Romance of Horn*, 24–26, 46; love and, 28, 30, 34–35, 39, 194
Rimenhild, in *King Horn*, 24, 29, 32, 38; love and, 30, 34, 88, 194
Robant, in *Boeve de Haumtone*, 57n
Robert le Diable, 92n
Robert Manning of Brunne, 189–90n, 193
Romance of Guy of Warwick: The First or 14th-century Version (ME), 53–54, 62–65, 75, 77n, 78n, 193; exemplarity in, 81–82, 95, 103, 196–97; justice in, 69, 79–80; religious values in, 104, 109–15, 208, 219–20; secular values in, 58–59, 60, 74, 87, 111, 217
Romance of Guy of Warwick: The Second or 15th-century Version, 133n
Romance of Horn, The (AN) (Thomas), 13, 18, 24–27, 34–40, 218; love in, 58, 63; secular issues in, 48, 65, 84; style in, 29, 31, 33, 50, 75, 76, 82
Romance of Sir Beues of Hamtoun, The (ME), 41n, 53, 55n, 193, 217; justice in, 58–59, 67–68; national feeling in, 60–62, 66–67, 82–83; religious values in, 63–64, 104–6, 107; style of, 54, 74–78, 80n, 81n, 87–88
Romance of Sir Degrevant, The, 66n, 67, 179, 210–11n

Romance of Tristran, The (Beroul), 152–53
Romances (genre), 10–11, 13–14, 83, 128–33, 134–35, 137, 158–59, 174, 211–13, 217–23; and generic mixing, 14–15, 92–94, 101–4, 127–28, 222–23
Romances, courtly, 12, 62, 134–46, 173, 211–15, 220–22; social behavior and, 176, 179–80, 198, 202–3, 209. *See also specific romances*
Romances, Old French. *See* Old French romances
Romances, pious, 12, 92–133, 134, 219, 222. *See also specific romances*; Faith; Identity, personal
Romances of English heroes, 16, 28n, 35, 86–90, 130–31, 217–19; centralization in, 12, 97; class consciousness in, 42–44, 47, 52, 66–67, 180; heritage in, 32, 40, 53–54, 74–75; legality in, 21, 23, 58, 68–72; society in, 13–14, 83, 137; style of, 27, 30–32, 78, 80, 134. *See also* Anglo-Norman romances; Middle English romances
Roman Curia, 97
Roman de la Rose, Le (Jean de Meun), 171
Roman de Renart, Le, 171
Roman de Rou, Le (Wace), 15
Roman de Thèbes, Le, 3, 158, 161
Roman de Tristan par Thomas, Le (Thomas of Britain), 135–36, 139, 144, 158, 189; love in, 6, 146–57, 171–72, 181, 182–84, 194–95; ideal vs. practice in, 174, 186, 187, 203, 211–12, 220
Roman de Troie, Le (Benoît de Sainte-Maure), 158
Roman de Waldef, Le, 6n, 13, 16, 41n
"Roman généalogique," theory of, 16–18, 41n, 86
Romans d'aventure, 89
Round Table, 178, 197
Rumble, Thomas C., 192n, 195n

Sabaoth, in *Boeve de Haumtone*, 56
Saint Laurent, 16
Saints' lives. *See* Hagiography
Salter, Elizabeth, 75–76
Schelp, Hanspeter, 103, 107
Schlight, John, 20
Schmolke-Hasselmann, Beate, 141n
Schroeder, Peter R., 206n
Sea, image of, 31–32, 33
"Secular hagiography," theory of, 92, 103, 115, 117, 127, 219
Seguin, in Guy romances, 78–79

Self-development, 88, 223; love and, 138, 148, 171, 200, 201, 208–9, 222; religious values and, 82, 103; society and, 83, 199
Sensuality, 162, 165, 172, 204
Sermons, 93, 94, 99, 219
Sexuality, 34, 46, 76, 188; passionate, 12, 137–38, 150–51, 162–63, 167, 207n, 220
Short, Ian, 143n
Sigar Estal, in *Lai d'Havelo*c, 52n
Sigfried, in *Chronicon Ghisnense*, 201
Sir Degrevant. *See Romance of Sir Degrevant, The*
Sir Gowther, 92n
Sir Tristrem, 158, 181, 184, 188–98, 203, 212
Sir Ysumbras, 95, 96, 115–17, 220
Social behavior, 11, 135, 197–98, 214, 217, 221. *See also* Courtly convention
Social integration, 101, 212; in love, 139, 171, 194; religious values and, 103–4, 111, 117
Social order, 2, 30, 40, 44, 91, 223; barony and, 11, 23, 52, 218. *See also* Class consciousness
Southampton, 16, 85
Southern, Richard W., 7n, 99–100
Speculum Gy de Warewyke, 197
Speculum Vitae, 96
Spirituality. *See* Faith
Staines, David, 43n
Stevens, John, 207n
Statute of Marlborough, 22
Stimming, Albert, 75
Subinfeudation, 19
Suddene, 26, 34
Suffering, 51, 80n; in brotherhood, 104, 121; in love, 152–57, 162, 183–85, 187, 191, 195, 209, 220

Tail-rhyme, 75–76, 190n
Tale of Gamelyn, The, 13, 67, 87n, 89, 90; justice in, 54, 71, 73–74
Tenure system, 7, 16, 18n, 55, 57
Terri, in *Guy of Warwick*, 64, 83, 112
Thomas (poet of Horn romance), 24, 26–28, 30, 35–36. *See also Romance of Horn, The*
Thomas de Newburgh, 17
Thomas of Britain, 24n, 146–57, 160, 171, 189, 193, 196; on fallibility, 139, 170, 183, 184, 186, 190–91; historical tradition and, 135–36, 142, 173, 181, 187–88, 211–12; on ideal vs. practice, 158, 174, 179, 194–95, 213, 220; insularity and, 143–44, 145–46. *See also Roman de Tristan par Thoms, Le*

Thomas of Erceldoune, 189
Thomas of Kent, 24n, 216
Thrupp, Sylvia, 10n
Tierri, in *Boeve de Haumtone*, 56, 57n, 60
Titles, baronial, 19, 23, 63, 223
"Tomas" (source of *Sir Tristrem*), 189, 192
Topoi, 34n, 143, 166n, 198, 202, 215
Touraine, 145
Tournaments, 140, 142, 158, 214; in *Ipomedon*, 159, 166, 167–68, 205; knighthood and, 178, 180, 197, 198, 199
Tradition. *See* Custom
Translatio studii, 139
Treupe, 122–23, 124, 126, 129
Tripartite structure, 88
Tristan, in *Tristan*, 146–57, 163, 186, 187n, 196, 211–12; inconstancy and, 188, 190, 195, 220; suffering and, 182–83, 184–85, 194. *See also Roman de Tristan par Thomas, Le*
Tristan le Nain, in *Tristan*, 155
Tristrem, in *Sir Tristrem*, 190–91, 194–95
Truth, 122–23, 124, 126, 129; authorial, 147–48, 161

Ubbe, in *Havelok the Dane*, 48n
Ulrich von Zatzikhoven, 163n

Values, Christian. *See* Christian principles
Values, secular, 31, 39, 64, 217; Christian values vs., 93–97, 101–17, 128–31, 219
Vance, Eugene, 89n, 138, 187–88
Veraie amor, 136–37, 150, 156
Vie du Prince Noir, La (Chandos Herald), 199, 202
Vie Seint Edmund le Rei, La (Piramus), 95
Violence, 83, 106, 137–38, 168–69, 187–88, 196
Vitz, Evelyn Birge, 114

Vows, 199; in *Ipomedon*, 159, 163–64, 168, 169, 205, 206–7

Wace, Robert, 3, 15
Wade, 60
Waldef, 15, 16n, 41n, 85. See also *Roman de Waldef, Le*
Wallingford, 16
Warren, Wilfred Lewis, 20n
Wars, private, 7–9, 18, 58
Warwick, 16, 17, 85
Wathelet-Willem, Jeanne, 17n
Wehrli, Max, 132n
Weiss, Judith, 60n, 61n
West, Constance Birt, 3n, 92, 109, 136, 179
Westir, 28
White Hart, badge of the, 178
Whittington, 57
Wikele, in *Romance of Horn*, 24, 25, 26, 35, 36, 38
Wilde, Oscar, 143
William I (the Conqueror), 7, 17
William II, 15
William of Albini II, 17
William of Albini IV, 17, 18
William of Albini V, 18
William of Malmesbury, 15
William of Nassington, 95, 96
William of Pagula, 93
William of Palerne, 210
Wittig, Susan, 30
Woledge, Brian, 143n
Women, 162, 187–88; behavior in love, 167–69, 172, 186, 204–5, 211; role of, 46, 58–59
Wymundham, 16

Yder, 166n
Ydoine, in *Amadas et Ydoine*, 179, 181–86, 188, 196n, 200, 221
Ysonde, in *Sir Tristrem*, 190–91, 195
Yvain, 168, 207
Yvain (Chrétien de Troyes), 194, 207
Ywain and Gawain, 194, 207, 210

Compositor: G&S Typesetters, Inc.
Printer: Braun-Brumfield
Binder: Braun-Brumfield
Text: 9/11 Palatino
Display: Palatino

THE LIBRARY
ST. MARY'S COLLEGE OF MARYLAND
ST. MARY'S CITY, MARYLAND 20686

DATE DUE			